ROBERT L. SCRANTON

ART

THE UNIVERSITY OF CHICAGO PRESS

Chicago and London

Library of Congress Catalog Card Number: 64-24964
THE UNIVERSITY OF CHICAGO PRESS, CHICAGO & LONDON
THE UNIVERSITY OF TORONTO PRESS, TORONTO 5, ONTARIO
© *1964 by The University of Chicago.*
All rights reserved. Published 1964.
Composed and printed by The University of Chicago Press,
Chicago, Illinois 60637.
Designed by Robert A. Eustachy

To My Wife

To My Wife

PREFACE

THE PRIMARY PURPOSE of this work is to provide an account of the aesthetic aspects of the arts of the ancient Mediterranean world, including Egypt, Mesopotamia, and the Aegean, through classical and early Christian times, from a consistent point of view. Through such a study, one may hope, there will emerge new insights into these arts as aspects of their own cultures and as the fundamental phase of the history of Western art.

To accomplish this purpose, perhaps not an entirely overweening ambition in itself, the disparity of materials involved seems to make it necessary to adopt a system of analysis with as broad and deep a basis as possible. The system employed and the concepts of art and style on which it is based are hardly revolutionary in the particulars, although in the whole system the particulars sometimes take on a novel character, and the system itself may not be entirely self-evident. Therefore the theoretical basis of the system is explained in general terms in an introductory chapter.

Though a full justification of this system in the face of competitors and a fully documented account of all terms and concepts used and rejected might seem to be in order, this would create a work in which the primary purpose would be thrown into the shade—perhaps utterly lost. In this dilemma I have seized on the horn that would preserve the primary purpose as much as possible. After all, I claim originality for the synthesis of the system, and substantially all of the particular concepts are in common currency in various formulations, though they may take on a slightly new color in my own synthesis. I have endeavored to avoid using concepts that are wholly indefensible in their own fields, and have lacked both temerity and sense of necessity to demolish alternatives; though I do believe my analysis is most meaningful, I recognize fully the values of others.

There is another dilemma in the fact that in so wide a range of theoretical and historical material and concepts many readers will find a perhaps exasperating combination of the commonplace and the unfamiliar, the interesting and the uninteresting. This dilemma I have ignored, feeling that only through the totality can anything be known, and not wishing to trim the presentation for any one specialty, but hoping for a varied audience of readers specialized or not but having in common an interest in the basic problems and a curiosity as to the meaning and perspectives given the various elements in the larger perspective.

There is also a dilemma, or at least a hard problem, in that by attempting to subject art to objective analysis one almost inevitably loses, kills, essential qualities of art itself—its spontaneity and immediacy, its subtlety and refinement, its element of non-intellectuality by which it transcends rational process. And, certainly, for the individual in his personal response to the work of art as an aesthetic experience, objective analysis must be carefully controlled and limited if the experience is to be complete and true. But the purpose of this study is not so much an "appreciation" of ancient art itself as an exploration of its meaning to the people who made it; to consider the art as evidence for history. In this purpose it is necessary to be objective, and particularly in dealing with matters in which objectivity is elusive it is necessary to be cautious, even ruthless. At the same time one may believe that if any insights should be gained at the cost of the surgery, once the shock has passed and the understandings have been assimilated to the subliminal sphere of awareness, the direct and personal appreciation of the art being studied will not have suffered and perhaps may have been deepened.

Yet another dilemma is presented by the problem of illustrations. At one extreme, theoretically, almost any object of any style should serve to illustrate the style as well as any other; at the other extreme, to demonstrate and document the propositions completely would necessitate reference to every representative of the style. In this dilemma I have tried to compromise, providing a limited number of illustrations, assuming that it will be easy for the reader to supplement these at his own need from the increasing number of books of plates in the various fields, of which some are listed in the second part of the bibliography.

The ideas and thoughts operative in this work began to come to me in 1933 in my first year as a graduate student, and it would be impossible for me to reconstruct the "credits" accurately and completely. The work is, for better or worse, positively or negatively, part of everything I have met. But without wanting to saddle with responsibility any of those to whom I owe deeply in one way or another, I will record at the least my debt to Franklin P. Johnson, Edward Rothschild, and John Shapley from the earliest years, and from a more recent period my colleagues in the Institute of Liberal Arts at Emory University, particularly Thomas Altizer, and Gregor Sebba, and also Robert Roelof of the Department of Philosophy of the University of Nevada, formerly of Emory University. I am specifically in debt to Emory University for funds and facilities to pursue the work on various occasions.

Aesthetic Aspects of ANCIENT ART

Aesthetic Aspects of

ANCIENT

CONTENTS

PLATES

PLATES

PLATES

PLATES

PLATES

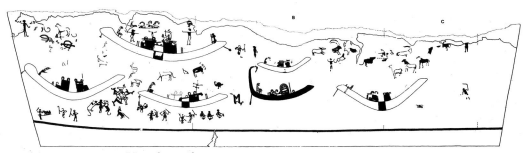

1. TOMB PAINTING, Hierakonpolis
Pre-Dynastic
Quibbell, *Hieraconpolis*, II
Courtesy of B. Quaritch, London

2. PALETTE OF NARMER (cast), Hierakonpolis (Cairo)
Archaic, First Dynasty, ca. 3200 B.C.
Courtesy Oriental Institute,
University of Chicago

3. TOMB OF NAKHT (painting), Thebes
New Kingdom
Courtesy Oriental Institute,
University of Chicago

4. Tomb of Ti (relief), Saqqarah
Old Kingdom, Fifth Dynasty, ca. 2500 B.C.
Steindorff, *Grab des Ti*

5. BATTLE OF RAMSES III (relief), Medinet Habu
New Kingdom, Twentieth Dynasty, ca. 1170 B.C.
Courtesy Oriental Institute,
University of Chicago

6. IKHNATON AND FAMILY, Tell el Amarna (Berlin)
New Kingdom, Eighteenth Dynasty, ca. 1350 B.C.
With permission of Staatliche Museen, Berlin (West)

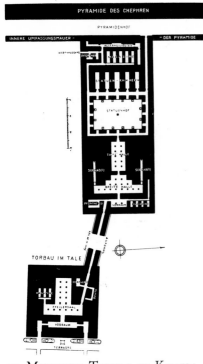

17. MORTUARY TEMPLE OF KHAFRA,
Gizeh
Old Kingdom, Fourth Dynasty,
ca. 2600 B.C.
Hölscher, *Grabdenkmal des Königs Chephrens*

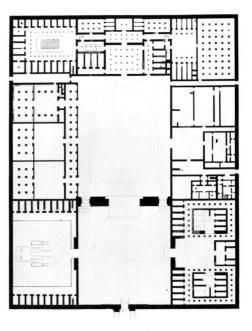

18. PORTICO IN SECOND COURT OF TEMPLE,
Medinet Habu
New Kingdom
Courtesy Oriental Institute, University
of Chicago

19. PALACE, Tell el Amarna
New Kingdom, Eighteenth Dy-
nasty, ca. 1350 B.C.
From H. Frankfort, *Mural Painting of
El Amarna*
Courtesy Egypt Exploration Society

20. PAINTED BEAKER, Susa (Louvre)
Iranian, "Susa I," fifth millennium,
B.C.
Courtesy of Musée du Louvre

21. BRONZE "STANDARD" WITH
WINGED IBEXES, Luristan
(Godard Collection, Paris)
Iranian
With permission of the owner

22. SEAL IMPRESSION, Jemdet Nasr (Louvre)
Courtesy of Musée du Louvre

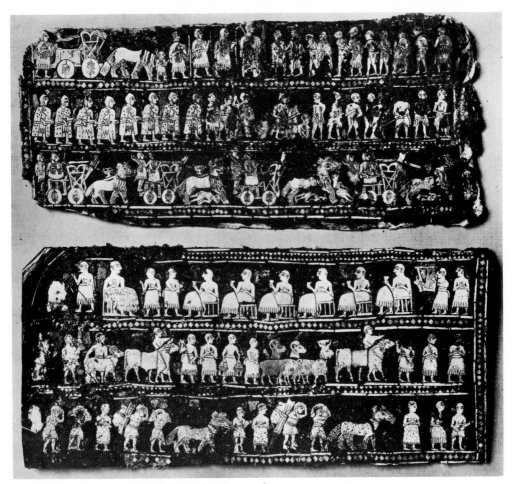

23. Mosaic "standard," Ur (British Museum)
Early Dynastic, ca. 2500 B.C.
Courtesy of the Trustees of the British Museum

24. STELE OF HAMMURABI (cast), Susa
(Louvre)
Isin Larsa, ca. 1775 B.C.
Courtesy Oriental Institute,
University of Chicago

25. STELE OF NARAM SIN, Susa (Louvre)
Akkadian, 2340–2180 B.C.
Courtesy of Musée du Louvre

26. Relief of sacred tree, Nimrud (British Museum)
Assurnasirpal II, ca. 880 b.c.
Courtesy of the Trustees of the British Museum

27. Hunting scenes, Nimrud (British Museum)
Assurnasirpal II, ca. 880 b.c.
Courtesy of the Trustees of the British Museum

28. DESTRUCTION OF ELAMITE CITY, Nineveh (British Museum)
Assurbanipal, ca. 650 B.C.
Courtesy of the Trustees of the British Museum

29. CULT FIGURES, Tell Asmar and Khafaje (Chicago)
Early Dynastic, ca. 2500 B.C.
Courtesy Oriental Institute,
University of Chicago

30. GUDEA, Telloh-Lagash (Louvre)
Neo-Sumerian, ca. 2100 B.C.
Courtesy of Musée du Louvre

31. BRONZE HEAD, Kuyunjik,
Nineveh (Baghdad)
Akkadian, 2340–2180 B.C.
Baghdad Museum
Permission of Directorate-General of Antiquities, Republic of Iraq

33. SCORPION MAN FROM DOORWAY, Tell Halaf
Syrian, ca. 800 B.C.
Oppenheim, *Tell Halaf*, III
Courtesy Walter de Gruyter & Company, Berlin

32. SPHINX FROM GATEWAY, Alaca
Hüyük
Hittite, 1400–1200 B.C.
Garstang, *Hittite Empire*
Courtesy of Constable & Company,
Ltd., London

34. BULL CAPITAL, Persepolis (Chicago)
Persian, fifth century, B.C.
Courtesy Oriental Institute,
University of Chicago

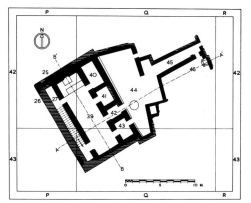

35. Sin Temple (II), Khafaje
    Protoliterate, 3500–3000 B.C.
    Courtesy Oriental Institute,
    University of Chicago

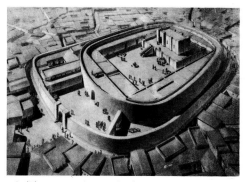

36. Temple oval, Khafaje
    Early Dynastic, 3000–2340 B.C.
    Courtesy Oriental Institute,
    University of Chicago

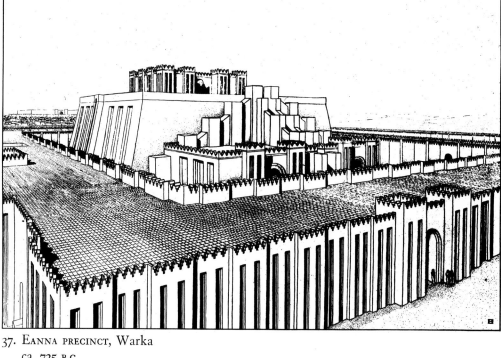

37. Eanna precinct, Warka
    ca. 725 B.C.
    Uruk-Warka, 9[te.] Vorl. Bericht

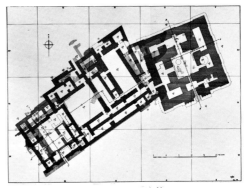

39. PALACE AND TEMPLE, Tell Asmar
Neo-Sumerian, ca. 2000 B.C.
Courtesy Oriental Institute,
University of Chicago

38. ROCK SANCTUARY, Yazilikaya
Hittite, 1400–1200 B.C.
Bittel-Naumann, *Yazilikaya*

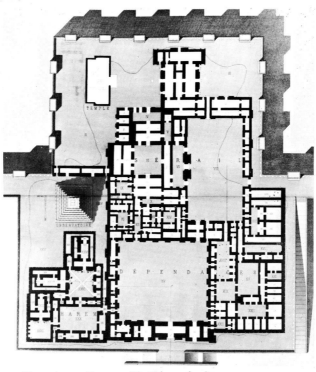

40. PALACE OF SARGON II, Khorsabad
ca. 725 B.C.
Courtesy Oriental Institute,
University of Chicago

41. PALACE, Tell Atchana
    Syria, ca. 1400 B.C.
    From *Antiquaries' Journal,* XIX (1939)
    With permission of the Society of Antiquaries

42. ISHTAR GATE (reconstructed), Babylon
    (Berlin)
    sixth century, B.C.
    Koldewey, *Ischt ar-Tor in Babylon*
    With permission of Staatliche Museen,
    Berlin (Ost)

43. COLUMNED TERRACE OF TEMPLE OF EANNA, Warka
Protoliterate, ca. 3500–3000 B.C.
Nöldeke, *Uruk-Warka,* IV

44. FACE OF PALACE TERRACE, Persepolis
fifth century, B.C.
Courtesy Oriental Institute,
University of Chicago

45. NEOLITHIC VASE
   ca. 3000 B.C.
   From Wace and Thompson, *Prehistoric Thessaly*.
   Permission of Cambridge University Press

46. EARLY MINOAN VASE, Vasiliki, Crete
   ca. 2500 B.C.
   Hirmer Verlag, Munich

47. KAMARES VASE, Crete
Middle Minoan, ca. 1800 B.C.
Hirmer Verlag, Munich

48. LATE MINOAN VASE, Aegina
ca. 1400 B.C.
Foto Deutsches Archäologisches Institut, Athens

49. EARLY HELLADIC VASE, Tiryns
    ca. 2500 B.C.
    Foto Deutsches Archäologisches Institut, Athens

50. LATE HELLADIC VASE, Korakou
    ca. 1300 B.C.
    From C. W. Blegen, *Korakou*
    Courtesy American School of Classical Studies,
    Athens

51. WOMEN AT FIESTA (fresco), Knossos
Late Minoan, ca. 1500 B.C.
Hirmer Verlag, Munich

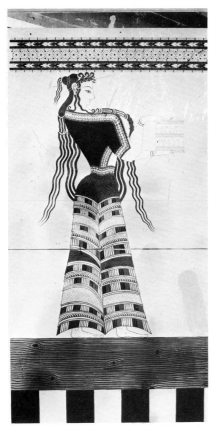

52. WOMEN WITH OFFERING (fresco),
Tiryns
Late Helladic, ca. 1300 B.C.
Foto Deutsches Archäologisches In-
stitut, Athens

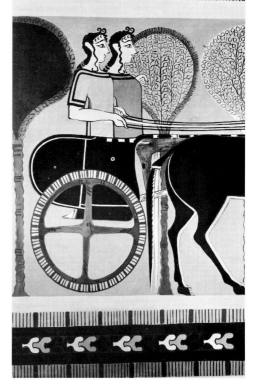

53. MEN IN CHARIOT (fresco), Tiryns
Late Helladic, ca. 1300 B.C.
Foto Deutsches Archäologisches Institut,
Athens

54. HARVESTER VASE, Hagia Triada (Herakleion), Crete
Late Minoan, ca. 1500 B.C.
Hirmer Verlag, Munich

55. GOLD CUP, Vaphio, near Sparta (Athens)
Late Minoan, ca. 1500 B.C.
Foto Deutsches Archäologisches Institut, Athens

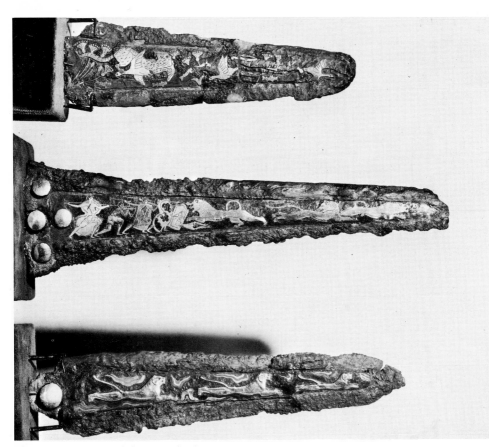

56. INLAID DAGGERS, Mycenae (Athens)
Late Helladic, ca. 1500 B.C.
Hirmer Verlag, Munich

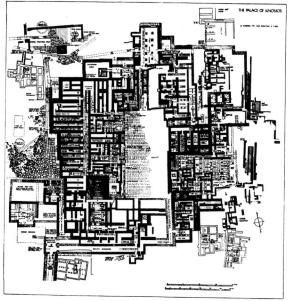

PLAN OF THE PALACE AT CNOSSUS

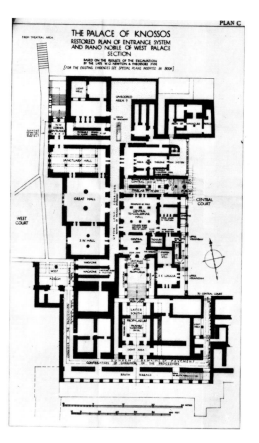

57. PALACE AT KNOSSOS
Late Minoan, ca. 1400 B.C.
From W. B. Dinsmoor, *Architecture of Ancient Greece* (3d ed.)
With permission of B. T. Batsford, Ltd., London

58. THRONE ROOM IN PALACE, Knossos
Late Minoan, ca. 1400 B.C.
Hirmer Verlag, Munich

59. RESIDENTIAL ROOMS, Knossos
Late Minoan, ca. 1400 B.C.
Hirmer Verlag, Munich

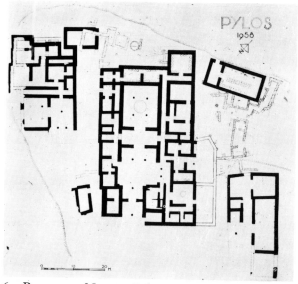

60. PALACE OF NESTOR, Pylos
Late Helladic, ca. 1300 B.C.
From *American Journal of Archaeology*, LXV (1961),
with permission

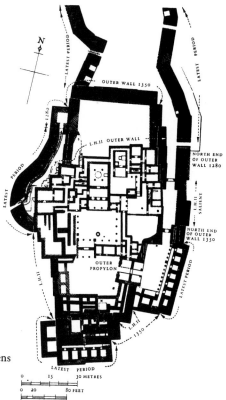

61. FORTIFIED PALACE, Tiryns
Late Helladic, ca. 1300 B.C.
Permission of Deutsches Archäologisches Institut, Athens

62. LION GATE, Mycenae
    Late Helladic, ca. 1300 B.C.
    Hirmer Verlag, Munich

63. Dipylon vase, Athens (Athens)
Geometric, eighth century, B.C.
Hirmer Verlag, Munich

64. Proto-Attic vase, Athens
Orientalizing, seventh century, B.C.
Foto Deutsches Archäologisches Institut, Athens

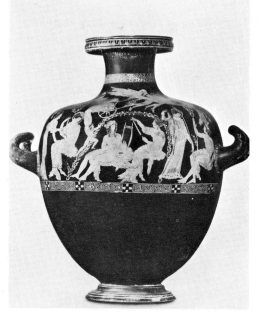

65. Vase by Exekias (Vatican)
Late Archaic, ca. 520 B.C.
Hirmer Verlag, Munich

66. Vase by Meidias (Florence)
Classical, ca. 420 B.C.
Hirmer Verlag, Munich

67. Relief vase, Athens
Hellenistic, third century, B.C.
Foto Deutsches Archäologisches Institut, Athens

72. Lapith woman and centaur from pediment of Temple of Zeus, Olympia
Classical, ca. 460 B.C.
Foto Deutsches Archäologisches Institut, Athens

73. "Fates" from pediment of Parthenon, Athens (British Museum)
Classical, ca. 440 b.c.
Hirmer Verlag, Munich, and courtesy of the Trustees
of the British Museum

74. Divinities and celebrants in Parthenon frieze, Athens
Classical, ca. 440 b.c.
Hirmer Verlag, Munich, and courtesy of the Trustees
of the British Museum

75. ALTAR OF ZEUS, Pergamum (Berlin)
Hellenistic, second century, B.C.
Courtesy Staatliche Museen; Berlin

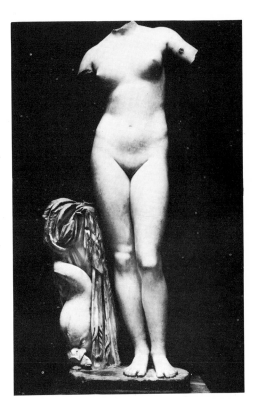

76. APHRODITE OF CYRENE, Cyrene
(Rome)
Hellenistic
Alinari, Art Reference Bureau

77. "Theseum" (Temple of Hephaistos), Athens
Classical, ca. 445 B.C.
Foto Deutsches Archäologisches Institut, Athens

78. Temple of "Ceres" (Athena), Paestum
Archaic, ca. 520 B.C.
Courtesy Fototeca di Architettura e Topografia
dell'Italia Antica

79. Temple of Isis, Delos
Hellenistic, second century, B.C.
Courtesy École Française d'Athènes

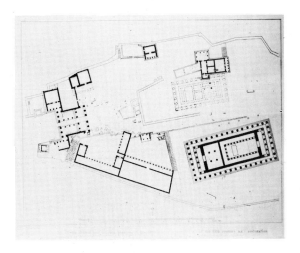

80. THE ACROPOLIS AT ATHENS
   From G. P. Stevens, *Restorations of Classical Buildings*
   Courtesy American School of Classical Studies, Athens

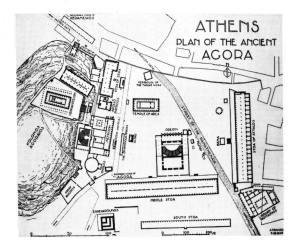

81. THE AGORA AT ATHENS
   From H. A. Thompson, *The Athenian Agora: A Guide*
   Courtesy American School of Classical Studies, Athens

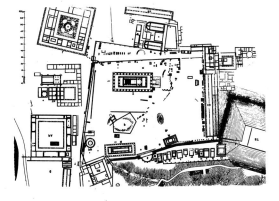

82. THE SANCTUARY AT OLYMPIA
   Durm, *Handbuch der Architcktur. Baukunst der Griechen*
   Courtesy Alfred Kroner Verlag

83. TOMB OF FISHERS (painting), Tarquinia
Etruscan, sixth century, B.C.
Alinari, Art Reference Bureau

84. ODYSSEY LANDSCAPE (Laestrygonians), Rome (Vatican)
Roman, A.D. first century
Alinari, Art Reference Bureau

85. Garden scene (Prima Porta), Rome
A.D. first century
Anderson

86. Harbor scene, Stabiae (Naples)
A.D. first century
Anderson

87. FUNERARY URN, Chiusi
(Chiusi)
Etruscan, seventh-sixth cen-
turies, B.C.
Alinari, Art Reference Bureau

88. L. VIBIUS AND FAMILY (Vatican)
first century, B.C.
Alinari, Art Reference Bureau

89. Altar of Peace (Terra Mater), Rome
ca. 10 B.C.
Courtesy Fototeca di Architettura e Topografia dell'Italia Antica

90. ALTAR OF PEACE (Aeneas sacrificing), Rome
ca. 10 B.C.
Courtesy Fototeca di Architettura e Topografia
dell'Italia Antica

91. ALTAR OF PEACE (main frieze: the imperial family), Rome
ca. 10 B.C.
Courtesy Fototeca di Architettura e Topografia dell'Italia Antica

92. ARCH OF TITUS (triumphal procession with spoils of Jerusalem),
Rome
ca. A.D. 82
Alinari, Art Reference Bureau

93. COLUMN OF TRAJAN, Rome
ca. A.D. 112
Courtesy Fototeca di Architettura e Topografia dell'Italia Antica

94. FROM ARCH OF SEPTIMIUS SEVERUS, Leptis Magna
ca. A.D. 200
Courtesy Fototeca di Architettura e Topografia dell'Italia Antica

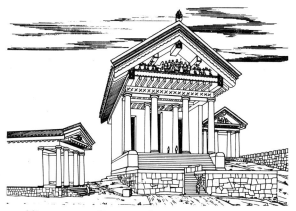

95. TEMPLES OF CITADEL, Cosa
third-second centuries, B.C.
From *Memoirs of the American Academy at Rome*,
XXVI (1960)
Courtesy of the American Academy, Rome

96. SANCTUARY OF FORTUNA, Praeneste (model)
ca. 80 B.C.
Courtesy Fototeca di Architettura e Topografia dell'Italia Antica

97. House of the Silver Wedding, Pompeii
A.D. first century
Anderson

98. Dining pavilion, Hadrian's villa, Tivoli
A.D. 120
Courtesy Fototeca di Architettura e Topografia dell'Italia
Antica

99. Basilica Nuova, Rome
ca. A.D. 310
Courtesy Fototeca di Architettura e Topografia dell'Italia Antica

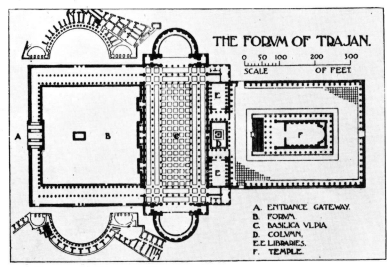

THE FORVM OF TRAJAN.

0 50 100 200 300
SCALE OF FEET

A. ENTRANCE GATEWAY.
B. FORVM.
C. BASILICA VLPIA.
D. COLVMN.
E.E. LIBRARIES.
F. TEMPLE.

100. FORUM OF TRAJAN, Rome

ca. A.D. 113
From Axel Boethius, *The Golden House of Nero*
With permission of the University of Michigan Press
(Copyright © by the University of Michigan, 1960)

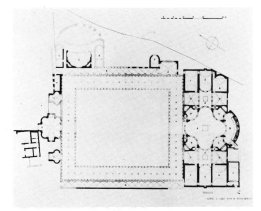

101. PALACE OF HADRIAN, Tivoli

ca. A.D. 120
From H. Kähler, *Hadrian und Seine Villa Bei Tivoli*
With permission of Gebr. Mann, Berlin

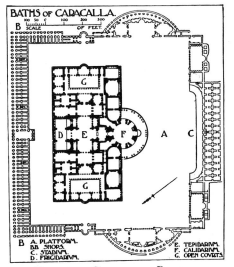

BATHS of CARACALLA.

100 50 0 100 200 300
B SCALE OF FEET

B A. PLATFORM.
BB SHOPS.
C. STADIVM.
D. FRIGIDARIVM.
E. TEPIDARIVM.
F. CALIDARIVM.
G. OPEN COVRTS.

102. BATHS OF CARACALLA, Rome

ca. A.D. 215
Robertson, *Greek and Roman Architecture*
Permission of Cambridge University Press

103. STA. COSTANZA, Rome

ca. A.D. 325

Courtesy Fototeca di Architettura e Topografia dell'Italia Antica
and Deutsches Archäologisches Institut, Rome

104. Apse Mosaic, Sta. Pudenziana, Rome
A.D. fourth century
Hirmer Verlag, Munich

105. Mausoleum of Galla Placidia, Ravenna
A.D. fifth century
Hirmer Verlag, Munich

106. S. Apollinare in Classe, Ravenna
A.D. sixth century
Hirmer Verlag, Munich

107. S. Vitale (apse), Ravenna
A.D. sixth century
Hirmer Verlag, Munich

108. S. VITALE (choir), Ravenna
A.D. sixth century
Hirmer Verlag, Munich

109. ROSSANO CODEX (parable of virgins), Rossano
A.D. sixth century
Hirmer Verlag, Munich

110. Sarcophagos (allegorical scenes)
Hirmer Verlag, Munich

111. Sarcophagos (symbolic scenes), Rome (Lateran)
A.D. sixth century
Hirmer Verlag, Munich

112. ORPHEUS, Athens (Byzantine Museum)
A.D. sixth century
Courtesy Byzantine Museum, Athens

113. NATIVITY, Athens (Byzantine Museum)
A.D. fifth century
Courtesy Byzantine Museum, Athens

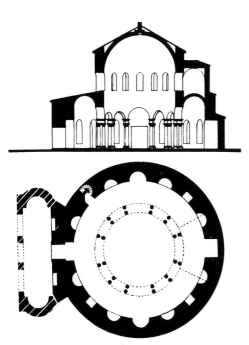

114. Sta. Costanza, Rome
ca. A.D. 325
From Volbach, *Early Christian Art*
Courtesy Hirmer Verlag, Munich

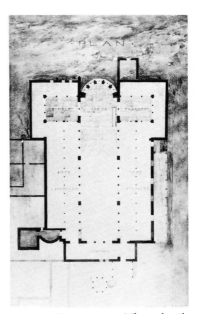

115. St. Demetrios, Thessalonike
A.D. fifth century
From Volbach, *Early Christian Art*
Courtesy Hirmer Verlag, Munich

116. St. Demetrios, Thessalonike
A.D. fifth century
Hirmer Verlag, Munich

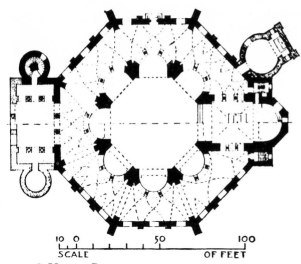

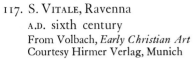

10   0   50   100
SCALE   OF FEET

117. S. Vitale, Ravenna
     A.D. sixth century
     From Volbach, *Early Christian Art*
     Courtesy Hirmer Verlag, Munich

118. Sancta Sophia, Constantinople
     A.D. sixth century
     From Volbach, *Early Christian Art*
     Courtesy Hirmer Verlag, Munich

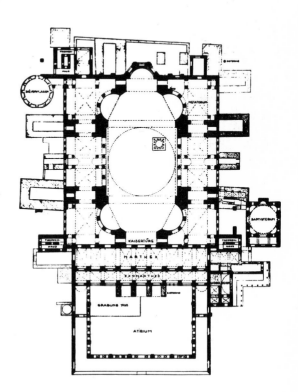

119. SANCTA SOPHIA, Constantinople
A.D. sixth century
Hirmer Verlag, Munich

Aesthetic Aspects of ANCIENT ART

Art "is always a vision, an attempt to express visibly what a particular age, a particular society, a particular person has viewed as the true nature and essence of reality, and this includes both the essence of man and of his relations to significant aspects of the world."

BRUNO BETTELHEIM

But what do they mean when they speak of different styles, unless they mean different visions of the world?

LEONARDO RICCI

Even today, even for man in the future, reality must include an awareness of the reality known to our ancestors. Just as the grown man is composed in part of the child, the boy, the youth of his earlier years of experience, modern man is partly his cultural past. No life can be full, complete, without awareness even of that experience which it lacks or explicitly rejects. Even today, even in the future, it is necessary to see what one can of the visions of the world known to man remote in time and place.

The past of Western man is imbedded in the ancient Mediterranean world. With all that has occurred since the submergence of that world in history there was his beginning, there his earliest youth. Its experiences were among the major experiences of mankind, and they are in the tradition of modern man. To recapture the experience of these visions there are, perhaps, various ways, but one, certainly, is through the arts in their various styles—for "what do they mean when they speak of different styles, unless they mean different visions of the world?"

Introduction:
The Structure of Style

O UR PURPOSE is to try to discover the basic and meaningful characteristics of the several styles of art that prevailed in the ancient Mediterranean world, and the first step toward this is to understand the relation of style to art.

The concept "style" is the usual basis for the historical study of art and it is crucial to the methods of archaeology in general. The distribution of works of art and other objects through time and place, their relation to the individuals or groups of men who made them, are considered primarily with reference to style. To recognize a style in terms of some systematic pattern of qualities, to distinguish similarities and differences among various styles and various phases of a single style, these are fundamental, practical problems. In spite of this, the actual, essentially valid fundamentals of style itself—its own nature, its own function, the rationales that determine the formation of a particular style—these are still not really understood. But for our purpose of surveying comprehensively the complex panorama of the styles of the ancient Mediterranean world it is necessary to take some specific positions, even if dogmatically.

By "art" we commonly mean a great variety of things—painting, sculpture, architecture, literature in its various branches, music, the dance, and those artistic expressions which seem to be secondary qualities of products essentially for practical use. When we speak of a "people" we usually mean a fairly heterogeneous lot of individuals living together under varying conditions over a more or less wide area through a more or less extensive period of time, during which they may have experienced many critical changes of fortune. Because of the accidents of history and external conditions or for some more significant reason, the art preserved from one people may be of a different kind than that preserved from another: there is much painting from Egypt and little from Greece; much literature from Greece and little from Egypt. To speak then of "the art" of "the Greeks" or "Greece" includes already so many variables of so many different kinds as to seem to baffle logical treatment; and to try to compare systematically "the art of Greece" with "the art of Egypt" may seem to involve, in addition, so many incomparable elements as to be meaningless.

If there is any reality to our concept "art" as including various "arts," we must suppose that there is something common to the several arts included. If we could identify the common elements, we should be able to see more clearly the generally basic qualities which constitute art, and to discuss any art from any time, place, or condition, at least in relation to these elements and qualities, and in terms of them to compare it with any other art from any other situation.

The Objective State of the Work of Art

It is possible that we might discover, or at least approach, these fundamentals through a dissection of the actual objects of art at hand. But what is the "actual" object of art to be dissected? A work of art may be conceived to exist in at least three states: one in the mind of the artist, another which he constructs in the objective physical world, and a third in the mind of the observer. Indeed, in those arts which must be "performed," like drama, music, and the like, other states may be seen to exist, in the minds of the performers and in some aspects of the production. Of these the only state practically available for examination is the second—the objective. The artist is seldom available to give an account of his own conception apart from his objective construction; the "observer," especially when we are dealing with the work of past generations, is equally elusive—unless we consider ourselves the observer, in which cause the enterprise becomes completely subjective. We must, therefore, begin with the work of art in the objective state.

But what, more specifically, is the objective state of the work of art? The artist has some conception which he wishes to endow with a form of existence that will be independent of his own mind and will continue to exist in its own form and material regardless of whether the artist himself may forget, change his mind, move away, or die. This fabrication must be of a sort that an observer, whether the artist himself or another person, can gain from it some awareness of the conception originally held by the artist. Sometimes the artist may insist that he has no concern with whether a second person ever sees the work, but the fact remains that the artist has attempted to create an independently existing thing of materials and forms constituting in some way a direct equivalent of something in his own mind, such that this could be recreated in another mind.

THE MEANS OF REPRESENTATION

What is it, however, which distinguishes the work of art so described from a mathematical proposition or a chemical formula or a recipe for making bread? Putting aside for the moment other considerations, for immediate purposes some characteristics of art may be derived from the proposition—dogmatic or hypothetic if necessary—that art involves aesthetic effects in the original Greek sense of the word, implying "apprehension by the senses." Since all apprehension—if we except intuition, divine revelation, and extrasensory perception—is through the senses, if "aesthesis" is to mean some distinct kind of perception it must refer to an immediate apprehension through the senses without intervention or interpretation by rational process. Of this a common and crudely simple example would be the soothing effect of certain colors and sounds; more generally it would be the awareness of colors and sounds, and other sensory experiences, without any thought about them, as one may simply feel comfortably warm or cool without putting this feeling into words.

It must be understood clearly and explicitly that in this definition of "aesthetic" there is no rigid reference to "beauty," nor is the aesthetic effect to be considered exclusive to art. In our usage, a work of art is a man-made object which possesses, among other attributes, aesthetic elements, but it is not necessarily beautiful. Other man-made objects, like bridges or airplanes, also possess aesthetic elements, and they too may or may not be beautiful, but they are not works of art because the aesthetic elements are accidental by-products of a design determined primarily by other factors. Natural objects, like flowers or sunsets, possess aesthetic elements, and, also, may or may not be beautiful, but they are not considered works of art because they are not man-made. Works of art, or other objects which are not works of art, may be evaluated in terms of their aesthetic qualities in our sense—i.e., the kind and degree of sensory apprehension they make possible—or in terms of "aesthetic" in some other sense—e.g., in terms of beauty, however beauty be defined—but these are distinct and different evaluations.

Thus we have two limited terms: aesthesis, meaning immediate apprehension by sensory means; and art, meaning human activity governed by aesthetic factors. As we have observed, objects which are not art may have aesthetic qualities simply by their own nature, as the curve of the cables in a suspension bridge or the aerodynamic lines of a military aircraft, but in most man-made objects there is usually some room for purposive imposition of aesthetic factors as a determinant in establishing some of the form, in addition to other factors controlling the form. The choice between a suspension and cantilever bridge might be an example; some of the lines of a rifle, the "style" of an automobile, the shape of household silver or chinaware—indeed most objects of use will be equally useful in any of several forms, and the ultimate decision of the form may have an aesthetic as often as an economic or other basis. To the extent, then, that aesthetic factors have determined the form of an object in use, the object may be said to be a work of art. Conversely, regardless of how affective its aesthetic character may be, if that aesthetic factor was not in itself a determining factor in forming the object, the object is not, simply because of that aesthetic factor, a work of art.

These observations are important not only in bringing into our purview the world of "minor arts" as commonly understood, but in suggesting the theoretical basis for an aesthetic element in the concept of "style" not only in art but in all other human activities that are not purely technical. Whenever, even in most practical activities, man makes choices from aesthetic motives, the peculiarity of his work may be understood, with art in the more conventional sense, in terms of those aesthetic factors.

Thus the distinctive feature of the work of art in its objective state is the structure of devices constituting sensory stimuli which are, in the artist's judgment, means capable of communicating his conception by reproducing a sensory experience, even though he may regard the process of formulating and constructing this stimulant as an end in itself, satisfying him in its completion. The dissection of the work of art in its objective state, then, is ultimately a matter of identifying and assessing the elements effective in stimulating the senses.

We are brought, then, to the final preliminary to the dissection—a reminder of just what the sensory stimuli are or can be. They must, of course, be devices capable of stimulating the senses, or some of them. The senses, however classified in technical psychologies, include chiefly and broadly those of sight, hearing, touch, taste, smell, and motion—all with various subdivisions; and they may also include some "organic" senses of obscure character that may be exemplified by anger and relaxation. Practically speaking, of course, not all of these are of concern in an account of what is commonly considered as "art"; we realize immediately that neither taste nor smell come seriously into the problem, especially in a modern consideration of ancient art. For practical purposes the arts are chiefly concerned with four kinds of sensation: optic, auditory, tactile, and kinaesthetic.

ELEMENTS IN THE MEANS OF REPRESENTATION

MATERIAL SUBSTANCES

The first purpose of the preceding discussion is to justify the attempt to identify in a work of art in the objective state those elements which are the means of stimulating the senses. If, now, we focus our attention on an actual work of art—for example, a painting—the question arises, where are these sensory stimuli? The direct stimulus of course is the light itself that strikes the eye, but as we examine the painting the most tangible thing about it as an independent object is the canvas and pigment of which it is made. It is worthwhile, then, to consider the nature and relative position of these material substantial elements in order to distinguish them the more readily from the more elusive elements. In general, with regard to the painting, we would say that these material elements—the canvas and pigment—are substances calculated to generate or project the sensory stimuli. There arises the problem of identifying similar elements, if any, in other arts.

If we examine first of all examples of commonly recognized works of art in painting, sculpture, and architecture, we find at once that they differ conspicuously but not consistently in the material elements of their construction. Paintings are constructed of pigments of various media—vegetable or mineral matter in vehicles of oil, water, and so forth—affixed to some kind of surface—canvas, paper, wood, plaster, stone. Sculptures are constructions of metal, stone, plaster, wood, paper (even pigment), too, though the materials which are normally primary in sculpture constitute simply the base for painting. Works of architecture, at first glance, also seem to be constructions of stone, wood, metal, concrete, or other familiar or unfamiliar materials almost any of which would be appropriate also to sculpture, but a moment's reflection will make it clear that these materials are actually secondary to the characteristic substance of building, which is space, formed into volume—the word understood geometrically. The forms of the walls and supports are essentially sculptural, in that they are plastically formed solid substances, but the empty volume formed by the walls and supports is the primary characteristic substance of the architecture. It does indeed strain the term "material substance" to make it include "empty geometric volume"; what we have done is to create a logical category and apply to it a term chosen almost arbitrarily, but in the end the operation will prove to be useful.

In dance, music, literature, and drama, there is more than one objective state of the work of art, unless the artist is performing his own work *ex tempore,* for whereas in painting, sculpture, and architecture the original artist constructs his work in the objective state once and for all, in other arts he must rely on a performer—an artist in his own right —to construct the work anew for each performance. In the dance, for example, the objective state is in the performance itself, in the physical movement of the performers. Indeed, there may be understood to exist simultaneously two objective states: that which is experienced internally by the performer himself as his body moves, and that which is experienced optically by the observer watching the dancer's movements. But in either case the body of the dancer is the material substance and the movement is the characteristic aesthetic stimulus affecting the senses directly or indirectly.

In music, the conception of the composer is usually preserved as a written score, but this is only an aid to memory or a series of instructions and not the work of art itself. In one sense the actual objective state of the work of music is the sound produced by the singer or instrumentalist, for even though this be the most ephemeral of the states of the work of music it is the only one in which the aesthetic stimuli as such have any existence apart from the mind of the artist or observer. But the sound corresponds to the light of a painting; the question is whether there is in music anything that corresponds to the pigment in painting. In one sense this correspondence is seen in the actual operation of the voices and instruments engaged in the performance, and indeed by strictly logical analogy it is precisely here that we should see the "material substantial" elements of music—in the operation of voice and instruments producing sound waves.

In literature, too, with some variations, the written words are mnemonic devices, like notes, to guide the "performance" of the work by a performer reading either to others or to himself. But there are, of course, considerable differences between music and literature, between the written notes of a score and the written words of a literary composition. In one respect the written words are like notes in that they indicate the formation of a certain sound by the vocal cords, and this sound has an actual impact on the senses. But though this sound has aesthetic significance simply as sound in almost any literary work, and the dominant significance in some, in most literatures the major importance of the sound is in evoking some meaning, and it is this meaning which embodies the material substance that provides the stimulus to the sensory receptor. For example, the word "moon" has a sound, and the sound in itself may be used for calculated aesthetic effects. But the sound "moon" also has a meaning: it denotes a celestial object familiar to everyone, and this meaning, the experience of the moon itself which the use of the word evokes, will stimulate in the hearer the sensation, within limits, that the actual sight of the moon would stimulate. (This is what is often meant by "imagery" in discussions of literature, though "imagery" in such discourse usually refers to the more colorful conscious meanings.) Thus a procession of words is a device to direct the mind to pass in review a procession of meanings or experiences; it is this array of meanings which is the substantial material projecting stimuli to the sensory system. This proposition might seem to violate our principle that aesthesis is direct apprehension by sensory means, in that we have introduced the mind, or a rational process, to translate the words into meanings. But it must be clear that the aesthetic reaction is between the meanings and the senses; the rational process comes between the printed word and the meaning. The printed word is not the work of art; the work of art is the construction of meanings which the reader, like the director of a play, presents to himself on the cue of the words. The aesthetic reaction, then, occurs as his senses respond to the mental performance.

Finally, in the drama, when we see a play actually performed we behold a composite form. The bodies of the actors, the scenery and properties of the stage setting, the sounds and meanings of the words spoken, are all material substantial elements in the actual performance —the objective state of the play. Even when we read the play instead of seeing and hearing it, we are in the position of a man reading a musical score or a poem: we are required to "produce," as it were, a mental performance of the drama, from which we may experience the sensations intended.

Thus our first effort to dissect the work of art in its objective state is to recognize the existence of the material substances of which it is formed. It is on this basis that we commonly make our practical distinctions among the arts—painting from sculpture, architecture from music or literature. But conspicuous and important though these elements are, they are only the material embodying and projecting the elements which are the characteristic essential of the aesthetic object—the actual stimuli to the senses. Thus, as pigment embodies or contains the substantial basis for light stimuli, so stone, volume, the dancer's body, instrumental and vocal performance, the meaning in words, embody or provide a substantial basis for the sensory elements in the work of art in its objective state.

Elements in the Means of Representation

CONCEPTUAL FORMS

Once again, if we focus our attention on a work of art, another element in its appearance seems to obtrude itself, and for various reasons it will be helpful to consider it next. To most people, the first step in the observation of a work of art is to say that it is a picture, for example, of a horse, or a statue of a man, or a poem about heroes. In any work of art the material elements and sensory elements are arranged according to some intelligible conception, and this conceptual element must certainly be recognized and accounted for. In the first place, some shaping of the material and sensory elements is unavoidable, and it is necessary to recognize the significance of the kind of shape. Second, these forms have their own role in producing stimuli, just as, in different ways, pigment and other substances do, and hence are a part of the aesthetic aspect of the work. The image of standing or running figures, of a battle, or of a garden, may evoke sensations of various kinds of motion, color, texture or sound, or even organic sensations.

In other words, the conceptual element is, or includes, the "subject matter" as commonly understood, or what is often called in discussions of painting and sculpture the "imagery" (not quite the same as "imagery" in discussions of literature). It is usually fairly easy to identify the conceptual form in a painting: it might be a human being or an animal or trees or flowers. However, in some kinds of art—geometric Greek vases or abstract paintings—there are no recognizable things, only geometric shapes. This at once suggests two different kinds of conceptual forms. The first are those derived from the world of natural objects, "naturalistic," intended in some sense to depict such objects; because of the variety of ways in which "naturalistic" has been used, this form might be called "iconic." And the second, those which are not derived from the natural world and are not intended to depict anything in it—this form then may be called "aniconic." The distinction is not so useful as it may seem, since it will be found that there is in fact very little aniconic conceptual form, most conceptual forms coming from the world of nature, however distorted. Most conceptual forms that might strike us as fanciful or fantastic are simply adaptations or distortions of natural forms; much that might strike us at first as pure geometry is actually derived by abstraction from natural objects. Nevertheless, it is useful when we can distinguish between something genuinely aniconic and something abstracted from nature. And in any case it is useful and meaningful to define as closely as possible the particular source of iconic conceptual form: floral, landscape, human—and so on.

The problem of conceptual form in architecture is complicated. With regard to the sculptural part of architecture—the walls and supports, the solid forms—the situation parallels that of sculpture, at least to some extent. We can say when a molding or a capital of a column takes its form from some floral inspiration or other source in the world of nature. But with the volume of a building, which we have tried to insist is the characteristically architectural substance, the problem appears in a different light. Moreover, in neither case are we likely to find an architectural conception worthy of the name with the direct purpose of depicting as such a natural form such as a man or a tree, though admittedly we do find houses whose design is purposely adapted to rock formations, airports with lines suggested by birds in flight, and possibly, though this may be disputed, domes inspired by the vault of heaven.

Introduction: The Structure of Style

From another point of view, we know that in a certain sense a good deal of historical architecture has depicted simpler, more primitive, and spontaneous kinds of building. Thus the Greek temple may reproduce in stone some details of wood or wood-and-mud-brick construction; the Persian hypostyle halls at Persepolis may well be simply elaborate versions of nomadic tents; a host of similar examples may be adduced to suggest that sophisticated architecture in permanent materials has commonly taken its form in details and in broader elements from prototypes in slighter materials. And, insofar as these prototypes may be said to have existed in nature, if the developed forms were modeled on them they may be said to be iconic—depicting natural forms.

But buildings like birds or rocks do not account for much of architecture, and though a Persian hypostyle hall may have reproduced a tent the question arises about the simpler prototypes behind developed styles—if "primitive," depicting no prior structural form, were they then aniconic? Or was their form derived from something in "nature"? In reality, that from which most buildings ultimately draw the forms of their volumes is the activity which is to take place within them (the use-function); that from which a structural member derives its form is the work it is to do (the structure-function). These functions are phenomena of the natural environment of the building, and thus, although we would hardly say that a theater depicts a dramatic performance, we must say that it derives its form from the performance—that in a sense its form does "reflect" the performance. In such a case the building's conceptual form would be analogous to the "naturalistic" iconic form more readily identifiable in painting. On the other hand, a building designed according to arbitrary geometric patterns without reference to its use-function, or walls and supports designed from the point of view of an arbitrarily conceived shape rather than from the point of view of its structure-function, would be analogous to the aniconic conceptual form of painting. The situation is not perfectly clear: in Islamic architecture, for example, there are domes which, though structurally hemispherical, are contrived by any of several means to have a more or less intricately polyhedral interior surface, molding a volume of curious shape that is purely arbitrary. Such a volume is not functional according to use or structure; whether it be regarded as iconic—"naturalistic" but fantastic—or a modification of natural shapes like stalactites or cloudy skies, or as aniconic—a rigidly mathematical form contrived in spite of use and structure—may be less clear.

In music, a definition of the conceptual form is easier to phrase though more elusive in essence. We may perhaps distinguish as aniconic compositions those which are simply demonstrations of harmonic theory—mathematical configurations expressed in sound. Those which adapt their form to some human activity—a march, a hymn, a song—would be naturalistic and iconic. Fortunately for us, it is unnecessary to develop this question in a consideration of ancient art.

Nor shall we be able to study the dance in antiquity, though here again the matter of conceptual form is relatively simple, since the dance usually involves the depiction of natural or fanciful beings and situations, though occasionally endeavoring to adapt itself to non-pictorial forms, and all this is fairly easily understood.

Literature may depict things and situations from the world of experience or create fanciful worlds based on nature; again it is difficult to find examples of aniconic literature. There are, to be sure, extreme examples of labored attempts to devise compositions in the verbal patterns of the prayer, the sonnet, and other conventional literary forms, devoid of any meaning whatsoever; there are also spontaneous nonsense verses and poetry written primarily for forms like the ballade and the rondel, and all these may be thought of as aniconic. But, more essentially, literature and especially poetry, when presented abstractly and not through the vehicle of some human character or experience, is aniconic to the degree that it lacks such a vehicle. Plato's *Symposium* and the thirteenth chapter of Paul's *First Epistle to the Corinthians* are both expositions of love: the former is cast in terms of a group of people at a banquet discussing a topic; the latter is cast as a series of ecstatic images emanating from a disembodied voice in a context rather abstractly allusive than pictorially formulated.

It is necessary, of course, to distinguish between the aniconic and the obscure. In modern works by Joyce, Stein, and others, the conceptual form is dominated by formal or theoretical relationships, and yet, however obscurely, they depict some natural creature, experience, or character.

The basic difficulty in discussing conceptual forms in literature lies in the fact that it is the meanings in the words which are the material substance, and almost any word is bound to contain a sense derived from nature or experience. Therefore it is impossible to divest literature of pictorial images, unless by substituting carefully contrived symbols for words in the manner of algebra or a logical exercise. But when these word-meanings, or "imagery," are used to formulate a picture of a thing or event or the like, or a configuration not derived from natural phenomena, it is then that we find ourselves confronting the "conceptual form."

In general, it may be said that substantially all art in all forms employs conceptual forms based on nature, in the sense that the sensory stimuli are arranged in patterns derived more or less from nature and the world of experience. We shall see that the question of fidelity to nature, or accuracy in rendering nature, does not affect this proposition, for a natural form may be abstracted or stylized to a degree of simplification or exaggeration that makes it almost unrecognizable— but it is still derived from nature. Hence the problem of distinguishing iconic and aniconic conceptual forms is fairly academic, though useful in a few instances of aniconic form and significant in clarifying the meaning of abstraction. The practical question, really, is the understanding of the scope of iconic naturalistic conceptual form, particularly in the arts of painting, sculpture, and literature. Here we find that styles may be more or less coherently distinguished as they show a preference for humanity—physically or in terms of character, thought, action, experience; for the animal world or some aspect of it; for the vegetable world or some aspect of it; or in nature or some part of it considered as environment. Thus on Greek vases the conceptual form is man and man alone; in Egyptian painting it is man in his natural environment; in Minoan art it is primarily vegetable and marine animal life.

ELEMENTS IN THE MEANS OF REPRESENTATION

THE SENSORY STIMULI

We have now distinguished two kinds of elements in the work of art in its objective state: the material elements, or substances, of which the work is composed; and the conceptual elements, or the forms or shapes according to which the sensory elements are arranged. We are at last in a position to consider the sensory elements—the stimuli projected by the material and conceptual elements on the nerve-receptor system of the observer.

To repeat, it is not essential to this accounting that there be an observer, or even that the artist anticipate an observer. The essential thing is that the artist constructs the work of art in terms of the sensory stimuli which in his own experience and understanding do in fact correspond to or stimulate the conception in his own mind. Again, once more, it may be recalled that the sensations most commonly involved in the usual arts are optic, auditory, tactile, and kinaesthetic.

Ordinarily we think of each of the arts in terms of a single kind of sensation. Painting and architecture are primarily visual, and so is sculpture, though more than any other this is tactile as well; music appeals to the ear. Drama and the dance involve more of the senses; literature, since the meanings of words can evoke many kinds of experience, involves stimuli for all senses. But in spite of the apparent limitations of some, all the arts involve all these senses, since all the senses possess the same fundamental characteristics and a stimulus received by one receptor—with some qualifications—can be apprehended, as it were, in terms of another.

In the first place it is clear that we are dealing in all cases with nerves—highly specialized in form and receptive acuity with reference to different kinds of stimuli. Crudely speaking, however, all four sensations—motion, light, sound, and texture—have a basic similarity in that the affective stimulus can be understood as successive impacts of something on the nerves at different rates. Light is a phenomenon of waves (or particles?) dispersed at different rates. The frequency determines what we call color or hue—low to high represented by the spectrum red to violet; the intensity of emanation or reception on a scale of low to high gives dilute or pure color; the volume of emanation or reception on a scale of low to high gives luminosity, or tone, from dark to bright. With sound we are dealing with waves or impulses of the air striking the nerves of the ear: the sounds vary in timbre by the character of the process producing the waves, but the height of pitch or tone varies with frequency, as low frequency gives a low, rough sound and high frequency a high, smooth sound; intensity ranges from gentle to strong; volume from faint to loud.

With the tactile sense we experience the direct impact of some physical substance on a nerve or nerves. If we think of this in a perspective of time, as when we sense a slow series of heavy impacts, drawing our finger over a surface, we call the surface rough; if a rapid series of small impacts, we call it smooth. Spatially conceived, the sensation of coarse sandpaper, with widely dispersed points of contact, is rough; fine sandpaper, with closely set points of impact, is smooth. As light and sound dissolve in insensibility at either end of a scale, so texture becomes a kind of smoothness which is really non-sensation when the point of contact with the body is continuous because of infinitely close-set points of impact or when the points of impact are so broadly spaced that they cannot be apprehended individually. Further, the intensity of the tactile stimulus is perceived in a scale of sensation from dull to sharp; the volume, from soft to hard.

Finally, in the kinaesthetic sense, motion is felt, in the first instance, by pressures created by the inertia of bodily substances on certain nerves. We are not really aware of motion itself, but of change of motion, whether change in speed or direction. If the change occurs in distinct impulses—at low frequency—we feel the movements as rough; if the change occurs in small, rapidly accumulated impulses, we feel it as smooth. Here, too, there is an ambiguity of time and space, so that we are often aware of a succession of stimuli in time as though it were a movement in space. Since velocity and acceleration are essentially matters of relationship between some unit of time and some unit of space—miles per hour, feet per second, telephone poles per minute *or* per mile as we drive along a road—whether we think of the time aspect or of the space aspect is not really important.

Thus, without deliberating all the limitations of all the permutations of the proposition, we glimpse the basis for the validity of our common conviction—that we can see and hear texture and motion in their various qualities, as well as seeing light and color and hearing sound. Whether we can "see" sound, or "hear" color, or "feel" either, is perhaps another matter, but need not concern us here. For our own purposes it is necessary only to observe that sensations of light, texture, and movement can be apprehended through the eye in response to visual stimuli designed in terms of frequency, intensity, and volume. A pattern of accents of light or color distributed over a surface may be apprehended both as light and color and as texture; distributed in linear form, they may be apprehended both as light and color and as movement.

All of this is obvious in painting. The purely visual stimuli are there—those that appeal to the sense of sight in and of itself—color and luminosity. But there is also the appeal to the sense of motion. Any pattern of accents established in colors, lights, dots, lines, or shapes may induce a realization of rhythmic beat, either in the movement of the eye from one accent to the next or as perceived in terms of distribution throughout a field, and the beat may be felt as motion through space or through time. A smoothly undulating line, indicated as drawn in color or light or dark, or indicated by sequences of elements of the pattern, or otherwise, creates an awareness of smooth movement; a violently angular line creates an entirely different kinaesthetic response; and so on. Finally, impressions of texture may be conveyed by arrangements of dots or points, or unbroken surfaces, or by a great variety of devices of color, light, or line. To this may be added also what we know of the textures or kinaesthetic qualities of the objects depicted, if they are recognizable.

Sculpture is essentially a matter of constructing tangible shapes with tangible materials. It is, par excellence, an art of the sense of touch, in which different qualities of surface—smooth, rippling, undulating, rough, granulated, and so forth—exist as physical qualities of the material as it has been worked. Moreover, the substances are arranged physically through three dimensions, establishing physical positions in space and bodily paths of movement through space. But all these sensations are also perceptible through the eye as in painting. One senses, through seeing, the textures, rhythms, movements. And, too, qualities of light and color may be provided in sculpture by the addition of pigment or by the use of different kinds of material, or by the treatment of the material to create actual light and shadow in different qualities, by shaping the forms or carrying the textures from absorbent granular surfaces to highly reflective polish.

It is worth emphasizing that the accents contributing to the apprehension of texture and movement may be implied rather than physically present in the work, as when we carry a movement initiated by a series of accents or lines to some other part of the composition.

If we think of architecture in terms of walls, floors, ceilings, roofs, and so forth, there is no difference in the sensory elements in this art from their nature in painting and sculpture. But if we insist on volume as the significant characteristic substantial element of architecture, ranging with pigment in painting and stone or metal in sculpture, we need some reflection to see how, in and of itself, it is effective in inducing sensory responses. Movement, for example, may be expressed in a building by what are essentially sculptural means: the vertical soaring of a Gothic nave is to some extent due to the ascending lines of the system of piers and ribs disintegrating finally to form the roofing system. Other senses are affected by the broad, smooth textures of the lower elements, the minutely shimmering textures of the upper reaches of the wall and pier systems, and the diffused brilliance of the luminosity of the higher surfaces contrasted with the subdued shadows of the lower. To a certain extent, these are functions of the sculptural and visual effects of the walls and windows. But the shape of the volume itself—narrow and long, horizontally and vertically—also channels the line of sight and movements to the ends or the top of the volume in a single, intense, full movement. The kinaesthetic effect of the volume, moreover, is not simply from its shape but from its own internal structure. In part, this is created visually from the operation of the lines of the wall structure, which tends to subdivide the volume into large forms in the lower reaches or minute particles toward the top; in part, it results from the different quality of the atmosphere itself induced by the varying luminosities—heavy and quiet at the bottom, scintillating and mobile above.

In general, architectural volumes have an impact on the kinaesthetic sense in three ways. One is by the actual movement of the observer, walking through a temple or a palace—the various shapes of rooms or parts of rooms and the doors or changes of level establish rhythmic accents of various kinds. Another is visual, as one becomes aware of the contours of the volumes, the lines of movement—directions—and the horizontal and vertical rhythms as the eye scans the interior. The most complete sense of movement is attained by combined vision and physical movement, as when one proceeds through a space while perspectives change and elements appear or disappear or change their form.

Color and luminosity of volume are an effect of lighting, direct and indirect, and the shadow and color of structural elements. A whole room, or part of a room, may have its own intensity or volume or even hue of luminosity pervading its atmosphere as well as coloring its walls. One may sense that a volume is soft and yielding, or crisp and firm—in part from its luminosity and in part from the shape given by the surrounding walls.

In music, the primary sensory stimulus is sound itself, directed immediately to the auditory nerve. With, indeed inseparable from, this are kinaesthetic stimuli. The rhythms of music, expressed either in the basic beat of the "time," in the repetition of phrases, cadences, movements, and other elements, may stimulate a direct kinaesthetic response of movement through time or in space of varying degrees of complexity. So also the rise and fall of tone and intensity and volume, the rhythm itself, or the quality of the melody—fluid and sweeping, or staccato, or something else—may arouse a continuous flowing movement or a disjointed, angular movement. So, too, the fluid movement, or a rasping or pizzicato melody, or different timbres of instruments or voice are evocative of responses of texture.

The dance is an art primarily of movement; indeed, it may be regarded as the most primitive of the arts in that it is simple, elemental movement and nothing else. In any case, whether it is presented directly to the performer in performance by his own movement, or visually to an observer, its stimulus is first to the kinaesthetic sense by rhythm, tempo, direction, and quality of motion. In this, just as in music, may be felt textures—smooth or rough, delicate or coarse.

In literature, of course, every sensory element may exist, though it is not always easy to identify the mode of its existence. For in literature the rational aspect of the work of art, which we shall discuss in more detail below, is strangely enough even more elusive than in the other arts since it blends more subtly with the aesthetic aspect. That is, the difference between a policeman's report of an automobile accident on a stormy night might differ materially from a novelist's account of the same event; the policeman would concentrate on the measurable fact and the writer on the way in which his characters were aware of the event. From the policeman's account we would get information which we could translate into experience, and we might then react to the experience. From the novelist's account we would sense the experience directly: feel the motion, chill to the dampness, and hear the sounds.

Thus, in their aesthetic aspect, the meanings of the words in literature must create sensory experiences of motion. From the policeman we learn that the automobile, proceeding at eighty miles an hour, ceased to move on impact with the bridge, and to a degree we understand what happened. But the same event described in "motion" words like speed, fast, sudden, crash, not to speak of more dramatic words, contains sensations of movement and tension that give us a more immediate awareness of the experience.

Apart from their meanings, words may appeal to the sense of motion in their rhythmic arrangement, not only in terms of sounds, accents, and quantities of pronunciation, as in poetry and poetic prose, and in terms of particular or similar words, phrases, and grammatical constructions, but also in terms of meanings, ideas, thoughts, pictures, and conceptions. Such rhythms may be apparent in single lines or through larger sections of a composition and may vary in a number of ways from simple alternating rise and fall of stress to complex patterns of various character or speed. The tempo of movement and its character as smooth or fluid or agitated or static or methodically pedestrian may also be suggested by the length and structure of sentences in relation to each other, or of paragraphs and other sections of the work, or of trains of thought and the ideas there developed. Potential movement, or controlled tension, may be felt in the structure or pacing of a work; large, "serious" words or sentences will differ in their quality of mobility from short, "casual" words, and this kind of difference may even induce a sense of lightness of weight with corresponding tensions.

Similarly, words may evoke visual stimuli as meanings in themselves apart from the thing being described. A description of a garden purely in terms of the botanical names of the flowers and shrubs growing in it may be sufficient to provide some readers with complete information about the scene in all its color, and the information will of course have its effect in stimulating the visual sense. But a description of the same garden in terms of color words like red, carmine, blue, emerald, or less specific words with connotations of color like "jeweled" effect an immediate optic reaction. Apart from their meanings, words that are plain or more or less unusual or elaborate, or such expressions or turns of phrase, are in a sense colorful in that they create a simple, monotonous effect or a rich and variegated one. So also figures of speech may evoke color sense, but more generally are "colorful" in the variety and surprise they create. Intensity and volume of light are contained in words like "bright," "dull," "shadowy," "clear," "suffused," "dark," "gloom"; they also recall that high-frequency sounds like "i" and "ee" tend (in English, at least) to be luminous, and low-frequency sounds like "o" and "ou" tend to be dark. Again, words implying various kinds of mood have a reference to luminosity, like "gay," "cheerful," "sad," "mournful"; and passages creating a sense of mood will normally produce, because of the mood, an atmosphere of corresponding luminosity.

In the same way, words evoke stimuli to the sense of touch through naming: "rough," "rippling," "undulating," "smooth," "fluffy"—appeal immediately to the tactile sense whatever their context. Or they may stimulate the sense of touch through their very sound, as in the preceding words and others like them—"limpid," "melodious," "rasping," "harsh"; and phrases, sentences, and paragraphs may be so constructed as to come smoothly, gratingly, or thickly in terms of sound, grammar, or meaning. The ambiguity of touch and movement is especially evident in the structure of writing: a sequence of regularly similar elements, equal and self-contained, may emerge as a series of starts and stops, or a kind of vibration, or a roughness; a flowing passage of even continuity may appear as a sweeping movement or a polished texture.

Finally, words affect the auditory sense in obvious ways. The actual physical sound of the word operates like any other sound, but the meanings have their own auditory effect: "strident," "bray," "hoarse," "singing" (especially as an adjective) "quiet," "calm"—such concepts appeal directly to the sense of touch.

ASPECTS OF THE ELEMENTS IN THE MEANS OF REPRESENTATION

THE AESTHETIC

Our survey of the elements of the work of art in its objective state has been for the purpose of developing a total view of the subject so that when presented with problems covering only a limited range of the field we may realize its position in relation to what is missing. But much of what can and must be said in a full analysis of art has been left untouched. Some of this depends on distinctions among what may be described as three aspects of the elements. So far we have been thinking in terms of the aesthetic aspect—the aspect which makes on the observer the characteristically definitive impact of the work of art—the way the observer is made to feel by the work of art. It is what Paul Valery has in mind in his "Commentaries on 'Charmes' " in *The Art of Poetry*[1] when he says "There is no question in poetry of transmitting to one person something intelligible happening within another. It is a question of creating within the former a state . . . [which]communicates it [i.e., the 'intelligible something'] to him."

In addition to this aspect, a work of art involves much technical skill and may include much that belongs in the world of intellectual understanding. Though these have little or nothing to do with the aesthetic impact in itself, they may have great importance in their own right, and if we are too understand the actual aesthetics of the work of art we must consider their relative position also.

[1] *Collected Works of Paul Valery*, ed. by Jackson Mathews, tr. by Denise Folliot. Bollingen Series XLV, VII (Pantheon, 1958), 157. A reference brought to my attention by Mrs. Vera Townsend.

ASPECTS OF THE ELEMENTS IN THE MEANS OF REPRESENTATION

THE TECHNICAL

The technical aspect has to do with physical construction and operation. There is a technical aspect to each of the three groups of elements—material, conceptual, and sensory. For example, the technical aspect of the material elements in painting would include methods of making and preparing surfaces for painting—wood, canvas, plaster; matters of pigment—composition of oils, tempera, water colors; methods of application, ways of holding the brush, and so forth. In sculpture, the technical aspects of the material would include the kinds of materials and methods of working them, the tools, the tooling. In architecture, it would be a question of the engineering or building, the calculation of stresses and loads, adhesion and cohesion, kinds and availability of materials and their characteristics; methods of actual construction—the craft of brick-laying, the tools and methods of carpentry. In literature, the technical aspect of the material elements—of words and their meanings—would include matters of phonetics, linguistics, lexicography, semantics, grammar, and the construction of figures of speech.

The technical aspect of the conceptual elements has to do with constructing the forms in the various media. In painting and sculpture, there are matters of iconography, anatomy, botany, zoology, and the like, and particularly in painting there are perspective and related matters on the basis of which naturalistic iconic forms are designed. In literature, there is similar material, and in addition a knowledge of character, history, and cause and effect in human relations. "Plot" is the equivalent of iconography applied to action, the pattern of incidents which constitute the special formulation of a narrative with reference to the verisimilitude or conviction of the mechanics of cause and effect. In architecture, the technical aspects of conceptual form involve problems of function. The particular requirements of liturgy, living, or business arising from their peculiarities must be accounted for in the volume of the building; the use of columns, piers, posts, walls, may be affected by technical peculiarities of structure-function.

Introduction: The Structure of Style

With regard to the sensory elements, the technical aspect includes problems of psychology—the processes by which sensory stimuli are received and made affective in the human being—and particular sciences of optics, geometry, and acoustics that have to do with the generation and projection of the sensory stimuli in the various arts. In literature, this is included in some problems of rhetoric: kinds of diction, figures of speech, ways of achieving emphasis, metrics, and symbolism help compose a science of the use of verbal artifices to guide practice in composition; it has to do with the skill or technique of applying words for sensory effect.

There are situations, of course, in which the technical aspect has a role in the aesthetic response. Indeed, a good understanding of the technical proficiency of an artist arouses a sense of admiration, an awareness of sure, clean economy and facility of action, that makes an aesthetic response so immediate that we speak quite naturally of the "art" of a surgeon or mathematician. If pressed we would probably deny that we mean anything aesthetic by this, and actually of course the action of the surgeon or mathematician is dominated by his own proper ends, not by aesthetic ends. But his special technical virtuosity does have aesthetic elements, and so also the technical virtuosity of an artist in the ordinary sense has its own aesthetic impact to add to the aesthetic impact of the material itself. One's knowledge of the weight or hardness of stone, the viscosity of pigment, that a figure of speech is a simile rather than a metaphor, and some understanding of the reason for the choice, may often affect in some way his aesthetic response to the whole. But this does not alter the fact that the technical aspect of the work of art is essentially different from the aesthetic, and the distinction should always be kept.

Aspects of the Elements in the Means of Representation

THE RATIONAL

In addition to the aesthetic and technical aspects of the work of art, the rational aspect should be distinguished as clearly as possible since it is frequently of great importance in the whole significance of the work, often inescapably obtrusive, and sometimes even distracting or misleading in the direct perception of the aesthetic impact. Although it may be insignificant in some instances, even then the observer is likely to be so concerned with the "meaning" or "idea" of the work that he is oblivious to anything else.

In general, the rational aspect is the knowledge or thought or reasoning that is demanded of the observer, as distinct from the skills and techniques required for the production of the work, or the state or awareness or perception that the work creates.

With regard to the material elements in painting, for example, the distinctions between certain substances like oil pigment or gold leaf have their technical aspect in the problems of application, their rational aspect in the theory or tradition of their use and in their commercial value (and perhaps otherwise), and their aesthetic aspect in "how they look." And so with the material substances in all the arts, there are always ideas, thoughts, theories, special understandings that one may have about them, apart from the technique of their use or their sensory impact.

The rational aspect of the conceptual elements frequently dominates one's whole attitude toward the work of art. While the conceptual forms may have their aesthetic aspect, their impact on the sensory system, of equal importance is their intellectual content as they depict or illustrate some action or idea. Their rational aspect lies in the way these works stimulate thought and cogitation about such matters. One's efforts to think through, to explain the artist's message, his meaning, his lesson or information as indicated by the characters in action and their interrelations—these are rational, intellectual activities. So strong is the tendency to regard the conceptual elements of painting and sculpture rationally that it is common for observers to be nonplused before a work in which the rational element is minimized—whether iconic or aniconic—and to feel that the rational aspect has been concealed in some way. Theoretically, of course, there is no reason why a work of art must have a significant rational aspect. . . .

The rational aspect of the conceptual form of a building would be the knowledge, interest, thoughts, and ideas one has about the use-function. In a church, the technical requirements of liturgy would establish certain requirements for the shaping of the building. The shapes of the volumes developed would convey their own aesthetic impact, but one's knowledge and reflections about the liturgy would be rational. This might affect one's perception of the volumes and color one's aesthetic reactions, though it would not necessarily do so. A person brought up in the Christian tradition is likely to have a stronger, and almost certainly a different reaction, influenced by his rational understanding of the spirit and tradition of Christian liturgy, when he encounters a Christian church, than he has, out of his rational understanding of the spirit and tradition of any other religion, if he encounters a religious monument of that religion. Or, in the conceptual forms determined by structure-function, we have an intellectual interest in seeing, for example, how the shafts and ribs of a Gothic ceiling system are developed logically and completely to account for accumulation of all stresses on a sufficient series of supports. And when we relate the sculptural program of the façade to our knowledge of contemporary dogma or history, we are quickly lost in the intricacies of the rational content of the work.

In literature, the "idea" or "theme" or "argument" of a work may have a part in the total effect: it may be part of the purpose of the work, or parallel the aesthetic purpose, contributing to it, but it is different in kind from the aesthetic impact. For example, the conceptual form of a play about Oedipus is the reaction of Oedipus to a situation. Considered technically this form is what we call plot—the structure of the incidents in the tragedy. The rational aspect is what Sophocles says or thinks about Oedipus and his problems, whether expressed in words attributed to Oedipus or the chorus, such as "Apollo brought these woes to pass . . . the hand that struck the eyes was mine," or "call no one happy . . . until he hath crossed life's border free of pain," or whether it is to be inferred from the logic of development. These interpretations of experience, these reflections about the responsibility of God and man —more recently our modern interpretation in terms of an "Oedipus complex"—all this is matter for thought, not sensation. The thought may indeed loom large in setting our mood for the reception of the totality of the work, sobering us by contemplation of the limitations of human powers, and in passing details this or that intellectual understanding may affect our state of being as we react aesthetically to the sensory impact of the play. But the proper aesthetic aspect of the conceptual form, and the distinctively "art" element in the play, is the way that these experiences of these characters make us feel—the actual sensations that we experience.

Finally, there is a rational aspect to the sensory elements themselves —to the lights, sounds, textures, and movements which are embodied in them and which arouse these sensations in our own being. It is, again, what we think about them—the self-awareness that we have of them. Occasionally, there is something a little more specific, as when we attach a special meaning to a special color—red means "stop" (or danger, or harlotry, or murder); certain shapes of lines may acquire conventional significance. But this is certainly of more restricted importance than the broader and deeper ranges of the rational aspect of conceptual form.

The Means of Representation

SUMMARY

In summary, then, we have found the work of art in the objective state to consist of three kinds of elements: material, conceptual, and sensory; and to exist, in all three elements, in three aspects: technical, rational, and aesthetic. Of these, the aesthetic aspect is the characteristic, fundamental, essential peculiarity of art itself. It is with this aspect that we are primarily concerned, and we shall deal with the others only when they have, as they often do for particular reasons, a significant part in the aesthetic response or in the definition of the style.

The Manner of Representation

A "style" is a characteristic way of doing something. The style of a particular art may include characteristic choices of material, conceptual, and sensory elements; characteristic emphases on the technical, rational, or aesthetic aspects; and characteristic ways of using the elements in the aspects chosen. Considered pragmatically and empirically—not only with reference to actual works of art but with reference to the traditional experience of historical and archaeological analysis, style may be characterized in terms of almost innumerable variables, but most of those which relate inherently to the aesthetic aspect, which we have seen is the universal but exclusive aspect—the definitive essence—of art, may be subsumed under a relatively few heads. These do not emerge in a sharply defined, clearly logical pattern of categories, though some more than others seem to be metaphysical in reference; some, physical; some, structural. The common factor is that they all have to do with variations in the manipulation of the elements—the elements being the "means" to the aesthetic effect, while the manipulation itself pertains to the "manner" of developing the means, to reflect Aristotelian terminology. For convenience and clarification we might outline the principles of analysis as follows:

I. ELEMENTS OF THE WORK OF ART IN THE OBJECTIVE STATE (THE MEANS)

	Aesthetic Aspect	*Technical Aspect*	*Rational Aspect*
1. MATERIAL			
pigment, stone,	HOW OR	WHAT IS	WHAT IS
volume, bodies,	WHAT ONE	USED AND	THOUGHT OR
performance,	FEELS	HOW THEY	UNDERSTOOD
meanings, etc.	BECAUSE OF	ARE	RATIONALLY
2. CONCEPTUAL	THEM	FASHIONED	WITH
iconic, aniconic			REFERENCE
forms			TO THEM
3. SENSORY			
light, color			
touch			
motion			
sound			

II. Variations in Manipulating the Elements (the Manner)

those pertaining especially to ontology
epistemology
signification
definition
configuration
dynamics
system
focus
cohesion

Variations in manner relating to ontology

One quality of the manner of manipulating the aesthetic elements derives from convictions about certain aspects of the nature of being—from ontological grounds—whether the artist treats things as particulars, as abstracted essences, or as something in between. This will be most evident in the conceptual form, where it will usually be fairly clear whether the subject matter—a man, for example—is taken as a unique individual, different from all others; as an ideal, or representative of a type or kind of humanity or of the animal world; or as some distilled essence of the human being—his mechanical structure, his spirit, his geometric form, or the like. The complete abstraction is a reduction of the form found in nature to some single element or principle—a single smallest common denominator. The extreme particularization is the totality of all the elements constituting a particular man at one time in one place in the world of nature. Between these extremes there is a continuous range of possibilities with, in the center, the "typical" or "ideal" man—the conception containing all, but only, the common denominators of mankind distinguishing him from other animals. Once again, the chief problem is in stating the relative position of any one example or group of examples in this range; the general principle is clear enough.

As applied to the material and sensory elements of the work of art, the concept of ontological character is not so obvious. In theory it is easy to say that particularism in movement, light, texture, and so forth is an emphasis on the uniqueness of that which is actually used, while abstraction is emphasis on some essence. In practice, it is difficult to do so in many situations, although it is important to attempt the distinction.

Variations in manner relating to epistemology

Another scale of qualities is based on epistemological premises— whether the artist treats things objectively or subjectively or in some way in between. Despite the difficulties, the distinctions are sometimes conspicuous in art and generally recognized in such terms as illusionism, impressionism, expressionism, and the like, though the use of these words has been inconsistent and even self-contradictory. In an illustration from conceptual form, the objective manner would put into the work of art in its objective state only definite, tangible equivalents for elements of the object depicted as they exist in the natural object—to reconstruct, so to speak, the natural object and thence allow the reaction between the observer and the depiction to occur as it would between the observer and the natural object. The subjective manner would be to include also specific reference to the observer—his involvement, his point of view, his relationship, his own effect on or contribution to the thing depicted or the depiction. The extreme objective method of rendering flowers would be to depict them with botanical accuracy so that the observer would see in the depiction everything that exists to be seen in the flower itself; the subjective method would be to include in the painting only those aspects of the flower which the observer would value or notice—a splash of color, perhaps—and devices suggesting the observer's attitude toward the flower, his feeling about it. The extreme of subjectivity would be a kind of expressionism in which calculated distortions of the objective form of the thing depicted would be introduced to heighten or exaggerate some facet of the subjective relationship.

So, too, color and light may be objective—specific hues applied in distinct pigments; or subjective—optical blends or suggestions by juxtapositions of pigments of various hues. Motion may be rendered objectively by complete lines and contours or by implied lines or directions. The sensory stimuli of words and meanings may be varied in analogous ways.

It might be well to allude to a possible complication—that it is possible to be objective about subjective experience, or vice versa. For example, in nineteenth-century impressionism and pointillism, it is assumed that man's experience of things is subjective, but the method is developed in terms of the objective facts of scientific optics. The implications and permutations of this ambiguity, however, are too complex to treat in general terms, though they may be elucidated in particular situations.

Variations in manner relating to signification

"Signification" has to do with whether things are to be taken literally, symbolically, allegorically, or in some other way. Much confusion arises from the range of meanings that have been attached to the word "symbol," and there is no hope of establishing a particular definition satisfactory to all, but we must try to define the sense in which we shall use the word here.

Generally speaking, a symbol is something that evokes a meaning far wider than the direct, specific significance of the thing itself. In this respect most words, numbers, and works of visual art are symbols. But for our purposes we may ignore this elemental symbolism of the devices of thought and perception, which we may call "basic," and try to distinguish other categories. For it is evident that some artists try to be "literal"—to say or paint a thing, a tree or an animal, simply in and for itself; others endow each object with secondary and tertiary and further meanings, layer on layer, beyond and apart from the immediate significance of the object itself.

These extended meanings may be intellectual or emotional in character. In the first case, one interprets the extension of the meaning by some kind of intellectual understanding or process. He knows that a wreath is an emblem of victory; that a shrouded woman is to be understood as "Death," and that the Slough into which Christian falls is despair and not a swamp; that Scarlett O'Hara constitutes an analogy with the American South. Thus intellectual symbols may include "emblematic," "allegorical," and "analogical" symbols, and perhaps others. Emotional symbols, on the other hand, are those which constitute some part of an experience, and they are used in such a way that our emotions are drawn into the experience and are likely to continue the experience beyond the extent of the actual symbol. Behind this there may be, or may have been, earlier in our lives, some rational understanding of the connections, but this is not always so and in any case does not operate significantly in our apprehension of the symbol. Such is true of effective ritual and myth and many psychological symbols.

The problem may be illustrated in the question of whether a depiction of a fish is to be understood simply as a fish or as a symbol of Christ. And whether the Christ is to be understood as God or a proof of God's love or an example of how one should live his life. Although such questions are most natural in the rational aspect of the work, they are equally significant in the aesthetic aspect, for although it may require a rational act to determine whether the fish is merely a fish or intended as Christ, once the conclusion is reached the interpretation may have a profound effect on the way in which the observer sees the fish and reacts to it. Similarly, a cross taken literally as a cross is a simple and relatively static pattern of lines, but taken as the Cross of the Crucifixion it is, for many people, a source of powerful dynamic force. Moreover, the fish, apart from its anagrammatic reference to Christ, is to some degree an emotional symbol only somewhat less vivid than the snake and some other creatures. In this it has a direct aesthetic value that may color the rational interpretation.

Not only the conceptual form but also the sensory elements may be treated in this way. An artist may use a red hue in the garment of a figure simply because it is red, for the sensory value of that color, or symbolically, because according to conventional symbolism it represents blood or fire or harlotry. A particular rhythm under some circumstances may have a symbolic meaning; light may be simply light or it may symbolize the Forces of Light. Though these meanings may be intellectually established, their symbolic meaning endows them with a particular and often enhanced value in stimulating the senses—and it must not be forgotten that the original intellectual choice frequently must have involved the artist's aesthetic sense of appropriateness.

Even the materials of art may have such literal or symbolic use: gold leaf in the background of a scene may stand for existence in a world of eternity, not the world of particular time and place that we inhabit; in literature, certain words, idioms, dialects, the use of foreign words, often mean something beyond the meaning of the word—may symbolize something about the characters using them, or the like.

In our own investigation, then, it is important to know whether an artist is using some kind of intellectual or emotional symbolism, and whether he uses it consciously or unconsciously, and whether the audience is or is not conscious of the usage.

Variations in manner relating to definition

Still another group of variables in the manner of handling the elements of the work of art has to do with what might be called the character of "definition": qualities such as clarity, vagueness, precision, looseness, definiteness, indefiniteness, and the ranges between them. We may speak in such terms of the material elements: whether the pigment is clearly apparent in the painting or subdued or obscured in some way, a factor which is represented in the choice between an oil or enamel and a water color or encaustic; whether the stone or metal or wood of a piece of sculpture is clearly such or presented in a way to be less readily distinguishable; the clarity of definition of a volume; the clarity or vagueness of words in their meaning or sound. We speak, too, in any of the arts, of a clear or confused or obscure movement, rhythm, color, sound, or texture. In the conceptual forms we recognize various degrees and kinds of definition in the forms depicted, their action, character, experience, thought. The quality of definition is one of the most evident in the manner of an artist of whatever medium; the great difficulty is in expressing the various shades of degree and difference.

Introduction: The Structure of Style

Variations in manner relating to configuration

Another group of variables has to do with what may be designated as "configuration," though in a rather special sense. This is the variety of treatment of aesthetic elements according to which they may be displayed either in line or serial progression; in expanse or surface; in three dimensions or mass; in four dimensions or more—that is, in space-time relationships.

In almost any painting, for example, line is evident either as a streak of pigment in the border of an area, or as the meeting place of two adjoining areas, or in the optical progression from one accent of color or form to another. But even a line drawing, of course, may be executed to produce a strong impression of solid, plastic, three-dimensional solidity. Therefore, it is not simply the presence of lines in a painting which make it "linear." It is rather the quality of the whole in suggesting a configuration of the elements which proceeds in a single direction along a single path or many paths. Indeed, a series of objects which may be understood to be solid and three-dimensional—representing mountains or people, for example—may be so arranged as to induce a sense of a single current of movement, a single chain of progression and association. Thus not only actual lines, but rhythms and movements, however induced, colors, lights, textures, the elements of the conceptual form, may be arranged in this way: in chain, as it were; in single progression.

In sculpture, line may be indicated by carving or engraving on the surface of the stone, or by the edges of two intersecting planes; and by the continuity between similar accents, as in painting. Characteristically, sculpture is an art of substance present in three dimensions; therefore, it is characteristically an art of mass. Nevertheless, in compositions of attenuated forms—even of wire—although the substance has its massive existence, it may be so attenuated as to evidence itself for all practical aesthetic purposes as line with independent physical existence.

In architecture, the plastic members of walls, supports, and the like may be treated with linear configuration like painting or sculpture, with linear arrangements of the elements of the walls, exaggeratedly slender columns, or in other ways. As for volumes, some, it may be said, are more spacious than others, and a volume which is simply a long, narrow corridor in comparison with others, would be linear. Moreover, an architectural composition calculated to channelize real or optical movement in a single direction may be felt to be linear in its configuration—as in a hall that may be relatively roomy but with everything focused on a single point at one end.

Linear configuration in literature is evident in the unbroken flow of simpler meters like iambics or dactyls; in the simple repeating rhythms of other kinds of accents; in the serial succession of color, light, sound, and texture as expressed in grammatical, rhetorical, and semantic terms; in the direct, chronological sequence in the unfolding of a story or the descriptions or explanations that are given substantially in terms of systematic listings.

The configuration of expanse, or two-dimension, or plane, or surface, refers to a manner of composition in which there is little concern for depth or solidity and the chief emphasis is on plane surfaces. In painting and sculpture, the interest is concentrated on the shapes of the plane surfaces, their textures or colors, their arrangement as part of a broader plane surface. Almost inevitably there will also be linear elements in the composition, but the dominant concern and quality lie in the potentialities of the plane surface.

In architecture, the same qualities may be developed on the structural parts of a building—walls, columns, and so forth—so that the emphasis is on the surface patterns rather than on the mass. Such would be the quality of a flat ceiling as opposed to a coffered or timbered one; a smooth, round, thick stocky column as opposed to one with flutes which reminds the observer of the solid material of which it is made; a flat, smooth wall as opposed to one treated with moldings to bring the surface into modeled relief. The "two-dimensionality" of the essential volume of a building may be seen in a structure like an Egyptian or Persian hypostyle hall, where the volume is, as it were, spread evenly through a broad rectangle, without a definite focusing axis as in an early Christian church or a clearly defined pattern of subdivision of the total space into major and minor elements of different sizes and shapes, as in a Renaissance church with its aisles, nave, apse, crossing, and dome.

Introduction: The Structure of Style

In literature, there is a difference between the kind of writing which presents a narrative simply as a series of events; one which attempts to give a panorama of actions occurring over a wide field; one which attempts to put such varied actions into perspective, proportion, and relation to each other; and one which attempts to bring out the processes of time and change among these actions. Similarly, a description or exposition may be little more than a list; it may be a panorama; it may attempt to make clear its subject in its proportions and inter-relations; it may attempt to deal also with the effect of time and change, or the relation of the subject to other things. The interest in dwelling on some theme or object, describing it at length but from a limited point of view, as distinct from characterizing it swiftly and moving on, or dwelling longer upon it in order to describe it from different points of view, is a recognized manner of treatment. All this has to do with conceptual form but reflects the treatment of the sensory elements. The movement in the work may be not direct and continuous in its various devices but measured and spaced in its definite quantities. One may perceive this distinction in metric form by comparing the continuous dactylic hexameters of Homeric verse with the elegiac couplet, which resolves itself into two-line sections each constituting a unit of pattern, and the set stanzas of early Greek lyric poetry such as the Anacreontics or Sapphics, where a broader and more intricate pattern of rhythms is established and repeated. A further step, into a third dimension, would be through the early dithyrambs to the developed tragic choruses, in which a lyric whole is made up of several triads each consisting of a strophe, antistrophe, and epode: the strophe represents one pattern, the antistrophe its equivalent, and the epode a foil for both; whereas the next triad of strophe, antistrophe, and epode may follow a different pattern of essentially similar construction. So also in the other sensory stimuli of language, words expressing expanse rather than linear move-ment of mass; figures of speech conceived and presented for their richness and extent rather than their concentration or profundity—in general, color, light, and texture in its various manifestations presented in breadth rather than depth.

Configuration in mass or solid form, or three dimensions, is that in which the painter, for example, tries to create forms that seem full-bodied or plastic. The movements are not only directional, or expansive, but project or recede. The sensory and material elements are endowed with fulness and body; the conceptual forms are relief-like and solid. In sculpture, the concern is not only for the various planes of the piece but for the prisms, cubes, cylinders, and spheres which combine to form the piece. These solid forms are the basis of construction and the focus of interest. In architecture, the physical elements are given an effectively solid shape and organization. For example, the pyramids at Gizeh, though indisputably geometric solids, each present the spectacle of one (or, from certain angles, two) triangular plane surfaces; an obelisk, however, is evidently a complex solid compounded of two pyramids (one truncated) of different degrees. The observer's attention is caught by this plastic organization. From the point of view of interior volume, the same principle applies: if the volume is a rectangular prism, or more particularly if it is subdivided so that it may be regarded as a cylinder, for example, surmounted by a dome and surrounded by series of rectangular prisms or of semicylinders, or a low ring, there is a definite manipulation of the dimension of height as well as that of length or breadth—a shaping of the volume on all sides, and all of equal significance.

This kind of configuration is met in that literature which treats an element of conceptual forms "in the round," depicting various facets of the subject. The movements of such a work of literature, both its simpler rhythms and more complex developments and trends, are various in tempo and direction, interweaving and interlocking to give a sense of depth and fulness.

Finally there is the configuration of space, or space-time, or the fourth dimension. In conceptual forms of painting and sculpture, this interest is evidenced in the suggestion of "real" space in which the several conceptual elements exist in some relation to each other. It differs from massive representation as a Holy Family of the northern Renaissance, existing in the space of a building, or a landscape, with perceptible spatial relations to other things in the space, differs from a Raphaelesque composition of Madonna and Child, solid and compact but existing alone. Relationship in time may also be evident if the figures are shown in movement so that the implication of a position prior to the position depicted and of one later than the one depicted have some bearing on the composition, or when the figure has a quality of being in movement from one position to another.

In architecture, apart from qualities of the structural parts of the building, the volume has "spatial" form if it is not simply a complex geometrical form but a grouping of such forms. This will be evident in a comparison of the Pantheon, which is a complex of cylinder and hemisphere with minor adjuncts, and St. Peter's or a baroque church, where one moves through a nave that is essentially a rectangular prism surmounted by a semicylinder, coming eventually to a cube surmounted by a hemisphere, with other shapes of volume projecting from the other three sides. In other words, if a volume is perceptible as a single shape, however complex, it is in three-dimensional configuration; if it is to be perceived as a series of separated but related shapes, it is in four-dimensional configuration. Such a configuration is more clearly evident in a large Roman bath, with the accumulation of volumes opening off the main hall and one another, than in a building as functionally unified as a church, but in essence they are the same.

In literature, the configuration of space-time is obvious in works employing the time-shift, as when part of the account is given as though from a point of view of one contemporary with the action, part from a point of view more or less remote in time. A similar effect is created when an account of an action is interrupted by a passage revealing one or more of the actors in some previous action or by an account of the broader scene in which the action occurs, or by accounts of other people involved in other, but ultimately related, actions. It is also the characteristic of that literature which dwells on the spatial aspects of environment—not simply in specifying the relative location of the various elements in it, but striving to impart a sense of the impact of the intangible qualities of the environment, its mood, its degree of constraint or release, the effect of the passage of time on the personalities being depicted—to create an impact of a similar nature on the reader. In a simple application of these devices (for example, the *Odyssey*), no tangible effect of the mobility of relationships is attained. The exact point, in the progression from the *Odyssey* to the works of Nikos Kazantzakis or Lawrence Durrell, at which the fourth dimension is achieved might be difficult to establish objectively; but the difference of the extremes is evident.

Dynamics

Another quality of the manner of manipulating the aesthetic elements of art may be designated as the character of dynamics. This is a relatively simple and familiar concept and refers to the degrees and kinds of energy with which the aesthetic elements may be endowed, ranging, for example, from the static to the violent. A "static movement," of course, would be a state of complete immobility. This is achieved in any art by keeping any movements in complete equilibrium, with a strongly symmetrical arrangement of equivalence of action and reaction, and slow, regular, definite movement. So, too, with colors and light, which would have to be pure and elementary—clear and flat—low or in neutral intensities; and so, too, with sound and texture, which avoid extremes and seek neutrality or equilibrium and strict compensation. The material elements in the work of art may often contribute to the sense of immobility especially through their technical and rational aspects, when, for example, in architecture the brute weight of stone, and the fact of its being laid dry, may enhance this effect. The choice of conceptual form may also contribute, of course, in the preference for scenes of inaction as opposed to scenes of action; of inert things as opposed to active creatures or, in a scene of action, of a moment of equipoise as opposed to a moment of intensity. But we shall see that the handling of the sensory elements may nullify the potential effect of the imagery, as when an Egyptian battle scene is so depicted as to be rendered static.

At the other extreme of dynamics is violence, where the movements are emphatic and eccentric, without compensation or equivalents, so that they compound themselves and stimulate rather than constrain. Color and light may be of high intensities (or extremely low), or subdued, or contrasted without being harmonized; their stimulative effect may be augmented by deviations from pure hues and juxtapositions calculated to be disturbing; a similar use of sound and texture in extreme, eccentric, and discordant combinations achieves the same effect. Certain conceptual forms, too, may contribute to the quality of violence.

System, focus, and cohesion

We come finally to the question of the arrangement of the factors we have been reviewing: the relation, for example, that the texture may bear to the pigment or the conceptual form, or to the choice of quality of definition, configuration, or dynamics, and to the ontological or epistemological presupposition apparent. This is the harmonizing, the proportioning of all that goes into the work, and might well be designated the "composition," save that "composition" has also other current uses of some ambiguity. In some respects these factors of arrangement have to do with a good deal of what is sometimes called "form," meaning the scheme or relationships among all factors in the work apart from the conceptual form. Once again, however, the word "form" has become extremely ambiguous and, even more important, it *ought* to refer to the totality of the work: the means employed, the manner of their use (including the arrangement), and any factors beyond these. Therefore, in spite of alternatives, the word "arrangement" is convenient in alluding to these qualities.

The qualities of arrangement may be subdivided as those pertaining to *system,* those pertaining to *focus,* and those pertaining to *cohesion.* System has to do with whether there is any regularity in the disposition of the aesthetic factors, or whether they are chosen irregularly, haphazardly, and indiscriminately. Focus has to do with whether there is a concentration of emphasis of the dominant over the subordinate or an equality or dispersion of emphasis. Cohesion has to do with the kind of structure or adhesion among the parts: whether the unity is fused or monolithic—the unity of inseparable oneness; or tectonic—the unity of separate, distinct parts combined in some order of mutual relation into an integrated whole; or organic—to restrict this word to the integrated unity of parts resulting from the growth or emergence of one part into another as in a plant form.

These categories are not so rigidly related as they might seem. A regular composition may be concentrated, as in a symmetrical façade with some dominant in the center, or free-field, without dominant, as in a chessboard; an irregular composition may or may not have a dominant feature.

THE OBJECT OF REPRESENTATION

We have completed a survey of the factors of means and manner in the work of art in the objective state—the factors chiefly pertinent to a study of style for most analytic purposes, although there does remain one other important factor which should be recognized before we leave our theoretical survey.

In speaking of the means and manner in the work of art, we imply that there is a process for which certain things are a means and that there are certain ways of manipulating the means—to some end. The end toward which the process is directed was stated at the outset: the induction in a spectator of a sensory experience first existing in the mind of the artist. The work of art in its objective state is a device to communicate from one mind to another, by aesthetic means.

The thing which is in fact being communicated is the artist's actual experience of something. Being "actual," it is real, genuine, true, in human experience. Although in some propaganda, advertising, pornography, and other special phenomena it may be false in a philosophical or ethical sense, even so it existed as a reality in the mind of the artist; exists, in the work of art; and may exist again in the mind of the spectator. In serious or spontaneous art, however, it is assumed by the artist to be genuinely real and true in an ultimate sense.

The "something" may be of such a nature that we have a name for it, as life or death, love or hate, good or evil, success or defeat—or, somewhat more concretely, humanity, divinity, a man, an event; or it may be of such a nature that we have no name for it—some apprehension, awareness realized, sense of rightness, which has never been distinguished by a name or defined in words.

This "something" is not the subject matter, the conceptual form of the work, though it may have reference to the conceptual form. That is, a picture of the Crucifixion represents not simply the event of the Crucifixion, but rather the artist's experience of the event—what he himself has known to be real and true in the event. The *Aeneid* does not represent simply or primarily the activities of Aeneas and his people, but more profoundly the artist's awareness of what it is to be a Roman. In understanding the meaning of a particular work of art, then, we simply yield to its formative influence and ourselves experience the truth or reality it conveys.

The truth, again, is not an argument or an assertion, such as "Death is a bad thing" or "Mankind is subject to fate." It is the actual badness or fatality itself. The artist has an experience which he believes is true and essential of death or the human condition; he causes the observer to have the same experience. The experience may remain wordless and unnamed in the observer, but he has been aware of it all the same. The artist becomes conscious of some quality of the world; he senses that the lines of a vase or the patterns of a musical composition will recreate in himself and perhaps in others that awareness or consciousness. In the light of broader human experience, he may be wrong in his conception of the truth or of the experience, but (ignoring questions of propaganda or purposefully misleading art) at least he does believe the quality to be true—real in the ultimate sense. He has a vision of the world or of some part of it as, to him, it really is; this he tries to instil in the observer in the form of a sensory experience.

Since the reconstruction must possess the qualities of the original experience, and the reconstruction is formed from our aesthetic means, the aesthetic means must be so chosen and manipulated as to embody and participate in the qualities and characteristics of the original experience. The basis for the control of the selection and manipulation is the vision of reality, and the selection and manipulation bear a direct correspondence to the vision. If we could understand fully the formulation of the aesthetic means, we would understand some of the vision.

This is said with reference to a single vision and a single work of art, but if the artist's several experiences of truth and reality represent a constant point of view—if they all reflect the same general understanding of the nature of reality—all of his works will use, fundamentally, the same aesthetic means in the same way, and this community of distinctive qualities in his work is his style at its basic level. And, so, beyond this, to the style of a time or place.

It is clear that in describing a style and explaining its problems we must use terms of this order to insure the validity of the analysis and its meaningfulness historically. Of course some aspects of the form of an object are derived from strictly functional requirements or technical capability, but these are relatively incidental and the essentially meaningful accounting must be in categories of the object of representation, the view of the world, embodied in the aesthetic forms. Moreover, although these aesthetic forms may be inherited, borrowed, or invented, these circumstances, for the most part, have no real significance in a particular work or style. The Egyptians had the means to complete the invention of the Doric style and adopt it, and the Romans, to borrow the Egyptian manner of painting. Why they chose as they did depends not on any control of knowledge, technique, function, tradition, but on their sense of what is essentially real. Finally, art forms do not constitute a closed system structured and changing in pattern according to laws of its own corresponding to the mechanical laws of physics or chemistry, nor is art an autonomous, intrinsic entity that in itself grows or decays or evolves, that causes or influences itself or other arts, in any analogy with biological processes. Each work of art, each style, is an original creation utilizing elements as they are found or invented afresh for an immediate purpose. And, yet, neither, on the other hand, is art an inert thing, subject only to vagary and whim or—within limits—to economic or social pressures. Art is a way of knowing and communicating, and it does have a rationale, a rationale based on knowing and communicating that which is known.

It would complicate our problem without advancing matters appreciably to consider in detail apparent exceptions to this basic proposition. In propaganda and advertising, for example, we seem to find art trying to express concepts that are not true and real, but if the propaganda or advertising is successful it means either that the public which yields to it does in fact believe the concepts to be true or at least temporarily has been persuaded to believe so. Or, we find Anatolian motifs in the art of late Roman northern Europe, or Pompeian rooms in American hotels, and we know that somehow or other the style has been imported across time and space; but we must conclude that either the reality expressed by the importation is itself found to be valid, however fleetingly, in the new environment, or the new environment has some kind of eclectic body of truth. Therefore these and other complicating aspects of the problem do not disturb the essential validity of our concept of style, and though the concept has been set forth in general, hypothetical, even dogmatic, terms, it may suffice as an explanation of the pattern to be followed in our account of the styles of the arts of the ancient Mediterranean world.

CHAPTER I

Egyptian Art

THE PEOPLE of ancient Egypt, relatively secluded and stable within the shelter afforded them by their peculiar geography, for almost four thousand years maintained a preference for certain aesthetic qualities in their art so that to some Western eyes there is little change in the style from pre-Dynastic times to the end of the Roman period. Of course, even a slight familiarity with the development of Egyptian art allows one to distinguish the early and late phases of the style, and a little more will enable one to perceive some peculiarities of various stages during the "classic" phase—the development from about 2700 to 1085 B.C., from the third dynasty or Archaic period through the Old, Middle, and New Kingdoms. However it may annoy the Egyptologist to be reminded of the lack of perception of the layman who thinks of all Egyptian art as tradition-bound and stereotyped, nevertheless it is a demonstration of the fact that (on the whole) almost any piece of Egyptian art is more like another piece of Egyptian art than it is like anything else—that there is a community of qualities which may be characterized as "Egyptian." It is this community of qualities which it is our primary purpose to identify; at the same time we shall endeavor to notice variations that may be significant in an understanding of the whole.

Egyptian Art

CONCEPTUAL ELEMENTS

The conceptual form of Egyptian art from beginning to end is iconic, derived from a wide range of nature. In early pre-Dynastic times the naturalism is limited: it reveals itself in patterns on ceramic vases, perhaps intended to reproduce patterns created in the weaving of basketwork; but even on these vases there are occasional representations of animals or human beings, and in some of the few tomb paintings of this period, as at Hierakonpolis (Plate 1), scenes of human activity are the rule. Throughout the main stream of Egyptian art universal naturalism prevails, although for purposes of ornament natural motifs are highly abstracted. In almost every case (including structural motifs), motifs derive from the phenomenal world of nature.

Considering the matter in more detail, we observe that in painting and relief sculpture (Plates 2–6) the conceptual form is centered on human activity—daily life in every aspect—so that it is possible to illustrate the entire range of social, economic, political, and religious life with all its appurtenances, animate and inanimate. Thus not only human beings but their tools and instruments, their furniture and dwellings, their gardens and natural environment, their domestic animals and the fauna of the world around them are depicted. Particularly striking is the depiction of public and historical events: battles, receptions, religious ceremonies, funerals, and the like. In all of this human life is the focus. The animals, gardens, and natural scenery are not depicted for their own sake, though the artist and observer may well have taken great delight in the sight of them, but as elements in the lives of men.

Before going further it may be well to note that the conceptual forms in Egyptian painting and relief sculpture exist chiefly in a rational rather than aesthetic aspect; that is, as can be established from external evidence, the elaborate description of human activity was meant to be understood as an objective record of these activities—a listing and description of what people did. It was not intended primarily to evoke feeling. The purpose of the pictorial scenes could have been equally well fulfilled by a written document or catalogue. The purpose of the

47

painting on the wall of a tomb was to provide a close description of the life, or kind of life, lived in this world by the man buried in the tomb, a life which he hoped would continue in the next. The description served as a charm or incantation on the principle of primitive magic, fixing permanently, or for the period of survival of the engraved or painted description, the shape of the activity desired; when thus fixed, the activity was confidently expected to persist. It is this conception which determined the imagery of much of the Egyptian sculpture in the round (Plates 7–8). These statues were portraits, intended to preserve the individual personality, or essential being, of the subject through the eternity of the afterlife. Thus the statue, though highly generalized in its depiction of most of the body, was endowed with a carefully individualized face, so that whatever might happen to the actual physical remains of the individual, in spite of all efforts at mummification, there might always exist a stamp of his person, the straw to which the spirit might cling to avoid losing its identity in some impersonal continuum. The validity of this interpretation is established in the theory of Egyptian belief in the afterlife and is underlined by the fact that not only were several portrait statues often left in the tomb to insure against the possibility that one might be damaged, but also—as further insurance against remote chance, at least in many of the tombs of the Old Kingdom—stores of spare heads, each an excellent portrait but lacking a body, were provided.

It is also apparent that the paintings and sculpture in the tombs were themselves substitutes for the objects depicted. Thus a man would place in his tomb all the furniture he cherished or wished to have with him in the afterlife—the clothing, the food, and all that was needed to continue his worldly existence in the next. He did so to the extent of his financial resources; only the richer kings came reasonably close to achieving the ideal. The corpse itself was mummified with all possible care, to the same end. There seems to be no indication that in Egypt the servants and attendants whom the rich man would wish to have about him were slaughtered and buried with him, though in many periods the custom of providing around the tomb of a king tombs for his family and chief attendants doubtless was intended to provide for a continuation of the same retinue in the afterlife that had been available in this. But for most people it was necessary to provide replicas of furniture, food, and attendants; this could be done in almost exhaustive completeness by making models, as was the custom in the Middle Kingdom, or by figures painted or in relief on the walls of the tomb. Indeed, even the kings who could afford to bury a fairly complete array of goods felt it desirable to supplement this hoard with paintings and reliefs.

Thus it is abundantly clear that the primary purpose of substantially all of the tomb painting and sculpture was a rational, practical one: to illustrate, and by the permanent form of the illustration, to preserve indefinitely, the objects and activities which the individual desired to retain in the afterlife. And, it may be observed, this is precisely the result achieved, though mayhap in a somewhat different form than was anticipated. To the modern observer, the decorative programs of Egyptian tombs are thoroughly fascinating because they are illustrative; one can seldom shake off the enchantment of this depiction of the manifold activities of Egyptian existence. In spite of the aesthetic qualities present in some, one's impression must take into account that they are, first of all, "interesting."

To say that the conceptual element exists primarily in its rational aspect is not, of course, to say that it is completely without aesthetic being. The fact that the forms are confined to scenes of human life—not heroic subjects or landscapes—is an active component of the aesthetic effect. Moreover, the subjects depicted are full of movement, color, sound, and texture in the variety and connotations of the activities shown. It is true, as we shall see, that these qualities are rigorously confined by various means, but they constitute a significant strain in the composition as a whole. On the other hand, it is helpful to point out that much of the aesthetic value of conceptual form is ignored. Its rational purpose is to preserve the desirable things in life, but there is no heightening of one's sense of what is desirable by, for example, a contrast with scenes of pathos or unhappiness. It gives a searching, if unimaginative, listing of things valued, with no development by contrast or nuance.

In all this we have been speaking of mortuary art, but the same

49

observations are true of other categories of imagery in painting and sculpture. Of these the most important are the historical and commemorative reliefs recording the triumphs of the monarchs and the gods; here too, we see depicted in exhaustive detail the daily life of a monarch or a general, and the purpose, quite openly and frankly, is a rational one, to make known the facts (as the king wished them to be known) in imperishable form, that they might always exist and that the life and activity of the king might be eternal.

To some of these generalizations there are some exceptions. During the El Amarna period (1370–1340; Plates 6, 10), and in the Saite period (663–525; Plate 11) and later, there prevailed a concern for a broader conception of the human being, physically and emotionally. Although normally in Egyptian art it is simply the *fact* of the individual and his activity which is significant, in the art of the El Amarna period there is an interest in his character, thought, experience. Thus one is bound to be impressed by the strange physical form of the members of the royal family, and the different attitudes they display in different kinds of situations, formal and intimate. Here, for once, we see the king and his associates in moments of weariness and imperfection, heightening by contrast the sense of what unimpaired vitality may be.

We must allude to the many representations of divinities in half-human, half-animal, form and to the special phenomenon of the sphinx, also a composite creature. Do such features in the conceptual form, it might be queried, constitute an element of fantasy? Actually, these forms are relatively limited in number, and throughout the historical period of Egypt, at least, seem to involve no free imagination or fancy. The gods, at least, seem to have been cast in their unnatural form at a very early period, and to have been generally accepted as existing so throughout the period of Egyptian art as we know it. Only the sphinxes, in their various forms, seem more freely manipulated and may be taken as illustration of some tendency toward fantasy in art.

So far we have been speaking of painting and sculpture as the most abundant and self-evident area of art for examination. In the field of literature we are handicapped by the scarcity of material, and by the difficulty of coping with a language which few people are likely to know well. Nevertheless, it seems that the literature offers little in the way of important contradiction.

The greater part of Egyptian literature which has been preserved consists of historical and religious texts, and among the latter the more numerous examples are mortuary documents of one sort or another, chiefly those embodied in the Book of the Dead, which consists of a sort of program to guide the spirit in overcoming the obstacles to his achievement of a desired status in the afterworld. Here everything that has been said about sculpture and painting would apply, save that there is nothing in the literature that corresponds to a portrait in any sense, except that some biographical or historical records of various individuals reflect their chief interests.

A few examples of what may be called prose fiction are among the rare works whose conceptual form has been developed. Of these the *Story of Sinuhe,*[1] of the Middle Kingdom, and the *Journey of Wen-Amon to Phoenicia,*[2] of the Twenty-First Dynasty, may be strictly biographical or they may be in part fiction; in either case the conceptual form does have a definite aesthetic in addition to its rational quality. The fears and longings, the final joy of Sinuhe, are brought out explicitly, creating an awareness of the nature of his experience beyond a simple account of his adventures; the story of Wen-Amon is developed with a plot structure involving selection of incident, passages of conversation, indication of setting, suggestions of emotional state, and character, and contrasts with other, happier situations, all of which deviate from the even tone of a factual, rational account and create a definite effect of pathos. Even among various ritualistic documents, some—especially *The Primeval Establishment of Order*[3] and *The God and His Unknown Name of Power,*[4] an account of a plot of Isis against Re—use the conceptual form from the aesthetic point of view: the former especially in its implied contrast of the desert-like calm of the afterlife and the turbulence of this; the latter in its description of the pain resulting from a snake bite and the (albeit colorless and factual) ruth-

[1] J. B. Pritchard, *Ancient Near Eastern Texts* (Princeton, 1950), p. 18.
[2] *Ibid.,* p. 25.
[3] *Ibid.,* p. 9.
[4] *Ibid.,* p. 12.

lessness of Isis in withholding the cure until Re finally reveals his secret name. On the other hand, one of the few indisputably fictional narratives (essentially a Märchen), the *Story of the Two Brothers*,[5] recites the familiar theme of Potiphar's wife in a singularly prosaic style.

From the body of Wisdom Literature, moral and pragmatic precepts addressed to individuals or a more general public, the *Dispute Over Suicide*[6] is a notable example of conceptual form conceived almost purely as aesthetic: it is a conversation between a man and his soul on the subject of suicide—a concept that verges on the fantastic. In contrast to the simple list of purely didactic maxims which constitute the main lot of this class of written work, so devoid of aesthetic elements as to be hardly worth considering as art, it illuminates vividly the aesthetic function of conceptual form in and of itself. More complex is the *Protests of the Eloquent Peasant*,[7] a tale on Märchen framework about a peasant who is robbed and persists in his claims before an official, who is at first merely bored, later, under the influence of the monarch, somewhat disinterestedly curious, in a series of eloquent appeals embodying moral and legal principles. The conceptual form, therefore, is both a vehicle for formulating the principles and a dramatization of these principles. It also conveys the value of perserverance. In all this the sturdy, forthright character of the peasant, which emerges implicitly rather than explicitly, has a definite effect.

In poetry, the most purely lyric works observed are the hymns celebrating various divinities or the triumphs of monarchs. Strangely enough, these seem on the whole more rationally conceived than some of the prose works we have discussed; they tend to be simply descriptive of the god or the event. Much of the description, however, is in figurative or allusive imagery, and the meaning is often conveyed in terms of the effects of the subject, as for example in the *Hymn to Amon Re*[8] in such phrases as "the cattle grow languid when thou shinest/ the love of thee is in the southern sky/ the sweetness of thee is in the

---

[5] *Ibid.*, p. 23.
[6] *Ibid.*, p. 405.
[7] *Ibid.*, p. 407.
[8] *Ibid.*, p. 365.

northern sky/ the beauty of thee carries away hearts/ the love of thee makes arms languid/ thy beautiful form relaxes the hands/ and hearts are forgetful at the sight of thee."

Thus we may say that, insofar as it is known, Egyptian literature, like painting and sculpture, employs naturalistic forms drawn from human activity, and the general significance of this is chiefly rational. There is less attention to the environment and furniture of human activity, more to character and emotion—at least in certain examples; and there is, in proportion, more attention to the divinities. The aesthetic aspect of conceptual form was more widely, and more searchingly, employed in literature than in painting and sculpture.

We come then to the question of architecture. Here again the conceptual forms are naturalistic, in the sense of being adopted from natural function (Plates 12–19). The spatial conceptions meet the requirements for which the buildings were designed; the structural forms are directly or indirectly the forms of unadorned construction.

Again our understanding is limited by the fact that most of the Egyptian architecture which has survived falls in only two or three of the major classes of buildings; very little, for example, is known today of Egyptian civic or domestic architecture. Surviving is an almost overwhelming array of religious monuments, including some of the most remarkable achievements in the whole history of architecture. Broadly speaking, these religious buildings may be divided into two categories: mortuary structures (Plates 12, 14, 17), and temples to the gods (Plates 13, 15, 16).

The function, and functional form, of mortuary architecture was based on the problem of the life of the individual after death. In the simplest possible conception, this problem could be—and was, in the earliest identified burials—met by the interment of the body together with a token provision of food. But the incessantly growing doubts and fears of the Egyptian with regard to the efficacy of the measures he might devise to preserve his self and its necessities began early to create more and more complex and elaborate arrangements.

Theoretically, perhaps, the first radical accretion to the simple interment would be a place where survivors of the dead person might bring replacements for the provisions buried with the corpse as the previous offerings were exhausted; and where the dead person might return, through his tomb, to a point of contact with the world of the living. For example, the Tomb of Aha at Sakkarah consists of five chambers formed by a timbered ceiling over walls in a pit excavated in the rock, covered by a large rectangular structure consisting of some twenty-seven cubicles. These cubicles were used for the storage of objects for the convenience of the dead monarch and his family buried in the underground chambers. The outer walls of the structure, thick and solidly made of brick, were designed in alternate projecting masses, like buttresses or compound piers, and recesses; and the walls sloped inward toward the top, forming a low, truncated pyramid, longer than it was thick. The whole was surrounded by two concentric brick walls, set close together; the exposed brickwork was covered with white lime-stucco, perhaps ornamented with colored patterns.

In the early Mastaba of Aha an offering room has not been clearly identified, but in the mastabas of the Second and Third dynasties such chapels are clearly apparent. Sometimes, in this and succeeding ages, they are built within the face of the mastaba; sometimes they project in part outside the wall of the mastaba. In either case they consist of a niche in the face of the tomb structure with a door depicted in relief on the wall; this was sufficient for the dead person to use in passing in or out of the tomb. In this room, in increasingly conventionalized forms, provision was made for the continued nourishment of the dead, either in the form of repeated offerings of food or (safer and surer) carved or painted depictions of meals, with appropriate charms. Thus at least the dead person was assured of a bare continuation of existence.

To this nucleus of interment and chapel provided by the mastaba at an early stage of its development, many kinds of variations were possible. For a period the superstructure of the mastaba was almost entirely solid, with only a few haphazardly arranged cells within its masonry, but with more or less elaborate combinations of cells or rooms excavated in the rock below. At times this subterranean complex was fairly extensive, with arrangements comparable to that of a dwelling, the whole being entered by a pit or ramp, or both, devised through the superstructure of the mastaba. At times, especially during the later days of the mastaba (the Fifth and Sixth dynasties), the rooms related to the chapel became more and more numerous and began to fill the body of the superstructure. The detailed function of these arrangements is not well known, but in general they seem to have been used during the burial rites for the storage of things to be used in the service of the dead and for the administration of such services. The complex usually included a large room with piers or colonnaded courts, one or more corridors connecting this to a chapel, the serdab (a walled-up room containing statues visible through small windows), and storage rooms. The walls were lavishly decorated with scenes of active life and charms for their perpetuation.

This remained, in spite of somewhat extensive modification, the real pattern of mortuary architecture throughout its history in Egypt. The pyramids, for example, are essentially the same in every respect (Plates 12–15). Whether the pyramid type developed from the mastaba through the stepped form so impressively conceived at Sakkhara or independently is immaterial to the question of use-function: the pyramid is the functional equivalent of the superstructure of the mastaba; within it, or beneath it, or both, were chambers for the interment of the dead (unless for fear of sacrilegious disturbance the corpse was buried in a place of special concealment nearby); and against the base of the pyramid was a chapel with its provisions for offering a "magic meal" and other services of the dead. Associated with this complex might be, as at Sakkhara, a whole village or town of other structures; or as at Gizeh, a veritable city of tombs; but the matters of chief concern were the chapel, or offering complex, and the interment complex, and some physical or symbolic connection between them.

The complex of Khafra at Gizeh (Plates 12, 17) illustrates clearly a division in function; there is a chapel on the bank of the river, connected by a long ramp with the burial and service chapel at the foot of the pyramid. Thus the necessity for provision of funeral facilities as well as perpetual attendance is made clear. In any case the ensemble is typical. On the river bank lay the small "Valley Building," simply a cubical mass of masonry containing a т-shaped hall entered from a transverse hall along the river side. The ceiling of the T-shaped hall was supported on rectangular monoliths. The ramp connected this building with the pyramid building, the first part of which consisted again of a transverse entrance hall leading to what is essentially a T-shaped hall, though the vertical and crossbars of the T are separated by doors. Behind this was an open room surrounded by rectangular piers; between this and the face of the pyramid was a series of narrow, labyrinthine chambers devoted to the more mysterious phases of the service. The false door or key point in the sanctuary lay in the innermost corridor against the enclosing wall of the pyramid.

Other great tombs, though superficially quite different, are essentially the same. The Tomb of Mentu-hotep III (Eleventh Dynasty) at Thebes (Deir el Bahri; Plate 14) was a striking conception, a pyramid rising out of a square block with an open façade of piers facing outward, resting in turn on a square-cut terrace with a piered façade facing the river; but for all its remarkable qualities in these respects, from the point of view of function it is like the others. There was a temple by the river and a causeway to the mortuary temple proper, the most conspicuous feature of which was the complex we have described; behind this, sunk into the face of a cliff, was a tunnel leading to the tomb itself.

Immediately to the north lay the extraordinary and beautiful Mortuary Temple of Hatshepsut (Eighteenth Dynasty), also with a river temple and causeway; no pyramid, but a series of terraces each with a piered façade (facing on enclosed or partially enclosed courts), culminating in a tunnel with mortuary chapels cut into the rock behind the highest terrace. In this case the actual interment was miles to the west, in the Valley of the Kings, but the conception of the nature of the afterlife was such that this physical obstacle and distance were of no significance in the function of the tomb; the false door in the rear of the mortuary temple along the Nile opened into the Valley of the Kings to the west as easily as into a chamber less than a foot away.

The conceptualization of the volumes of mortuary architecture is a fairly complex and shifting matter. Certain fundamental factors remain consistent throughout: provision for the ritual of burial; provision for the preservation of the dead king and his possessions; provision for the dead to keep in touch with the land of the living; and provision for the maintenance of ritual attendance. All of this had a predominantly rational basis in the final decision on detailed or broader aspects of design, but it also had a pervasive and inescapable effect upon the atmosphere of the buildings: the sentiments, such as they may have been, which the Egyptian normally entertained toward the land of the dead, its inhabitants, and the act of departure from this world; the intricate, mysterious impenetrability—the sheer scale and cost—of the efforts made to achieve the rational purposes; the character of the ritual celebrated in these rooms—such factors have real importance in establishing certain predispositions on the part of the observer in the presence of the monument, and continue to color his perception.

Although it is not a matter of conceptualization of volume, there is a special question concerning the pyramid from the point of view of conceptual form. If it was embodied in mortuary architecture as a symbol of Re in the cult of Re, this fact would be significant in the impact of a pyramid tomb complex. But even if it developed structurally from the mastaba through the step pyramid, by the time the true pyramidal form had become fixed in royal tomb architecture the association with Re was undoubtedly made by most observers, so the effect was essentially the same. (Conversely, the Sun-temple of Neuserre near Abu Gurob [Plate 13] must have carried to the cult of Re some of the atmosphere of the mortuary complex.)

One of the most vivid examples of the aesthetic impact of conceptual form is the contrast between the typical Old Kingdom mortuary complex, such as that of the Pyramid of Khafra at Gizeh, and the Mortuary Temples of Mentuhotep of the Middle Kingdom and Hatshepsut of the New Kingdom, both at Deir el Bahri. In all three cases the functional basis of the conceptual form is the same, but in the later buildings everything which possibly could be so treated was turned outward and made to face the sun and air, instead of being closely confined in cavernous restraint. The difference in effect of the corridors of piers flanking broad open courtyards instead of completely enclosed labyrinthine corridors; of broad, open, elevated ramps ascending from terrace to terrace instead of covered ways and processional halls cannot be minimized. Some of the difference is sensory—a matter of movement, light, and color; but a good deal of it is conceptual—activities in the world of light or in the world of dark. The pyramid in the Temple of Mentuhotep plays quite a different role from the Pyramid of Khafra; it is not the seal of the burial, either actually or by pretense. Its purpose is to a large extent sensory, as we shall see, though as conceptual form it brings to the temple complex the atmosphere and connotations of the grand burials of the Old Kingdom. Thus typologically (and it should be emphasized that both the Temple of Mentuhotep and that of Hatshepsut are now unique and may not represent the styles of their respective eras) it is a transition from Khafra to Hatshepsut, in whose temple all is new; all is, so far as function will permit, the opposite of Khafra.

With regard to the architecture of temples to the gods, the fundamental functional basis in the conceptualization of volumes seems to have been that the temple was a dwelling, or at least temporary residence, of the divinity, who was richly attended by human servitors who had need of accommodation for their possessions; that the divinity would be pleased by rich and imposing offerings; and that though the divinity could be approached in appropriate degrees by human worshippers, divinity required and deserved a considerable degree of privacy and reserve. Thus the typical form of a temple (Plate 16) consisted of a small sanctuary embedded in a maze of smaller corridors and chambers, approached from one end by an anteroom or vestibule, which in turn was approached through a hypostyle hall, a large, completely enclosed hall filled with columns. It was entered from a large rectangular open court, usually with columns on all four sides, the side entering the hypostyle hall often taking the form of a deep colonnaded porch. Externally, the entire complex had the outline of a simple rectangle, and the chief—and frequently the only—entrance was through a large gate complex leading to the open court on its axis opposite the sanctuary. The gate complex normally took the form of two towers or pylons in the form of truncated pyramids—quite shallow—or with the external form of inward-sloping trapezoidal walls, flanking a relatively small door. The whole was approached by a formal avenue often lined with sphinxes or other sculpture. This was the schematic plan of the great temples and most of the minor temples of the New Kingdom (and presumably, although remains are almost non-existent, of earlier periods) and of the Ptolemaic and Roman periods, the differences being chiefly individual, with a somewhat greater sense of discrimination of parts in the later buildings.

There were special adaptations and forms to be found in many temples; frequently there would be unusually elaborate storage space; sometimes additional sanctuaries for special purposes; but on the whole these are likely to be lost in the general maze of rooms surrounding the sanctuary. What is likely to make one Egyptian temple impressively different from another is that, in front of the main entrance, other hypostyle halls, courts, pylons, were added indiscriminately though usually in an increasing crescendo of scale. They had no functional basis—they were simply duplicates of what had already been provided —and served to glorify the man who caused them to be built. The result was a more or less extended and impressive processional development from the external world to the sanctuary and the god himself. In this the rational element is high: the secreting of the god, his isolation from the world, and the development of his majesty and mystery by the provision of a series of imposing and even forbidding elements to be traversed before he might be approached. Aesthetically this would operate with considerable effect: the presence of the sublimity and mystery of the god, who was to be supposed as immanent in the remote recesses of the complex, would undoubtedly be of real significance in the spectator's reaction to what he beheld.

So far we have been speaking of the conceptualization of volume derived from the function; it remains to consider the more sculptural forms of structural elements like walls and supports (Plates 16, 18). In this sphere it is evident that the developed style of Egyptian architecture is largely a matter of repeating in stone the forms spontaneously evolved in an architecture of mud brick and reeds and light wood. Massive elements like pylons and walls are smooth and structurally unbroken— monolithic, as it were—expanses of mud brick, which almost invariably have a contraction, or inclination, or batter, toward the top, as would be appropriate in mud brick; and they are frequently crowned with flaring moldings which are not only carved or painted to suggest palm fronds, but are readily identifiable in the palm and reed copings still visible today in mud architecture in rural structures. In other supporting elements, such as piers and columns, the characteristic form is that of a plant—a reed or bundle of reeds, lotus, or some similar form. Sometimes, particularly in the early dynasties, these forms are rendered in stone in strict imitation of the appearance of the reeds or plant form—as woven mat walls with massed bundles of reeds for ribbing or support. In the New Kingdom it is more common to see a column conceived as an entire and distinct plant with stem and bud, standing as the sole support for a ceiling beam.

Since the buildings we have under consideration are made of stone—often heavy, massive, refractory stone like granite and syenite—and not mud brick or reeds, and the spaces created are vastly greater than could be formed by mud and reed construction, the question arises whether these forms in stone do not constitute fantasy. In certain respects, it must be agreed, they do. Nothing could be more illogical or disturbing, really, than the conception of the ceilings and roofs of the great halls and porticos at Karnak and Luxor being supported on reeds and lotus and palm stems. But even in these examples, the floral basis for the form of the column is generalized and abstracted to the point of moderating this effect of fantasy, if not entirely dispelling it. On the other hand, the substitution of stone for mud brick in walls and pylons is not a radical one; stone, like mud, is inert—it has no inherent dynamic beyond that of gravity; the differences are simply in scale. Thus the stone in the walls is related functionally to its use in the same way mud brick is; and there is nothing fantastic in its Egyptian use. Moreover, the plant forms of the columns and moldings, though derived from vegetation, have been recast to include the surface character of carved stone: there has been an effective fusion of the shape of the plant, the substantial character of the stone, and the mechanical role of the support in the structure. It is in the last respect that the fusion is weakest; the erection of the plant form on a simple disk base, with a simple block cap making a bearing for the ceiling beam, is incongruous.

Egyptian Art

SENSORY ELEMENTS

MOVEMENT

The most vivid stimulus to the kinetic sense in Egyptian sculpture and painting is line—outlines (either in the sense of the boundary between one plane surface and another, or actually drawn borders) of men, animals, plants, objects, hieroglyphs; elongated forms (bodies, arms, spears); the organization of compositions largely in terms of long, narrow, horizontal bands—and the consequent linear arrangement of all the figures and their interrelationships in one of these bands, with the lines of columns of hieroglyphs introduced freely into these compositions. These lines—individually, by the tendency they have to lead the eye from place to place; and in combination, when they occur, as often, in such profusion as to scintillate and cause the eye to jump and quiver—are the basic stimulus to the sense of movement. Closely related are the rhythms set up by parallel or duplicating figures in the imagery or line patterns, which create movements broken or pulsating in more or less measured ways, instead of physically continuous movements.

In literature the movements are chiefly in the phrasing and the rhythms, based on repetitions of words, phrases, ideas, either exactly or with slight modifications often suggesting a special overtone of movement. "I stretch out my arms and I tie them up for thee; I bind the barbarians of Nubia by ten-thousands and thousands, and the northerners by hundred-thousands as living captives. . . . I have commended to the earth in its length and breadth so that westerners and easterners are under thy oversight." Or (also from the *Hymn of Victory of Thutmose III*),[9] more characteristically and less pointedly expansive: "I establish thee in my dwelling place. I work a wonder for thee: I give thee valor and victory over all foreign countries; I set the glory of thee and the fear of thee in all lands, the terror of thee as far as the four supports of heaven. I magnify the awe of thee in all bodies; I set the battle cry of thy majesty throughout the Nine Bows." The most significant quality of the rhythmic patterns is discussed in another context, but at least it is evident from these examples how the rhythms

[9] Pritchard, *op. cit.*, p. 373.

are accentuated by repetitive development of ideas and words. As for stimuli to the kinaesthetic sense by the sound of the words, or by the particular concepts of movement involved semantically in particular words in the Egyptian language, it is fruitless to raise the question; there must be too few moderns sufficiently familiar with the ancient language of Egypt for such discussion to be useful.

In architecture, kinaesthetic responses are stimulated first of all by the movement of the spectator. The pervasive processional concept: the avenues leading to the temples; the monumentalized entrances; the succession of court, porch, hall, and sanctuary—so often, and so naturally extended by the addition of other courts, halls, and porches—in the temples to the gods; and the causeways and ramps so prominent a feature of mortuary complexes, remind us of the importance of physical movement. Moreover, in most interiors the walls or columns or both were so thickset that it was impossible to see more than a small part of the unit from any one position; it was necessary to move about even through each room, excepting the simplest corridors or rectangular chambers.

Optically there are many stimuli to the kinaesthetic sense: the rhythmic ranks of columns and piers; the lines of architraves and outlines of pylons and gates and ramps and avenues; the wall surfaces and columns alive with reliefs, paintings, and inscribed writings.

We have paid some attention to the aesthetic aspect of conceptual form in Egyptian art, in the sense that the subject matter of a painting or piece of sculpture or literature, or the uses for which a building was constructed as reflected in its form, have an effect on the emotional disposition and reactions of the observer. There is another way in which these forms may be effective aesthetically; as we have noticed briefly, motion is also contained in the conceptual forms. Thus the familiar spectacle of the Egyptian portrait, the figure standing firmly on one leg with hands at rest, is logically interpreted as of one at rest, although the other leg, sharply advanced, is suggestive of movement (Plate 8). Another characteristic pose, particularly in relief and painting, a figure with legs extended as in a mighty stride, carries a suggestion of forward movement; whereas the common pose of a seated figure, in its character as conceptual form, is immediately understood as one of lack of movement. It is hardly necessary to list all the poses that one encounters in paintings and reliefs, nor indeed would it be possible, so rich in this kind of suggestion of movement, color, and texture is the imagery of Egyptian relief sculpture and painting. In this respect, the play of conceptual form in sculpture in the round is sharply restricted; and in literature it is limited in curious ways. There is not so much movement as might be expected, considering that so many of the texts are historical; usually the facts of movements are given in the most prosaic way, with little sense of movement. Exceptions may be seen in the *Tale of Sinuhe,* whose alarm, retreat, and wandering in exile are the main theme of the story, and the story of Wen-Amon, whose frustrations and delays on his extensive travels are of chief interest. In the *Story of the Eloquent Peasant* (Middle Kingdom), the peasant's initial trip into town, the obstacles to his passage contrived by the designing townsman, the peasant's circumvention of these obstacles, and the subsequent goings and comings of peasant, king, and official all create an image of things in motion that is fairly intricate and certainly unusual. But for the most part the movement in literary imagery is in brief details and touches—often vivid, like the swift flight of a falcon, but seldom extended beyond a flash of impression. At the same time, many of the narrative documents as a whole have a kind of momentum developed by the businesslike way of reviewing a long series of events, however prosaically.

LIGHT AND COLOR

The Egyptians were evidently acutely conscious of color and used it freely in all the visual arts: significant aspects of the use of color may be seen most clearly in the manner of its use rather than the fact. Their consciousness of what they were doing is evidenced, among other ways, by the fact that the paintings in one tomb may be in a wide range of hues, in another, almost pure black and white. Statues in the round were often fully painted to render the anatomical forms and garments more naturally; sometimes they might be granted the monotone of some particular material—black or green basalt, syenite, or granite. In architecture, the use of different colored materials and the practice of covering most surfaces with paintings or painted carvings are well known. The most conspicuous demonstration of Egyptian love of color is in the minor or industrial arts—jewelry, furniture, and the like—where the widest range of rare and common materials in all kinds of colors and textures was lavishly employed with unparalleled success.

In literature, as we have noted, there is a curious lack of actual designation of colors by name in the imagery, and again we are in no good position to judge phonetically or semantically the color connotation of individual words. We do see lavish color of the rhetorical kind in the rich, involved, oft-repeated figures of speech, ornate titles and phrases of address, and the elaborate periphrases by which relatively simple actions are stated ("I cause them to see thy majesty as a fierce lion/ As thou makest them corpses throughout their valleys").[10] Comparable to this is the rich combination with architecture of sculpture in the round, where statues of gods and kings, sphinxes, obelisks, flagpoles, and the like are used as luxurious ornamental supplements to simple architectural forms.

In view of the generous appreciation of color, the apparent lack of awareness of light is a matter of interest. But the paintings lack luminosity: they are depicted in abstraction, so far as light and atmosphere are concerned; nowhere does one encounter a shadow or shade, rarely the darkness of night. So it is also in relief sculpture, except for the basic fact that it is the shadow in an incision which makes the line of a relief contour; and we shall note in another connection the character of later New Kingdom relief, creating garish shadow by broad, crude slashings of the stone. In sculpture in the round, light and shadow play little part. In architecture, light and shadow are important, but independently; that is, in the brilliant Nile sun the shadows are so deep and open light is so dazzling (under average conditions) that from a position in the sun it is difficult to see into a shadow, and vice versa. Thus the colonnades and covered halls make welcome retreats from the glare of the open court, but from the point of view of optical sensation,

[10] Pritchard, *op. cit.*, p. 373.

aesthetically speaking, the contrast is so great that visually it is a simple matter of bright and dark, with no intermediate tone or interest. There are certain exceptions, the more appreciated because of their uniqueness. For one, the early morning light in certain positions is suffused to permit one to sense the interior of a colonnade as part of the composition of a courtyard in terms of space as well as light and color; in this regard, the sensation of Hatshepsut's temple at Deir el Bahri in the early morning is indescribably perfect. Also, in some smaller temples like that of Khonsou at Karnak the tremendous open courts of the great monuments of Egypt were replaced by smaller courts with a higher proportion of the space covered by the roof; that is, they were more peristyle rooms, with the result that the brilliance of the light in the open area was cut down, enabling one to see from the entrance past the court through the hypostyle hall through open and closed structures beyond—vistas of light and shadow of some effect.

A remarkable limitation of the sensory suggestion of color is its absence in the conceptual form of literature; rarely are colorful objects described. There are occasional references to gold or precious stones; to the Green Sea; and sporadic instances of other kinds; but on the whole one looks far in the preserved writing for specific descriptions of things in terms of their color. The same might be said of light, for although there are frequent allusions, especially in the hymns to the light of the sun and the contrasting dark, there is never a suggestion of anything between these two flat extremes of night and day. And, also remarkably, considering the potential of literature in this regard, there are few evocations of sounds: the lowing of cattle which awoke Sinuhe in the desert stands out as a vivid exception.

TEXTURE

Finally there is the matter of texture, in which Egyptian art achieved extraordinary qualities: the rich and sensitive exploitation of the various kinds of materials of which the buildings and statues, jewelry and furniture, are made and the intricate, finely produced textures of a decorative kind created by modulated and carved surfaces. These textures are almost always the textures of the material used, not of the iconic form itself. That is, a papyrus swamp may be represented on a relief as a sheet of reeding—a sensation originally suggested by the stalks of papyrus, optically perceived but converted to a stone surface tactically appreciated (Plate 4). In architecture, the polished sheen of the faces of the pyramids, the chalky facets of the limestone columns or piers of Hatshepsut's or Zoser's mortuary complexes; the shimmering surface of a pylon, the soft warmth of the smooth, deeply carved columns at Karnak, are typical of Egyptian sensitivity to texture in building.

Manner

ontology

We turn now to qualities of the manner of using these means. In the first place there is the extraordinary contradiction in Egyptian art between the consummate mastery of their individualized portraiture in sculpture in the round and the tendency in all other aspects of art to prefer types or abstractions. At one extreme is a firm particularism—a conviction that the reality of things lies in their phenomenal individuality; at the other extreme is a conviction that lies somewhere between idealism and thorough abstraction—that the reality of things lies in certain generic qualities or characteristics subsisting among certain selected elements of the things: for example, the reality of a papyrus swamp lies not in the particular state and disposition of the particular reeds, animals, and birds that existed at a certain time; instead, the reality consists in the fact that the swamp has water, reeds, fish, fowl, and animals each endowed with kinds of qualities of value which are always present among all examples in some degree, though not equally in all. To both points of view the problem in art is to embody in the work the qualities which are real from that point of view, particular or generic. The curious feature in Egyptian art is that both attitudes sometimes seem basic and concurrent.

66

Egyptian Art

The particularist attitude, however, is concentrated on and all but confined to the problem of identifying and perpetuating in the world of eternal life the individual men and women of this life, either through the magic processes of burial or through the magic effect of written records. All the efforts, through mummification, portrait statuary, written documents, used in mortuary rites to preserve the individuality of the dead, are to this end; the historical documents carved on stelae and temple walls and otherwise written down, the ruthless energy with which monarchs carved their names on monuments of all kinds, erasing the names of their predecessors while they devised such means as they could of preventing their own successors from erasing their names in turn; the widespread primitive principle, seldom so developed and respected in highly sophisticated cultures, of the magic power of the real but secret name of an individual (or thing) as being invested with the vitality and power of his existence—all of these focus on the intense preoccupation of each Egyptian to preserve himself for eternity.

But this preoccupation was not based on any very clear conception of what, exactly, the self was. The Egyptian recognized a physical body, an immaterial element called a *ba,* and another immaterial element known as a *ka,* but these were never completely rationalized into a clear system, unless briefly and locally. (Compare the inability of moderns to agree on any systematic conceptualization of such commonly used terms as mind, spirit, soul, ghost.) Moreover, when it came to capturing his individuality the Egyptian seems to have been content, as we have seen, with whatever was evidenced in the face. Therefore it is clear that the particularism reflected by portraiture lies in a not unnaturally confused area of Egyptian thought and represents only one facet of a complex riddle.

Apart from portrait sculpture, it is clear that Egyptian art deals in types with a fair degree of abstraction. In the conceptual form this is especially true of the human figure, which appears almost invariably in a few limited poses, in a few typical costumes. It is also true of the activities depicted. These activities, as we have observed, are almost limitless in covering the entire range of human life, but never is an activity depicted as being a particular one—a particular baking, for example, on a particular day in a particular place—but always as a *kind* of activity. Moreover, we note the same kind of activity repeated over and over again: in a single tomb there will be an extraordinarily varied repertoire of scenes—but almost any other tomb of the same size and degree of luxury will have almost exactly the same repertoire.

Thus the conceptual form is depicted in highly simplified typical forms, and with this the sensory qualities of movement, color, and texture also recur to produce the same restricted range of types of effects. This is inevitable to some degree because of the repetition of the forms, although a vastly wider range of composition, in every respect, has been achieved in depicting the Last Supper from early Christian to modern times than was ever achieved in the depictions of the ceremonial meal set at the magic *ka*-entrance to the Egyptian tomb. That is, even preserving the same forms the effects could have been varied in terms of color, texture, and scale, but such variety was seldom attempted, apart from degrees of material and technical excellence.

Figures of men are ordinarily red; of women, white; conventional colors are generally assigned to different elements of conceptual form. The swamp scene in the Tomb of Ti, with the same textures of water and reeding, recurs in many other tombs. There are, no doubt, many differences in detail. Each painting has its own special colors and textures, but within limited ranges, within specified types. This tendency is dramatized by the occasional exception, as in the Tomb of Amenhotep II at Thebes, with the severe black and white color scheme of the main chamber.

What we have been discussing, of course, is the conventional character of Egyptian art in all its phases throughout all its history, its tendency to repeat and cherish any quality once established, its adherence to the forms and patterns accepted in the early days of the Old Kingdom. We are simply saying that the reason for this "traditionalism" or conservatism—or the immediate reason—is the conviction that important qualities are simple and constant. This conviction remained with the Egyptians throughout their history and justified them in accepting without resentment some typical formulation of qualities.

Egyptian Art

To this notion that Egyptian art is "conventional," that it accepts and adheres to types of qualities rather than particular manifestations, can be opposed not only the exceptions of certain periods, like that of Ikhnaton (Plates 6, 10), but also a fairly persistent current of aliveness to particularized detail under certain rather special conditions. In reliefs concerning Hatshepsut's expedition to Punt, the peculiar flora and fauna of the country, the remarkable figure of the Queen of Punt, even strange items of social and economic life are depicted with absorbing attention to detail. Less conspicuously, but more profoundly, certain creatures like antelopes and donkeys are often rendered, even in the most conventional compositions, with notably sympathetic expression of their aliveness and the grace of a particular animal in a special pose or the humor or pathos of some rustic incident. Occasionally, one sees the anatomical structure of a human figure in a relatively complicated position, bending or twisting, quite absorbingly depicted, in contrast to the awkward convention of shoulders and waist in simple standing figures. It is commonly supposed that for most elements of the conceptual form of a decorative program there were standard patterns in an artists' manual, but when on his own responsibility, faced with a problem of conceptual form not covered by the manual, the artist was sensitive and capable of close observation and original invention. This involves no real contradiction of the general conception of Egyptian art as tending toward the abstract; it simply reveals the process. The more familiar a phenomenon was, the more thoroughly it was reduced to its essentials. A phenomenon which presented itself for the first time had to be observed, understood, and reduced to essentials in terms of the understanding achieved. This is a metaphysical problem; its results are perceptibly different from those of imperfect observation, or stylization by hasty, mechanical, inept repetition, or simplification by carelessness. So the novelties of the land of Punt had to be analyzed before the question of whether a "Puntian tree" could be reduced to the same simplified form as an Egyptian tree. The question of whether the grace of the antelope, the nimbleness of the donkey, the fluffiness of a bird, were among its essentials had to be considered before an answer was established; indeed, it might be raised more than once.

Aesthetic Aspects of ANCIENT ART

EPISTEMOLOGY

It seems clear that Egyptian art is fundamentally one which tends toward abstraction, though not to an extreme. It tends to conceive of phenomena in terms of their types or kinds. Furthermore, these types and kinds are derived to a large extent from sensory apprehension, largely controlled by logic, of the inherent phenomenal qualities of the object. Epistemologically, the Egyptian attitude might be described as logical objectivity. One of the more obvious examples is the depiction of the human body, almost invariably represented, when in the common pose of standing in relatively quiet participation in an activity, with legs, hips, and head in profile, chest and eye shown fullface. The figure, in other words, is constructed of certain typical, visual patterns, arranged not as they occur in actual vision but with the most characteristic visual shapes abitrarily combined into a single logical but improbable form. It is an act of logic as arbitrary as hieroglyphics (or any system of writing or language), where standardized ideograms are arranged in whatever combination is needed to suggest a particular combination or relation of ideas: thus legs & waist & shoulders & arms & head equal man. The point is that the parts of this ideogram are evidently conceived as having objective existence in the concept "man"; their combination in one arbitrarily logical scheme may stand adequately for "erect man"; in another, for "seated man." Almost naïvely, the more important an individual, the "bigger" he is, as we say; this quality of importance is conceived as having objective existence, and in the work of art the conception has a logical, objective equivalence in the mathematically larger size of the important individual.

The depiction of a scene of any complexity, for example a papyrus swamp or a garden, follows the same logical objectivity. Rivers are inhabited by fish and animals of various kinds; boats float on the water; the blossoms are at the tops of the papyrus reeds; in a swamp there are many different birds and animals. All this objective fact is objectively indicated in carvings and paintings by tangible physical counterparts of all the natural phenomena under consideration (in their important essentials); and the situation is revealed by thorough, sober logic in the broader as well as smaller details of arrangement and exposition. Still speaking of conceptual form, this objectivity is easily apparent in the literature, in the bare, factual reporting of events.

There is also an almost studied objectivity in the rendering of sensory stimuli. Lines of movement are drawn or carved in full; rhythms are developed by painted or engraved accents of one kind or another; colors and textures are fully painted or carved in every detail; nowhere is anything left to impression, guess, suggestion, allusion.

The objectively real qualities of the many kinds of material employed (and carefully sought out) are also developed and revealed with elaborate concern. The colors and textures inherent in various kinds of stone—the hard polish of the igneous forms, the polish or soft matt surface of various kinds of limestone, the color and special textures of faïence and metals and wood—these are among the outstanding refinements and successes of Egyptian art, a direct expression of the objective conception of the qualities of the materials. The granite or basaltic monolithic piers of some buildings, the more yielding contours of limestone columns in others, the shallow, crisp, gemlike engraving in the granites, the undulating, putty-like contour of relief in softer stone are evidences of the same attitude.

SIGNIFICATION

Egyptian style is a somewhat abstract idealism, objectively known; it is also completely literal. All the elements in the art are to be taken for what they are or seem to be, and not for what they might symbolize or as they might be understood in terms of allegory or analogy. A battle is a battle, a dog-headed god is a dog-headed god; red is red, a color for enjoyment and rarely a symbol of some meaning beyond itself; the same may be said of all other aspects.

There is, of course, a sense in which red is something other than red, a bird something other than a bird, as we have seen—in the sense that red is one of the identifying characteristics of the male human and birds are one of the attractions of hunting or one of the denizens of a swamp. But these meanings are as literal as language can be, and have no tendency to be anything else.

There is another sense in which a bird, a hawk, for instance, may be intended to represent a soul or a god—a god, not an otherworldly being but a force of nature. Here again, however, these equivalences are literal in the extreme—literal and logical and matter of fact, a form of emblematic symbolism. There is no emotional symbolism involved, no welling of immediate understanding which comes with the unconscious recognition of the motif.

At least, this would seem to be a legitimate inference from the thoroughgoing ideographic literalness of the usual manner of depicting a concept in terms of the sum of its details. It is impossible for a modern to imagine exactly the reaction of an ancient Egyptian in the court of Ikhnaton (Plate 6) to the pictorial signs of Amon or Aton. The sunburst, the scarab, the *ankh,* and no doubt other configurations may have had a meaning well beyond their "lexicographical" definition, and this is, of course, symbolism; but the extent and intensity is impossible to judge. Much thought has been expended on the possible symbolism of the pyramid or the obelisk; no doubt these were figures which were easily and naturally associated with Re, and the sight evoked his name and meaning; whether the impact of this evocation was more forceful than the total impact of aesthetic qualities we can probably never know. Nevertheless, on the whole, it seems most reasonable to suppose that the symbolic content of Egyptian art and thinking was low and their normal way of using and interpreting the materials of their art was more than ordinarily literal.

DEFINITION

Of the more directly sensory qualities in Egyptian style, the manner of definition is one of the most characteristic—remaining very nearly constant throughout the entire history of Egyptian art—and one of the more difficult to designate in unequivocal, unambiguous, objective terms. It is, roughly speaking, a quality of precision: definiteness, distinctness, in some ways exactness, that is in certain peculiar ways unique and remarkable.

The movements of Egyptian art, for example, have this quality of precision in their abbreviated simplicity, their exact repetitions, the sharp, definite, distinct rendering of lines, accents, and other factors stimulating the senses to awareness of movement. In painting and relief sculpture, one of the conspicuous characteristics of the sensory elements is the extraordinarily definite and distinct outline contour, a precise, deeply cut line in relief which often constitutes most of the carving in the relief; or, in painting, the arbitrary, often heavy contour line which surrounds a figure or object, although the border between the smooth silhouetted figures in flat color against another plain, flat color in itself is enough to make a vivid contour line. Relief, especially in the Old Kingdom, might be worked out by reducing the background plane to a general level surface behind the figure plane, but the contour line around the figure would be a bold, quick shearing of the surface, not a graded modulation of one plane to another; and indeed this would be reinforced by the difference in coloring and often by a supplementary incision behind the background plane. The delineation of subsidiary detail—clothing, jewelry, anatomy—would be similarly sharp and distinct, though usually a grade less emphatic; but the primary forms of all elements, whether human, animal, or hieroglyphs, would have the same strong grade of treatment; the secondary aspects of these elements, if differentiated at all, would have an approximately even and weak grade of treatment.

With regard to the conceptual forms, too, the kinaesthetic effects are developed in the same clear-cut, recognizable way. This is evident in the poses of the human or animal figures and the arrangement of vegetable forms: forms which quickly become familiar, not only as conceptual form (i.e., as people, animals) but as geometric or typical patterns, and thus facilitate and accentuate the rhythmic response. Because of the easily identified component elements of a composition, the arrangement as a whole and the component details may be assimilated rapidly. Apart from these stereotyped poses, conceptual form is made to contribute to the kinaesthetic response by whatever uncompromising distortion of form might seem convenient; arms are elongated, curved almost unnaturally; fingers are arranged at will.

In another respect the kinaesthetic use of conceptual form reveals the same precision: in the extraordinary pains that were employed to preserve intact individual silhouettes to avoid overlapping or confusion of lines of one figure with those of another. In many an Egyptian frieze there will be scores of human beings, the background will be filled with accessories of all kinds and with hieroglyphics, and yet there will be few overlapping elements. Of course this is by no means always true, and scenes of agricultural activity, the hunt, and war often involve figures superimposed many times over. But in most cases the superimposition will be most carefully rendered to leave important contours unbroken; a herd of donkeys, for example, may be rendered as one donkey, complete with any number of heads and forequarters projecting successively in front and in the background. This rhythm of heads, combined with the single broader element of the body, is a convenient contrast with a rhythm of exactly equal figures shown entire, but it is equally distinct and definite in terms of the number and kinds of accents. It is only in the last phases of the New Kingdom that this distinctness in the rhythmic elements of a pattern is lost in a generalized shimmering of light and movement, though even then the carving itself is boldly, even harshly, vivid and distinct.

In still another respect the quality of precision appears in the movements of a composition of painting or relief: in the clear-cut changes in scale with which the artist gives positive, self-evident importance to any person or thing that is logically important in the conception, and kinaesthetically a weight that is sensory as well as intelligible. Its downward movement or static resistance creates a major accent, a powerful dominant, in the rhythmic pattern.

In its rational aspect, the conceptual form does not always seem carefully and precisely defined. There is no consistent effort to depict a human being with complete anatomical accuracy or to clarify the relation of one part of the body to another in various poses. If it were convenient to indicate such details clearly, the artist might well do so, but often he is content with a leg or an arm appearing from some impossible direction behind the body, or a skirt which crosses the waist but not the thighs. But there is full, forthright clarity in the depiction of those forms that did interest him, *as* they interested him—the unhesitating conjunction of utter particularism in the face, complete abstraction in the body.

Turning now to sculpture in the round, we find this same precision in contour outline of the figure as a whole, details within the figure, and the actual carving. In some figures depicted as almost completely enveloped in a smooth tunic of some sort, as is characteristic of the women of the Old Kingdom, the rationale of the conceptual form allows the drapery to soften some of the contours beneath, but normally the junctures of the planes of the carving will be distinct and strong. Generally speaking, the geometric character of the pose of the truly Egyptian figure and the fine, sharp carving of all lines and planes give special distinctness and definition to the directions, angles, and qualities of movement.

In literature, the ideas, expressed in relatively short, clipped phrases or sentences of simple, stereotyped form, produce clear, distinct rhythmic patterns in which there is, perhaps, little subtlety but a definite momentum. The movement of conceptual form—especially that movement of the free progress of the narrative—is uncomplicated, simple, and straightforward.

In architecture, the forms are, for the most part, also simple and precise. The façade of a temple, for example, with its gate between pylons, is hardly complex. A colonnaded façade of piers or columns resting on a floor or slight step, with only the simplest kind of entablature above, is equally distinct in its forms. The plan of a temple complex belies the name; it is hardly "complex" either in the courts or halls which constitute the first elements or in their relation to each other, and though it may be admitted that the congeries of rooms and passages around the sanctuary is something of a maze, it will be observed that the elements are almost exclusively long narrow rooms opening at right angles off long narrow corridors: the delineation is still precise and distinct, though the over-all pattern may be otherwise.

In the movements and rhythms of the volumes, and of volume with relation to volume, as with the movement of the lines and rhythms of the design of structural members, the quality of precision—definiteness, distinctness, exactness—is predominant.

In one important element of architecture this quality of precision is elusive: in one aspect of the spatial movement of a large hypostyle hall. At Karnak, for example, if one takes a position well in the center of the square defined by four columns, in the center of the crossing of a colonnade corridor of each major axis, there is, to be sure, a precision in the ranks of columns leading in front and behind, to right and left, that has a strong effect. There is a definite, rhythmic vista along each axis of the room, from wall to wall (or door to door, if one is on the central crossing of the major axial corridors), and nothing is visible except these two corridors; nothing is made aware to the senses except these particular, well-defined movements. On the other hand, if one retreats close to any column, out of the direct channel of these dominant movements, so that he is able to see at off-axial angles into the ranks and files of columns all about him, he may easily find himself deprived of any sense of the precise, regular rhythm of the axial corridors and feel an un-organized, quite generalized extension or continuum of space and movement on all sides, unbounded by definite walls or borders. As a matter of fact, this is characteristic of movements in other kinds of Egyptian art: as long as one accepts a specified point of view, everything is distinct and definite: but if one refuses this specified point of view, some of the precision may be lost.

The same remarks can be made of the treatment of other aesthetic elements—color, light, texture. It is unnecessary to dwell at length on these; there have been frequent if casual allusions to the concepts, and they are neither obscure nor of prime importance. In Egypt, there was a preference for a few, easily distinguished pigments, and these colors were used generously and in clear contrast. Similarly, light, as we have said, is never employed in chiaroscuro or shades, always simply in full contrast to unadulterated dark, if at all. So also the particular texture of each area is distinctly rendered and kept separate from others in the composition. The most familiar example is the panel showing Ti hunting hippopotami (Plate 4)—the jewel-like distinctness of the various textures, the reeding, the stippling of the river, the perfect flatness of the bodies of men and animals, the delicate etching of the wings and fins, the more complex but nevertheless distinct textures of other elements. The impact of the conceptual form—the people, animals, and activities delineated, from the point of view of emotion or sensuous reaction as differentiated from the information and instruction they may contain or the part they may play as framework for an arrangement of the purely optical sense stimuli line, color, texture—this too is singularly precise. Thus, to use the same example of the relief of Ti hunting, one is presented with all the details of a pleasurable experience—the charms, beauties, and opulence of the swamp with its flowers and wildlife, the many kinds of fish as well as hippopotami, the lively activity of the beaters nimbly maneuvering their attack against the hippopotamus, the servant quietly seeing to the lunch, the master's complete control of the situation—to enjoy, to participate, to retreat, to ignore. All this is distinctly indicated, spelled out, as it were, in simple phrases.

CONFIGURATION

A quality of the manner of Egyptian art which is perhaps less equivocal is its configuration of expanse, or two-dimensional, or plane surface. This, too, is a quality that pervaded Egyptian art from beginning till end, though in the same periods, and generally from the Saite period on, there were strong tendencies toward a more massive configuration. In the initial phases—Neolithic and pre-Dynastic—the configuration was linear, as exemplified by the figures of the early tomb paintings at Hierakonpolis (Plate 1) and some of the painted pottery of the time, which depict the elements of conceptual form in terms of wirelike forms and develop patterns in which parallel or concentric lines predominate. Of course even in these early works there is a tendency toward plane-surface forms, as when a ship emerges in a pattern resembling a comb: an open surface representing the hull contrasted with a rectangular surface of close parallel lines representing the oars; or triangles or semicircles are developed out of parallel or concentric lines; or solid triangular forms are used; or the bodies of men and animals spread out like blots, though the legs and arms may remain thin and stringlike. The sculpture of the period is also marked for its linear qualities; the elongated, slender forms of the bodies of certain early clay figurines with unusually mobile, attenuated arms; the emphatic linear ornament on some of the early figurines, though the patterns tend to take plane forms—differently patterned or textured triangles, squares, circles, and so forth. Rather striking is the vivid contour line of the earliest slate palettes, generally in the form of animals and conspicuous for their rich, flat surfaces and equally remarkable for the strong effect of linear movement. In pre-Dynastic material it is evident that interest in plane surface in painting and sculpture emerges in a tradition of linear design.

By the First Dynasty, with the Palette of Narmer (Plate 2), there has been achieved a degree of two-dimensionality in configuration which remains almost constant in Egyptian art for the next two thousand years. The dominant movement is that of the plane surface; the organization is in terms of these surfaces, one way or another. There is almost no feeling—no attempt, even, to search—for a third dimension of depth or solidity of form. It is true that, in the Archaic period, the hieroglyphs in the Stele of Hesire have a massive development and an independence that is unparalleled in later Egyptian art; even the figure of Hesire himself has a "body" that could hardly be matched until Ptolemaic times. But in spite of this stirring of interest in three-dimensional configuration, the expansive concept remained characteristic.

It is exemplified in the Palette of Narmer in a number of ways. The movements are exclusively in two dimensions—or one; that is, a line, whether the contour of Narmer's figure or that of the necks and tails of the giraffe-lions, pursues its sophisticated course in a fairly intricate pattern, but the pattern never goes into depth; it always wanders along the single plane which is the surface of the palette. Even the tentative interlacing of the necks of the giraffe-lions, where overlapping is to be expected, is in an unbroken plane (and optically almost so). More obviously, the larger forms of the design are plane surfaces or areas. Thus the top of the palette is divided into four zones, transversely; the central zone is subdivided into the circle, the plane forms of the animals and the man, and the plane forms of the background; the figured upper band is subdivided into a rectangle on the right formed by two rows of stacked corpses (or parading soldiers?), a rectangle formed by a row of standard bearers, a rectangle formed by the king with two attendants and some symbols; and each of these rectangles is further subdivided in obvious ways. On the back the plane areas are less completely indicated, but primarily there are the shapes which constitute the figures of Narmer and his foe; the shape of the falcon and other devices in the upper right, comprising a rectangular subdivision; and the shape of the individual on his own base line behind Narmer. And so on, into the most minute portions of the design, all the parts are flat and plane.

So far we have been speaking of movement, for a plane surface is created by the sweep of a line in a single direction; but it is clear that in the Palette of Narmer these plane surfaces are distinguished chiefly by texture. The textures, however, are flat and without depth or body. The conceptual forms, too, are distorted to contribute to a sense of flatness—the frontal shoulders, for example, with the feet and head in profile; the frontal horns of the bull in the lower zone of the top of the palette, with the rest of the head in profile.

It will be hard to find in Egyptian relief or painting examples which deviate in any significant way from this predilection for the plane surface, for two-dimensional rendering of movement, texture, and conceptual form. In painting, the preference is for even tones over a surface, without body or depth or great intensity. There is sometimes a degree of modulation of color that seems to suggest an attempt to model the figures, particularly those of birds and animals; this, to Western eyes, at least, is likely to seem extraordinarily restrained and subdued— perhaps even unintentional. In the El Amarna period there was briefly a more consistent interest in the third dimension, not well developed; and from the Saite period (Plate 11) through Roman times the third dimension—the mass, the solid form—are almost constantly evident in a restrained but insistent way. Thus, for example, in a relief of around

350 B.C. from Sakkhara, representing the goddess Nut spanning, archlike, a complex of other symbols, there are all the traditional qualities of the liquid-smooth litheness of the figure (particularly the arms, which completely ignore anatomical form and structure in favor of the movement of the line), the arbitrary plane surface textured smoothly or otherwise along the arch of the body or rippling in the hair and fingers; and the pervading flatness of the whole conception; but in spite of all this there is an inescapable suggestion of mass in the thighs, the breast, the ear, the face. Similarly, other works, particularly paintings, from Saite through Roman times, tend to a more or less forceful indication of the massive form. But in almost every case the plane remains dominant.

Egyptian work of sculpture in the round is also an organization of plane surfaces. Typical works such as the Old Kingdom statues of Khafra or Ranofer, for all the ponderous bulk of the arms and other limbs, are done with chief attention to the appearance of each section of the surface. Thus the headdress and the various parts of the head, the torso, the arms, hand, and fingers, the thighs and drapery are all individually interesting in terms of plane or curving surfaces of different shapes and textures and not of the solid geometry of the figure. This is particularly evident when, as often, a rippled surface suggested by a bit of drapery terminates, replaced by the smooth surface of skin, with no change in relief to suggest that the drapery, or rippled surface, had been lying *on* the skin; or when an elaborate necklace is simply incised and painted on the skin of a throat; or when a hieroglyphic text is carved on a flesh surface, perhaps overlapping from a surface belonging to a chair or wall. The ultimate in this conception of sculpture in the round as surface is seen in a statue from the New Kingdom (Plate 9), where the design consists substantially of a cube from which projects a tiny head; on the sides of the cubes are inscriptions. In other words, the body— understood to be seated—has been reduced to the six faces of a cube, which are conveniently used for displaying written statements; and the object is identified as a statue by the addition of the head. Because of the physical existence of sculpture in the round in three-dimensional mass, it is bound to possess the movements and sensuous qualities of mass; but insofar as a material which exists in three-dimensional mass can be treated as though it were an organization of plane surfaces, Egyptian sculpture may be so described. The fact is made all the more vivid by the exceptions, notably from the work shop of Thutmose at El Amarna and from the Saite and later periods (Plates 10, 11).

Similarly in architecture, though one is accustomed to think of the tremendous masses of material and the vast size of many of the famous buildings, the sense of bulk and weight is largely rational or an effect of the dynamics to be considered below; there is little emphasis on the massive, three-dimensional form of space or structural elements and much emphasis on the two-dimensional, expansive spaces and plane surfaces. For example, the pyramids—largely because of the unparalleled size and scale of the great pyramids at Gizeh, partly because a pyramid is an easily comprehended, geometric solid, partly because one knows that the pyramids are near-solid masonry—are likely to occur to one as dramatic examples of massive form in architecture. This is true in only a very special way, however, and what one sees in beholding a pyramid is one, or at the most two, triangular surfaces. If seen from the corner, the pyramid presents two surfaces that are recognizable as two faces of a solid form, but no more than is unavoidable in the unyielding fact of its physical constitution; and from the point of view of planned design, the pyramid was intended to have been seen squarely on a single side, from the central axis, whence only a single triangle would be visible, with no hint of physical mass. Furthermore, as originally designed and constructed, the developed pyramids were finished with each facet absolutely smooth and polished, emphasizing the surface and its shape, detracting from consciousness of the material. In their present state, the pyramids at Gizeh seem much more massive and solid than originally intended, for the smooth sheath has gone and one sees the blocks of the successive courses of masonry of which the mass is built. The alternate projection and recession of these component masses, the rough texture of the triangle, and the broken lines of angles of the pyramid serve to remind us of the material behind the façade.

It is illuminating to observe the brief phase of interest in the stepped pyramid. Aesthetically, the mastaba—a low structure with sloping sides, essentially a truncated pyramid, characteristically with its faces planed smooth—is like the true pyramid in this emphasis on the surface rather than the mass. The stepped pyramid, with its appearance of being a series of mastabas piled on top of each other, cannot avoid the effect of the re-entrant lines and recessive planes in creating a feeling of constructed masses. But this effect was not preferred, evidently, for it was used for only a few monuments and then abandoned in favor of the true pyramid.

In the early mastabas and in such features as the enclosing wall around the pyramid complex of Zoser at Sakkarah, the wall face is sometimes rendered in alternating, buttress-like masses projecting in front of the smooth wall; the various faces were elaborately treated in the form of alternating panels, pilasters, or various structural forms from brick, wood, or reeds. These effects often have a quality of configuration in mass, but on the whole, when an entire wall is treated uniformly in this way, it usually presents itself as surface ornamented in more or less complex patterns of textures.

In general, however, it is significant that after the lively experiment and variety of the Archaic period, Egyptian architecture subsided into a faithful treatment of its structural elements in terms of plane surface. The great temples were surrounded tightly with tremendous walls which presented only a single, unbroken sweep of smooth expanse to the spectator (Plate 16). The entrances were between pylons which appeared to the spectator only as a sheer expanse of smooth or ornamented surface, though in structural fact they may have been truncated pyramids; the columns and supports within the building were smooth rectangular prisms or cylinders—frequently modified slightly to suggest plant forms (Plate 18). It is the film of surface that is evident to the eye, that impresses the senses. Every surface—the face of a pylon or a papyrus-bud column—is decorated with scenes in relief or documents in hieroglyphic. The surfaces are areas for the display of ornament or information or sensuous texture of their own. The columns in the colonnaded porch behind the court of Amenhotep III at Luxor, for example, reveal by the contrast between the compound forms in the lower element and the smooth cylinder of the element below the capital the difference between the lack of massive configuration of a smooth cylinder and a modeled shaft. But even the reed-bundle form of the columns of Amenhotep at Luxor or of the entrance corridor at Sakkarah, compared with the fluted columns from the South House or Temple T in Zoser's pyramid complex at Sakkarah, or fluted columns from Hatshepsut's temple at Deir el Bahri, is in fact more impressive for the swollen, bulging surfaces than for carved form in massive configuration. Though there was much interest in massive configuration in the archaic period, and though polygonal, compound, and even fluted columns appear sporadically thenceforth through Egyptian architecture, the predominant and characteristic forms were those exploiting the qualities of surface.

So, too, the volumes in Egyptian architecture have the essential quality of expanse, or development in two dimensions, rather than in three. To take the characteristic completely enclosed form, the hypostyle hall, the spatial effect is primarily one of extension from side to side (Plates 15, 19). One proceeds along the main axis of the hall with corridor after corridor of columns opening at right angles on each side; the space is a succession of sweeping ranks and files of columns and corridors, whether one moves on the main axis from front to back, or the almost equal axis (longer, not so high) from right to left. The third dimension, of height, is impressive in any particular view upward, but is always limited, confined, never developed into a phase of the whole volume. Basically, the space is a rhythmic movement of successive lateral directions; second, it is an amorphous flowing of space in uncontrolled expanse horizontally in all directions from any single point. In smaller hypostyle halls, again, the arrangement of the axis of primary motion from front to back, with an axis of predominant length from right to left, emphasizes the horizontal expanse of the space. In an open porch, like the porch opening off the court of Amenhotep III at Luxor, there is a great expanse of columns behind which colonnades and corridors recede in unbroken, regular ranks and files—an even expanse rearward. In the courts themselves, or at least the larger ones, the primary effect is breadth and openness; only in smaller buildings do the proportions become so confined as to suggest height. Even in the great processional alleys leading to the temples, the rows of sphinxes on either side, confronting each other across the line of passage, introduce cross-rhythms and lateral emphasis that give a breadth, an awareness of right and left, that prevent the avenues from being simply linear movements in one direction.

In literature, the equivalent of this two-dimensional configuration can easily be identified in the manner of composition of poetry in terms of relatively short declarative sentences, often in groups of several beginning in identical or closely similar ways, usually arranged in blocks or paragraphs that seem to have a rather more distinct unity and completeness, more definite beginnings and ends, with sharper transitions from paragraph to paragraph than is common in classical and post-classical European literature. This technique produces a rhythm that may be compared to that of mowing a field with a scythe, stroke repeating stroke, culminating in swath after swath, or to the rhythm of progress through the hypostyle hall or sphinx alley, with the succession of lateral vistas or accents measured off like palings in a fence.

In the second place, the "imagery" of word and metaphor is disconnected: it is not compounded to construct a single, completely integrated conceptual form but sparkles and gleams at random from innumerable points and facets. In the *Hymn of Victory of Thutmose III*,[11] as translated by Wilson (other translations show the same quality in different words), the more lyric part consists of a series of groups of lines with a repeated pattern of line beginnings:

> I have come . . .
> (variation) . . .
> I cause them . . .
> (variation) . . .

The effect is almost exactly that of stanzas rhymed in a fixed system with the same two words or syllables ending the first and third lines of every stanza, as in a ballad or rondel. But this is an extreme development in Egyptian literature; it is cadence of phrase and image which makes rhythm rather than accent, meter, or rhyme. But the unusually close parallelism of this form to forms more familiar to us

[11] Pritchard, *op. cit.*, pp. 373–75.

gives us the opportunity to see essential differences. In the first place, this use of the same two "rhymes" in all the stanzas, while it unites the stanzas, prevents them from being thrown into modulated relief by contrast and variety of rhyme. In the second place, if we examine the stanzas, we find that the first proclaims that the god has come to trample down the Djahi (Phoenician); the next, that he has come to trample down those of Asia, the East, the West, the islands of the Mitanni, the islands of the Sea, the Libyans, the ends of the lands, the "front" of the lands, and Nubia. This geographical formulation could easily have been used to construct a definite, over-all shape of space; but we have in order three sets of easterners, a western section, two lots of islanders, another group of westerners, the near, the far, and then the Nubians alone. Each of these sections is complete and vivid in itself; together they make no coherent formal unit. Each stanza closes with a picture of how the god causes the people to see him: as lord of radiance, equipped with adornment, a shooting star, a young bull, a crocodile, the avenger, a fierce lion, lord of the wing, jackal of the Southland, Horus, and Seth. The effect is that of a litany in which innumerable individually apt and telling pictures are created, unrelated, but all uniting in a shimmering, tapestry-like fusion. In this process it is the cadence which makes the unity for both larger and smaller internal patterns and the multiplication of detailed effects, so that any incipient tendency to the deeper development of any theme is lost in the aggregate, the particular kinds of color or movement or texture.

DYNAMICS

Preciseness of definition and the two-dimensional character of configuration are prominent among the qualities which constitute the individuality of Egyptian style. The most specific quality, perhaps, may be seen in the dynamics of the style. Egyptian art is, on the whole, essentially static and unmoving, with forces either inert, mutually canceled, or otherwise contrived to create a condition of immobility.

A good deal, for example, of what has been said with regard to the precision of Egyptian style is appropriate also with regard to its static dynamics. For that which is precise and definite is fixed, determined, available. It is possible, of course, to be precise about degrees of high velocity or violent exertion of energy, but in the very precision some of the dynamic quality of the speed or force is lost, aesthetically at least. The fixed quantity has always some quality of the static; it is a moment, a particular phase of the movement or release of energy which has been abstracted and pinned down for examination. Thus when the Egyptians depict an act of violence in the swirl of battle, as when Narmer brandishes his mace to brain his foe, the act, its content of movement and energy, is stipulated by convention and even the tension in the drawing is fixed for eternity. The fact of the act—perhaps, indeed, the fact of the intensity of the act—is immobilized and reduced to static permanence.

Another characteristic of Egyptian design tending toward immobility is the discreteness of the parts, the lack of any vital, interpenetrant connection between one part of a composition and another. In a wall painting, the surface may be divided into several sections, most of them horizontal bands, with a few larger rectangles to provide for more important figures, even though, rationally, they may be parts of the same scene. Or a scene may be rendered thus discretely even without the formal division into panels: the swamp scenes in the Tomb of Ti, for example, with the underwater zone at the bottom, beneath the surface zone, the stem zone, and the foliage zone. By a mental effort one can bend the plane, so to speak, to see in elevation those parts which are to be seen in elevation and in perspective those which are to be seen in that way, but the process is mechanical and the interconnection arbitrary. Even more striking is the ordinary scheme for a garden, in which the pool is rendered as a rectangle seen from above, with the fish in it in profile as seen from the side; the four views from the center of the pool are individually rendered right side up, each one correctly, on the appropriate side of the pool but without integration with the other sides. In this and in other ways, both as conceptual form and as pure sensory stimuli, the parts of a composition are relatively separate. The possibility of developing a strong movement of any kind through the whole is eliminated, and the individual sections remain inert. In literature, one of the striking qualities is the full stop to each period, which inhibits a free flow of rhythm.

Still another factor in the static quality of Egyptian art is the impact derived from the rational aspect—the conscious recognition of the physical mass and weight of many characteristic buildings and statues. The realization that they are indeed physically immovable more than most things made by man is always impressive and often overwhelming.

Perhaps the most important factor in the static dynamic is the preference for movements in terms of horizontal or vertical lines, usually fixed in full rectangles—the chief variant being the triangular form with the base horizontal—in harmony with a mechanics of unalleviated gravity, of geologic stability. Active, vital movement is produced in art by more varied, eccentric lines and angles and by curves. Curves there are in Egyptian art, but they are minimized (if possible, almost everything is reduced to straight lines), and when employed the curved lines are firm, economical, restrained, and often repeated in exact duplication. Angles must be eccentric to some degree to create a sense of real movement; thus a normal standing figure in Egyptian sculpture, with one foot advanced, has a slight suggestion of movement in spite of the postlike immobility of the one vertical leg because of the independent, eccentric angle of the advanced leg. On the contrary, a striding figure, with one leg advanced at the same angle as the other, is retarded because the legs make an equilateral triangle with the apex on center; it has a quality of movement only because of the direction implied by the imagery, i.e., by the arrangement of feet and face indicating that the figure is supposed to be moving and that the movement is eccentric, or to one side, without compensation. The extraordinary stability and immobility of the pyramid, which is often translated, rationally, into "mass," is primarily a result of the completely self-contained, downward-focused forces represented by the lines of the sides converging on the apex and descending thence through the central axis to the broad, flat, horizontal, base. It might be noted that late pyramids, like those at Meroe, which are appreciably taller than wide in comparison to the "ideal" forms at Gizeh or an imaginary pyramid much wider than tall, would have distinctly more mobile effects: the one, of shooting skyward, the other of collapsing or spreading outward. In spite of the lively subject matter of some of the historical documents, and in spite of the evident interest in what happened displayed by the narrator, the opportunity to create a flow or violence of movement is refused.

In short, the whole of Egyptian art shows a tendency to reduce forms to relatively discrete geometric patterns of rectangles or regular triangles, horizontal, measured, and definite. Inevitably this limits the possibility of developed movement and reduces it to a minimum. The result is an effect of immobility and static rest which in some circumstances is overwhelming, but always serves to capture and perpetuate the imagery, to suggest to the senses permanence and fixation.

SYSTEM

We come then to the question of composition, the manner in which the factors we have been considering are combined and integrated. In general, we would probably recognize a certain regularity to the system of arrangement and its strongly concentrated focus; the character of cohesion may be less easy to specify.

The regularity of the system is perhaps easiest to perceive in the systematic way in which a wall surface was subdivided for painting. Departures from the regular succession of evenly ruled panels were admitted, to be sure, for specific reasons, but clearly as departures from the basic system. One thinks, too, of the avenues of sphinxes, with long rows of beasts contemplating the passing scene like the regular lines of soldiers drawn up along an avenue for some procession, the regular rhythms of column and colonnade, and pylon and court, in the architectural compositions. Regular, too, is the beat of rhythm in the lines of poetry and hymn, the patterns in costume and jewelry, the plan of the workers' quarter of a town. Irregularity appears chiefly within large groups, where there is some miscellaneous arrangement, like the fish in the river where Ti fishes (though the reeds in the swamp grow with perfect regularity) or where much is crowded into small space, as in the Palette of Narmer.

FOCUS

More conspicuous is the concentration of focus, the emphasis of dominant over subordinate. This is the secret of the pyramid, the tremendous power of the simple convergence of all lines on the apex. It is the principle of the conventional design of the entrance to the Egyptian temple complex, with the door passage flanked so impressively by pylons that the door itself is overwhelmed visually but is nonetheless the dominant feature because of its powerful flanking supports. It is the principle of processional movement which determines the general scheme of an Egyptian architectural complex, everything being subordinated to the processional act—at least until it is lost in the inner recesses of the sanctuary. In sculpture in the round, it is the common dominance of the head and its attributes over the rest of the work; in relief and painting, frequently, and in the minor arts commonly, it is often revealed in the formal, bilateral, heraldric symmetry; in literature, it is the strict adherence to the point of a chosen subject, with complete disregard of digressions of any kind.

There are some mannerisms of Egyptian composition where this principle of concentration, of dominance and subordination, is not so conventional, in terms of European attitudes. For example, it may express itself in a relief or painting by the physical enlargement or diminution, without regard to natural scale or linear perspective, of some man, creature, or object which has special importance in the conceptual form. Moreover, there are occasions when Egyptian style seems to strive to minimize the effect of dominance. This is conspicuous in a major hypostyle hall, where the axis of movement is transverse to the longer axis of the volume itself; the larger columns have a direction intersecting the direction of the more numerous if smaller columns. This is a rather obvious effort to neutralize movement and create immobility. Similar is the T-shaped arrangements of the mortuary temples of the Old Kingdom, the contraposition of lines of movement in terms of volumes.

The over-all arrangement of a large surface, like a pylon, is not likely to be sharply and fully focused by major and subordinate borders, panels, and the like; it is likely to be treated as a whole. The field of decoration is not simply dominant in the conception; the field of decoration *is* the whole conception. In the elaborate decorative programs of tombs or temple walls, it is relatively more likely that a given wall or section will be planned with an over-all dominant in the ordinary sense; even if it were, it could hardly be seen from a single point of view. Rather, the whole decorative program, including many walls and corridors, leads to the ultimate dominant of the point of greatest liturgical significance. This may be invisible from most positions— unknown and unforeseeable; and the dominancy may be rational rather than aesthetic. Still, the unity of the program, the system of subordinate and dominant, hangs on this.

The focus of the arrangement, then, need not be with reference to a visually logical boundary, nor need it be in terms of elements that seem logical according to our own conventional categories. Thus a texture, the hard gloss of a statue, the surface of the walls of the entrance hall to the processional temple of Khafra, the mellow softness of the limestone of another statue, the major parts of the great Theban temples, may be the strongest focus of arrangement. Normally, however, there is some focal dominant, and this is usually fairly strong.

COHESION

Another peculiarity of Egyptian style is what may be called, to coin a word, *monoidal* organization, as opposed to a structural or organic organization. Something of what is involved here has already been implied in the reference to the organization of a pylon decoration without definite base moldings, frames, crown moldings, and so forth, calculated to show the structural relation between the ornamentation, or the ornamented surface, and the pylon itself. Rather, the ornamented surface is at one and the same time two different things, but undifferentiated—a decoration and a wall. In the ornamentation of many of the columns in a building, the structural distinction between the column as a weight-bearing functional entity and its surface as something ornamented is ignored. But this quality is revealed more fundamentally and clearly in two other peculiarities of Egyptian architecture. One is the monolithic tendency by which an entire structure is conceived as a single piece of substance, one thing, without parts, without the necessity for construction. The prime example of this, of course, would be the pyramid, especially in its original appearance with polished, seamless surfaces; monolithic in essence, a single form without parts. It is revealed in some respects almost as impressively in such buildings as the river temple of Khafra's pyramid complex (Plate 17), with the great monolithic rectangular piers supporting the ceiling, without base, without capital, without form other than the plain rectangular prism, an unconstructed entity. More subtly, the essential attitude on which this preference is based is revealed in the phenomenon which it is the delight of guides to point out—that certain blocks in the walls at the interior corners are L-shaped (to a certain extent) and appear on each of two adjoining walls. When the building was erected, large, roughly worked blocks of stone were stacked one upon the other, leaving spaces approximately the size and shape of the rooms desired; then the rough surfaces of the blocks were smoothed. But this is not construction in the sense of fitting pieces to create a desired shape; this is more like carving a space out of a block. In fact, the whole T-shape of the volume of the temple has exactly this effect of having been carved like a cave. Indeed, many Egyptian temples, including such famous examples as that of Rameses at Abu Simbel, are entirely rock-cut.

From another point of view, architectural forms like walls and pylons follow the forms originally developed in the undifferentiated amalgam of mud brickwork in vast bulk; a design of door with flanking pylons is encompassed by a single molding; a range of square piers with architrave looks like a smooth wall cut with slots (Plate 18).

Another expression of this monoidal quality, superficially different but nevertheless fundamentally related, is that when something was put together of pieces that are evidently parts of a constructed whole it was done in such a way that these parts retain a strong quality of their own separate entity, with a minimum sense of structural relation to associated members. A column system, whether it consists of simple geometric prismatic forms or elaborate floral forms, is likely to carry capitals or imposts of plain rectangular shape, which have no sensible relation to the shape below and look what they are—chunks of stone stacked upon the support in a purely arbitrary way.

In sculpture and painting, the individual figures are structurally integrated only insofar as the conceptual form involves a structural pattern; that is, insofar as a man is constructed of legs, pelvis, torso, and so on, and insofar as the observer recognizes this in seeing a statue, the statue has that structure. But the sculptor or painter does nothing to clarify this structure—to show in what way the lower leg is related to the thigh, the thigh to the pelvis. Drapery may be indicated simply by engraving the body form. A seated figure is one with the chair on which it sits. In composition, the figures are arranged in mechanical or blocklike relationships, effective in the ways we have described above but not in suggesting a unity consisting of structural elements operating effectively among themselves. Thus a wall or stele will be composed of bands over bands, interspersed with panels of various sizes; except that the highest rests on the lower, there is no structural principle operating among them. Temples may be enlarged repeatedly by the mechanical addition of units—pylon, court, hypostyle hall. The cohesion is that of a chain. In summary, the elemental "atomic" quality of the Gizeh pyramids; the mechanical, inert construction of the Zoser pyramid, in terms of a few separable mastaba-like forms, each preserving a strong sense of its own completeness; the more nearly integrated composite structures of parts in the Sun Temple of Neussere or the mortuary temple of Mentuhotep III, will illustrate the range of experiment in arrangement among the Egyptians, from pure monolithic design to a recognizable approximation of tectonic form, but one so simple and with such emphasis on the component units that structural logic as a thing in itself hardly emerges. And even this extreme is rare.

Egyptian Art

SUMMARY

To summarize, then, the most significant peculiarities of the Egyptian style in its choice of means is emphasis on the conceptual form of human activity and the lack of interest in light. The manner is characterized by precision of definition, two-dimensional configuration, static dynamics, a rather abstract idealism of conception, objectivity of apprehension, literalness of signification, a rather strongly focused but not consistently regular arrangement, and usually a "monoidal" cohesion. Translated into the "vision of the world," the "essence of reality," this means that there is a literally and objectively existing reality, precisely defined and regular in its system, but unstructured, indissoluble, permanent. It is, however, not the particular phenomena or the material substances that are real and true but the rather simplified patterns of non-material form. The most important realities, to the Egyptian, were those that indeed we know well from our physical and sensory experience in this world—those that are in fact involved in the optimum well-being of physical man in the mortal phase of his existence, though of course they do have eternal existence transcending the terms of man's mortal life.

There were in all periods modified or divergent views expressed in works whose style deviates from tradition and convention, and there were certain periods in which there occurred widespread divergent movements of consistent character. Most of these have been alluded to in passing, but it may be useful to review them systematically.

First of all, the initial stages in the emergence of Egyptian art, in the pre-Dynastic period before about 3200 B.C., not unnaturally present some anomalies. Chief among them is the proclivity toward linear configuration, or perhaps it would be more accurate to say the evident survival of linear tendencies while two-dimensional proclivities develop, even in the use of linear pattern.

The Archaic period, or the first three dynasties, from about 3200 to 2680 B.C., was a period of lively inspiration and imagination, and active invention. Opening with the reign of Narmer, it reveals at the outset the normal pattern of Egyptian style fully developed in characteristic measure; but throughout the period there was a gradual development of three-dimensional configuration and a more fundamental structural composition. These tendencies, together with less fundamental but varied and intriguing experiments in conceptual form, textures, and all other aspects of art, culminated in the reign of Zoser around 2780–2761 under his architect Imhotep; but by the beginning of the Old Kingdom and the Fourth Dynasty the spirit of inquiry had given way to the spirit of finish and perfection; the range of values had been explored; the desirable values had been identified and accepted; it now remained to achieve them in the most excellent way possible.

Except for isolated exceptions, that is, particular attempts to formulate the values in a special way for definite purposes, there is no fundamental deviation from the pattern from Cheops to Ikhnaton, from about 2670 to 1370. There are minor stylistic variations, more or less apparent to the expert, distinguishing the broader periods, the dynasties, and the reigns of these thirteen centuries, and beyond question these distinctions have importance and meaning, but they lie well within the pattern we have outlined. Just before the reign of Ikhnaton, however, under his predecessor Amenhotep III or perhaps even before, but becoming common and generally typical only during the brief reign of Ikhnaton (1370–1352), more fundamental differences prevailed. Conceptual form became the human being himself, physically and emotionally, as distinct from his occupation, activities, and amusements. Otherwise there was an interest in configuration in the third dimension, in mass; for a more centrally idealistic, rather than abstracted, concept of reality, an idealism, indeed, that tends toward particularism, but a broader particularism than the facial identification of personality characteristic of the rest of Egyptian art. One discerns a somewhat less static dynamic, a greater tension in some of the lines, a deeper vitality in some of the conceptual forms.

But this deviation, too, quickly passed, and Egyptian style resumed the cultivation of the values to which its culture had been dedicated. During the Nineteenth Dynasty there was a shift in the quality of the dynamics; the sober, static forms of tradition gave way to an evident, though not very profound, tendency to something more violent: the colors become more garish; linear movements become exaggerated and less carefully controlled; perhaps accidentally, the deeper carving of hieroglyphs, partly intended to guard against erasure, introduced an energetic contrast of shadow; there was a greater generalization of conception, less precision of detail in conception and execution, that slackened the control of traditional art. In the later Nineteenth and Twentieth dynasties, the tendency toward a more violent, mobile dynamic (as compared to normal Egyptian standards, of course) reached a climax in the violent battle scenes on the walls of the temple at Medinet Habu, where it was accompanied by a resurgence of linear configuration and a renunciation of the long-cherished emphasis on surface and geometric shapes.

After a few centuries of relative conventionality, the stirrings of the final movements of the ancient Egyptian style begins with the Saite Dynasty. Chiefly this evidences itself in a renewed concern for mass and the third dimension in sculpture. The degree to which this interest makes itself evident is particularly clear in Plate 11.

The fulfilment of this new tendency does not come until the Ptolemaic period. Egyptian sculpture from this period, not taking into account true Greek work done in Egypt, may hardly seem Egyptian at all because of the full development of three-dimensional form and the concentration on the man or the animal rather than on what he or it does. There is a greater sense of structure; in a basalt dog in the Louvre, the neck and head above the collar are structurally integrated to the body below in terms of line and geometric solid form but not in terms of conceptual form (i.e., canine anatomy). The separation at the collar has no relation to the structural logic of the dog's skeleton and musculature. Probably the basalt hawks of the period, like those in the Metropolitan Museum and the British Museum, are more typical. They preserve the abstract-idealized forms of Egyptian tradition and the taste for full surfaces, with a forceful rendering of the massive structure of these elements. In architecture, the spatial imagery of the buildings changes little save again to introduce a greater degree of structural order. The porch has greater importance, establishing a definite entrance to the temple proper from the forecourt; the sanctuary is a distinct building, or tabernacle, isolated and therefore emphasized, separate and therefore structurally contained, within the inner complex of rooms. The relief compositions on the pylons of the temples at Edfu and Philae show a tendency toward clarity and organization lacking in earlier buildings. The chief figures show a greater fulness of form, with accompanying contrast of light and shadow and emphasis on the outline. In relief compositions in general, there seems to be a more logical structural system of dominance and subordination in various aspects of design. Finally, in the realm of painting, the decoration of the Tomb of Petosiris at the dawn of the Ptolemaic period shows conventional Egyptian work with the particular novelty of obvious massiveness of configuration and a little less abstraction in conceptual form.

It is worth noticing that there are evidences of foreign influences in Egypt during the three most "unconventional" phases of Egyptian art: pre-Dynastic, El Amarna, and Ptolemaic. From the first, a knife handle from Gebel el Arak seems, in the carving on one side at least, to be markedly Mesopotamian in style; during the second there were certainly close contacts with the Aegean; during the Ptolemaic and Roman periods Egypt was under the direct political control of the Greeks and the Romans. But whether or not the "Mesopotamian influence" in pre-Dynastic times came from abroad, it was almost entirely ignored, forgotten with the multitude of other individual stylistic expressions of the time. There were contacts with the Aegean from the time of Thutmose III at least, although almost wholly disregarded until the later days of Amenhotep III (the El Amarna style had its beginnings before the actual accession of Amenhotep IV-Ikhnaton). And it is a remarkable fact that the beginnings of tendencies toward certain "classical" traits began before there was important contact with the Greeks. Indeed, it is somewhat disconcerting to discover that at the time the Greeks were thought to have been discovering sculpture in Egypt, Egyptian artists were carving in a style considerably more "advanced" than the early archaic style which the Greeks, who are thought to have copied from them, employed.

In short, while not denying the fact that there were definite influences from abroad at these times in a direct transmission of artistic influences, it may still be maintained that these could become effective chiefly because for other reasons the Egyptians were predisposed to see in them the solution to problems of expression of convictions already developing in their minds. That is, a recognition in the El Amarna period of a greater degree of freedom and mobility in reality; that reality may be to a degree transitory; that feeling and emotion may have reality and value. And, in the later period, that reality of matter, substance—previously denied by the emphasis on surface—should be admitted and expressed by emphasizing three-dimensional massive form.

CHAPTER II

The Art of Hither Asia

U<small>NREALISTIC AND IMPRACTICAL</small> though it may be to count the art of Egypt from pre-Dynastic through Roman times as one, there is a far clearer unity than is true of the art of westernmost Asia during the approximately equivalent period of from before 4000 B.C. to the time of the Sassanians. In Egypt, at least, there is a well-defined geographical unity imposed by the Nile Valley, and a basic ethnic and social unity of some complexity. In Hither Asia none of these unities prevails. There is, of course, the valley of the two rivers. Mesopotamia itself is a geographical entity of some distinctness, but it is less rigorously confined. Even so, it does not include the Iranian plateau, which figures conspicuously in the cultural development of Mesopotamia, especially under the Persians. Assyria, in the upper reaches of the rivers, is distinguishable from lower Mesopotamia as Upper and Lower Egypt scarcely are. And one should include the Anatolian plateau, the Syro-Palestinian coast, the Arabian deserts, all of which play some role. Ethnically, one might be inclined to think in terms of a basic unity in Semitic stock, but neither the Sumerians, Persians, Mitanni, nor Hittites were Semitic, nor do the Semitic Akkadians and Assyrians blend as completely as do the Egyptians of the Delta with those of the Sudan.

In Egypt, periods of political unity throughout the land were generally periods of cultural achievement, and periods of disunity were less productive of art, but in western Asia there is no easy parallel between cultural and political power. In the protoliterate period, before approximately 3000 B.C., the territory from the Persian Gulf to the Assyrian plains seems to have been a cultural unit more or less, participating in the periodically varying fashions of the Sumerians, though doubtless divided politically into a vast number of local communities each organized as the estate of the local god. Although occasionally one or another of these divine states would gain some degree of ascendance over its neighbors, it was not until the Semitic Akkadian Sargon I that anything like a man-centered, politically based empire state was developed to organize the affairs of a considerable number of these communities. The collapse of this political superstate around 2180 was followed by a resurgence of the Sumerian system with people like Gudea of Lagash and Ur-Nammu of Ur achieving some level of dominance; then followed the increasingly firm hegemony of Tsin and Larsa, culminating in the Babylonian Empire of Hammurabi in 1792–1750 B.C., reconstituted after its collapse by the alien Kassites around 1595. From around 1300 the Hittites and Mitanni of Anatolia and Syria maintained rival empires, but all were doomed to fall eventually to the Assyrians who reached their height in the ninth and eighth centuries. A brief resurgence of Chaldean Babylon in the early sixth century gave way to the world empire of the Persians under Cyrus in the mid-sixth century and the Seleucid Empire following Alexander's conquest in 323. The Romans who succeeded to the Seleucids in 89 B.C. eventually resigned the region to the Sassanian conquerors of the Parthians in the third century of our era. But most of the preserved objects we know came from the protoliterate, early Dynastic, neo-Sumerian, Assyrian, and neo-Babylonian periods—a heterogeneous list of political patterns; the Akkadian, Kassite, and Mitanni empires have left little behind them.

And yet, throughout this varied landscape, through successive ethnic and political waves, there persisted in art certain common qualities that make it natural to consider this art during several thousands of years as one. The task is both simplified and complicated by the fact that as compared with Egypt and the classical world there are relatively few major monuments preserved from Hither Asia, and new discoveries disturb generalizations in a way that is hardly true any longer in Egypt and Greece. But the effort to see the theme, and its variations, has some rewards.

Conceptual Elements

The conceptual form in the art of this world is pervadingly naturalistic, with significant tendencies toward fantasy. Even the early pottery from Susa (Plate 20), whose striking designs seem at first glance to be aniconic, probably takes its form from the patterns resulting from the sewing of bark or leather vessels. The vivid depiction of antelopes, birds, and other animals incorporated into the designs find their essential inspiration in nature, whether they are abstracted from actual forms or "naturalized" from the superficially aniconic forms drawn from sewing. Quite commonly through the succeeding course of the art of Hither Asia, natural forms are highly abstracted in formal arrangements that often suggest aniconic design but remain, essentially, naturalistic.

The naturalism has, of course, a fairly definable range, and this range varies from time to time and place to place. At the core is always the human being, most commonly engaged in acts of worship or at war. Particularly in the Assyrian palaces—especially Sargon's palace and in the Persian palace at Persepolis—much is made of the overwhelming supremacy of the monarch as well as of his fearful prowess in subduing challengers. It is also noteworthy that divinity as such, in fully anthropomorphic form, seems to appear commonly in the art of lower Mesopotamia but rarely among the Assyrians and Persians.

As far as is known, there is nothing in Mesopotamian art corresponding to the minutely detailed depiction of the manifold aspects of daily life so characteristic of Egyptian art. Scenes of peaceful activity—notably the inlaid "standard" from Ur (Plate 23), the Stele of Ur-Nina from Telloh-Lagash,[1] and the hunting and camping scenes from the Assyrian reliefs at Nimrud and Nineveh (Plates 27, 28) tend to

---

[1] H. Frankfort, *Art and Architecture of the Ancient Orient* (London, 1951), Plate 33.

illustrate some particular aspect or matter of concern about a ruler or the monarch, and the range of activity is noticeably limited.[2] On the other hand, there is a continuous and thoughtful interest in landscape.

It is also to be observed that animals, especially more or less fantastic animals, play a considerable role in Mesopotamian art, if normally a supporting one. The inlaid sound box of a harp from the royal tombs at Ur includes many characteristic motifs.[3] One panel shows a hero between two man-headed, bearded bulls (such bulls appear again at the portals of Hittite [Plate 32], Assyrian, and Persian palaces); another, a young goat on its hind legs attending a scorpion man (scorpion men somewhat different in form and perhaps unrelated guard and support the arched gate of Tell Halaf [Plate 33] in Syria in the ninth century). Fantastic animals, in the sense of composite creatures (Plates 22, 26) like giraffe-lions, man-headed bulls, sphinxes, griffins, and chimeras, recur in varying form from protoliterate phases to Persian times and later; the history, with the varying forms and characteristics of strangeness, may be traced with fullest continuity on the seals,[4] but the impression is supported by isolated details from other kinds of art.

A particular form of what may well be regarded as fantasy is the depiction of animals "out of character." On the sound box of the harp from Ur (although these may be men in costume) and on seals, animals whimsically conduct themselves like human beings. More fundamentally, representations of animals are given a structural function in architecture—at the bases of walls, the supports of gate piers and arches, as supports for columns—often as anthropomorphic columns. This is fantasy, though as we shall see it may have a basis in the rational aspect of the conceptual form.

There is a difference between the fanciful animals common in Mesopotamia itself and the fanciful animals characteristic of the Luristan bronzes (Plate 21) and related objects, even in later Persian art, in which the fantasy seems to be directed by the ornamental function of the animal on the object on which it is depicted, rather than in some

[2] Frankfort, *op. cit.*, Plates 84–114.
[3] *Ibid.*, Plate 38.
[4] *Ibid.*, Plates 39–40.

conception of the animal itself. Thus these animals may emerge—almost flow—out of the handle of a vase or the end of a bracelet in a series of naturally incompatible but ornamentally effective and fancifully intriguing forms to culminate in a goat-sphinx, for example, or something similar. The result is an object of grace or vigor rather than terror.

Finally, Mesopotamian conceptual form is distinguished by a delight in man-made objects; jewelry, textiles, and similar products are frequently exploited in the other arts, either directly, when the jewelry or embroidery of the costume of some human figure in a relief composition is elaborately depicted in great detail, or indirectly, when the rosette forms derived from floral motifs developed in weaving or embroidery or the various weaving patterns themselves are employed for borders or panels in decorative schemes in other materials.

The peculiarities of the conceptual forms of the art of Hither Asia may be illuminated by a particular point of contrast with that of Egypt, with regard to the degree to which it is rational. In Egypt, as we have observed, the rational aspect is perhaps the dominant consideration. A composition involving human figures embodies or summarizes information about certain human or divine activities, largely as a matter of intellectual interest; the aesthetic effect of these activities, though it exists, is in and of itself relatively minor, and the chief aesthetic effect comes from the sensory elements of the art rather than the conceptual form.

In Hither Asia, the rational facts and details of the conceptual form are ordinarily of little concern intellectually, as a matter of knowledge; the matter of chief importance is the effectiveness of the facts and details in evoking feeling. Perhaps the most "rational," in our sense, of the elements of Mesopotamian imagery are the fantastic monsters which guard the gates of Assyrian, Hittite, and other palaces and cities. These creatures were evidently intended to be portraits—indeed, virtually fetishes—of divine powers which were literally relied upon as agents to ward off danger. The form of these creatures was presumably an intellectual matter; it was a given fact to be studied and duplicated, not a conception to be evolved by an artist for sensory reasons to evoke some feeling. Nevertheless, that they did evoke feelings appropriate to the situation, and that the fashion of using them for such reasons spread, may be suspected.

But such instances of almost purely rational conceptual form, together with some religious scenes like that on the Stele of Hamurabi (Plate 24), where the monarch is described literally in some kind of communion with divinity obtaining sanction for his acts, are exceptions in the body of the art of the region. Even historical scenes of campaigns and hunting in Assyrian palaces (Plates 27, 28), which might be thought to be the most rational of all in inspiration and control, have been already described by others [5] as calculated, in terms of conceptual form, to evoke sensations of fear of the irresistible power of the monarch among visitors to the palace. Especially indicative of this is the frieze from the palace of Sargon which relies less on narration, more heavily on sensory elements; similar in this respect are the friezes of the palaces of the Persian kings (Plate 44). In general, then, it may be said that the choice of subject matter—the conceptual form—of the art of Hither Asia is determined by aesthetic rather than rational considerations. Conceptual forms are significant chiefly for their role in the aesthetic experience, not for what they depict. Scenes of war and armies are not records or illustrations of military events and other human affairs; they are vehicles of sensory stimuli. They are, in short, examples of conceptual form in its almost purely aesthetic function.

In literature, too, conceptual form is fundamentally naturalistic, and the element of fantasy makes itself felt with considerable conviction. The body of written material from Hither Asia is great, though how much of it should be considered literature may make a question. Few of the extant legal or historical documents have any conscious aesthetic aspect; nor do the extremely interesting documents of a practical nature prescribing the conduct of ritual. But there are still many documents of aesthetic character among the hymns and prayers, and the ritual or epic poems, including most conspicuously the Epic of Gilgamesh, known in both Sumerian and Semitic versions. In all of these the conceptual form is, essentially, naturalistic with a human focus. It deals with human

[5] Frankfort, *op. cit.*, p. 78.

beings and their actions, usually of a heroic nature; or with the gods, humanly conceived, and their heroic actions. Animals figure but little in the literature.

There is also a considerable element of fantasy. This is evident not only in the strange forms of some of the creatures described, like the god Marduk, but more fundamentally, for example in the unnatural birth and being of Gilgamesh's companion Enkidu, the adventures of Gilgamesh beyond the mountains of Maashu, the remote world and strange history of Utnapishtim, the mysterious plant of immortality which Gilgamesh brought from the bottom of the sea, and in numerous examples of genuine Märchen material that pervades the literature. Although sometimes these can be paralleled superficially in Egyptian literature, in Egypt the fantastic is believed to exist among the natural phenomena of the world of everyone's immediate experience, with nothing strange or marvelous about it. In Mesopotamia, fantasy belongs to another aspect of the world, which exists in addition to the world of natural human experience, inhabited by gods and demigods and only by the rarest exception an occasional human being, though evanescently merging and interpenetrating the natural world. Thutmose III and Amenhotep II [6] soberly vaunt superhuman feats of archery in actual life, but Ugaritic Aqhat's bow [7]—a plausible enough instrument in itself—involves him in the affairs of the world of divinity and becomes momentarily the magic price of immortality. The voyage to the land of immortality was a matter of hard and immanent fact to every Egyptian; Gilgamesh's search for converse with the gods in the land of Utnapishtim is a heroic venture beyond the horizon of ordinary experience.

It may be significant that works of this character were produced from the beginning of the second millenium or earlier, and one may wonder at the absence of comparable original writing from later periods. But the Ugaritic documents are from the second half of the second millenium; the early literature is preserved in copies made for the Assyrian royal libraries, and they must have been read in the eighth century. The

[6] J. Pritchard, *Ancient Near Eastern Texts*, pp. 243–44.
[7] *Ibid.*, pp. 149–53.

supreme monument of literature of this world, the Old Testament, kept current in the first millenium a world in which God spoke from a burning bush in the desert or handed down the Tables of the Law from a mountain peak; angels wrestled with human beings; and (though these events occurred for exceptional men in a moment of crisis) the Red Sea divided to allow a whole people to escape a foe. These are actions beyond the ordinary; they are miraculous by any account; and even if they occurred in history, they occurred as part of the converse of God with man—they are part of the conceptual form of his expression and, no doubt, had their aesthetic effect.

Once again we may feel that the conceptual form in the literature of Hither Asia, natural or fantastic, is distinguished by its aesthetic rather than its rational aspect. This is not to suggest that Gilgamesh is merely a piece of decoration, as might be maintained of a figure of a soldier from the walls of Susa or Persepolis (Plate 44); nor need one deny the effect of Egyptian exaggeration for affecting understanding. But the Epic of Gilgamesh is not primarily a body of information about activities which took place or might have taken place, nor is Gilgamesh simply a man about whom something may be known. The poem, is, to be sure, rational in the sense that it is a statement of certain views or understandings about mortals and mortality, immortals and immortality, but it is not simply information about them or a discussion of pertinent problems. It is an attempt to convey an awareness or sense of these views and understandings through aesthetic stimuli as well as rational exposition, and the formulation of the aesthetic stimuli is achieved through the person and actions of Gilgamesh and the others. We are informed that Gilgamesh was one-third human and two-thirds divine; without this information we would have realized his superhuman qualities by his action and feelings. Utnapishtim philosophizes about human affairs and relates the story of his survival of the flood—the attempt to destroy man for his faults—but the ethereal, semianimate character of Utnapishtim as Gilgamesh encounters him, his direction to Gilgamesh to find the plant of immortality and make his mysterious return, evoke in us an awareness of the existence of power not otherwise clearly perceived. What Gilgamesh was, and what Enkidu was, and what they did and felt and experienced, these are in and of themselves important and valuable, and they evoke feelings in the auditor so that his experience is sharpened and enlarged through Gilgamesh's experience. The unreality, moreover, of Gilgamesh's penetration into a world beyond this one in search of the means of immortality accentuates the aesthetic reaction and intensifies the awareness beyond the ordinary possibility of an expression of the same concept in the real environment of the natural world—certainly more than ordinary argumentative or expository discussion. And all this is evidently intended and preferred in Mesopotamian literature; their interest in what the heroic figures did was less than their interest in the feelings of the hero in response to his actions.

It no doubt adds great color to our impression of Mesopotamian literature that it is based on the Gilgamesh epic. Perhaps if our opinions could be based only on Assyrian historical documents our ideas might be different. But in the present state of our collection of preclassical literatures, the smaller fragments from Hither Asia—the other Sumerian and Semitic documents apart from the versions of Gilgamesh in each language, the Hittite and Ugaritic fragments, both narrative and lyric—seem to be of about the same general character if seen from the point of view of conceptual form: naturalistic, human (heroic and divine), with effective elements of fantasy. They are couched in terms of fictitious but natural as well as fanciful characters and actions involving experience on a heroic scale in which the particular action of the figures is of less importance in itself than it is in evoking feeling in the auditor.

The remains of architecture in Hither Asia are less abundant and less impressive than those of Egypt. A good deal of this difference can quickly be explained: there was relatively little stone used in building in Mesopotamia, since it had to be imported, and excellent stone was hardly available even so; instead, brick was used. Some of the brick was well-baked and durable; some was only sun-dried and decayed as soon as it was uncared for. The result was that most of the buildings of Mesopotamia, large and small, are preserved only in their lower foundations and make little show. Furthermore, although the potentialities of brick allow for the creation of large and elaborate volumes once the proper kinds of bricks and techniques are evolved, it is also true that until this technical stage is reached they are strictly limited. Therefore, only certain kinds of structures could be created out of this material. Nevertheless, the world of Hither Asia has much that is valuable in architecture, and much that is instructive.

The conceptual form of this architecture is various, in general and in detail. Both religious and domestic architecture were developed in some degree of elaboration, taking together all the periods of all places. Religious architecture begins with the relatively small temples of the protoliterate and early Dynastic periods (Plates 35–37). From the point of view of interior arrangement, these buildings are simple rectangular halls with usually a sanctuary at one end consisting of a statue on a slightly raised platform and somewhere in the longitudinal axis of the hall an altar. Normally, the major entrance to this hall was on one long side, although there might also be entrances on the end of the hall. The building might contain smaller rooms on either side of the hall, or even across an end, and there might be a second story. The entire structure was erected on a platform which might be only a few feet in height or, as in the temple at Warka, on a base some forty feet high with sloping sides. The history of the temple at Khafaje illustrates clearly a further element—the court and service buildings which developed along one side of the shrine.

In later temples these essential features remain. There is a tendency to separate the shrine from the rest of the main hall by spur walls, which ultimately suggest a narrow room for the sanctuary transverse to the long axis of the hall. Sometimes, then, the main body of the original hall became an uncovered room or court. The entrance at the end of the hall opposite the shrine, giving direct access to the street or exterior of the complex, was more and more formally and impressively developed, although there still persisted the ceremonial entrance at the side connecting it with the courtyard.

There is also a tendency to fuse the kind of structure we have described with the ziggurat. The ziggurat is essentially a stepped pyramid on the top of which is a shrine, conceived as a transitional place for divine passage from heaven to earth. It is a shelter, as it were, erected on the top of a mountain—a "waiting room," or "anteroom," or "room one passes through"—where the god might meet humanity.[8] Apparently the slight elevations on which the more primitive temples were erected could have been similarly interpreted, and all temples would stand on some elevation; but not all temples stood on ziggurats or even in conjunction with ziggurats. The specific function of the ziggurat is not completely clear. Nevertheless, it was used effectively either as the base for some shrines or in conjunction with other shrines, and it constitutes one of the characteristic features of Mesopotamian architecture. Apart from its stepped form, its distinction, and chief area for individual treatment, lay in the method of access to the peak. In the typical structure, there was a steep flight of steps on a separate foundation projecting from the center of one face of the ziggurat; in the building at Ur there were also steps on platforms attached to the face of the ziggurat, and paralleling the face, the three flights joining at a sort of gate house part way up. At Khorsabad in the eighth century, the chief ziggurat of the palace complex was provided with a ramp spiraling up around the core instead of separate, level stages of the main structure with added steps.

The significance of these arrangements from the point of view of conceptual form is considerable. In the first place, the interiors are not much developed or very elaborate; apart from the slight distinction of the sanctuary in the main hall, there is no organization of the interior space. This could possibly be attributed to a failure of the Mesopotamians to conquer the technical problems of their medium, so that their interiors, spatially speaking, were completely controlled by technical considerations; in other words, functional but not aesthetic. There is an aesthetic significance in the firm adherence to the side entrance, the "bent axis" approach, whereby one enters the ultimate chamber from the side and is compelled to make a ninety-degree turn to face the focal point of the room. The particular reason in this cultural context can hardly be defined, but its significance is attested by its permanence in spite of the greater and greater elaboration of the secondary entrance on

[8] Frankfort, *Art and Architecture of the Ancient Orient*, p. 6.

the primary axis. Furthermore, the elaborate development of glazed brick and tile is, to a large extent, an exploitation of the aesthetic possibilities of a structure-function device.

But the most interesting feature of this conceptual form is that while it makes little of interior space, it makes much of exterior space. The relation of the court to the shrine is studied and developed (though no more, to be sure, than in Egypt), and the effects of raising the shrine on a platform, and the more complex series of platforms in the ziggurat, are almost unique. For the ziggurat implies a series of positions that a person might take at successively higher levels, not only physically, by ascending the stairs, but optically and in imagination, each with its own different relation to the courts, other structures, and the city as a whole, and culminating in the shrine at the top. It is unlike the Egyptian pyramid, even the stepped variety, in that it is accessible and invites ascent; the Egyptian pyramids are remote and inaccessible, except in a spirit of bravado, which has nothing to do with basic function.

Although religious buildings from other areas of this world are known or suspected, they are less well understood. Structures which are called temples at Hittite Boghaskeuy present significant peculiarities in their symmetrical entrance halls which, in some cases, though not all, mark the longitudinal axis of the major element of the complex—a rectangular court with columns or piers on one or more sides. The sanctuary itself seems to have been normally in a secluded room, difficult of access, of simple, purely functional character. A remarkable structure at Yasilikaya (Plate 38) consists of an architectural complex evidently intended to organize and accentuate a natural rock sanctuary.

There is little religious architecture from the Persian world, which in itself is a significant commentary on the non-material principle of Persian religion. To be sure, the religious position of the king made his palace a religious monument—but perhaps no more than those of other oriental monarchs.

Domestic architecture, in its turn, presents a similar variety, exemplified chiefly in the royal palaces. Of these one type is presumably Sumerian, from the neo-Sumerian town of Eshnunna at Tell Asmar (Plate 39). The palace lies between two temples, each almost square in plan, facing at slightly different angles on the same street. Each could also be approached from the side, from the palace itself. The palace consisted of an open court with a row of private rooms behind and a complex of formal rooms on the right as one entered. The entrance to the palace had notable peculiarities: from the street one entered a moderately plain door opening upon an approximately square room; through the left wall of this room was a door leading to a long, narrow corridor with a door at the opposite end leading into another long, narrow corridor with a door at the opposite end. This door gave access to a short hall with an axis at right angles to that of the corridors. From this hall a door on one long side, opposite the entrance from the corridors, opened into a series of rooms along the front of one of the temples; a door on one short end (to one's right as he emerges from the corridors) opened onto the central court. In this entrance complex, consisting of five doors separating two small and two long, narrow rooms and involving two right-angle turns in z-fashion, one naturally suspects motives of defense; and this suspected, the fact that the doors connecting the corridors are not in line suggests the attempt to break a line of fire. If these suspicions are justified, the military basis and presumably rational emphasis of the building's conceptual form seems dominant. But the assumption may not be true; the reasons for the arrangement may be aesthetic. In any case, the principle of off-center, broken-line flow of movement seems to be pervasive.

Continuing a formal course through the palace, from the outer entrance to the courtyard, one finds the entrance at one corner of the court and a paved path from the entrance to a great door in the middle of the side at the right; this door gives access to the middle of the long side of a narrow hall called the throne room. There is a door at each short end and one at one end of the long rear wall, leading to a much larger rectangular hall which was the largest and most formal room in the complex and surrounded by smaller rooms of irregular shape.

In general, then, this conceptual form, apart from the eccentricity of its lines of traffic, is extremely simple: it consists of courts, rectangular halls, and narrow corridors with little differentiation of form or schematization of arrangement.

Almost the same generalization can be made of Assyrian palaces (Plate 40). They stood on terraces, for defense; they were vastly more extensive and elaborate; they were more complex, including more sanctuaries, more official and private units or quarters; but essentially the unit consisted of a court with a monumental entrance, surrounded by service quarters, with a monumental entrance at one side leading to a more or less grandiose official or domestic apartment of rectangular halls of which some would be likely to be notably narrow. Entrances and lines of traffic would still be eccentric and tend to occur on the long sides of rooms. One quality which seems to emerge at Khorsabad is that of composite function: the palace was almost a city, with religious, administrative, police, and domestic sections more or less clearly defined and separated. The same fundamental division is evident also at Tell Asmar, though on so small a scale as to be little apparent at first impression.

The region of Syria seems to have produced a quite distinct type of dwelling, called a *bît-hilani,* which came to be most clearly defined around the eighth century, though its origins have been seen as early as the time of Hammurabi (Plate 41). It consists of a remarkably open entrance, usually a broad doorway without flanking elements but with one or more columns in the center, opening into a transverse room, the unit constituting a definite but distinctly open portico. Behind this lay another transverse room with a hearth, this being the main room of the complex; and behind or around this room were smaller, more private rooms. A structure of this kind involves a number of peculiarities. First, it is much more definitely an exclusive unit than the Sumerian-Assyrian palaces where any number of courts with accompanying apartments may be accumulated in almost any arrangement. The *bît-hilani* has a limited number of specialized rooms in definite order and cannot be combined easily with other units of the same type.

One reason for this exclusiveness is that apparently the *bît-hilani* did not include a courtyard as an essential feature. Some houses of this type opened on to courtyards, but others seemed to open on to streets or *plateias,* without courtyards. In those examples where courtyards exist, the impression is of a fusion between Mesopotamian and Syrian

III

traditions, perhaps for the very purpose of developing larger, more palatial dwellings than the *bît-hilani* would have provided.

Finally there is the totally different and unique type of structure developed by the Persians: a square hall, the ceiling upheld by regular rows of posts or columns. The main entrance was symmetrically arranged on one side, which might be distinguished on the exterior by one or two rows of columns extending the whole length of the side between antae, or between square rooms at the corners. This structure may have been used as a gate house, an audience hall, a throne room, or for any domestic purpose; the plan of Persepolis is composed of nothing but rooms of this sort, in addition to noticeably few courts and corridors.

The more formal examples of this type of structure are elevated on terraces with imposing flights of stairs—an element presumably derived from Mesopotamia or Assyria—but the origin of this kind of hypostyle hall must certainly lie in the nomadic tent or pavilion, which, in its more luxurious, "monumental" form, would have consisted of a great sheet of cloth supported on rows of poles. Even the entrance porch *in antis* would be paralleled in tent architecture by the door flap elevated by special poles for ventilation and easy access.

Thus the conceptual form of architectural volumes may be said to be fairly undeveloped, "iconic" and "naturalistic" in the sense of corresponding generally to function of use and structure. The same may be said of the conceptual form of structural members, so far as these are known.

The most striking distinctions of Mesopotamian architecture from this point of view are the lack of columns and piers in any significant scale; the development of wall surfaces in rectangular projections and recesses, often intricately compounded; and the use of glazed brick or tile for facings inside and out. All of these are direct responses to the use of brick in construction. Brick supports, though developed under some special stimulus for the construction of columns or cylindrical pillars in protoliterate times, are bulky and inappropriate in creating spatial forms. On the other hand, ceilings in brick architecture must be vaulted, in which case they do not need columnar supports; or wood, in which case the wood can equally well be used for supports if required.

The possibilities of glazed brick for surface ornament was recognized in protoliterate times with the mosaic work at Warka (Plate 43) and occurs again at Kassite Warka in the fictile statues adorning the temple wall on the exterior, and increasingly in later periods through the Persian, when fantastic animals in glazed tile adorned the gates of Chaldean Babylon (Plate 42) and warriors and lions the palaces at Susa. This is a thoroughly natural use of the peculiar qualities of ceramics in architecture: a patently surface ornament fusing with the wall itself, the mosaic and animal (and other designs) revealing the wall as a mono-lithic entity. Similarly, the recesses and projections of the wall surface in tower or buttress-like forms are simple variations in bricklaying that have a functional value in strengthening the wall from point to point and are decorative as well.

In Persian architecture, to be sure, supports are common. These supports are tall and slender and often ornamented with elaborate capitals incorporating animal forms (Plate 34). There is some possi-bility that the animal forms had an apotropaic function, like the monsters guarding Assyrian and Persian portals, but it is more likely that the proportions and ornament of these columns derive from their origin as tent poles. The capitals correspond to bronze ornaments for pole ends, known, for example, from Luristan. As used in the palaces, their slenderness is adapted to the use-function of supporting a high, airy ceiling with a minimum of obstruction in the space below.

Finally we might note the conspicuous lack of rational emphasis in the architectural volumes in Assyria and Persia, where the long, narrow Assyrian halls and the approximately square Persian halls each seem to serve many kinds of purposes. In other words, either the use-functions themselves were not highly differentiated or the differentiations did not necessitate specific forms of volumes, so that the kind of volume preferred for sensory reasons was employed for as many use-functions as possible.

The conceptual form of the art of Hither Asia, then, may be regarded as basically naturalistic. That of the pictorial arts and literature is tinged with fantasy, and its naturalism tends toward the heroic. In general, the aesthetic aspect of the conceptual form is more apt to be emphasized than the rational.

SENSORY ELEMENTS

MOVEMENT

The sensory stimuli present in the art of Hither Asia are not fundamentally different in nature from those of Egyptian art, though they are used to rather different effect, particularly in movement. Linear movement—the line of outline—is important, but the line of inner detail is of greater effect, proportionally, than in Egyptian art. Line plays an even greater part in Asia than in Egypt in the development of textures; there is an unusual variety of conformations, most of which have prominent, distinctive kinaesthetic affects. The bronze head of an Akkadian ruler (Plate 31) found at Nineveh has extraordinarily intricate textures of hair and beard rendered in complex patterns of interleaving or intertwining strands, and quite apart from the patterns or textures this treatment creates several varieties of vivid movement. The same tendencies, similar even in details, recur in the art of the region through Persian times, and the same fundamental spirit is pervasive. In the beard of the god Abu from Tell Asmar (Plate 29), of protoliterate times, the line of the full angular waves of the beard and hair and also the details of the face (outline of eyes, the line of the brow) are strong stimuli to kinaesthetic response. Of quite a different order are the elongated forms of the Iranian animals from Luristan, reflected in some Persian art, and the ornamental animals and especially seal designs of certain periods; in all of these the shapes of the conceptual form are attenuated and made to function obviously as channels of movement, narrow and vivid. Finally, there is stimulus to the kinaesthetic sense in the band compositions that characterize Hither Asia almost as much as Egypt. From the Standard of Ur through the Assyrian palace wall friezes to the files of soldiers and courtiers on the terrace walls at Persepolis, the characteristic large-scale design is in terms of single-register bands. Even the much more sophisticated (and exceptional) Stele of Naram Sin (Plate 25) is conceived as a series of superimposed registers slanting up the field, or perhaps zigzagging up the slope, and the remarkable panoramic compositions of later Assyrian relief adhere to the concept of narrow, horizontal bands.

Perhaps the most vital source of movement in the art of this region is rhythmic or repetitive accents, often multiplied to a point of vibration. Most obviously, this is a fairly simple repetition of broad, generally similar accents—the various figures in a relief composition or cylinder seal (Plate 22); more fundamentally and effectively, it is the repetition of elements of detail in costume or anatomy, whether the broad simple overlaps of the robe of the god on the Stele of Hammurabi, the ranges of feather-like lappets in the skirts of the late early Dynastic Sumerians (Plate 29), or the vibrant, scintillating movement of the infinitely repeated detail of beard or costume in works of almost every period. The principle reappears in other manifestations: the hard, brilliant accents of form and color in the inlaid harp from Ur, the staccato characters in the lines of cuneiform, the conventions for mountains or water in landscape relief.

In architecture, the outlines of buildings are simple—plain horizontals and verticals, apart from battlements and serrated balustrades. Stairways introduce some diagonal lines, the components of the multitude of horizontals and verticals of the treads and risers. The more telling effect is produced by the lines which normally resolve into textures. The most characteristic is the pattern of vertical lines created by the succession of rectangular projections and recesses—towers, bastions, buttresses, and framed panels. These rectangles function doubly in organizing vertical movements by the direction of each line and horizontal movements by the general horizontal direction of each frieze of lines, and also as a fairly vibrant movement of rhythmic repetition of various kinds of accent. This is an aesthetic equivalent for the colonnades of other architectures, although the two can never be the same. The wall must remain a wall, and impenetrable; the colonnade is always in varying degrees open and penetrable.

Architectural volumes contain definite kinaesthetic effects: the bent-axis approach in the simplest and most primitive sanctuaries, persisting throughout; the elevation of the deity within the sanctuary; the compounding or rising levels as the religious structure expands; the compounding of gates and courts in series leading to the sanctuary—all provide elements in one or another plan of rhythmic accent and line of movement. The relative poverty of invention in this area, however, is obvious; there are many, and some very impressive, variations on the theme, but the theme is limited.

The exterior volumes have their special qualities. Vertical movements is varied. Volumes are usually broad and low, but some courtyards are surrounded by impressively high walls, and ziggurats penetrate the high, open volume above their courtyards. Horizontal movements are indicated in part by the horizontal ranging of wall ornament, in part by the terracing of the buildings—each terrace establishes a horizontal sheet or slab of direction of space through which to move—and in part by the uniform, relatively low heights of the walls of courts. The volume takes the mold, so to speak, of the re-entrant forms of the surrounding walls, and thus the rhythmic contours.

Movement in literature is, first, in the stress-meter of poetry. Normally it scans in lines of two sections, each with two stresses; each stress is a combination of a phonic accent and a thought unit. This pattern is employed by the Hebrews almost to the exclusion of any others; in other early Semitic literatures there are slight variations. One noteworthy aspect of the system is the complete coincidence of sound-stress and meaning-stress (including both conceptual form and "imagery" in the narrow sense) and grammatical division. The result is a cadence, more pronounced than in Egypt, if only because of the regular combined accent, but similar in substance to that of Egyptian literature, though different in manner or quality, as we shall see.

Some suggestion of the rhythmic effects may be taken from the tenth and eleventh tablets of the Akkadian version of the Gilgamesh epic. The simplest kind of repetition would be (Utnapishtim speaking in Tablet X, vi, 1.26): [9]

[9] Pritchard, *op. cit.*, p. 92.

> Do we build houses for ever?
> Do we seal [contracts] for ever?
> Do brothers divide shares for ever?
> Does hatred persist for ever in the land?
> Does the river forever rise up and bring on floods?

Here there is a simple, consecutive rhythm that changes direction, as it were, but in single progression; each line is different. At the beginning of the eleventh table Utnapishtim speaks in a kind of couplet: [10]

> I will reveal to thee, Gilgamesh, a hidden matter
>   and a secret of the gods I will tell thee;
> Surippak—a city which thou knowest
>   [and] which is on Euphrates' banks set—
> That city was ancient, [as were] the gods within it
>   when their fear led the great gods to produce the flood.

The rhythm of larger elements is illustrated in what follows, when the god gives instructions to Utnapishtim as to how to make his ark, and he weathers out the flood. The story is blocked out in sections—the advice, the construction, the loading, the storm, the time afloat, and so forth— each having its beginning and end, with a definite break between, each creating an independent surge of interest with a definitely rhythmic character.

Not only brief passages or phrases but long sections may be repeated for rhythmic effect, as when Inanna leaves with her messenger Ninshubur (in the *Descent of Inanna*).[11] There are forty lines of instructions, almost all of which is repeated (in the indicative, not imperative, of course) as Ninshubur follows them out. The halting, surging movement by parallel states and repeated lines is well exemplified by the disrobing of Inanna item by item, gate by gate, with the same question, the same answer, repeated. In the Semitic version of the *Descent of Ishtar*,[12] the style is essentially the same, but more restrained. To be sure, Semitic style can easily produce a triple repetition, as when the hunter's father advises the hunter to get Gilgamesh to provide a courtesan to ensnare Enkidu; Gilgamesh does so, and the courtesan

[10] *Ibid.*, p. 93.
[11] *Ibid.*, pp. 52–57.
[12] *Ibid.*, pp. 106–9.

does her work, in the same phrasing. But it is said with brevity and restraint, and the action proceeds so quickly that the repetition is not burdensome.

In the pictorial arts there is a good deal of movement, but one may observe that with the exception of the Assyrian hunting reliefs the movement is relatively restrained. The figures walk slowly or proceed in masses or large groups, in ceremonial dignity or military discipline, or formal precision. Rarely does one encounter action that is quick, light, and vivacious. Even in the Assyrian battle reliefs, in scenes of great confusion, individual figures are steadily and cautiously, if boldly, concentrated on a particular job. Rarely in these reliefs, more often in the hunting scenes, something of the verve of a race or a spirited onslaught is depicted, but more often the movement is better characterized as methodical. In sculpture in the round, most figures are standing quietly or seated. In literature, despite the heroic adventures of Gilgamesh and the others, their conflicts are marked by power rather than speed.

LIGHT AND COLOR

Color played an important role from the earliest times. It is most dramatically preserved in the cone mosaics of Warka and the royal graves at Ur. Ceramic glaze, colored minerals, and other substances were lavishly exploited with extreme effects. The sculptures from Tell Asmar show the use of pigment on statuary, and the fragments of painting from Zimrilim's palace at Mari, of about 1800–1750 B.C., show the same interest in other fields. It is a matter of special interest that as early as protoliterate times, in such works as the base of a cup from Tell Agrab, there are touches of "colorism"—the contrast of fully lighted forward surfaces and unalloyed shadow in cutaway areas. In a sense this is a play on light, but the contrast is so great that it normally makes itself felt simply as white and black. In its present state, the contemporary head from Warka is also vividly coloristic, and though presumably the deep-cut eyes and eyebrows were intended to hold some inlaid material, the inlay itself would probably have been of some sharply contrasting colorful material, like that used for the eyes of the god Abu from Tell Asmar.

In architecture, color seems to have been used lavishly, as in the grand conceptions of the great ziggurats, with each stage painted in a different color and exterior and interior walls sheeted in great expanses of tile or paint. As colorism, the light and shadow effects would have been vivid on the walls with projecting "towers" and recessed panels. Both color and colorism recur through Persian times: the glazed-brick figures from Susa, brilliant in various hues; the ornament of the stairs of the audience hall of Darius at Persepolis, reduced, at short distance and in slanting light, to simple patterns of light and black.

In the literature a good deal of color emerges from allusions to natural phenomena and to jewelry and costume—that is, from the conceptual form more than from actual color words. Modern understanding of ancient languages does not permit a satisfactory evaluation of their color content, beyond the fact that they are rich in figures of speech of all kinds. Different ways of expressing an idea—parallelisms, indirection, metaphors, similes, and so forth—were important in sustaining the metric patterns. But the fondness for a series of parallel expressions, one differing from the other only by a component—the key noun, common or proper, or a verb—suggests a relish for the connotations and qualities of individual words in themselves.

TEXTURE

Texture is perhaps the special interest of the artist of Hither Asia; at least here he achieved his greatest variety and originality, and on this he expended most efforts. The attempt to reproduce actual textures of embroidered cloth and jewelry in the sculptural rendering of figures is a conspicuous illustration of this, as is the elaborate patterns of hair and beard. This effort serves partly to recall the textures of the conceptual form itself, but also allows for great variety in the physical texture of the sculpture, from the intricate fine textures of some Assyrian work (Plate 26) through the sharply defined forms of Persian to the full, heavy undulations of early Sumerian. In contrast are the high gloss of flesh and other smooth textures of sculpture, both stone and ceramic, related to the deep glazes of architectural ceramic tile. In architecture, too, there are the rich textures created by the modulation of wall surfaces and contours and by the distinctions between various kinds of wash paint applied to the brick. The relief-ornamented wall surfaces of the palaces produce a wide variety of texture. The minor arts are striking for the textures of the stone, metal, and enamel, quite apart from the work on them. In literature, this quality is harder to establish, without the actual sound of the words and their meanings, but it must be said that there is less allusion to texture, perhaps, than might be expected, though somehow the reader—or some readers—are brought to sense the soft flesh of Innana or Ishtar, or of the prostitute who wins Enkidu.

MANNER

The aesthetic means of the arts of Hither Asia reveal some degree of coherence and distinctiveness. The peculiarities of the manner of their use vary from time to time and place to place—and people to people—throughout the region, and thus they serve to distinguish several styles within the sphere. But because of the small number of preserved monuments it is not always clear whether a recognizable style is that of a time or region or "school" or even a particular artist. While aesthetically this makes no difference, historically it is quite important. Nevertheless, it presents problems too intricate to be analyzed systematically in this study, the primary purpose of which is to identify, insofar as possible, qualities that pervade the whole region throughout its history.

ONTOLOGY

Ontologically, the art of Hither Asia is similar to that of Egypt: the work is fundamentally neither particularistic nor highly abstracted, but its idealism allows tendencies in both directions. This is clearest in the conceptual form of relief, where, generally, one never sees an individualized face or figure: human beings are indistinguishable except for size or costume. Animals normally take only typical poses; even when viewing the vivid lions of the Assyrian hunting relief, one thinks of the creatures as "charging lion" or "wounded lioness," typical figures from common scenes. Occasional features tend toward a greater abstraction: trees and landscape are depicted in highly simplified form; certain conventions of rendition of anatomy become almost stylized and independent patterns. Even greater abstraction marks the Iranian sphere of Hither Asia, from Susa pottery to Sassanian work. But there is also a certain amount of particularism, in ways that seem significantly different from parallel tendencies in Egyptian art.

This suggestion of individuality appears at the very beginning, in the head from Warka, and may be observed in occasional works of almost every succeeding period, though observers may differ in their feeling as to the individual quality in particular works. The basic question, however, is whether the individuality which is indisputable in some works is a matter of portraiture, an attempt to endow each statue with an individuality of its own imaginatively created, or simply a reflection of different concepts of an ideal form. We have no independent evidence as we have from Egypt on this point; but the recognizable similarity of the strongly personalized heads of Gudea (Plate 30), the strong sense of personality in the heads from Warka and Bismaya and other less fine heads, and perhaps the death mask heads from Jericho combine with the lack of personality in the heads of gods to suggest that the individuality of the statues derives from the models. Moreover, although there seems to be no individual personality in the figures in relief, there is not infrequently an individuality or particularism in the scenes represented. The Stele of Eannatum presumably represents a particular conquest but not in any sense particular incidents from the conquest—simply "the way we won." Even the Stele of Hammurabi, where the giving of the law was possibly a single occurrence, represents only a "traditio legis," not historical confrontation of king and god. Such scenes are the common type in Egypt, but there are also particularized Assyrian reliefs in which the pictorial narrative is as specific in detail as the written narrative which accompanies it. The cave-sources of the Tigris on the Balawat bronzes are particular places at a particular time. The scenes of Sennacherib's war in the marshes are not simply "war in marshes," like the "hunting in swamps" scenes from Egypt; this is a specific campaign, and the events depicted are unique. In the scenes from Assurbanipal's war with the Elamites, the particular death of a named individual is recorded in visual and written terms (even more specific than in Egyptian scenes of battle)—*this* man got killed in *this* melee. The camp scenes which flash so intimately to our view may in fact be "a moment in camp," but the particular collocation of elements in some of the scenes suggest that they were drawn from life, that they constitute an effort to specify the situation on a particular occasion. On the whole, we must say that, especially in Assyrian reliefs and to some extent in other reliefs, particular events were frequently rendered with some amount of historical and topographical detail, though almost always, of course, in fairly broad and typical lines.

In literature, since the conceptual form is largely of divine or heroic personages and places, there is little opportunity for particularism in terms of actual prototypes, but even with this taken into account the general impression is idealized. Thus in the Gilgamesh epic the hunters and prostitute who effect the enticing of Enkidu are scarcely personalities; the prostitute, sketched briefly, has a genuine human warmth but no features. And certainly the major figures and events are broadly generalized, though sometimes in terms of intimately special qualities or feelings, as the great sympathy between Gilgamesh and Enkidu. Strangely enough, even the Assyrian historical documents, with their formal records of the campaigns, seem to lack fidelity to actual details: the phraseology which Shalmanezer repeats in recording his several campaigns with the coalition of Syrian kings is so similar for each campaign that the boast of a coalition annihilated loses conviction with reiteration.

Legal documents from Mesopotamia reveal a possibly meaningful parallel to the tendency to particularism noted in the pictorial arts. The establishment of innumerable types of situations covering the infinite variety of historical events in every life is the essence of this law: not simply the eternal triangle of a man and two women, or a woman and two men, but every conceivable variation of this theme is set down as a type, and definite legal action is specified for each type. The cause and effect relation between law and art cannot be established in this study, but the search for types below genus to species is apparently a common phenomenon in all fields.

In architecture, the lack of existing monuments makes generalization unwise, but even the few known buildings fall into quite clear types or forms, as we have already seen; as far as structural forms are concerned, there is a certain amount of individuality but within a relatively stand-ardized basic form.

This tendency toward the typical is evident not only in conceptual form but in the sensuous elements of the arts; the same devices for creating the same kinds of motion are encountered throughout the entire range of each art. It is true that in certain periods a greater variety of patterns is evolved, and not all are found in other periods; but this variety is used for profusion and not for its potentialities in improvising. So, too, with textures. As for color and light, there is too little evidence to be useful.

EPISTEMOLOGY

Throughout Hither Asia for the most part, as in Egypt, things had their own existence apart from the minds and reactions of men; this existence was knowable and worth knowing. It is true that in Asiatic art the conceptual form is of greater importance for its effect on the observer than for the information it embodies; but it is the effect created by existing phenomena, distinct from the observer and objectively known by him. It is also true that in this realm the regions of Hither Asia differ rather conspicuously, so that what may be said of one time and region does not apply equally well to another.

The region of Mesopotamia itself—with the art of the early Sume-rians, the Babylonian Semites and Kassites, the Assyrians—seems to represent about the same range of objectivity. There is some degree of the Egyptian logical objectivity in the change in scale: important figures are large, less important figures small. Generally, and especially in Assyrian historical reliefs, careful attention is given to the inclusion of all the facts of an incident; a city does not disappear in a cloud of smoke, for we see the soldiers throwing it down stone by stone; a battle is not a blur of frenzied movement, for an ascertainable number of soldiers are engaged in definite operations. There is, as well, effective use of non-objective means. Some few exceptions to the practice of objectivity should be mentioned: the confusion of the battle of the defeat of the Elamites is dramatized by multiplying the number of figures until they become a swirl of lines; the calm of night is expressed by the bare openness of the camp scene. Normal practice, almost conventionalized, is the expressionistic treatment of musculature, the "flying gallop" design of speeding horses, the taut or shrinking curves of the backbones of charging or wounded lions, the distorted claws of fanciful beasts.

An even greater extreme is represented in the art of the Hittites, not so much in the rendering of the figures as in the relation of the figures to the environment. Thus the warriors (or heroes or gods) on the jambs of the gates at Boghaskeuy are not in themselves essentially different from the figures in an Assyrian relief, but carved as they are, singly, on the rugged substance of the tremendous mass of the spring of the arch of the gate, they are endowed with an extra vitality, vigor, and power expressed by the apparent geological formation of the block. A similar infusion of superhuman forces into otherwise ordinary figures is evident in other gateways and especially in the natural rock-face carvings of other Hittite sites. One of the most effective is the sphinx gate at Alaca Huyuk, where the head and forequarters of the sphinxes emerge from a partially shaped mass of stone which merges into the gate, expressing, as it were, the residence of unfathomed power within the stone. All this represents a decided contrast to the meticulously rendered seraphim of Assyrian gateways, where the artist includes an extra foot so that the entirety of his conception may be objectively present from each significant point of view.

Another extreme of sensitivity in the art of Hither Asia is in the Iranian area. A lively expressionism appears in the ceramic art of early Susa and is never completely lost. The distorted animal forms in Susa pottery, the Luristan bronzes, the later Achaemenian jewelry and decorative work, and the vivid, restless movements to which forms are adapted are expressive of a feeling, a kind of experience on the part of the thing depicted. What is expressed may or may not have an objective existence, but in either case it cannot be objectively perceived. Its state of being is non-material and not perceptible. Its existence, its quality, can be known only in its effect on the observer, and this effect must be produced by substitute means. The substitute involves the fantasy of the imagery, the vitality and near-infinity of the movements. Of course this expressionism is lost in the official art of the Persian Empire. The lion attacking the bull on the stairs to the audience hall of Darius at Persepolis is a formal version of such a theme in objective terms. But in the minor arts, and revived in the Sassanian and later periods, the expressionistic style remains.

A final observation regarding this question in Hebrew art: the Hebrew mind seems to have been notably objective in its view of natural phenomena and human experience in general, and conspicuously so in regard to religious law and practice. But it achieved a unique distinction of conceiving its highest value, its supreme and only God, as a Being objective, to be sure, but to all human intents and purposes not objectively knowable. He could be known in objective disguises, of course, in pre-prophetic days, as when He led the people in a pillar of fire or a pillar of cloud; but at least from the days of the prophets He was regarded as knowable only in His works, His relations to the human spirit. The writings of the later period—the prophets and the apocalyptic writers—speak their thought not in objective or even impressionistic but in expressionistic terms.

SIGNIFICATION

Although the arts of all the peoples of Hither Asia represent an essentially idealistic ontology, their epistemology is varied, with examples from the extremes of objectivity and subjectivity. On the other hand, they seem to find community in the essential literalness of the arts, in which respect they seem to parallel the manner of Egypt. There is, of course, a certain amount of symbolism on a fairly rational plane in the conceptual form—indeed, no doubt a good deal more than is now understood. The headdress resembling a series of cows' horns, tubular forms rising up behind the head and circling to come together in front in a vertical movement, is a symbol, mark, or emblem of divinity; the eagle or vulture on the Stele of Eannatum may well be a symbol or emblem of something; the scale-like pattern representing mountains from Sumerian times onward is in a sense a symbol. But these are not symbolic in any profound sense. More meaningful—though whether it is symbolic and, if so, in what sense, is hardly known—would be the harpy-like form of Lilith in the Babylonian terra-cotta relief (p. 134, *n.* 15) and, even more, her position on the paired lions, an arrangement which recurs frequently throughout the region, particularly in later Phoenicia and Palestine. Yet most symbolism of this kind, along with much else from the sphere of religious iconography, has more to do with theology than aesthetics, though undeniably the same psychological impulse that created a harpy-like divinity would revive at the stimulus of a visual representation of such a creature. The Assyrian sacred tree, in the artificial formulation of a network of palmettes, exemplifies a special problem—whether the tree, theologically speaking, symbolizes something in religion, or *is* something in religion, in the nature of a fetish or baetyl. The objects which demonic figures present to the sacred tree in various Assyrian reliefs no doubt are symbolic ritually and theologically, and hence to some degree aesthetically.

Apparently most of this might be characterized as a conscious use of intellectual symbolism, with some unconscious use of emotional symbolism. The art works include these symbols as part of the material being illustrated—part of the rational content; when recognized in the conceptual form as being depictions of symbolic objects, their aesthetic content is enriched, but for the most part the artist is not augmenting any symbolic content they may possess in themselves or using that content in a new symbolic structure.

There are some examples worthy of note of primary, clear-cut, conscious use of emotional symbolism. One is the net in which Eannatum's enemies are enmeshed. More esoteric is the absence of divinity in early Assyrian reliefs. In the altar of Tukulti Ninurta I from Assur, for example, the two figures pray before an altar with no divinity present; on the altar is a plain, rectangular object with a sword-like object resting against it, the emblem, we are told,[13] of the god Nusku. Frankfort says that it cannot be established whether the god is omitted from scenes of Assyrian devotion when approached on familiar terms by Babylonian monarchs because of the greater elevation imagined for the Assyrian god above humankind or because of the unformed, numinal character of the Assyrian god; but in either case the spectacle of two men praying before substantially nothing may be a symbolic formulation of the rarefaction of the nature of the god to whom they pray.

Also symbolic is Assyrian and Persian architectural organization of ziggurat and palace by which access to deity or monarch is repeatedly delayed; the god is to be found, remote on a high elevation, at the heart of the complex. That this is more genuinely a matter of symbolism than is the more literal and aesthetic seclusion of the Egyptian monarch and god is evident from the fact that although the god was thought to manifest himself in high places, it was enough to raise him only a few feet above the surrounding level.

Finally, in Mesopotamian literature it is hard to distinguish anything consciously symbolic. The myths recounted involve much unconscious symbolism, but it seems to be presented literally. Among the Hebrews, of course, the prophets and apocalyptic writers indulged freely in highly conscious symbolism, mostly emblematic or allegorical.

DEFINITION

With regard to the quality of definition, we find no vagueness, softness, or coarseness; nor, excepting perhaps in the Iranian sphere, is there anything that would be characterized commonly as finesse or delicacy. And yet the prevailingly sharp, bold definition is not quite the equal of the precision of Egypt. In Egypt, the precision and distinctness of definition includes an element of external control imposed by the artist; the artist is easily the master and delineates with sure skill. The boldness of the Asiatic is more vigorous, obvious, direct, and heavy-handed; where the Egyptian makes an incision, the Asiatic hews a line. In this as

[13] Frankfort, *Art and Architecture of the Ancient Orient,* p. 66.

...In other respects Egyptian art is thoroughly sophisticated, in a broad sense mannered, a matter of artistry and virtuosity; Asiatic art is more naïve, spontaneous, natural, and immediate. On the other hand, to anticipate, Hither Asia lacks the quick, sketchy drawing of Minoan Crete. Egypt and Asia both lack the sober, exacting clarity of classical definition which demands that the relationship of details of all aspects and elements be simply and directly evident; they are content to deal with certain kinds of relationships and to leave others alone; for all the precision and clarity of rendition of the costume and the other details of the winged genius from the citadel gate at Khorsabad, the attachment of the right arm to the body, anatomically speaking, is wholly perfunctory and obscure. To say simply that definition in Egyptian art is precise and in Asiatic art is sharp and bold is meaningless, of course; and yet, properly understood, there is a real distinction.

The delineation of conceptual form in its larger entities is fairly consistent throughout the geographical and temporal area. From the protoliterate period on, relief and painting, so far as can be observed, are characterized by bold depiction of individual figures. In a frieze, the Standard from Ur (Plate 23), the Persian palace reliefs (Plate 44), or the seals (Plate 22), the figures generally are in strong distinction against a neutral ground; even more than the Egyptian they tend to proceed in single file, without overlap, so that each one stands out sharply. The Assyrian reliefs, particularly the later reliefs, often reject this sharpness for massed effects, although this does not always produce clarity. It is sometimes a puzzle to recognize the animals or analyze the monsters, especially on the seals; it is sometimes difficult to see what is going on, as for example in the steatite vases from Bismaya and Khafaje; the nature of the skirt-like garment worn by the Sumerians is still not perfectly understood; and costume throughout the entire range invariably conceals the body so thoroughly that its existence can hardly be suspected. In other words, in the sphere of sculpture, although the figure as a whole is delineated with bold, sharp outline and certain chosen features, hair, jewelry, embroidery, may be similarly executed, much of the possible content of the figure is ignored. One more remarkable example of this contradiction is to be seen in the topmost panel of the inlaid front of the sound box of the harp from the royal tomb at Ur. The delineation of the hero between the two bull-men is certainly sharp and bold in the contrast of the materials and the outlines, but the disposition of the front legs of the bull-monsters and the arms of the hero are thoroughly confusing: two of the bull-monsters' legs seem to be the arms of the hero. The articulation of the monsters' heads is disturbing. Some of this must be due to the difficulties of the technique, and the confusion is extreme; even so, the panel dramatizes the characteristic.

The conceptual form in literature is equally sharp and bold in its larger outlines, though there may be some confusion today because of the ragged preservation of the texts and imperfect understanding of the language. It too is marked by an incompleteness and lack of full clarity of minor elements. Gilgamesh and Enkidu, Aqhat and the divinities of the mythological literature, all emerge as firm, clear-cut figures; their strength is strong, their passions passionate, their actions forthright; the reader is carried along with the main current and does not question the gaps in the chain of causation; the heroes leap from act to act, conclusion to conclusion, in easy strides which allow for broad, bold spectacle and avoid the delay of niggling connections.

Finally, the conceptual forms of architecture are for the most part sharp and bold in their scale, simplicity, and abruptness, particularly in the great emphasis on the quality of a gate or entrance as a divisive element, utilizing ramped or stepped approaches, towers, apotropaic demons, and so on.

The boldness of the treatment of movement is one of the distinctive features of these styles. Of the Sumerian style is this particularly so; the large angling of the beards, and bodies, and the lappets of the skirts of the costume of the protoliterate figures from Tell Asmar (Plate 29); the broad and obvious zigzag lines in several tiers in the lappeted skirts of later Sumerian figures; the carefully uncomplex contours of bird and lions in the vase of Entemena; in general throughout Sumerian sculpture, the broad, large-scale, repetitive movement is characteristic. Semitic work is similar, but more refined. The bronze head from Nineveh (Plate 31), is broad and bold in its general organization of strands and duplicated forms; but the greater number of these strands or other elements, in comparison with a similar Sumerian design, the more imaginative modulation of the forms into spirals interconnecting in several directions or square or triangular plaits, the careful engraving of individual hairs within the strands, are all symptoms of the more detailed treatment found in Semitic work even at an early date. This remains a remarkable and exceptional object for its period; more typical, perhaps, is the Stele of Naram Sin (Plate 25), but once again the diagonal composition and the variety of the rhythmic accents of the figures at the right avoid the obviousness of the heavy monotony of the Standard from Ur or the Stele of Eannatum, without sacrificing boldness. The Babylonian goddess Ningal has a costume of overlapping bands of wavy vertical lines, essentially the same as the Sumerian lappets, rhythmic and yet given a closer unity by their multiplicity. This movement achieves an ultimate extreme in the costume of the god on the Stele of Hammurabi (Plate 24) where the bands are smooth, but the elimination of the verticals creates a new sharpness of distinction between the bands, since the only lines are those separating them. Among the Assyrians the sharp boldness of the broader, over-all movements persists—indeed, it is given a greater prominence by the increasing elaboration of linear pattern depicting the ornament of the costume and beard, which is rendered with increasing crispness and incisiveness. Broader lines, of landscape for instance, are usually indicated with full weight and prominence; outlines of figures of men or animals, bows, towers, and walls of cities stand out with unimpaired clarity. And, remarkably enough, in the latest phases, along with scenes which have dissolved to a shimmering texture of indistinguishable lines, there are others with a few broadly separated figures, with movement of line and rhythm so bold and sharp that they could not be duplicated easily.

Sharp boldness is achieved in the movements of literature, also, most obviously in the establishment of rhythms—the unconcealed, identical repetitions of words, phrases, grammatical forms—as well as ideas and situations, rather than by veiled allusions and similarities. In Sumerian, again, this is particularly obvious—quite as much, often, as in familiar

European folk stories of the Gingerbread Man or Chicken Little or the Three Bears in those versions where much is made of exact repetition of the replies and answers in similar, successive situations. The modern ear is accustomed to a degree of variation sufficient to allow each recurrence of the pattern a distinct, different, and individual character without losing the rhythm; but the Sumerians and the Semites, though to a lesser degree, yielded to the bare theme with little modification. In Sumerian poems, many apt remarks or acts come many times over, as in *The Paradise Myth of Enki and Ninhursag.*[14] Among many instances, Uttu, importuned for favors by Enki, demands "cucumber, apples, grapes"; Enki goes to a gardener and says "Bring me cucumbers, bring me apples, bring me grapes"; the gardener "brought him cucumbers, brought him apples, brought him grapes"; Enki goes to Uttu and says, "I, the gardener, would give the cucumbers, apples, grapes"; to Uttu, Enki "gives the cucumbers, gives the apples, gives the grapes." It is not clear in the text as preserved (and, it may not be clear in the original text) how this intercourse resulted in the sprouting of a series of plants; Enki asks his messenger Isimud the "fate" (Aristotelian *entelechy*) of each plant, and Isimud replies,

> "My king, the [—x—] plant," he says to him;
> he cuts it down for him, he eats it,

repeated as many times as there are plants. And there are other passages based on the same principle. In other words, it is evident that the author and those he wrote for enjoyed the most emphatic kind of simple repetition.

In the *Paradise Myth* are instances of greater sophistication: Thus when Enki lay with Ninhursag, his first mate,

> She took the semen into the womb, the semen of Enki.
> One day being her one month,
> two days being her two months,
> three days being her three months
> [and so on, in complete series, to]
> Nine days being her nine months—the months of "womanhood."

[14] Pritchard, *Ancient Near Eastern Texts*, pp. 37–41.

This rhythmic pattern, incidentally, is familiar in Negro spirituals and other American folk music. In the *Paradise Myth,* when Enki next embraced his daughter Ninmu in her turn,

> She took the semen into the womb, the semen of Enki.
> One day being her one month,
> two days being her two months,
> nine days being her nine months, the months of "womanhood,"

omitting the days and months between two and nine; and when Enki next comes to the daughter of this mating, Ninkurra,

> She took the semen into the womb, the semen of Enki.
> One day being her one month,
> nine days being her nine months, the months of "womanhood,"

omitting the days and months between one and nine; and when Enki next comes to the daughter of this match, Uttu,

> She took the semen into the womb, the semen of Enki,

with no mention of days or months. In short, in this series the author has avoided straight repetition, perhaps relying on the momentum of the first statement to induce the movement when it is repeated or perhaps seeking variation.

It is hardly necessary to enlarge on a point which a casual reading of the texts leaves obvious, that the rhythms and movements in Sumerian are bold and heavy; it is more difficult to state the degree of difference in which Semitic literature is rather more modulated and varied and yet thoroughly and emphatically frank and sharp in its definition of movement. The finest examples, of course, are the poetic passages in the Old Testament.

The movements of architecture are also notably sharp and bold, most conspicuously in the characteristic pattern of a wall surface with vertical lines and panels formed by projecting corners, simple and compound, of towers, bastions, or simply ornamental piers. These provide vertical movement with the lines themselves and horizontal movement with the rhythm of lines both individually and as they are grouped to make sections more or less densely lined or open. In all this, once again, the patterns are characteristically simple, emphatic, and repetitious. Interior spaces are so simple and uniform that little opportunity arises for the development of patterns of movement; in the larger palaces, progress from court, room to room, would induce in the viewer the sense of a monotonous rhythmic pattern.

Other sensuous elements are employed equally boldly; and, again, it is in the Sumerian that the most conspicuous examples of this quality appear. The use of color in the treasures of the royal tombs at Ur, with compositions of various materials in pure colors—gold, lapis lazuli, and other substances—has an effect which is vivid and perhaps even garish. The colored tiles in the temple at Warka are not subtle, and are arranged in broad, bold patterns. Semitic art has the same boldness of color, if the paintings from Mari are typical. By Assyrian and late Babylonian times, some of the starkness of the early color schemes has yielded; the tiling of the Ishtar gate at Babylon is hardly garish, though it is a forthright, sharp, and boldly defined pattern of full hues. The tile work at Susa is notably less vivid, with something approaching pastel colors in merging rather than contrasting harmonies. Typical of the Asiatic attitude toward color is the treatment of the ziggurats, with each stage distinguished by a different color; considering the scale and large forms of the structure, the great sheets of color, one above the other, must have been striking.

The peculiarities in the delineation of textures in sculpture have been anticipated in the discussion of movement. The figures from Tell Asmar are composed in substantially three textures, smooth, lined, and ridged, each boldly conceived and sharply differentiated and executed. Generally there are two or three gradations of the lined surface. Other protoliterate and early Dynastic work shows the same textures in varying forms as well as a sort of chain mail texture developed in the lappeted skirt and feather designs (see the eagle on the vase of En-temena). The Stele of Eannatum, on the other hand, shows a considerable variety of textures, including cuneiform-filled surfaces. These textures may be taken as the chief quality of the stele. Certainly in the later Sumerian revival the textures of the Gudea group show a sophistication almost Egyptian in quality—the polish of much of the figure, with special textures at the corners of the drapery, in the clasped hands, along the eyebrows, in the brim of a hat. Akkadian work of the kind represented by the head from Nineveh is a remarkable example of elaborately patterned rhythmic movement fused with imaginative textures; altogether, this is an extraordinary achievement, unique in its time.

The sculpture of later Semitic and Kassite dynasties is commonly more sophisticated than the Sumerian, though not the equal of the head from Nimrud. It is useful to compare the relief of Lilith in the Norman Colville collection with the Sumerian bronze relief from Al Ubaid and with the vase of Entemena.[15] The two kinds of feathers of the birds, scale-like mountain ground line, hair of the lions, wrinkles on the bird claws of Lilith, and the various textures of her wings and headpiece are a sharply varied lot of foils to the two kinds of smoothness, the dead flat of the background, the tautness of her skin and flesh. Succeeding ages exploited hair and embroidery, in Assyrian work producing the most intricately imaginative variety; throughout, these textures are sharply and boldly defined. In Persian work, there is a tendency to a curious hard, superficial, stony gloss which deadens the sharpness of detail.

CONFIGURATION

As in Egyptian art, the most conspicuous singularity of the art of Hither Asia is its two-dimensional configuration. In some phases of the art of Hither Asia other factors work to rid the configuration of the obvious flatness of Egyptian art and some Asiatic art, but the basic interest is still on the film of surface.

The protoliterate alabaster vase and gypsum trough from Warka, the steles of Ur Nina and Eannatum and related works, the standard and other objects from Ur, the Stele of Hammurabi (to some extent), the Assyrian and Persian reliefs, are all characterized by broad, even, more or less rigidly flat frontal planes with relatively little or no modulation to suggest mass. Concurrent with these are works which seem, in one way or another, to have a quality of mass, though this impression is often misleading. For example, a cup and a cup base from the Tell

[15] Frankfort, *Art and Architecture of the Ancient Near East,* Plates 56, 27A, and 32.

Agrab of protoliterate times have a chunky quality, but this may be the result of an attempt to produce a coloristic pattern of a light primary plane with heavy shadows. There is a clear fulness and mass to the face of the head from Warka, but the forehead and the hair above the region of the eyes are simply patterns of variously shaped flat areas. The figures from Tell Asmar illustrate in vivid form one of the characteristic mannerisms of the sculpture of the region. There is a definite sense of the conical shape of the skirt and the other solid geometric forms which make up the figures; curiously enough, these shapes are less impressive as solids than as surfaces. The contrasting lined and smooth sections of the skirt seem to attract greater attention than the massive, post-like quality of the figure. There is the single, flat surface of the torso, the shoulder, and the upper arm, constituting a silhouette of this part of the figure, with the area between arm and chest punched out; the arm itself is smooth and round, more or less like a cylinder, and it is this rounding sweep of surface, in contrast to the flat spread of surface of the front, that is basic. In short, though this group from Tell Asmar exhibits a considerable variety in itself, these statues strike one as having been made of sheet metal trimmed and occasionally beaten into shape, an effect which remains even when we know that some of the forms are the outcome of certain techniques in clay or soft stone. There is something behind these shell-like surfaces, as we shall see, but it is not the continuous, substantial, material or mathematical mass that constitutes the lower face of the Warka head or the figures of more genuinely massive configuration as developed in classical art.

In later Sumerian art, as more elaborate textures are developed, the emphasis on the curving surface as differentiated from the cylindrical or conical mass is more apparent. There are, to be sure, individual, local, and temporary variations in the extent to which some degree of solidity is suggested. In the copper relief from Al Ubaid there is not only a demonstration of the massive form of the various elements of imagery but a demonstration of spatial relationships, for the creatures are inclosed by a heavy frame from which their heads project freely. The figures of the Gudea school have sections of impressive massive quality, especially in the arms, but normally the surface is interesting in its own right, as indicated by the indiscriminate application of cuneiform text to some sections. The striking arrangement of the hands, block-like to a degree, is not wholly intelligible as such; it is more vividly a matter of surfaces.

Semitic relief, like the Stele of Naram Sin and the Code of Hammurabi, has a special quality of being less a matter of silhouette than of half-figures sliced vertically and applied to the flat background. For all this they do not seem to gain in fundamental mass, and for the most part appeal as tubular surface. In later relief, in Assyria, the flat silhouette is normal, as, in Persian times, a flat silhouette in rather higher relief. Babylonian, Assyrian, or Persian sculpture in the round is nearly cylindrical or conical, with richly decorated patterns again emphasizing the surface rather than the shape of the mass. In some other examples the figure is rectilinear—the winged bulls, for example, seem to be in front or side view, as relief, and not in the round—or like the statue of Assurnasirpal II from Nimrud, which is plank-like in structure and intended to be seen only from the front.

Assyrian relief presents a remarkable series of investigations into various techniques of spatial configuration. The earlier historical reliefs, for the most part, adopt the Egyptian system of continuous bands of composition in which figures are arranged side by side, simply. In later reliefs, however, increasing experiments are made in what may be regarded as various kinds of perspective. Figures are in rows above and below each other, not separated by lines (whether intended to represent various stages of distance or simply larger numbers of figures than would be possible otherwise). Bands may depict subjects in proper spatial relation, like the relief showing Sennacherib's army fighting on both sides of a river, with the river in the central band. Figures may be scattered, depicted in vertical profile on map-like depictions of landscape, like Sennacherib's war in the marshes at Nineveh. There may be panoramic effects with figures emerging from the background, as in the sack of Hamaan from Nineveh. Certain camp scenes include both interiors and exteriors. Finally, in some respects most remarkable, are reliefs from Nineveh of herds of animals, the individual beasts represented at considerable intervals and irregularly over an empty ground, drifting, as it were, in open range.

In general, though sculpture of Hither Asia has many instances of tentative configuration in mass or space, the dominant interest is in surface—in expanse. In spite of a fairly widespread tendency to conceive figures in curvilinear rather than rectilinear forms—a tendency which we shall analyze in another connection—it was neither the purpose nor the effect to create compositions of solid forms; it is still the quality of the surface, fluid, with more mobile than rectilinear planes, that is paramount. Characteristically, in such sweeping curves, variously textured; in the rectilinear planes of the great majority of the work (taking into account Hittite, Syrian, and Phoenician production as well as that of Mesopotamia); in the evident relish for textured surface in detail and in the large; and in the predilection for a broad spread of ornamented wall surface in carvings of monotonous depth so that the total result is an even shimmer as of a tapestry; in short, in most details and in total effect, the sculptural style of the region is essentially two-dimensional.

The two-dimensional quality of the configuration in architecture is most conspicuous in the treatment of wall surfaces, in part, as suggested, in the instances where they are ornamented with sculpture, in part in the several other ways in which tapestry-like effects are created, with glazed tile or the patterning of the wall in towers and recessed panels. The latter concept, of course, is actually a three-dimensional form, with projecting and receding elements; and the sharply rectangular forms are easily handled to give depth and mass. In fact, however, the regularity of projection and recession, the number and the even monotony of the lines and component surfaces, creates a general impression of a more or less vibrant texture. The towers are not so much blocks in massive projection as phases in an angular, undulating façade. Only at major gateways was a significant massive effect produced, with unusually large towers flanking a gate passage, poised on a platform at the head of a flight of steps. Again, the ziggurat is more evidently a structure of block on block than is a pyramid. But even in these examples of tendencies toward massive configuration, the practice of generalizing major surfaces to a single expanse with the use of lines, panels, or ornaments belies the impression of solid material. In other words, the more emphatically the attention is drawn to the surface, the more remote is the reminder of the mass of which the façade is the surface.

As for volume, the characteristic exterior form is a generalized horizontal expanse. Insofar as a building is erected in terms of broad terraces, these terraces suggest flat horizontal layers, and projected into space optically, or as the lines of the building extend themselves, they materialize the horizontal expanse. We have noted that a vertical movement is normally contained within shallow strata bounded by horizontals above and below; it is not a projection into infinite height. Thus externally the dimension of space is horizontal in all directions; even in narrow halls or gate courts, where the height might create a well-like volume, horizontals along the wall and at the top restrict the vertical dimension. Around a ziggurat or a terraced entrance there may be a sense of two additional strata superimposed, but each is infinitely extended in all horizontal directions.

As for interior volume, we are inadequately informed. As we have already observed, the design of interior spaces seems largely rational or functional, with little variety or aesthetic manipulation; the chief distinctions of a temple interior are a raised sanctuary at one end of a rectangular room (sometimes isolated in a separate room at the end of the main room) and a "bent-leg" axis (the entrance on a long wall, the sanctuary in the middle of a short wall). Certain, more general distinctions include the absence (as a general rule, in Mesopotamia) of long, narrow corridors and a generous tolerance for entrances off-axis. Even in a complex as elaborate as the palace at Khorsabad, a corridor is replaced by a series of rectangular rooms crossed along the short axis. Thus any strongly dominant single axis is avoided; movement in any one direction is restrained by cross currents. The bent-axis recognized both directions in the room—if not equally, at least separately. In short, all horizontal directions are recognized. Although we are not in a position to discuss vertical directions, there is nothing in the information available to us to suggest that there was any effort to mold, so to speak, the space of an interior in any significant way: emphasis on the vertical was minor, supplementary to the horizontal.

Finally, the highly specialized Persian hypostyle hall is an obvious example of a space calculated largely in two dimensions, or horizontal expanse. The rooms are square, with columns ranged equally according to the two axes, neither of which is emphasized in any significant way. The vertical range of the room is subdivided in horizontal strata by the forms of the columns—bases, shafts, capitals; and the ceiling beams re-affirm the horizontality of the whole.

Configuration in literature is likewise expansive rather than continuous or massive. As in Egypt, this is implicit in the characteristic repetitive movements, large and small, involving successive patterns of parallel meanings, phrasings, constructions, and so forth. They inhibit a free, quick progression through the course of the narrative or train of thought but do not develop a multilateral figure or one with substantive depth. In the account of the Creation in the first chapter of Genesis, the narrative emerges in a series of panoramas; the "Evening came, and morning, the first [second, third] day" punctuates the series too effectively to ignore, framing each day, or unit of creation, sharply and boldly. Each unit is developed in parallels:

> Let there be light!
> And there was light;
> and God saw that the light was good.
> God then separated the light from the darkness.
> God called the light day, and the darkness night.

One dwells on the phenomenon of light, not searching its depth or revealing its various aspects from different points of view, but lingering over a single facet or impression. The tendency of the cadence of the units is to develop a swinging continuity with a growing momentum; the bold organization in terms of day-units, with rhythmically repetitive accents in the several units, develops linear progression in the narrative as a whole. But the measured punctuation of "Evening came, and morning, the——day" terminating each surge, followed by the beginning of a new movement "And God said——," prevents the development of free movement because each stage represents a concept marked out for its own attention and assimilation before another is approached. To be sure, from a certain perspective, and when the measure of the rhythm is felt, one senses a relentless progress along a single line at a slow, heroic pace. But the movement is that of a succession of panoramas, not a flowing stream; a series of still photographs, not a motion picture. Finally, it is revealing that this passage, in spite of its theme, does not reveal the shape of a universe or the formation of the elements in a tangible and clearly stipulated spatial relationship. The composer has not developed his subject in mass. Nor is there a shift in the point of view on each topic or variety in the form of expression of each day's task, to develop other dimensions to the configuration.

Such qualities are characteristic of both the Old Testament and the New Testament, though not always evident in those books in which the rational aspect is dominant, the books of the Law and the more intently historical sections. But the predilection for such qualities may be revealed in unusual places—in the free acceptance of genealogical lists, for example, in literary work. Such lists, though ostensibly the barest kind of linear outline of successive events, become patterned expanses of texture and color. An example of strictly linear configuration occurs early in the book of Matthew, but if this example is compared to the generations of Adam in Genesis 5 it will help to make clear the quality of expanse:

> After living one hundred and five years Seth became the father of Enoch; Seth lived eight hundred and seven years after the birth of Enoch, and was the father of other sons and daughters. Thus Seth lived altogether nine hundred and twelve years; and then he died.
> After living ninety years Enoch——

and so on through nine generations, each closely parallel to the others, linked in the same standard formula. It is a pattern of patterns, like a rug or a tapestry. Even in a book as complex as Job there is a lack of action; after the briefly stated, matter-of-factly inflicted catastrophes of the first two chapters, the remaining action consists of the discussions of Job and his friends in an atmosphere of suspended shock and emotional tension and the closing addresses of God. The conversations themselves are composed broadly, quietly, reflectively, though there is a vivid contrast between the reservedly determined benevolence of Job's friends and Job's own restrained yet burning resentment. On the whole, the various sections are characterized by thoughtful calm; an even, discursive dwelling on some aspect of a theme. Taken as a whole, however, the several discourses hardly constitute a systematically rounded, complete development of a problem or emotional state.

Other literature of Hither Asia employs the same configuration of expanse, as is clear in detail, though the incomplete state of most of the documents obscures the fact. Nevertheless, the Gilgamesh epic, narrative of heroic adventure though it may be, is retarded in its movement not only by the embroidered expression of particular statements and descriptions of small incidents but by long, discursive conversations. The definite beginning and end of the epic and its composition in terms of three or four major episodes—the arrival of Enkidu, the fight with Huwawa, the search for Utnapishtim, the visit with Utnapishtim (the story of the flood)—tend to give it a structure, but not a structure in depth or mass. There is a wealth of imagery and sensory stimuli but it undergoes no pronounced development, nor does it study or depict a subject systematically from different points of view or elaborate a sensuous theme in contrasting or complementary forms.

DYNAMICS

The question of the dynamics of the art of Hither Asia is particularly elusive because of the difficulty of identifying the quality and giving it its proper name. Indeed, one might incline to doubt whether there is a dynamic quality common to such works as Assyrian reliefs (including the lion, taut as a steel cable, rearing up before Assurnasirpal's chariot; Plate 27) and Sumerian statuary (including the oily placidity of the representations of Gudea; Plate 30). And yet Assurnasirpal meets the lion's charge with suicidally careless vacuity, and Gudea's arms are as powerfully developed in their mighty, vivid forms as those of any Assyrian god or hero. Thus apparently incompatible elements—a potentially violent, brutal power, and a sleek, luxurious, turgidity—occur side by side in some form at almost every time and place. There is, however, a common factor in both, the quality of abundance; that is, whether it is a matter of strength and violence or ease and luxury, it is the amount, the quantity, that is emphasized. There is a fulness, a richness, an opulence of vigor or material wealth. In short, the pressure toward satiety of whatever commodity is the dynamic of this art. Significantly, the satiety is not achieved; there is a resistance to the pressure, in most cases, that results in a tension of expansive versus restraining force sufficient to leave a fundamental note of vitality and active energy to preserve the work from unadulterated sensuousness. But the dominant note is the swelling increase of material goods.

More specifically, opulence is evident in the characteristic contours of Sumerian figures from protoliterate times: broad, round, almost shapelessly dumpy forms and big eyes, nose, arms—everything big and bulging. This is not only a matter of conceptual form. The patterns of movement—the swelling curves of line and surface—which have been described as representing geometrical solidity, more accurately represent the ultimate restraint to expanding pressure from within, the swelling growth of the content of the figure. They suggest opulence as the taut surface of a stuffed sack suggests opulence. So, too, the rich, bursting curves of details like the contours of eyes and beard, and the uninhibited fulness of color, tend in the same direction. In the Gudea style, the large, full curves of body and face, the well-fed self-satisfaction of the man as a man, the glistening, oily texture of much of the figure, the heavy musculature of his arm, all combine to suggest an extraordinary degree of plenty. This quality, as an ideal, is achieved most fully in the treasure from the tombs at Ur, whose effect derives so much from sheer mass and bulk of metal and color and amount of ornament, carried well into an extreme in the goat in the tree, the bearded bulls on the harps, and the woman's headdress. Even in such simple and restrained compositions as that of the silver vase of Entemena, the fulness of the outline of the bird's wings, for example, too distended to retain any grace or subtlety, reveals the basic concern. In this vase, too, is apparent the characteristic effect of symmetrical horizontal forces in establishing, so to speak, a deadlock of conflicting energies, a palpable restraint or containment of abundant force.

Semitic work has the same characteristic, evidenced in somewhat different superficial form. Figures are lavishly ornamented, to the degree of repletion; physical forms are swollen tautly, as in the nude Akkadian Lilith (p. 134, *n.* 15), or expressionistically strong, as in the men and animals of Assyrian relief. Movements are full and round, colors rich and abundant, textures profuse—the totality an impressive opulence. The expressive rendering of certain muscles in man and beast, and the exaggerated ferocity of claws and similar features of some Assyrian creatures, often seems to create a kind of contradiction (Plate 26). It is incongruous when these expressionistic renderings of power and energy occur with equal force in benign figures standing at rest and in figures in earnest struggle. But the fact that the force and ferocity of muscular power that they express is accompanied by the elegance and richness of other aspects of the figure shows that this brute force is simply one of the several goods with which the concept is endowed in abundant profusion.

So, too, the swollen forms of Hittite sculptures, the turgid ornamentation of the later Syrian and Phoenician work, the effete elegance in infinite profusion and minute detail, and the luxurious polish of Persian work—the lavish color and ornament that we encounter throughout the art and architecture of the region find their common basis in the gluttonous passion for never-ending accumulation. The pressures of the style are revealed in the taut compositions of forces represented sometimes by axially symmetrical heraldic patterns with strong forces in direct opposition, sometimes in the coiled-spring effect of the spiral compositions of the offering tables from Sumer, like the Stele of Ur Nina. In different ways, the impressive concentration on the entrances to architectural complexes and the long-extended eccentric lines of movement within build up strong potentials of energy.

The opulence of literature is seen to a considerable extent in the figures and words having to do with material goods and bodily pleasures—eating, drinking, productivity, wealth. In the great cosmic crisis of the flood (Tablet XI, 1. 25),[16] the gods tell Utnapishtim to

> Give up possessions, seek thou life.
> Despise property and keep the soul alive!

[16] Pritchard, *Ancient Near Eastern Texts*, p. 93.

but "Aboard the ship take the seed of all living things." And the ship is a monument of technical achievement on which Utnapishtim loads whatever he has of silver and gold and living chattels. When the waters recede, Utnapishtim sacrifices to the gods cane, cedarwood, and myrtle:[17]

> The gods smelled the savor.
> The gods smelled the sweet savor.
> The gods crowded like flies around the sacrificer.
> As soon as the great goddess arrived
> She lifted up the great jewels which Anu had fashioned to her liking.

But the real expression of the quality is in the richness and fulness of the movements—the unwearying enjoyment in large rhythmical patterns and the untiring expansion of repetition and parallels in developing these patterns. At its highest level, and the aspect which makes the literature great, is the determined attempt to express in an outburst of feeling something felt to be tremendous—and *by* that outburst. This is the power of the Psalms and the prophets, the welling-up and passionate outcry, without restraint, of a feeling or idea, until the unanticipated restraint of exhaustion and the limits of imagination are reached. Some such passion, urgent but unformed and without aim, is apparent in the Gilgamesh epic and other early works.

SYSTEM

The composition of the art of Hither Asia is, again, not remote from that of Egypt. It has a regular system—in some respects, a little more so than that of Egypt; a more generalized focus than that of Egypt; and an essentially agglutinative cohesion, in contrast to the monoidal tendency of Egyptian art.

The regularity is most easily seen in detailed passages, in the patterns in hair and textiles, for example. In early Sumerian skirts, the entire garment is a pattern of exactly equal lappets ranged regularly in even rows. In the infinitely more elaborate and elegant Assyrian and Persian costumes, the garment is rendered in terms of innumerable minute,

[17] *Ibid.*, p. 95.

wavy lines, all exactly the same; or of many rosettes, all substantially the same and spread evenly over the surface to fill it completely. Gudea's headdress (hair or hat?) is an evenly disposed pattern of identical snail-curls, covering the surface completely; and from the early bronze head from Nineveh through other later Semitic, Assyrian, and Persian works, hair and beards are a triumph of the most meticulously detailed arrangement in precisely ordered, regular schemes of ringlets or strands. Other recurring patterns are the conventions used to suggest mountainous country in regular, scale-like ranges and the formalized depiction of feathered wings. Many patterns, more or less conventionalized, are encountered, all characterized by this pervasive regularity. It is also characteristic of the towered and paneled façades of buildings of the region, regular to the point of monotony, and the endlessly repetitive rhythms of the literature.

FOCUS

A dominant focus is evident in those designs in which there is also a complete and almost rigid symmetry, beginning with the gypsum trough from Warka and the copper relief from Al Ubaid and continuing with notable frequency throughout the subsequent period. This symmetry often produces heraldic compositions, as in the examples named; it is also exemplified by the hero fighting two bulls on the inlaid box from Ur. It extends to complex designs where such formal symmetry would seem more difficult to contrive, as in the religious scenes on the Stele of Urnammu. There seems to be a less emphatic focus in Assyrian work, but perhaps this is due to the nature of the preserved material: extended narrative relief hardly lends itself to precise mirror-duplication. But certainly there are notable examples of such composition in the depictions of griffins or other beings attending the sacred trees.

It must be borne in mind, however, that axial symmetry is by no means universal. It would appear, for example, that the wall designs in the most formal rooms of the Assyrian palace, like the throne room of Sargon at Khorsabad, were not symmetrical in general or in detail.

Instead, there was a strong focus on the largest and most important element, representing the monarch, approached from one side by two attendants or suppliants. Nor, on the whole, were the characteristic forms of architecture symmetrical. Furthermore, even in strongly symmetrical designs, the concentration was often neutralized in some way by the compulsive restraint of force—the persuasive internal expansion. A striking example is the relief from Al Ubaid, where the bird-like creature in the center is intended to be the dominant, but the stag-like creatures facing away from it set up a movement of interest which undermines the effect of the bird; and the outward-looking, strongly illuminated, conspicuously antlered heads of the stags at each end establish points of interest that are at least the equal of the bird. Attention is distracted from the central dominant and directed to a series of features scattered over the surface of the composition, equalizing or generalizing the focus. The effect of the symmetrical duplication of scenes on the Stele of Urnammu is to divide attention between the two parts of the composition.

In the Assyrian palace there was a definite emphasis upon the entrances, although at times this was somewhat subdued. It is characteristic that on the Ishtar gate at Babylon the ornament consisted of a series of creatures of about the same size, disposed at equal distances over the surface of the towers, with light borders at the edges, the whole suggesting a fabric covering the tower. In the Iranian sphere, it is especially striking that the Luristan bronzes, for all their symmetry, lack any single absorbing element; each detail is as important as another. And in the Persian hypostyle hall there was no point of focus. In literature, too, there is a curious minimizing of beginnings and endings, so that a work (a psalm, for example) is without climax. There is a kind of monotony to it. There are, of course, examples of a tendency toward stronger focus in the Stele of Naram Sin, in the entrances to Hittite and Syrian buildings, and in other ways. In general, the fabric of Asiatic art is even and monotonous—not monolithic, for it is composed of many parts, but monotonous in the sense that there is no climax or focus or, in some way, it is neutralized.

The Art of Hither Asia

In its cohesive character the art of Hither Asia is agglutinative: though composed of parts, the parts are not articulated. Like its brick walls, the parts submerge their identity in the whole. There is no foundation, shaft, or coping; there is simply the aggregate of many small segments. The parts are seldom lost, as they are in Egypt; their identity is preserved, and they contribute to the textures and movements of the whole. But these discrete units are uniform in their regularity and lack of concentrated focus, and they do not act as separate elements in an emergent tectonic structure of a new order. Once again, the design of the Ishtar gate at Babylon illumines the matter: the border does not frame, or contain, the animals; it is simply another motif in the panel. The sense of a work of architecture as something built of separate working parts did not exist, if only, indeed, because the working parts did not exist in fact. The work of architecture was simply a homogeneous mass of bricks in which one brick played precisely the role that every other brick played. But the same attitude is evident in the pictorial arts: the area of decoration is filled with "bricks" of the details of decoration. The work of literature—the epic narrative or lyric song—does not have an articulated beginning, middle, and end; it simply begins and stops.

SUMMARY

In spite of the many differences among the many styles of Hither Asia, they all possess a common character which distinguishes them fairly readily from products of other parts of the ancient Mediterranean world. Stylistically, one may list the use of movement, color, and texture in a naturalistic imagery in which human forms predominate, but with tendencies to fantasy; used with sharp, bold delineation in two-dimensional configuration, with a kind of turgidity or opulence of dynamic, composed in a generalized, agglutinative regularity, conceived ideally, objectively, and, in the main, literally. This might be understood to express a vaguely pervasive "Asiatic" view that reality exists, objectively and literally; sharply, boldly, even rudely defined; broadly systematic but consisting of discrete parts, interacting but not interpenetrating, straining with internal forces. Once again, it is not the particulars of phenomena that are real but their non-material, prototypal forms. The most important realities, again, are those we actually know in our common experience, particularly emotional, and including things that come to us in imagination.

Within the preserved material there does not seem to be evidence for the clear growth that occurred in Egyptian art during the pre-Dynastic and Archaic periods. The style appears, so to speak, full-fledged. Later changes are representative more of ethnic than of temporal style. There is much variety in expression of individual values and attitudes. For example, among the earliest objects that might be counted as art are the remains of the pottery of Susa, in which the manner of linear configuration is still very much alive though adapted to a configuration of expanse; there is a dynamic of thoroughly free energy and an expressionistic rendering. But this is not, in all probability, the direct-line ancestor of the art of Mesopotamia and the lands to the west; no doubt it had its influence on Sumerian art, but its direct line of descent is through the Iranian peoples of the highlands east of the Two Rivers to the people of Luristan and the Persians.

The Sumerians, who dominated the region of the Tigris and Euphrates through the protoliterate and early Dynastic periods (the fourth millennium, and until about 2340) and again briefly during the neo-Sumerian revival (2125–2025), seem to have presided over, if they did not in every case initiate, the creation of the basic style we have been considering in various arts. The essentials of the style of sculpture, architecture, and literature were quickly developed, and there is little trace in preserved remains of any genetic process. It is true that, particularly in the protoliterate period, there is a wide variety of style and invention, and a more ebullient, spontaneous, and unrestrained exploitation of the various qualities of the style than at other times and places; whether this is an effect of the genetic process, some quality of

Sumerian personality, the co-existence in Sumerian society of different ethnic strains, or something else has not been determined.

In any case, the heirs of the Sumerians in the land of the Two Rivers—first the Semitic Akkadians (2340–2180), then (from 2025) the Semitic powers culminating in the Babylonian Empire of Hammurabi and the non-Semitic Kassites (to around 1100)—continued to employ the Sumerian style, though with greater discipline and greater refinement. Little is preserved on which to base judgments, but the chief difference between the work of this circle and the earlier Sumerians seems to be in the loss of the uninhibited extravagances of Sumerian art, replaced by a more concentrated intensity.

During the last centuries of the second millenium, the Hittites, Mitanni, and peoples of Syria and Palestine began to develop their independent cultures and art. They were heavily dependent on Mesopotamia proper for the framework of their styles both through the direct influence of the general cultural dominance of Babylon and the use of Babylonian artists; and there may also have been more fundamental characteristics of these peoples which made them either predisposed to accept Babylonian style or to develop something parallel on their own. In any case, each of these peoples developed a distinct individuality within the style. The Hittites preferred a higher degree of subjective, even expressionistic, rendering and a more fundamental concern for symmetry and tectonic structure, especially in architecture. So, too, the Syrians had a greater concern for tectonics and mass; especially noteworthy is the tendency of the *bit-hilani* to integrate the structure with the exterior and the observer. Much of the manner of northern Syria derives from a stylization of Mesopotamian motifs.

Assyrian work, beginning in the thirteenth century and most abundantly represented in the palaces of the ninth through the seventh centuries, brings us again to the region, the direct tradition, and the stylistic norm of Mesopotamia. Greater finesse, refinement, elaboration, richness, and more vivid expressionism are its general peculiarities, though the fundamentals remain the same. In the ninth century, expressionism is more intense and powerful; it is co-ordinated with an interest in conceptual form on a larger scale than individual creatures—the character and activity of large groups and movements. During the same period there is a notable attempt to leap from a two-dimensional configuration to one of space-time.

Finally, after the brief neo-Babylonian period, the Persian heirs to Susa and Luristan absorbed the rest of Hither Asia and assimilated or employed its culture and style, injecting it where possible with the expressionistic linear restlessness of Iran, a fusion which remained vital through the political domination of the Seleucid kings and the Roman conquerors.

CHAPTER III

The Art of the Early Aegean

THE THIRD major area in the early development of the European tradition was the Aegean—the sea, the islands, and the coastal regions lying north of and including Crete. In the years before approximately 1000 B.C., this region was the home of a number of peoples with styles of art and culture that are in some ways fundamentally distinct from each other, but which historically and in some aesthetic qualities are more closely related to each other than they are to the styles of their contemporaries outside the Aegean or to their successors and descendants.

The broader differences among the peoples and the singular position of the inhabitants of Crete are attested by the evidence of archaeology, linguistics, tradition, and mythology, though contemporary written history is not preserved. As early as 3000 B.C, or the time of the Archaic period in Early Dynastic Egypt and the protoliterate period in Mesopotamia, Crete was the home of a people living in a neolithic culture. There is no clear indication of their antiquity in Crete—certainly many hundreds of years—or of their home before they came to Crete. But after 3000 their development can be followed in broad outlines. The Early Minoan period, encompassing approximately the third millenium, saw the development of many towns with many marks of sophistication and elegance, though few of monumentality, indicating a constant if gradual consolidation of economic and cultural patterns. The Middle Minoan period saw, about 2100 B.C., the founding and growth of the increasingly magnificent palace of Knossos, coming to a climax in the third Middle Minoan period around 1700–1550. During the last period, and several times during the succeeding First Late Minoan period, earthquakes wrought damage requiring repairs and modification of the palace. Minoan civilization was evidently flourishing, and the Cretans enjoyed relations of dignity with Egypt, as evidenced by Egyptian records, paintings, and Cretan objects discovered in Egypt itself. About 1400, at the end of the Second Late Minoan period, a catastrophe left the palace at Knossos in ruins. At the same time there seems to have been certain changes in the style and culture of Minoan Crete. By 1000, the civilization, its monuments, its people and its traditions, had almost entirely disappeared.

In this "history" one is struck first by the absence of incidents, events, and personalities. The general impression is that for the most part the people lived undisturbed on their island. Along with the monotonous character of Cretan history goes the lack of large and ambitious monuments: no grand tombs and great temples, only the palaces and houses. But every indication points to a high level of refinement, accomplishment, and affluence.

In the islands and on the mainland of the Greek peninsula (not to include in this cultural province in this era the western coast of Anatolia, too little known to be discussed effectively) developments were of an entirely different order. The neolithic culture of these regions, which exhibits a variety of archaeological characteristics relating some elements to the north and other elements to other areas, was superseded around 2500 B.C. by a highly distinctive culture to which the arbitrary designation "Early Helladic" has been given; the Early Helladic peoples evidently brought their culture from abroad (perhaps Asia Minor) and superimposed it on a conquered population whose communities they burned and occupied. Around 1900 B.C. these people, in their turn, were overwhelmed and their culture was superseded by an invasion of northerners, presumably a tribe of the ethnic ancestors of the Greeks, Indo-Europeans living north of the Black Sea, speaking a primitive Greek, and cultivating primitive Hellenic institutions of religion and society. The Middle Helladic period, from 1900 to about 1600, is marked by relatively plain and austere remains; but, suddenly, the same forms appear in rich and luxurious substances—gold vases instead of clay—and the tombs of princes (the shaft graves at Mycenae) are treasure troves comparable with those of any other time or place. The First Late Helladic, the ensuing Second Late Helladic period of about 1500–1400, and the Third Late Helladic period of about 1400–1100 (often called the Mycenaean period because of the traditions and the awe-inspiring fortifications and tombs of Mycenae) apparently represent different phases of the development of the culture of the Hellenic folk in their new home, the differences resulting from the stimuli of successive arrival of various tribes, Ionians, Aeolians, and Achaeans, coming in from the north and of contact with Crete and the world to the east and south. Helladic culture reached a climax of a kind in the wars of the thirteenth century in Anatolia, Syria, Egypt, and North Africa in which the Mycenaeans participated, an age symbolized in the Trojan War, traditionally dated 1194–1184. Within a few years, perhaps under the impact of the arrival of the last, Dorian, tribe of Hellenes, Mycenaean civilization and the rest of Aegean culture disintegrated, to be almost entirely forgotten save in legend.

In general, then, we have to distinguish several geographic and ethnic entities: the neolithic people, or peoples, of uncertain derivation; the Cretan Minoans; the Early Helladic mainlanders from Anatolia; and the several Hellenic tribes from eastern Europe and Central Asia.

CONCEPTUAL ELEMENTS

In the arts of these various peoples the conceptual form exhibits a considerable variety. In Crete, in the neolithic and Early Minoan periods, the designs on the pottery are apparently aniconic patterns of straight lines and angular shapes, with no likely origin in any forms existing in nature. In contrast, in the second Early Minoan period the spouts of certain types of pitchers were elongated to an exaggerated degree and modeled and painted to suggest the head of a somewhat grotesque bird (Plate 46). In the decorative repertoire of the pottery of Early Minoan III, patterns are made up of lines which are frequently curved and quite generally different in spirit, but still probably aniconic, i.e., not derived from shapes of the natural world. The designs of the Middle Minoan period, however, are drawn with increasing frequency from natural forms (Plate 47). These are, to a large extent, floral, sometimes abstracted and formalized, only slightly reminiscent of their plant origin, at other times full of the spirit of the original and closely imitative of its form. In the Late Minoan period (Plate 48), there is an extended interest in forms drawn from marine life—the nautilus, octopus, squid, and other less easily identifiable forms of sea life, often extremely lifelike, though, as time goes on, increasingly formalized and then stylized.

Decorative painting on a larger scale, from Middle Minoan II, is characteristically devoted to the rendering of landscape with birds, animals, or occasionally human figures. Commonly, the flowers or rock-like configurations are the more prominent, together with the irregular wavy bands and lines of light and dark which possibly were suggested by the uneven shadows cast upon the ground by clouds or trees. Marine life is less common. Human subjects appear in the miniature frescoes of Middle Minoan III, representing festive scenes at court (Plate 51). Long friezes of attendants or soldiers lined some of the corridors, and friezes of fowls bordered some rooms. Occasionally a fantastic creature, a griffin or the like, constituted the chief element in a design; occasionally inanimate objects are used to form a design, as in the frieze of shields in the King's Megaron at Knossos, or aniconic patterns and interlacing spirals replace human or animal figures.

Vases were decorated with figure designs in relief. As it happens, the three most famous vases from Crete—the Boxer vase, the Chieftan vase, and the Harvester vase (Plate 54)—depict human beings, but fragments discovered of vases with octopus designs suggest that this proportion may be only an accident of preservation. Sculpture in the round, represented chiefly by a relatively few figurines in ivory or ivory and gold, depict priests, priestesses or female divinities, and one or two athletes. Smaller reliefs, as on signet rings, may depict religious scenes or simple configurations of humans, animals, or fantastic figures. Thus there is a wide variety of conceptual form but almost all are within the realm of naturalism, with a focus on the flora and fauna of landscape.

In architecture, the most distinctive creations of the Minoans were the palaces. The few tombs which have been discovered are works of functional construction rather than architecture, with the exception of two or three which should be discussed individually rather than for their general features. A considerable number of private houses—that is, dwellings of small scale with only a few rooms—have been found; their distinctive qualities are seen also in the more palatial dwellings. No separate temples or civic or other public buildings have been identified.

The form of the palace is unusually instructive, especially as its history is suggested on the site of Knossos. Through the neolithic and Early Minoan period this site had been occupied by the houses of a village or small town, of which numerous remains have been dis-covered; at the beginning of the First Middle Minoan period there took place a major re-planning and reconstruction of the town. In this reconstruction a large, level, rectangular area was cleared in the center, around which were arranged quadrangular blocks of buildings, sepa-rated by streets or alleys; there were also at least two other courts. Many of the corners of the insulae were not squared, but rounded. Even in the First Middle Minoan period, some greater degree of integral unity was felt in this complex than in a simple accumulation of buildings along streets as in a village; the blocks were treated with continuous façades; there seems to have been an attempt to consolidate and organize the plan. During the remainder of the Middle Minoan period, the course of development was to convert the insulae into apartments, the streets into corridors; to bring the town under one roof and make of it a single building. In other words, it is a living example, so to speak, of the imposition of an architectural (i.e., aesthetic) form on a rational, functional construction. Of course, the "rational, functional construc-tion," the village, may or may not have had an "aesthetic architectural form" itself, but the act of consolidating this village and molding it into a building is a clear act of establishing a new aesthetic form without altering, extensively, the basic functional form.

Thus the rational aspect of the conceptual form is retained from the old function. Presumably the entire community, with all its interests and organization, was given a single home. The aesthetic aspect is the new impression resulting from numerous major and minor modifications, achieving a degree of unity and making a quite different effect. Some other Cretan palaces, though not all went through the stages of this development, were constructed on the same lines as the palace at Knossos: a courtyard, around which were several complexes of apartments of differentiated use, separated and joined by endless, narrow corridors. They, too, employ the same conceptual form, though without the same functional history.

Within this larger plan, smaller elements also reveal certain distinctions of conceptual form. Of these one of the most widely dispersed and characteristic is the residential unit, of which a large, luxurious, and fully developed example is the King's Megaron at Knossos (Plates 57, 59). The nucleus of this type of apartment is a quadrangular space formed by a wall on one side and either screen walls of piers on the other three sides or two adjoining screen walls of piers and one solid wall. At one side, along the base wall and separated by one of the screen walls, is a space enclosed by the base wall itself, a wall opposite the base wall, the screen wall separating the second room from the primary room, and one or more columns opposite the screen wall. These columns separate the second room from a light well. At the other end of the complex, accessible from the nuclear room, was a corridor along one side or along two adjoining sides of the primary room. This fairly definite scheme of spatial organization, though developed with some variety, seems to have been a core unit in dwelling apartments. In addition, at convenient but not standardized positions, were stairs winding down from landing to landing, halls with ceilings supported by one to four columns, and bathrooms and other minor rooms.

Halls or rooms larger than the ordinary, and distinguished by approximating to a square in plan, are found in the palaces, with the ceiling supported by two columns. A few halls with ceilings borne on a double row of columns or piers are also known. Among the most remarkable, and potentially significant, are those which have been hypothetically restored for the *piano nobile* at Knossos (Plate 57B). In one room, approximately square, the space is divided into three aisles by one row of three columns and a parallel row of three rectangular piers. Quite apart from complications introduced by the arrangement of entrances, this has the effect of subdividing the space in several interlocking ways, depending on a shift in point of view (see below, p. 175). In some formal rooms was a lustral basin, a rectangular pit, approached by stairs along one or more sides. Porches, or formal entrance halls, and more or less independent propyla are frequently encountered. The simplest is a plain room with entrances unadorned save possibly by a column or pier; it served as anteroom or transitional room from one section to another. The most complex of these is the later south propylaeum at Knossos, an H-shaped hall with two columns between the ends of the H on the north and two corresponding columns in the room on the south, enclosed within a wall pierced by three great doors and closing the space between the ends of the bars of the H on the south. It is significant that these arrangements are more or less standardized and more or less separable; a large structure might utilize several different forms and combinations of these forms.

A distinctive feature of these rooms is that spaces are defined not only by walls, columns, and piers in the ordinary sense but by screen walls or walls pierced by a number of doors closely spaced, or by doors separated by narrow pier jambs. These screen walls have the effect of providing the complete, flat definition that a defining surface like a wall does, as opposed to a colonnade or line of piers, while permitting complete freedom of interpenetration of space and movement and a unique kind of lightness. Although the Minoans were thoroughly familiar with columns and used them freely, they did not develop the potentialities of full colonnades. Some courtyards were lined with colonnades; a curious arrangement of alternating piers and columns existed in the courts at Mallia and Phaistos. But these piers and columns probably supported galleries and had a subordinate place in the total effect. One should not overlook the obvious use of colonnades and ranges of piers where they occur, of course; but it remains a fact that there are apparently no examples of fully developed colonnades as the later Greeks or even the Egyptians used them.

Even more characteristic than these types of rooms or apartments are the endless, tortuous corridors which characterize the larger buildings; they were long, narrow, and frequently meaningless as preserved. These corridors, the long, narrow storage chambers at Knossos and elsewhere, and the great central courts are the broad identifying features of these remarkable palaces.

Certain elements of conceptual form in the detail of Minoan architecture are noteworthy. Particularly striking is the column without a base, with a broad, spreading echinus in the capital and the shaft narrower at the bottom than at the top. This is sometimes supposed to reflect the use of trunks of trees upside down, either to discourage the sprouting of new shoots if the wood were too green or to augment the bearing surface of the column at the top. A common motif in pictorial depiction of architecture is the "horn of consecration"—two vertical elements connected at the bottom by an element with the profile of a compound bow. Sometimes these horns appear in series as a coping design; sometimes between, or even underneath, columns. Whether they have any relation to a kind of altar is uncertain.

On the mainland, neolithic pottery exhibits a variety of patterns, all, however, aniconic (Plate 45). One style tends almost exclusively to angular linear patterns in vivid colors; another to curvilinear patterns, notably spirals and running spirals. In Early Helladic times, painted designs are in smaller proportion. The ornamentation of ceramics is in terms of polished, burnished, or generally diffused color rather than patterned designs (Plate 49). The most vivid and characteristic Middle Helladic ware, "minyan," is not decorated with designs; instead, it relies on even texture and color. Other wares have painted and incised aniconic designs of rectilinear and curvilinear forms.

The conceptual form of Late Helladic pottery is derived from Crete (Plate 50). Motifs drawn from marine life and vegetable life are particularly favored; only in monumental wall frescoes do depictions of human figures or large animals occur. Even here there is a difference: Cretan paintings, so far as they are known, were confined to action of a relatively calm and peaceful nature—ceremonial and religious scenes, daily life in the Minoan court. Mycenaean subjects commonly are drawn from the life of hunting or war; even what may be taken as a ceremonial scene shows the participants riding in chariots, where the Cretan would walk the corridors of his palace or the neighboring fields of lilies (Plate 53). The distinction designates the Vaphio cups (Plate 55) as Cretan, though they were found on the mainland, because of the bucolic bovinity of the scene in contrast to the embattled vigor of the hunters of the Mycenae daggers (Plate 56). In this particular case, of course, it would be easy to create the style ourselves by our attributions, but these attributions are completely harmonious with the indications from more definitely localized products. Late Mycenaean pottery is highly abstracted and stylized but strives for the same traditional motifs, though depictions of human beings do occur.

The conceptual form of neolithic architecture on the mainland is various and has not been fully understood. There are examples of both cylindrical and rectangular structures, and it is often thought that they may represent different cultures, for they occur separately. (And yet a modern rural complex in some parts of Greece today will include both types, both made of straw or reeds on a low socle of mud and stone.) Cylindrical structures were also known in the islands, as indicated by a marble model of a group from Melos. At certain sites, as at Dhimini and Sesklos in Thessaly, have been found examples of a form in which quadrangular rooms are arranged in sequence between two parallel walls. At the front is a porch formed by the ends of the two walls with a pair of columns between. Elsewhere there are buildings which do not fall within either of these types, nor are they related to other known types.

In the Early Helladic period, a similar variety is evident. At Tiryns was a circular structure some ninety feet in diameter (its internal plan, the nature of its external walls, if any, and almost all other details are unknown); but at Myli Lernae below Argos has recently been found a large rectangular building with impressively thick walls, containing corridors, stairways, and a number of rectangular rooms of various sizes. Otherwise the common form of building is rectilinear and irregular in plan.

Middle Helladic buildings are often apsidal—rectangular structures with a porch or anteroom, a central rectangular room, and a semicircular or apsidal room at the end. Normally there was a hearth in the middle of the main room, and columns along the axis of the building supported the roof. In Late Helladic times, this megaron was identifiably the basic type: the main hall, rectangular in form, with (usually four) columns symmetrically disposed to support the ceiling, possibly an anteroom, and usually a porch composed of the projecting side walls with columns between the ends. In a building of any size this unit would invariably face on a quadrangular courtyard, entered from the side opposite the megaron by an H-shaped gateway, neither the megaron nor gate being on center.

In Late Helladic times, one of the characteristic architectural forms was the palace as distinguished from the house. The palace consisted of one or more megarons in a maze of smaller rooms, storerooms, bathrooms, and other unidentified apartments, with corridors, stairways, and anterooms providing innumerable avenues of movement throughout (Plates 60–61). The plan seems to have been a fusion of the megaron and the Minoan palace. The megaron and its courtyard remain the central traditional Helladic feature, embellished as much as possible with elements of Minoan architecture, chiefly in matters of decoration, details like the peculiar column (narrower at the bottom than at the top) and the labyrinthine plan of the whole structure. For another difference, the Mycenaean palace or, at least, royal community, was normally protected by an extraordinarily massive fortification. Ponderous walls of tremendous stones, somewhat squared but set in heavy mud mortar and not tightly fitted, relying for effect on thickness and height rather than towers; elaborate entrances between overhanging walls and projecting bastions; such are the conspicuous characteristics of the fortifications (Plate 62). The curious manner of running vertical joints through the mass of masonry at intervals, with more or less slight projections of one face of the wall beyond the other at the joint, may have had an aesthetic basis; in any case, the totality of the fortification makes a powerful impression. Certainly the design of the entrance to the palace at Mycenae, with its portal adorned by the sculptured group of lions flanking a column, was determined in part by aesthetic considerations.

The Art of the Early Aegean

Apart from the palace complex, Mycenaean architecture is distinguished by another noteworthy form—the tomb. In fact, Mycenaean architecture developed several varieties of burial structure. Of these, the shaft grave, being simply an excavated pit subsequently refilled, could scarcely figure in formal architecture as such—though the provision of circular enclosures for groups of such graves does have an architectural character. Nor could the chamber tomb, a quadrangular room excavated in a hillside, approached by a downward sloping passage or dromos, be counted among works of formal architecture, though the chamber itself was closed at the entrance by a door to be walled up after a burial so that the chamber would remain open while the dromos was filled with earth. Characteristically, the dromos had sides sloping inward toward the top, which is either an aesthetic or traditional form of only slight functional significance. Still, the irregular shape and lack of finish of the burial chamber shows clearly that it was not regarded as a work of finished, developed architecture.

The tholos tomb, of which the Treasury of Atreus at Mycenae is the greatest example, is another matter. The distinctive shape of the vault, the careful design and workmanship of the door, the ornament of bronze rosettes over the curve of the vault, the careful finish of the masonry throughout, and the sheer scale and costliness of the tomb itself all make it perfectly clear that the builders of the structure had aesthetic intentions, and no one who sees the structure will wish to dispute them. There has been much debate as to whether the characteristic pointed dome was derived from domed chambers or burial mounds elsewhere or was simply a refinement and polished development of the chamber tomb or a projection of the circle in which shaft graves were sometimes arranged. The domed chamber in the tholos is not in all cases the actual burial room; burial often took place in a quadrangular chamber opening at the side of the domed room. Thus the domed room may be thought of as a ceremonial hall rather than a burial vault. But not all tholos tombs have the special burial chamber at one side, so that there is a possibility of amalgamation of two traditions. In either case, there is a clearly functional quality about all elements of the design—dromos, door, ceremonial hall and/or burial chamber; the more or less conical shape of the great hall is a result not of any abstract conception of form but of the structural scheme of rings of stone of diminishing diameter placed one above the other until the apex is reached.

It is revealing to summarize the qualities of conceptual form common throughout the Aegean area, in the major cultures at least, in contrast to the styles of Egypt and Hither Asia. To begin with, Aegean conceptual form stands with Mesopotamian art against Egyptian in being primarily aesthetic. Indeed, it has less of the rational emphasis than is found in the art of Hither Asia. Almost all of the known pictorial decorative programs are incidental—there are no historical records in pictures as such—and many compositions (representations of ceremonial processions and blue boys or monkeys picking saffron) are hardly to be understood as records or illustrations. Some compositions, like the palace fresco and some bull-leaping contests, the Boxer vase, Vaphio cups, Mycenae daggers, Tiryns boar-hunt fresco, are vignettes of real life, but the observer is not ordinarily preoccupied with the complexity of detail. In architecture, the function of the building is not dramatized. In general, it is as it is with the octopus on the vase: a knowledge of the limpness and ductility of the tentacles of an octopus adds appreciably to one's aesthetic response to the rendering of the octopus floating over the surface of the vase; but it is this impression alone which the artist is developing—he is not concerned with instructing us in the anatomy of the octopus.

Another quality of conceptual form of some general application, though more prominent in Minoan than in Mycenaean art, is the concentration on nature apart from man—on plants and marine life particularly. Perhaps a reflection of this may be seen even in architecture, in the smallness and openness of communities and the luxurious interplay of interior and exterior living space in dwellings; perhaps even in the apparent preference for open-air tree shrines over enclosed temples. Though some of these qualities may be perceived in Mycenaean art, there is here a greater weight on human life, on vigorous action; buildings are more tightly enclosed, courtyards less extensive, and underground tombs—a type of architecture as exclusive of the environment of nature as can be conceived—play an important role.

The Art of the Early Aegean

SENSORY ELEMENTS

MOTION

Movement, even apart from its expression in the kind and activity of the conceptual form, is thoroughly pervasive of Minoan and, in varying degrees, the arts of the mainland. In Crete there is a lightness, freshness, lack of serious concern in the subject matter: the real but almost fanciful worlds of the sea; the warm and pleasant hillsides of lilies and crocuses (not oaks and roses); the gay and carefree life of a court society. The interests, in general, which are embodied and reflected by the conceptual form of the various arts are the relatively casual ones of ordinary daily existence, not, for example, the problems of cosmos or empire. Once again, although Mycenaean art may be closer to Minoan art than it is to either Egyptian or Hither Asiatic art in this respect, it is perceptibly distinct from Minoan. Violent, even grim, subjects of war and hunting occur and are significant for the more sober, vigorous, energetic movements, colors, and textures they involve.

Movement is conspicuous in painting and vase painting, first in the wide variety of linear pattern—the formal spirals in varying degrees of elaboration; the bands of borders; the involuted lines of topography in landscapes or the bands and intervening edges of light and dark; the lines depicting lily, octopus, and man. It is, moreover, vividly present in the rhythms of the elements of frieze bands—horns of consecration, shields, marching figures or flowers; and in the more intricate compositions of line, color, and texture developed in certain borders like the border around the bull-fighting panels from Knossos, or the borders in designs resembling wood grain. There is movement also, which is a result of the reduction of a surface to a multitude of small shapes or broken lines, like the figures in the miniature fresco of the festive group at Knossos, so that the eye cannot follow every detail but records only a generalized effect of shimmer or scintillation. In all these respects Minoan and Mycenaean art differ only slightly. But the neolithic art both in Crete and on the mainland differs from later styles in that the movements are chiefly in pure lines (not outlines or bands), in the rhythms of repetition, and in the reaction to shock and block of fractured and frustrated momentum.

In sculpture—insofar as the relief vases, figurines, and a few miscellaneous carvings of other types may be regarded as sculpture—the principles are the same. When the conceptual form involves human and animal figures, forms are attenuated and delineated by emphatic line; the anatomical forms themselves are often attenuated and tensions are exaggerated. Of this the Harvester vase is an extreme example, and in the same vase the pattern of the winnowing forks over the men's heads is a seething movement of lines with the rhythm and agitation of broken texture. In Mycenaean work, though this may be only an accident of survival, there is apparently a greater predilection for incised work, with the resultant loss of solid shape and the concomitant increased importance of the lines themselves.

Movement in architecture is developed to an unusual degree in complex and subtle ways. The buildings, the palaces, though large in extent, are lightly constructed of relatively small units. The columns, in contrast to the conventional classical column which, thicker at the bottom than the top, embodies a conception of the accumulation of mass to buttress a support, is often narrower at the bottom, embodying a conception of a force emerging, rising, expanding (as in some modern ferroconcrete designs, though less effective in the Minoan). There is, of course, the obvious kinaesthetic stimulus of a double colonnade, creating two aisles and thus establishing a sense of movement parallel to the line of columns. Furthermore, Minoan architects evidently distinguished between the centralized, channelized movement of the aisle-nave arrangement and the divisive, plough-like movement of the single-row arrangement. They also recognized and employed in elaborate and intricate combinations the kinaesthetic effect of a façade in projecting a movement to the front. A colonnade along one side of a building constitutes a line parallel to the wall of the building, but since it looks away from the building, or constitutes the face of the building, the observer is inclined to conceive of it in terms of movements, toward and into or out and away from the building. This obvious effect was employed in less than obvious ways by the Minoans when they treated in different ways the several sides of a room or space so that each constituted a distinct façade, as it were, with its own line of in-and-out movement. In the throne room (Plates 57–58), for instance, the side of the room with the throne is from one point of view an important face with movement toward and away from it; the narrow ends of the room, containing the doors, tend to develop an axial movement at right angles to that projecting from the wall of the throne. In the *piano nobile* central tricolumnar hall, which is actually about square, a double row of supports creates a nave and two aisles with a resultant movement on the axis of the nave; but the rows of supports are different, one columns, one piers, so that each row constitutes a façade facing the other with opposing movements at right angles to the nave movement.

Another peculiarity of Minoan architecture which stimulates the kinaesthetic sense is the bent-axis of many elements and the eccentric and unpredictable line of communication. We shall discuss these in greater detail in another connection, but among their effects would be increased awareness of lines of physical movement and the realization that paths of communication through space do not coincide with any of the aesthetic axes described. In the tricolumnar hall, the entrances, of which there were several, none matching, were at irregular points along the walls and connected by broken lines of passage. None of this is easily perceptible, and the act of concentration required to ascertain the relationships heightens their effect.

Finally, the low, heterogeneous, broken outline of the palace on all its façades constitutes a quickened line; the lack of regularizing colonnades, though these have kinaesthetic powers of their own, leaves the chief effect to the broken outlines.

On the mainland, of course, the distinctly Mycenaean features— megaron, propylon, tholos tomb—represent quite different handling of kinaesthetic stimuli but contain no movements which were not present on Crete. Indeed, the Mycenaean buildings contained far fewer kinds of movement. In certain kinds of work, Mycenaean buildings, unlike Minoan buildings, have a sense of the downward movement and pressure of ponderous masonry. The powerful fortresses, colossal tombs, and large-scale sculpture in stone generate a sense of great weight, sobriety, and vigor.

LIGHT AND COLOR

One of the more immediately striking qualities of Minoan art is the variety of colors employed. Paintings, in the sense of wall frescoes, were executed in a wide range of hues, and many styles of pottery are vividly polychrome. Faïence and other colored glazes were developed. Several kinds of metals were used—often with other materials—in a single product—gold and ivory figurines, cups and bowls of bronze, gold, or silver inlaid with other metals and enamel. In architecture, too, one is particularly struck by the variety of color and the generosity with which it is applied. In these respects, Aegean art may not differ in essentials from the arts of contemporary Egypt or Hither Asia, but it does differ from the arts of later Greece, where polychromy was much more limited.

But it is in the consciousness of and interest in light that Minoan art—and, indirectly, Mycenaean art—is most conspicuous and indeed all but unique. This is startlingly expressed in fresco not by reliance on the illusion of light and shadow, by hues of high and low intensity, or by representation of the fall of light and shadow upon a subject but by arbitrary, conventional bands and patches of light and dark splashed across the expanse of the subject (Plate 58). With their wavy contours, these bands do not seem to represent an effort at pictorial rendering; they simply introduce light and dark according to formula. Perhaps the formula was suggested by the way light and shadow in nature fall in uneven lines and patches. Even in some gold-relief there is a suggestion of this kind of lighting. In its own way the conceptual form is filled with light—the flowers and the trees. There is an extraordinary suggestion of the shifting lights of the submarine world in the sea floor depicted on the gold cup from Dendra.

In the design of a building (Plate 57) the abundance of light wells is, of course, a direct response to a practical need for illumination for simple visibility and ventilation in lower stories; yet there is no reason why illumination might not have been provided through windows or galleries on the exterior walls or facing on courtyards. The predilection for light wells would seem to imply a preference for the particular kind of illumination such a device provides, namely, a suffused, quiet light combined with a relatively free circulation of air. The result was striking: the brilliant open air of the courtyards of the palaces, the luminous hues of the distant landscape visible from most parts of the buildings, and the cool, even, almost tangible half-light of the inner rooms. In the smaller details, the use of colonnades, however limited, and the broken lines and masses of the façades, caught shadows and contrasted with the harsh light of the courtyards.

In the matter of light, Mycenaean art seems simply to follow the Minoan tradition with little suggestion of spontaneous interest in the ways light might be used to further aesthetic ends.

TEXTURE

The use of a wide variety of textural materials in all the arts is suggestive and requires no elaboration. Perhaps an indication of extreme curiosity in the use of texture would be the fantastic "barbotine" ware of the Early Minoan period and less strange combinations of clay and pigment in other styles. And, of course, there is the rich variety of textures in the conceptual form of landscape, costume, marine animals, and so on. But texture is much less emphasized in Aegean art than in the arts of Egypt and Hither Asia.

MANNER

The relation between Minoan and Mycenaean strains in Aegean culture is further indicated by marked similarities and differences in the manner of manipulating the sensory elements of art. Once again, it is necessary to recall that the two spheres influenced each other; the place an object is found is no proof of the place of manufacture or of the origin of the artist. There was much mutual modification of style through the years.

ONTOLOGY

Minoan art is clearly not particularistic; light, color, movement, are seldom individualized but used in fairly standardized forms. So far, no examples of sculpture or painting with historical intent have been discovered, with the exception of a fragment of silver showing a city under siege, and even this may be no more particular than a scene on Homer's shield of Achilles. There are, to be sure, certain individual figures, like the figurines of the praying man from Tylissos and the stout, dowager-like praying woman and the figures of society ladies depicted in the miniature fresco at Knossos. But even here there is little suggestion that a particular individual is represented; the personal vitality of such figures is shared equally by all the figures on the Harvester vase, and none has the individual physical identity of the Egyptian "Sheik."

In the depiction of natural objects, birds, flowers, and the like, there may be some difference among the various specimens, but all are rendered broadly according to formula. In floral subjects, where the elements of grace and delicacy and color are to be emphasized, effective formulations are repeated without variation. Blooms or leaves are not always solidly attached to the stem; they flourish independently, joined to the mother plant, if at all, by a token stem. Lilies are reduced to the fleur-de-lis; a clump of crocuses is arranged in a spread too regular for nature, too full for idealization or typification of the crocus as a type, in order to convey the richness of the first crocus of spring. Rosettes and other abstracted forms are common not only as pure design but in positions approximating those of a rendition of nature. Particular marine forms are reduced to selected forms.

In architecture, there is a certain idealism, in the sense that the buildings we know were conceived according to a type that concealed individuality. All of the major palaces were built around courtyards and included many of the same features: the more or less stereotyped domestic apartment, lustral areas, "theatral areas," storage quarters, and a maze of narrow passages. There was much variety within these types, and the open arrangement in the domestic quarters, with screen walls and wide passages, makes it possible to manipulate hangings and screens to vary the forms of the volumes and to adapt to various temperatures, to groups of various sizes, and to degrees of formality or informality.

Mycenaean art would seem to be, at bottom, more abstract than Minoan art. It is true that the richest manifestations of this style, represented by the Late Helladic frescoes and minor arts and such early products as the gold daggers from the shaft graves, show Minoan influence. In the grave stele from the grave circle at Mycenae, however, the figures are also reduced to almost linear form. More significantly, throughout the range of the style there is a tendency to make almost identical formal patterns of all motifs, marine forms as well as floral, and in the latest phases these formal patterns are stylized to the point where they would be unrecognizable without corroboration of their origin. Even in the "fine phase" of the palace frescoes, the trees of the chariot fresco were almost precise duplicates of each other in form if not in color; the branches follow an undeviating pattern and lack even such variations as seen in vegetation in a Minoan fresco. In architecture, the megaron and propylon do not vary in essence, though the larger megarons may have a second anteroom between vestibule and hall and the smaller private megarons may be cramped and distorted by their position. It would not be feasible to make a categorical distinction on ontological grounds between Minoan and Mycenaean work, but broadly taken the differences are apparent.

EPISTEMOLOGY

In general, then, Minoan and especially Mycenaean art range on the abstract side of idealism. From the epistemological point of view, Minoan art seems to be fairly subjective—"expressionistic." The distortion of the human figure, tending toward a general slimness and litheness, is unlike the patently non-natural formulas of Egyptian figures, with full-front torso and the rest of the body in profile. The distortion seems to represent violence done the physical body of the subject to create an impression of a limber, wiry physique. In miniature work (as on some of the molded vases and frescoes), this distortion becomes caricature, creating a definite impression of some aspect of the subject depicted. The lacy leaves of a branch, the soft feathers of a bird, the lithe tentacles and powerful suckers of the octopus are exaggerated to increase the force of the impression they make. The onyxlike quality which seems to constitute the essence abstracted by the Minoan artist from clusters of stones in a rocky landscape is elaborated to the point where the original association with the stones of landscape is forgotten. The impression is reinforced by the use of the same pattern to represent other objects—clouds, for example.

The women of the Cretan court in the palace fresco give a general impression of vivid and sparkling animation. This is true of individual figures: pert nose, large, lively, saucy eye, raffish swirl of a lock of hair. None of these features would be recognizable in and of itself—the nose is no more than an impression of a nose. The combination of these features into an animated figure is our response to expressive suggestion. Furthermore, the first recognition one has of the character of the scene is not from these details (illustrative, so to speak, of conceptual form) but from the general effect of a restless, sketchy line and swirling light and color. From this comes an impression, strengthened and pointed, of the alert glances, vivacious manners, and bright expressions of a gathering of gay and sophisticated young women.

Expressionism in architecture is not easily discerned in the present state of preservation of the monuments and the little we know of their use, but it may be detected in the lightly raised paths marking lines of traffic across some courts and in the painting of wall surfaces to express the structure-function of the wall behind the plaster.

In Myceanean art there is apparent an equally strong expressionistic tendency in the distorted attenuation of the figures on the grave circle stele and the lion-daggers and in the "flying gallop" of lions and other beasts in hunting scenes—and in those vases in which structural parts are emphasized by curves or moldings.

SIGNIFICATION

Finally, there is the question of whether the elements of Aegean art are to be understood literally or symbolically. It may be that we know too little to have grounds for discussion. It may be that the Minoans used conscious symbols freely, particularly when one considers the double axes engraved on the piers in palaces, the strange ceramic knots, and the shells and other curious objects found in what were apparently sanctuaries. And yet it is perfectly possible that the people regarded these objects not as symbols but as fetishes; that is, they did not think of the objects as symbolizing or representing power but as being powerful or embodying power. And when we consider that apart from these objects there is nothing in Minoan art or culture which seems to constitute divinity physically or immanently, except as divinity might manifest itself in the body of a bird or woman or tree, it appears that the Minoan concept of divinity may have included such fetishes.

Even if the Minoans did think in terms of conscious symbols in their religion, it is less likely that their art embodied consciously chosen symbols. The double ax depicted in a Minoan fresco is, first of all, a real ax which played a part in the situation depicted whether or not the ax is to be considered symbolic; or the ax serves simply as an element in a decorative pattern. There seems little likelihood that the boy (or monkey) gathering saffron, or the priest-king wandering through the field of lilies, or the griffins by the throne were conscious symbols; in all probability they were understood directly in their own terms.

Columns or pillars not infrequently appear in contexts that have a strong suggestion of symbolism. Not only do they occur alone, as in some medallions or in some paintings (it may be a question, in the Hagia Triada sarcophagos, whether the postlike objects are pillars or double axes with heavy staffs) but also in some combination, as in the palace fresco where columns stand on horns of consecration. The most urgent suggestion comes from the Mycenaean area, where, over the main entrance to the fortress of Mycenae (Plate 62), two lions guard a pillar. Observers usually look for a "meaning behind" this group: do the lions represent divinity or a royal house, and in what sense? Does the pillar represent the physical structure of the house, or the "house" in a dynastic sense, or the people or nation symbolized through their religion or part of it? It seems futile to press any of these speculations, but it does seem possible that some kind of symbolism is involved. The alternative would be that the column is a literal fetish or charm guarded or adorned by literal beasts. Similarly, in the frescoes and medallions which show pillars resting on altars or horns of consecration, there may be a symbolic use of the column.

Of course, if we allow that there is a tendency to conscious symbolism in Aegean art, we may find a flood of examples (all unintelligible) in the seal stones. On the whole, however, it seems unwise to risk such an hypothesis; there are few of the symbols one might expect to find in this cultural area, and many devices which we may take to be conscious symbols equally well may be something else.

DEFINITION

Delineation in Minoan art has a consistent clarity in the sense that the movements, colors, light, textures, and conceptual form are normally simple, broadly conceived with relatively little detail, and normally in isolation or in near-isolation, with little overlapping. Important elements in a design are brought out in clear, unbroken contour, in isolation. So, generally, there is little merging or fusing of colors, textures, or other elements in any composition; the distinctions are plain and clear.

This clarity, however, often does not extend to making clear the articulation or even the identity of the individual conceptual forms; contours, wall surfaces, and the supports of a building may be clear enough, but there is no real effort to clarify the lines of passage, for example, distinguishing entrances and major and minor elements of a façade. Particular units may be clearly defined, only to be lost in the intricacies of the ensemble. In painting, dashes or sweeping lines are common instead of firm lines and contours. The lines are often like those of a charcoal pencil rather than of a pen or fine brush—thick without being heavy, with uneven edges, continued by repeated application instead of continuous sweep. The execution of designs in engraving and modeling is often similar in spirit, with quick, sketchy lines instead of complete and controlled contours. Of course, there are examples of unbroken lines and movements followed through extended periods, but rarely is there enamel-like, polished precision; usually there is some device to break the finish.

Mycenaean art, distinct from Minoan art, has a greater degree of firmness and completeness in its delineation. It is less sketchy and vivid. Lines in a fresco are likely to be full, even, unbroken; the forms of eye and lip, for example, are complete and clear insofar as they are detailed. The trees in the fragment of the chariot fresco from Tiryns (Plate 53) are heavily outlined by a broad band which follows the whole profile of the tree, with the outermost leaves of the branches individually aligned in the band. This broad, somewhat deadening device to delineate the general shape of the tree contrasts with the absence of any such objective, over-all outline in Minoan art. The sketchy rendering of the leaves and branches resembles Minoan work, though the individual branches and leaves are more strictly distinguished. In architecture, although there are many other factors behind the fact and form of the defensive walls of a palace, the Mycenaean fortifications are a vivid example of the firm, full definition of the typical complex as differentiated from the irregular, elusive outline of the Minoan palace. In the interior plan, the megaron and gates, simple and regular in their plan, are more clear-cut both as independent units and as organizing elements in the complex as a whole. The methodical arrangement of men and animals in the hunting daggers from Mycenae produce a matter-of-fact clarity of arrangement, though it lacks perhaps the delicacy and grace of Minoan work.

CONFIGURATION

Among the notable peculiarities of Minoan art is the configuration, which is linear, or in a single dimension. This is evident in the choice of conceptual form: the kinds of flowers, the fondness for tentacled creatures of the sea, the long corridors, narrow halls, and winding stairs. The same is true in relation to movement: the development of spiral patterns of all kinds, the stone and wood veining of borders (and the borders and friezes themselves), and so forth. For more detailed consideration, a figure like the griffin in the throne room fresco is indicative. The outline is a strong, bold sweep of line. There is almost no modeling of the figure to suggest its mass, and there are attempts to minimize the expanse of the figure, as is apparent in the prominent pattern at the shoulder. Although it centers on a broad, full rosette, the pattern consists of interlocking spiral lines so that the suggestion of the area of the circle is minimized and the movement of line is emphasized. It is true, of course, that these particular lines are broad and flat and in contrasting colors. From the back of the beast's neck project lines spiraling to an end, in themselves linear movements and at the same time supporting and concentrating the movement of the line of the neck itself. The lilies in the background are slender, the blossoms reduced to quasi-triangular areas. Most dramatically, the bands of shadow reduce the composition to four parallel horizontal lines, enlivened by the line created by the sharp contrast between the bands. The total composition is a two-dimensional plane, but the composition in terms of areas rather than lines is minimized by the pervasive horizontality, the vivid movements, the irregular areas which do not emerge as definite shapes.

Similarly, the saffron-gatherer fresco is so lavishly treated with undulating lines that the shapes they enclose, amorphous and incomprehensible as they are, make little impression. Even in the great tall friezes of shields where two-dimensional forms are obtrusive, and certainly in the friezes of marching or running figures, or birds and wild life, the frieze arrangement, the extensive development of linear patterns wherever possible, and the failure to elaborate two- or three-dimensional forms beyond a minimum, suggest the linear form. In general, one finds a novel and effective linear emphasis in almost every composition.

There are, to be sure, examples of Minoan art with well-developed two-dimensional qualities (for example, the Hagia Triada sarcophagus), and in general the art is rarely wholly linear but is usually to some degree perceptibly expansive. Nevertheless, it is fair to say that few styles have achieved the degree of sophistication which Minoan art achieved while remaining so close to primitive linear dimensions.

So also in sculpture—in the relief vases and figurines, and we might also include the gems—the lines are prominent, while surfaces and certainly the solid masses are not. On the one extreme is the Harvester vase, a swirl of linear movement. The bulls on the Boxer vase from Hagia Triada are broad, sweeping surfaces with a definite suggestion of meat; and in the Vaphio cups there is, again, a strong feeling for the bulk of the animals. These last, at least, are exceptions, and the indication of mass remains inchoate and tentative. Figurines are much attenuated or, as in the snake priestesses with their voluminous skirts, elaborated with linear patterns of costume or snake.

In architecture, apart from the corridors, stairs, and halls, and the painted wall ornamentation, one-dimensional effects of a more subtle nature appear. In an Egyptian hypostyle hall there is a sweep of movements along each axis of the building, marching with the essentially similar ranks and files of columns and corridors, like the threads of warp and woof in a fabric. In Minoan architecture, when a movement in one direction is established by one device and a movement in another direction, transverse or adverse, is set up by an unrelated stimulus, the two movements do not fuse in a single fabric but remain distinct and sensible as separate movements in different directions. Thus the hall in the *piano nobile,* with three piers facing three columns forming the nave in a square room, has the line of movement of the nave, the transverse movement looking out from the piers across the nave, the transverse movement adverse to this of the columns looking toward the piers, and the several threads of movement through the room from one entrance to the other. All these fuse in a way, but as an interlacing of movement rather than as a plane; and they maintain their individuality, each a movement in a single line. Of equal interest are the low buildings, usually widely extended, with colonnades limited in extent, if used at all, to provide longitudinal lines rather than the outward sweep of a façade. These structures emphasize the line of surrounding buildings rather than, say, the expanse of a courtyard.

In Mycenaean as in Minoan art, linear movement is abundant, but there is often a distinct tendency to enlarge the flat surfaces, to develop the geometrical shapes. It is the silhouette of the tree which is emphasized in Mycenaean work, rather than the spidery branches, though the branches may be seen contributing to the texture and movement of the surface of the silhouette. The highly distinctive tendency to symmetrical arrangement, which we shall discuss below, is also capable of creating two-dimensional effects. For example, a Minoan squid with its tentacles undulating loosely in many different patterns preserves the value of each tentacle as a unique line of movement. The Mycenaean octopus, with the four tentacles on the right and the mirror image of the four on the left, immediately becomes a flat surface with a design arranged on it, a sheet folded in the center and then flattened out. Similarly, the patterns of hair and costume on the figure of the queenly woman from Tiryns (Plate 52) confine all the movement within a single plane and in relation to other movements in that plane; the movements are no longer free and searching, each by each. Even in so linear a design as the hunting scene with the great rush of movement along the blade, the animals are silhouetted broadly, and the scenes are arranged to give full value to the surface qualities. On the other hand, there is little evidence of interest in three-dimensional, massive form, unless perhaps in the tholos tombs.

Finally, the most clear-cut example of an exclusively linear art that we have encountered is that of the mainland in the neolithic period, represented here by a vase (Plate 45).

DYNAMICS

The dynamics of Minoan art is closely consonant with the peculiarities of definition and configuration. In general, it is characterized by a lightness and exuberance, an eccentricity or lack of symmetry, unlike the other arts of the ancient Mediterranean. Particularly, it is different from the static permanence of Egyptian art, and it is perceptibly different from the pressing opulence of the arts of Hither Asia. Whereas in Asiatic art there is an everpresent abundance, a growth and swelling, in Asiatic art this meets with a powerful restraint that circumscribes and contains it; in Cretan art the lushly vegetating, ebullient energy meets no restraint and expends itself in complete freedom and mobility. Specifically, this is exemplified in the patterns of endless interlocking spirals in which the movement flows unchecked and endlessly; in the shapeless patterns of light, rocks, and hills in the landscape frescoes and the unbounded, all-over patterns of some styles of vase decoration. It is evident in the fondness for the sea in general, and the tentacled creatures in particular, whose energies expel themselves through boneless tendons to merge with the fluid forces of the environment. It is also evident, though usually in a somewhat different way, in the fondness for vegetable motifs on land, with their forces channeled in narrow stems to expand and burst forth in bloom.

It is this quality of dynamics which explains the characteristic shape of Minoan vases. Commonly, they have high centers of gravity (the greatest diameter well above the central point of the height) and relatively small feet, with the base minimized. The profiles consist of a single luxuriant sweep of line from bottom to top—an unchecked flow of movement of generous contour. This is the exuberance of a movement extravagantly conceived and freely fulfilled.

The conceptual form, too, reveals the same tendency. In Minoan art the activities depicted, while often extremely animated, are seldom strenuous; the bullfighters soar lightly and effortlessly over the beasts, and the bulls, in spite of their weight, charge in an almost dreamlike movement across the ground; the warriors drift briskly along the corridor; the priest-king moves without effort, in majestic calm, among the flowers. Occasionally there will be a scene of more intense action: strangely enough, the fresco, depicting an officer inspecting or setting a guard, in which the figures are all standing at attention, the soldiers bracing themselves in taut rigidity, seems to have a greater concentration of energy under tight control than many more violent scenes.

In architecture, this exuberance manifests itself in a variety of ways. One is in the extent of the palaces, which are expanded unreservedly, seeming to wander over the terrain in response to will and whim. Another is in the swelling, almost explosive quality of the columns rising from tight, neat bases to expanding, even-spreading, and bulging members at the top. Still another is the manifold diffusion of lines of movement and the extraordinary eccentricity, or asymmetry, we have already observed. This appears in such features as the "divided flow" entrance or passage, where traffic is diverted to right and left of a central pillar or support; by the bent-axis in many volumes; the L-shaped corridors or halls which are a natural corollary of the bent-axis plan, as in the domestic quarter at Knossos, but which are apparent also in L-shaped arrangements of different character in the "theatral areas," with seats on two adjoining sides. It is also evident in the multiple, conflicting axes of important rooms such as in the *piano nobile* at Knossos; the location of entrances—even major ones—in corners or off-center on a wall; the strangely inconsequential arrangement of corridors leading from the southwest entrance of Knossos with access to the grand entrance of the *piano nobile* but leading ultimately by an awkward extension to an insignificant point at the end of the main courtyard. In general, the lack of symmetry, the lack of strong dominants, and the common practice of eccentric arrangement are characteristic. The exceptions, such as the symmetrical design of the façade at the narrow end of the court at Phaestos and some of the major rooms at Phaestos, seem to demand special explanation which may, indeed, lie in their location on the south coast facing Egypt. But, in general, throughout Minoan art, the basic dynamic quality seems to be one of free mobility and spirited and vivid exuberance.

In the matter of dynamics, Mycenaean art lacks the completely free, relaxed mobility of Minoan work. The forces are constrained in symmetrical arrangements and two-dimensional planes; but they are, at the same time, more vigorous. The result is a fairly sturdy balance, conspicuous in the plan of megaron and propylon and in much of the pottery, where the symmetrical patterns bring one force into perfectly compensated balance with another. It accounts for the peculiar quality of the lion hunt dagger from Mycenae (Plate 56), where the main stream of movement goes from hilt to point, only lightly checked by the position of the head of the second lion. The third lion, in the center of the composition, turns his back on his comrades and faces the approaching hunters, thrusting himself toward them. His position reverses the movement of the design and brings it back to the center. This is true not only of the conceptual form but of the lines—the long, sweeping, lightly curved lines of the fleeing animals, the more roundly curved profile of the resisting beast, and the angular forms of his hindquarters at more or less right angles to the main line of movement. It is revealing that even as the lion seems to be lunging forward, the hind quarters seem to be gripping the ground. This is an effect of conceptual form and the direction and kind and degree of torsion of the lines.

On the whole, the dynamics of Mycenaean art is not only more vigorous but more firmly controlled than that of the Minoan. The result is a kind of balance—not, to be sure, the impressively static balance of the Egyptians, or the firm restraint of opulent pressure in Hither Asia, but an organized, directed release of energy.

Finally, in the neolithic art of the mainland we note a distinctly different manner—a dynamic of violence, agitation, electric shock.

SYSTEM

There are more definite characteristics in the area of arrangement. In Minoan art the system tends toward irregularity. This is most conspicuous in the plans of the palaces, which, in large part, are strikingly haphazard accumulations of apartments and quarters. At Knossos, the effect is unusually strong, perhaps because the palace is a natural agglomeration of structures through several centuries. Elsewhere, and in the reconstructions of Knossos, are apparent efforts to impose some degree of regularity. But even so, and even in closely conceived units like dwelling quarters, the arrangement has as its most attractive features a casualness and a lack of regular system. So, too, in much of the painting—fresco or vase—the order is not one of regular rhythm, binding every element directly to all the others, like meshwork, but of immediate connection, binding each element to its neighbor, like a chain. The distinction is most noticeable in contrasting some rigorously ordered pattern like the late shields on the stairwall of the domestic quarters or the procession in the south corridor at Knossos and the frieze of partridges.

Mycenaean work is much more regular. The arrangement of vase designs is according to system, not impulse; a scene of action is marshaled; even the trees in the Mycenaean chariot scene are ordered as in a formal park. More striking, perhaps, are the regular checkerboard patterns of the floors of the great halls, and the ceiling patterns, like that at Orchomenos, and the designs of spirals in regular ranks and files. Most impressive is the regularity of the axially symmetrical design of megaron and gate.

FOCUS

Within the somewhat irregular system of Minoan art the focus is relatively weak. This quality, indeed, constitutes one of its most distinctive pecularities in contrast to Egypt and Hither Asia, as indeed to much of the art of Europe.

In fresco, the tendency is hard to identify, perhaps because few complete specimens survive. In vase design, the characteristic is pervasive. In the patterns on most of the vases the devices are seldom centered; they lie at odd angles and at casual spots on the surface, covering the surface more or less uniformly. Again, this contributes to the sense of easy mobility and relaxation but deprives the design of a thoroughly co-ordinated focus. Most obvious is the lack of any special dominant in architectural design, either at entrances or elsewhere.

Mycenaean architecture presents a marked contrast. There are controlling dominants in elevation and plan, in the pylons and megarons; individually, the megarons and pylons are axially symmetrical, with the main axis open to the flow of traffic. Within the megaron there is a strong dominant in the hearth and throne dais, although the dais is at one side and not on axis at the end.

A striking contrast is the treatment of the octopus motif, which in Minoan art is thoroughly casual and freely spread out and in Mycenaean art is rigidly symmetrical with a strong central focus. This is true of the floor panels and of the vases, where, moreover, the patterns are arranged symmetrically on the prominent symmetrical axes. Most striking is the Mycenaean manner of depicting Minoan style, costumes, and hairdress (Plate 52); the horizontal flounces of the skirt are arranged with rigid regularity and divided, somewhat illogically and unnaturally, in the center to achieve as much symmetry as is consistent with the conceptual form, thus producing a garment that resembles a divided skirt. Strands of hair fall in groups of three strands, the strands regularly reproducing each other, the group symmetrically disposed in front and behind. The effect of this (in part at least) is to identify a point of focus in an otherwise undifferentiated expanse. The outstanding example of such a point of focus is the heraldic design of the sculpture over the lion gate at Mycenae. Some distinctive features of Minoan style, like the inconsequential play of light and dark across a scene, tending to conflict and dilute the more disciplined effect, are avoided in Mycenaean art.

COHESION

A corollary of the free-field, generalized system or arrangement in Minoan art is the lack of any strong sense of tectonic structure. Not even in architecture do we find a feeling for the smaller composite elements of the whole. Generally the columns lack bases, and when bases are included they are exiguous—slight disks on which the columns stand, with no developed form or character. The capitals, though they may be large and conspicuous, emerge flamboyantly from the shaft as though they were a swelling of the shaft instead of a separate member. Rarely is there organization of the superstructure over the columns to suggest the composite elements of an entablature. In the characteristic screen wall of the domestic apartments, the conception is one of openings cut in a sheet of material rather than of post-and-lintel construction. Miscellaneous rooms, all within a relatively narrow range of size and all relatively small, preclude any sense of ordered, logical, tectonic structure. In the vases, bases are seldom emphasized, if they exist; the profile of a vase is commonly one exuberant curve from beginning to end. Figures in sculpture or painting are seldom articulated; the emphasis is on fluid unity rather than the unity of composite ordered parts.

Lacking a tectonic structure, Minoan art has an organic structure similar to that of a tree or other plant; the composing units are microscopic cells, and the broader elements of composition emerge from each other and blend into each other. Of course, it is possible to depict such an organism in terms that will clarify the broader structural elements by defining the significant points of articulation in the area of emergence. Minoan artists preferred not to define the articulations in this way but instead sought to follow the same principle of emergence. For this reason the parts of a design tend to serve as transitions or to create whole, relatively undifferentiated patterns. Between such vividly differentiated components as the bands of light and dark across a fresco, the uneven, wavy lines bounding the separate areas allow a degree of interpenetration and detract from the establishment of distinctly apprehended firm forms of a structurally articulated whole.

In contrast, again, the structure of Mycenaean art seems characteristically a tectonic one rather than spontaneous and organic, the characteristics of Minoan work. A Mycenaean vase is more likely to have a well-defined, clearly articulated foot, shoulder, neck, and rim instead of a single sweeping curve from base to top. The Mycenaean palace consists of a series of courtyards with connecting pylons; the formal public area with its chief megaron and its court are strongly differentiated and segregated from the sensibly smaller, more intimate and casual living areas; the megaron itself is boldly distinguished from but integrally a part of its special court and has a vigorously articulated porch (and vestibule) and hall; there are other megarons, at least at Tiryns, and a maze of smaller rooms. All this is like a wall of large blocks and small stones packed between the joints; it possesses an "architectural" quality in its cohesion which the generalized casual parataxis of elements in Minoan architecture clearly lacks.

SUMMARY

Summarizing early Aegean art, we distinguish readily several styles. In Crete the native style throughout is characterized by conceptual form drawn chiefly from nature—notably vegetable and marine—but not primarily human; and the conceptual form is employed more in its aesthetic aspect than rationally. The materials are slight and varied. The aesthetic elements of movement, light, and color are most conspicuous;

texture is also noted, but to a lesser extent. There is a tendency toward abstraction approached subjectively; the kind of signification remains in some doubt. Beyond this, the style employs a sketchy kind of delineation, clear but not definite and precise; the configuration is predominately linear but includes two dimensions; the dynamics are strikingly mobile. In arrangement there is an irregular system (with the focus not emphasized) and organic cohesion. Finally, the style is notable for the intimacy and directness of its relation to the spectator. In the long history of this culture, there were, to be sure, many variations upon this theme and some fundamental deviations; particularly toward the end, a direct influence from the mainland is perceptible.

On the mainland itself, the art of the neolithic period is remarkable for its emphasis on movement and color in aniconic conceptual form; the objects known to us are almost entirely ceramic. There may be sensed a tendency toward particularism in the variety of designs; they are objectively rendered, and presumably lack symbolism. The style is vividly clear, almost exclusively linear, and electrically forceful in its dynamics. Arrangement is irregular, unconcentrated, undifferentiated.

In the succeeding Early Helladic period (although we have not dealt with it in our previous survey, the evidence being exiguous) the material is again almost exclusively ceramic. The conceptual form presents a curious anomaly: much of the pottery is decorated, if at all, by irregular color patterns produced in firing; other pottery imitates this effect in paint. This could be regarded as iconic conceptual form, in being drawn from the function and nature of the material and technical processes themselves. Pottery with designs are purely geometrical patterns, some of which may be drawn from basketwork, and, in a sense, are iconic. It may be described as idealistic and subjective, and hardly symbolic. The art is plain, two-dimensional, and relatively static, though the eccentricity of the shapes of some vases and the lack of pronounced feet or bases give it a kind of instability. The arrangement is somewhat irregular and concentrated, the cohesion organic.

Mycenaean art represents the developed phase of the style which begins with Middle Helladic, under Minoan influence. Materials are varied but include more ponderous substances than Minoan. The conceptual form is iconic, drawn from the more vigorous aspects of nature—war and hunting rather than peace and agriculture—though Minoan marine and floral motifs are freely borrowed. The chief sensory stimuli are movement and color. Mycenaean art tends more toward abstraction than Minoan, and perhaps toward expressionism; the signification, again, is in doubt. It is matter of fact in its solid clarity, includes two-dimensions as well as line, is vigorous, and is balanced dynamically. In arrangement it is regular, focused, and architectonically cohesive.

To the Minoans, then, reality is subjective, at least to some extent, and sketchily though clearly defined; it is irregular and diffusive, but fully integrated and interrelated in its parts in a kind of organic continuum. Reality consists not in particulars but in essences, which are of the nature of non-material, non-substantial, continuously mobile energies. To the Minoans, the important realities were those common to all living nature—life itself, the flow of life force in all living things. To the Mycenaeans, on the other hand, while they too viewed reality as subjective and existing as non-material forms rather than as substances or particulars, reality was more stable, more clearly and completely defined, more regularly and structurally ordered. The important realities were those of human life, especially its stern and vigorous side.

CHAPTER IV

The Art of the Classical World

W HEN ONE THINKS of "classical art," he often, and not unnaturally, thinks of Greece and Rome as a unit, as exponents of a single
style distinct from "Oriental" or some other entity. Indeed, to distinguish Greek from Roman as we intend to do is to distinguish things
more intimately related than those we combined in the chapters on
Hither Asia and the Early Aegean. And yet, because of the specific
importance of Roman art in later European art, it seems worthwhile
to make this distinction.

GREEK ART

The end of the second millennium before Christ brought shock
and upheaval to the ancient world. Though they hardly destroyed the
political and cultural patterns of Egypt and Hither Asia, their effects
were everywhere crucial and in the Aegean catastrophic. In Egypt and
Asia, the balance of political power was permanently redistributed,
and new measures of energy, from new sources, were released in the
sphere of cultural development. In the Aegean, the cultures of Crete

and the Mycenaean world were virtually annihilated in a quick series of events that were genuinely cataclysmic, so that almost all cultural activity is lost from view for several centuries.

During the thirteenth and twelfth centuries B.C., there was a general restlessness among the peoples of the Aegean and the Mediterranean beyond, possibly stimulated by the arrival of a wave of Indo-European peoples including the Dorians, the last of the major Greek tribes to enter the peninsula. Among its effects were the migrations of earlier Greek stock from the Hellenic peninsula to the western coast of Asia Minor in the eleventh and tenth centuries. Subsequently, in the eighth century, tradition reports the founding of many colonies in Sicily and the west and the shaping of nation states. The "geometric" style of the minor arts of metal and pottery of the period gives a name to the whole culture of the time.

In the seventh century, shifting economic conditions and the stimulus of the foreign contacts of the preceding century led to fundamental social and economic turmoil and political reforms. Increasing trade and colonization through the entire length and breadth of the Mediterranean and Black Sea brought an overwhelming flood of novel cultural ideas from all sides, chiefly Egypt and Hither Asia, reflected in the unassimilated agglomeration of "orientalizing" motifs in the ornamentation of various objects of art.

The beginning of the sixth century saw the culmination of these movements in men like the statesman Solon, who was besought to make order of the chaos in Athens. There followed assimilation and integration of the many elements, traditional and foreign, which had come into the stream of Greek culture. In this "archaic" period developed the primary, severe stage of the style that is usually meant by the term "classic Greek." A new stimulus came with the end of the sixth century, which brought to Athens the democratic reforms of Cleisthenes, and the Persian Wars, which stimulated the formation of an empire and the production at an unequaled rate of Greek art, literature, and philosophy to make the fifth century truly a Golden Age. In spite of political reverses, these forces continued to nourish cultural productivity through the fourth century, the age of Plato, Aristotle, and Demosthenes.

The Art of the Classical World

In 334 began the world conquests of Alexander the Great, continuing until his death in 323, an epic adventure of genuinely critical import in world history. By uniting the civilized world east of Italy—European Greece, Hither Asia to India, and Egypt—in a single realm, and bequeathing it to Greek rulers, all of a single cultural tradition, he created a situation in which the perspectives of individuals and states alike were brought into new scale and cultural interchange and mutual assimilation were not only easier than before but much more spontaneous and, indeed, an essential prerequisite for continued existence. In this world appeared not only new nations but also new cities—Alexandria, Antioch, Pergamum, and countless others less large and famous—cosmopolitan in spirit and rooted in the new age rather than the past. Like the early cities of Greece, they caught and formed the mainstream of the new culture.

Thus the Hellenistic age, beginning with Alexander, represents a direct fusion of three older traditions: Egypt, Hither Asia, and Hellenic Europe. But the dominant strain was Hellenism through the end of the first millennium. By then a tide from the west, which began with the Roman conquest of Macedonia in 168 and culminated in the conquest of Egypt in 30, became visibly effective in various ways. The new tide scarcely recast the shape of the culture, but it has sufficient importance to deserve a special accounting from its own roots through its mergence with the Graeco-Oriental components of the ancient world. It is proper as well as convenient to consider the stream of Hellenism from the Dark Age and Homer to the time of Christ as a single period, in spite of internal differences.

Conceptual Elements

Through this relatively short but rich history, and through the many forms of aesthetic expression, the conceptual form remains remarkably constant. With the apparent exception of the pottery, the chief product preserved from the Dark Ages and the "geometric" period, which is seemingly aniconic in its ornament, the art is a thoroughgoing naturalism of a specific and limited kind.

From the tenth and ninth centuries, almost nothing survives except a few vases. The ornament consists of some parallel lines laid on as the vase spun on the wheel; the contrast of large areas of dark with large areas of light; and a rare scattering of more elaborate motifs—squares, triangles, swastikas, zigzags, checkerboards, and diamonds in simple or moderately complex patterns. In the tenth century, the amount of decoration is severely limited and the prevailing character is that of the solidly colored ground; by the eighth century, in the fully developed geometric, the decorative patterns, more intricately developed but the same in kind, may cover the entire surface of the vase (Plate 63).

It seems beyond possibility that the designs represent anything in nature in any useful sense; they can hardly be stylized or formalized animal or vegetable forms, no matter how abstracted. The earlier, largely linear, designs may be called aniconic, though they take their form from the natural processes of making a vase. The more elaborate patterns were probably developed in weaving; in vases, taking their form from pre-existing things, the patterns are in fact iconic, though we do not mean that the vase-painter intended to depict a woven fabric on the vase.

With the exception of the ornamentation on geometric and proto-geometric pottery, the conceptual form of Hellenic art is substantially naturalistic (Plates 64–76). Whether it be the literature from Homer to Meleager or, for that matter, the work of Greek writers of Roman and Byzantine times, the pictorial form of literature derives from nature; so also that of painting, sculpture, and the minor arts. Similarly, the conceptual form of architecture is derived from the natural functions of structure and use. Nothing is fanciful, nothing arbitrary.

Within naturalism, conceptual form is restricted very largely to animal life, and within animal life, largely to humankind, and the emphasis is largely on the human being as such, his "ethos" rather than his activities, although his activities ("praxis") and experience ("pathos") are frequently depicted for what light they shed on the man himself.

Nowhere in Greek art do we encounter an interest in landscape until the last phases of Hellenistic art. Rarely is landscape admitted even to the extent of a quasi-symbolic tree trunk, as in the Alexander mosaic; when we see a cowherd with his cattle in a valley (Plate 69), the tree and the line of the hill are not present as landscape but as setting for an action. But there is no use laboring this point, for Greek art is notoriously barren of landscape even as setting for its compositions.

From the literary arts also has come a general impression that the Greeks were insensitive to landscape. That they were aware of natural beauty is clear from the many allusions to nature in the fragments of Alcman and Alcaeus, the ode to Colonus of Sophocles, and innumerable passages from Theocritus, and indeed almost all the poets from the time of Homer. But rarely is nature the central form. Most of the allusions in Homer and the other poets are imagery in the narrow sense: devices to provide color, light, motion, and the like. The passages from Theocritus are remarkably sketchy—mainly part of the atmosphere, and not presented as the prime subject. The fragments from the earlier lyric poets remain fragments so that we do not know the original emphasis, although we have little doubt that accounts of nature were secondary. Although we may be sure that the Greeks were, on the whole, sensitive to landscape, responding to its beauty and its impact on the senses and emotions, Greek artists seldom, if ever, chose landscape as the central formulation of aesthetic devices.

Though there are some references in literature to the interest of famous painters in flowers and fruit, the exact form this took is not clear, and among preserved remains of Greek art there are no examples of still life or other depictions of plant forms as such. Nor in literature is there any concentrated attention on plants, though multitudes of allusions to plants and flowers of all kinds are used for color and not as objects of interest in themselves. It is seldom that anything approaching a description of a plant is offered.

It is, of course, perfectly true that in formal ornament—borders and decorative patterns—floral motifs are common. Often these were more or less highly abstracted and formalized, as in the Lesbian leaf patterns and various kinds of anthemia; sometimes they were more freely close to nature. But, once again, such uses were strictly secondary, and rarely did patterns of this sort become the chief matter in a composition.

With regard to animals, the situation is somewhat different. There exist many vases, especially Archaic and earlier, in which the central design, which would commonly be of a man or a group of men, is an animal or group of animals; major works of sculpture were worked out in animal forms as in some of the Archaic pediments of the Athenian Acropolis or the bull of the Areopagus and Myron's cow. Horses commonly appeared with riders (or as parts of centaurs), and they often (notably as centaurs) assume at least equal importance with the human element. It is clear that in the visual arts animals often were used as the basic and dominant form, although the proportion of such work in the totality of painting and sculpture would surely be small. In literature, on the other hand, animals are conspicuous by their absence; except in Aesop, they receive as little attention as plants.

Though the humanism of the conceptual form of Greek art needs little argument, it may be useful to discuss its limitations. In contrast to other cultures, those of Egypt and Hither Asia, the conceptual form of Greek art is based on the person experiencing and sometimes on the experience itself, but not on the thing experienced. In Egypt, the conceptual form is (largely) human activity, with a rational emphasis; one is primarily interested in what is going on and how. In Hither Asia, the conceptual form is once again action, events, the doing of something, with perhaps greater aesthetic than rational emphasis; there is less concern for what and how than for the sensory effect of the action. In the arts of Egypt and Hither Asia we see the harvesting of fields and the sacking of cities; in Egypt we learn how harvesting was carried out and the significance of the conquest, and in Hither Asia we are impressed by the abundance of the harvest and the ferocity of the monarch. In Greek art, however, the major concern is the person who experiences and his experience; the action—what he does and what happens—merely illuminates this person. Even in the Parthenon frieze, the action—the procession and worship of the goddess—is depicted reasonably and clearly, yet the narration of this event is simplified to an extreme, and never do the events in themselves absorb our attention. On the other hand, the enlargement of the figures to fill the entire space, so that the sense of a procession as an event in time and space has been excluded, allows the figures to dominate the impression (Plate 74).

Indeed, of all classical Greek reliefs, the Parthenon frieze would come closest to the concept of the event being dominant; in most sculptural compositions the event is of practically no concern. One is always made aware by some detail that the relief depicts a battle of the gods and giants, or the Greeks and Persians, or Greeks and Amazons, or Lapiths and centaurs; but the viewer is not interested in these scenes as battles—how they were fought and who won; the emphasis is on the participants and the effect of the event upon them (Plate 72). Very few sculptural compositions depict a historic event, particularly in the classical period; and even in a Hellenistic rendering of a contemporary scene, like the wars of Pergamenes and Gauls, the contemporary event is lost among depictions of mythological events. This lack of interest in the particular event is significant in several ways; here it simply illustrates the lack of concern of the Greek for the events *qua* events; to the Greek the human being, divine or mortal, was in himself the object of interest, together with his experience.

Perhaps there is a need to emphasize that concentration on the human being as such as the conceptual form of Greek sculpture does not mean simply concentration on human anatomy, although quite commonly, and for useful, practical reasons, the history of Greek sculpture is often written in terms of the manner of rendering anatomical forms. It is evident that Greek sculptors were interested in anatomy, in varying degrees and with varying emphases throughout the entire development of the art, and at times certain artists may well have felt that anatomical structure and detail was the ultimate conceptual form. But sculptors who possessed supreme skill and acute observation, like those responsible for the Parthenon, were selective in their choice of anatomical detail to be rendered, and in the Hellenistic period some sculptors introduced arbitrary and gross exaggerations. In other words, the human being who was the source of the conceptual form of Greek art, in addition to being an anatomical mechanism, was also an ethos, pathos, and praxis—a "kind of being" that experiences and acts; the anatomical structure was simply part of the "kind of being," and something of the sculptor's understanding is reflected in his emphasis on and interpretation of anatomy.

One often has the impression that drawings on vases differ from sculpture in that they are widely varied in their subject matter and depiction of human activities. In the major works of vase painting, however, we find the same characteristics as in sculpture. Exekias (Plate 65) is not really so much interested in a game of dice as in the concentrating players. Today, a scene of revelry certainly has a greater interest for its action, but there must always have been a large share of attention for the figures and their experience. (This is especially clear when only a single drunken figure is depicted.) In vases decorated with genre scenes, a different proportion of emphasis appears, and the "subject matter" or action takes a larger place, not only as a matter of interest but as a vehicle of aesthetic communication. It is notable that in Greek art such imagery is found chiefly in distinctly minor works.

In literature, the dominance of the person over the activity is in some ways even clearer. Comparing the *Iliad* and *Odyssey,* one would admit immediately the greater significance of event in the *Odyssey.* The *Iliad* has an extremely simple story, almost artificially protracted. It includes many actions of considerable interest, but few people today enjoy it simply as an adventure story and even in times of antiquity (when it was memorized and recited) it can hardly have been the story itself which held the interest. Rather, the main characters dominate the scene: Hector—and Hector's fate; Achilles—and his fate (indeed, even in the *Odyssey,* Odysseus and his fate is the major theme). The pattern of action and event, however vivid and exciting, serves chiefly to develop and intensify our picture of the man and his experience; without these, both poems would disintegrate in a turmoil of incoherent incidents.

Apart from the major action, there is an abundance of minor incidents. These are the passages, often in stereotyped form, which present the performance of a sacrifice, setting sail in a ship, enduring death on the field of battle. Similar are the vignettes of life which serve as similes—the woodsman, the dairy yard, the fisherman. These are passages of vivid narrative, and whatever other purpose they serve they seem also to rely for the effect on the outline of action itself. But these passages are largely "imagery," in the sense of figures, allusions, verbal touches, to create color, movement, and other sensory stimuli in molding the primary forms of action and experience. Once again, it is not so

much the action itself that is of primary interest—except to the anti-
quarian. We are not diverted by varieties of sacrifice or ways of
preparing food or of setting sail; the same action, relived in the same
way, recalls the same experience, and it is the experience which is
evoked for its sensory impact. We are, to be sure, shocked by the variety
of ways men are killed, but our interest is not clinical; retelling keeps
alive the horror of the oblivion of death.

In lyric poetry there is little room for incident, though the formulation of an Anacreontic in terms of a visit from a storm-tossed Cupid
emphasizes the possibility of such narrative form against the fact of its
lack of favor. Insofar as it can be determined from the fragments, few if
any of the elegiac iambic or lyric poems were cast in the form of an
action interesting for its own sake; even the Homeric hymns, not
excepting the hymns to Demeter and Apollo, where plot interest is
hardly to be disputed, are formed rather on personality than incident.

In dramatic and quasi-dramatic forms, including the dithyramb, we
would expect action and event to loom large. Here, strangely enough, it
is in the choral dithyramb, or such works as Bacchylides' *Theseus,* that
event dominates form. In contrast, there are few tragedies in which
action is the dominant form. In the first place, the essentials of all the
stories were well known to the audiences before the first production; to
these essentials, most plays add little. In the second place, little of the
action is presented. The dramatic effect of most of the plays depends on
something other than plot: Medea's murder of her children is dramatic,
though hardly as an event, since we do not see it nor is it described in
detail. Almost none of the sparse action of the *Oresteia* happens within
view of the audience; there is, to be sure, a great deal that happens of a
spectacular sort in the movements of the rich choruses, but the action of
the story occurs off-stage, and insofar as it figures aesthetically in the
drama, it is presented by report. There are a few plays—like Euripides'
Electra, Iphigeneia in Tauris, and perhaps others—in which there is a
real or apparent complex of actions of genuine interest and fundamental
formative significance in the arrangement of the play. The controlling
factor in the development of Sophocles' *Oedipus the King* is the cause
and effect in the chain of circumstances and events leading to the

revelation of certain facts; the "prime mover" in the process may indeed have been Oedipus himself, if not some aspect of the divine, but the larger form and most of the details of the fabric of the play are determined by the events themselves.

Again, this is not to say that Greek drama is without action, and vivid action, in occasional incidents, in the stirring reports of messengers, in such speeches as Clytemnestra's vision of the watchfires bringing the news of Troy's fall from mountain peak to mountain peak, from Ida to Mycenae; or in more than one choral ode involving some such report or picture of action. And, surely, these touches have aesthetic impact in a variety of ways, even if they remain subordinate.

In an analysis of Greek literature, the histories of Herodotus, Thucydides, Xenophon, and others cannot be ignored, and in the present context it might seem that by their very nature these works must needs contrast with the characteristics of Greek literature we have been discussing. For surely in history, if anywhere, event is what gives form to the account. And yet the fact that in the work of Greek historians event is molded by character and personality constitutes one of the singularities of Greek historical accounts. It is fundamental to Herodotus that he narrate incident in terms of the chief participants and their characters; the bearing of the incidents on the participants, the experience of the participants, is his ultimate interest. Whatever more philosophical view of history he may have had, Thucydides openly casts his story in terms of its leading figures—Pericles and Kleon, Nikias, Alcibiades—and tends to personalize his protagonists Athens and Sparta when they speak through their representatives or when Athens speaks anonymously through her envoys to Melos. Xenophon's *Cyropaedia* is the extreme instance of this quality, since here a historical and sociological treatise is cast in the form of a man almost wholly created for the purpose.

In later literature, without attempting to deal exhaustively with the subject, one easily finds grounds for continued application of this characterization. Preference for this conceptual form led to the Platonic dialogue, a philosophic discourse cast in the quieter form of the expression of human personality. The details of Socrates' life are few, but we have a full picture of his person. Oratory, judicial as well as political, which might have taken a form of logical conviction without aesthetic persuasion, actually employed both on equal terms, and the conceptual form in the most outstanding works, even where there might have been alternative choices, was from the human personality. Thus, Demosthenes' defense of his crown is an analysis of himself as a personality and statesman; his analysis of the crisis in Athenian policy is framed on the person of Philip. The *Idyls* of Theocritus, and the others, though they include passages of action, never develop a plot as such, only a personality or a mood. The so-called idyl of the festival at Alexandria is more aptly called a mime; others are often disappointing in their failure to develop a potential theme of action. Even the *Argonautica* of Apollonios Rhodios, which of the major works of Greek literature depends most—or was intended more than any other to depend—on action and the suspense of adventure, the work being largely a compilation of heroic adventures from all sources woven into one great task, finds its unity in its hero, and surviving influence and interest rest in its formulation of mood and emotion.

It is true that from earlier days there had been a strain of literature in which action seems dominant. This is exemplified in Aristophanic comedy, where the action interest is at least as large as anything else in the plays, though rather distinctly separated. In the New Comedy, personality came to assume a more positive dominance in an integrated conceptual form, though a more sophisticated plot gives a new vitality to the events themselves. But this strain of dominant action remained minor in Greek literature until the Hellenistic period and the development of the cycle of romances. Although no romance from this period survives for detailed analysis, they seem to have taken their form almost exclusively from patterns of event and action; the personalities of the participants, and their experience, become more and more stereotyped and casual.

In summary, the conceptual form of the pictorial and literary arts is the human being and his internal life—not his environment, associates, or activities; and the emphasis is not simply descriptive, clinical, informational (rational) but aesthetic, working primarily on or through the senses. Through the history of Greek art there is some development of this conceptual form as understanding of the human being was deepened and enlarged and as factors of manner varied. But fundamentally it remains the same.

The conceptual form of Greek architecture, like that of the other arts, remains little changed, fundamentally, throughout its entire history. The most common forms of Greek buildings include the temple and related religious structures; the stoa, of many purposes, civic and religious; assembly buildings, including both open theaters and enclosed halls; and houses. Their special character from the point of view of use-function, and the peculiarities of the major structural forms from the point of view of structure-function, deserves some consideration (Plates 77–82).

The chief purpose of the temple seems to have been to provide protection and shelter to the more solemn and valuable objects of worship and cult possession. The temple, in the normal Olympian cult, was not intended to provide space for acts of worship except in minor personal devotion, as a worshipper might stand before the image of the god in solitary prayer; the official rites of worship took place almost entirely in the open air—the procession, the sacrifice with attendant hymns and prayers, the devotional acts like ritual dances or other mimetic performances, dedicatory contests and the like, all occurred in the open around the altar and outside the temple. Thus the temple served only to house cult objects and treasures of the divinity and the image of the god when it was not active elsewhere. For such a purpose a temple need be only the simplest kind of enclosed room, which in fact it always was essentially and often was in superficial effect, in the small *prostyle* or *distyle in antis* temple.

Such an interpretation, it is true, is at odds with the spirit of the theory of the descent of the Greek *distyle in antis* temple from the Mycenaean megaron, in which the megaron was essentially a living space and not a storeroom. But if the Greek temple is in fact the descendant of the Mycenaean megaron, the chief difference is surely in the disappearance of the living facilities. We must assume that in the dark ages the priest-king abandoned the megaron for another dwelling, leaving the megaron solely for the protection of the divine spirit. In the process such significant living elements as the hearth, the courtyard, and (with reference to the later phases) the Minoan adjuncts were stripped away.

Thus the interior of the cella served the purpose of a box; if it had a porch this was partly for adornment and partly to shelter the entrance. If the building became peripteral, with one or two rows of columns on all sides, this development had nothing to do with the cult or other religious needs; it may indeed have had distinct and valued aesthetic effects, but from the point of view of use-function its purpose can only have been to provide free and easily accessible protection from sun or rain. Though this may seem a trivial reason for the tremendous and costly colonnades of later temples, and certainly was not the most important reason, it was with little question the only use-function of the arrangement.

Though the forms of worship, normally followed in the open air, had definite patterns, there was no definite pattern to the arrangement of the sanctuary in which they were held. Indeed, Greek worship of the Olympian gods required only an altar that could be approached with sacrifices. It might be protected by enclosing walls and the sanctuary adorned and elaborated to a lavish degree by temples, stoas, and monuments both architectural and sculptural, but nothing in the arrangement was imposed by rite except the space needed to move about the altar and the path to approach the altar. Ritual might often include ceremonial acts of ablution or a more or less intricate series of liturgical acts along the way to the altar, but seldom did these demand architectural provision. Thus the Greek sanctuary has no discernible pattern of arrangement among the various monuments fixed by local tradition and ritual, or indeed by any other motive beyond aesthetic preference.

Even more common than the temple in ancient Greek architecture, though less well known today, was the stoa (Plate 81). In essence, it was a wall with a row of columns before it, the two supporting a roof covering the space between. Of this elemental type is one of the most famous of the ancient stoas—the stoa of the Athenians at Delphi. But by elaborating on this simple base a wide variety of forms might be achieved. There might be, for example, a second row of columns and one or two rows of enclosed rooms behind the columns; with any of these ground plans there might be a second story; in some locations, particularly on steep slopes, the stoa might be three or four stories high—though the main façade would never be more than two. The building might be elaborated with wings at each end—either with the columns facing the center, creating a u-shaped plan, or with slightly projecting, forward-facing, templelike façades at each end of the building or at the ends of the bars of the u. Along the front, as an almost essential element of the structure, was normally a narrow cleared space, often terraced. Beyond this, apart from minor arrangements in the category of furnishing or equipping, like the installation of water pipes to bring running water to various rooms, individual wells in each room, dining facilities in each room, food-container counters in the doors of the rooms, or other facilities, one might find examples of stoas enclosed wholly or in part, or left open on all sides, or otherwise adapted structurally to provide the functions of sleeping quarters, storage, passage from one public area to another, or other particularized functions.

But through all these variations persists the common basic form: the long, narrow (or wide and shallow?) roofed area, normally completely open and freely accessible on at least one side. The basic use-function is obvious, to protect from rain while allowing a maximum of light and air and accessibility. The stoa is, in terms of its tradition, simply a canopy spread in a public place to shelter any of an almost infinite variety of functions. But, again in essence, the structure is really only auxiliary: it is a retreat from the primary place of activity, the market or other open place in front of it. Therefore, it is not usually conceived as a covered or partially enclosed area, facing in all directions or accessible from all sides, but as a narrow, borderlike element, facing toward the primary space and accessible only from that space.

Gymnasia and palaestrae (Plate 82, upper left) were two other closely related types of structure close to the heart of Greek culture. These buildings, intended to provide for the necessities of athletic exercise and contests and related activity, consisted usually of open areas lined by colonnades facing inward. A palaestra might be surrounded uniformly on four sides by a peristyle colonnade completely enclosing the central space. This scheme might be abandoned for sufficient reason, as when, for example at Pergamon, the buildings had to be laid out on narrow terraces and the provision of an approximately square central area was not feasible; instead, it was long and narrow, with stoas on one or both sides. Thus the gymnasium, like the agora, was essentially the *area;* but in the palaestra the colonnades were integral with the area; with it they constituted a building. These colonnades, like stoas, might be freely adapted to the particular use to which they might be put— practice courses, dressing or bathing rooms, or even lecture rooms or schoolrooms.

Related to the gymnasium and palaestra, in turn, would be the stadium, and to this the theater. In the stadium, too, the centrally functional part is simply open ground—the running course or open space for athletic display. But the structural part, the seats along and across one end of the running course, was an inseparable part of the totality, since its use-function was to provide for the watching of the contests. Seldom, however, did the architectural development reach beyond the stands; shelter from the elements was not provided. Whether this was a purely aesthetic choice or a practical one—a consequence of factors of structure-function, in that the Greeks were unable to roof a space large enough to contain both spectators and the athletic course, or of a weighing of costs against probable conditions of use; or whether it had some relation to factors of use-function, in that some objection existed against athletics within doors—is not possible to determine.

In the theater, the use-function is similar: a matter of spectators witnessing a performance; and the approximately semicircular shape of the theater as opposed to the elongated shape of the stadium is a direct reflection of the different kinds of performance. So, too, is the peculiar adjunct to the theater, the scene building with its parascenia and later proscenium. The whole development of the theater, from its early form in which the circular orchestra was paramount and the theatron and stage buildings secondary and even temporary; through the fifth and fourth centuries, with the increasing elaboration of the stage building; through the Hellenistic period, with the diminution of the orchestra and the greater prominence of the proscenium and the stage on its roof—all this is a somewhat mysterious but evidently direct reflection in the conceptual form of the building of the use-function—the practices of the drama—for which it was intended. As the style of play changed, so changed the style of theater.

It is difficult to analyze domestic architecture, in view of the limited variety of monuments surviving. It seems to be true, however, that Greek houses were normally not designed for exterior forms; they lined the streets behind continuous walls with little distinction. Little is known of palaces, though the Leonidaion at Olympia is sometimes taken as representative of monumental domestic architecture: here, the exterior is designed as a continuous colonnade (Plate 82, lower left).

There would appear to have been more than one traditional type of Greek house, but most seem to include some kind of interior court. In the type common at Priene, this seems to have been conceived as a genuine court, or yard, on which the house, a complex of rooms, faced; the complex of rooms might lie along two or three sides of the court, and the other sides would be enclosed by a wall or passage; but the separateness of the court as an outdoor yard would be maintained. Another type, found at Olynthus and Delos, was also marked by an open space as the focus of the rooms, but this open space seems to have been treated as a room itself. That is, whether it had columns on only one side, as in the typical pastas house at Olynthus, or columns on three or four sides, as in the peristyle house at Delos, the space open to the sky was a genuine living room in the house, treated with plants and pools, like its modern survivor that we sometimes call the patio, but not simply a yard or court on which the house faced. By way of clarification, one may point to the features of the colonnaded garden characterizing the more luxurious Pompeian houses, which is not a room, nor yet a court, but a garden associated with the house and surrounded by colonnades; and the atrium of the traditional Roman house, which is a room enclosed and covered but with an opening in the roof and ceiling to admit light and afford an outlet for smoke. To be sure, more or less

sophisticated architectural treatments of these various kinds of sp
produced forms which blend the feeling and tradition of one with the
other, but the essential forms remain: the court (taken as an integral
part of the design, as at Priene, and the Mycenaean megaron, somewhat
differently in the Mesopotamian-Assyrian tradition, and quite differently in the Minoan tradition); the patio or peristyle room (with possible representatives in Egypt—certainly in Egyptian temples; possibly
in early Helladic Greece; possibly also an original development in
classical Hellenism) and the Roman atrium or room with a hole in the
roof.

But apart from the peristyle room, the other features of the Greek
house are unimpressive. There is the characteristic design of the Olyn-
thian dining room, square with a border along the edges; and there are,
of course, special adaptations of kitchen and bathroom; but for the most
part the rooms are simple spaces of little distinction. All this reflects,
quite directly, the use-function of the dwelling; a place for family needs
only, where the household affairs may be conducted in seclusion and
with such benefit of sun and air as conditions permit. The rest of life was
lived in public.

In general, then, we find that Greek architecture takes the forms of its
volumes—its conceptual form—direct from use in the simplest and
most logical way possible. The forms yield freely to the particular
demands of particular uses, but the adaptations are always minor. The
Greek style is, then, for all its precision, thoroughly natural in its
conception and development.

The conceptual form of the structural elements is also iconic, both
architecturally, from the standpoint of structure-function, in taking a
shape from the structural role that the elements play, and sculpturally,
in taking a shape depicting some form in the world of nature.

The respects in which sculptural forms in architecture are shaped after
natural forms is obvious and, architecturally, relatively superficial.
There is to be included here the whole array of architectural ornament:
moldings of all kinds and in some degree the particulars of the various
orders as commonly conceived. Thus the rich array of architectural
moldings, with some few exceptions, are derived from natural motifs:

the palmettes, lotuses, anthemia, and acanthus motifs, which appear in many forms throughout the entire history of classical architecture, are clearly derived from nature. The bead-and-reel motif is conceivably an independent, arbitrary creation conceived in the process of working a simple torus, as the torus and scotia themselves may have been, though in all these cases the impression is created that they are imitated from forms in woodwork. In any case, the relation of the Lesbian leaf, the egg-and-dart, and the tongue patterns seems close to the bead-and-reel in the Archaic stages, as though they were variants developed for variety. A motif more common in Hellenistic than earlier times has a less evident natural model, if indeed it has any—the key, or fret, or square maeander.

Another kind of problem appears in regard to the details of the orders. Some minor elements are iconic from nature: such as might appear around the neck of an Ionic column or on an Ionic frieze, or in the viae of a Doric cornice, the acanthus leaves distinguishing the Corinthian capital, or the egg-and-dart on the echinus of an Ionic capital. But the major elements of the various orders can hardly be said to be shaped according to natural forms of the external world unless this be understood in the sense that they depict the forms of wooden construction whose tradition remained in stone architecture long after the structure-function of the various elements had disappeared even from wooden construction (Plates 77–79).

The peculiarities of the Doric entablature sometimes have been explained according to the hypothesis that the architrave was originally a wooden beam bearing a flat plank (whose edge shows as the taenia) on which rested posts with a protective facing consisting of three small vertical blocks (forming the triglyph) held in position at the bottom by nails driven through a cleat and the edge of the plank into the bottom of the blocks (the heads of the nails being represented by the guttae, the cleat by the regulae). On this series of posts rested another plank carrying the ends of the rafters whose under surface shows as the mutules, to which were nailed the boards of the roof itself (the heads of the nails show as the guttae of the mutules). But the theory is robbed of complete conviction by several considerations. One is that another equally plausible theory accounts for the various features in reverse—with the metopes as the posts on the architrave, the triglyphs as a grating between the posts. This theory is based on wood and brick construction rather than wood alone. Another consideration is the failure of either theory to account for the peculiarities of the columns—the fluting, and especially the particular kind of fluting, the echinus, and other details perhaps too minor to be of concern.

The peculiarities of the Ionic order are susceptible to similar, though less specific, interpretation. The bases, and the various kinds of bases, of the order are readily understandable in terms of stone disks supporting a wooden shaft; the capital is purely decorative, derived, no doubt, from Hither Asia but modified under the influence of the suggestion of a partially unrolled scroll to the characteristic form. The architrave is too simple to "explain," with its three fasciae, which may be the faces of three superimposed planks or flat timbers, supporting the dentils, which would be the ends of the rafters. The carved frieze, which substitutes for the dentils in the early examples, where alone the difference might have any meaning in terms of this kind of interpretation, was without particular explanation.

None of the interpretations of the classical forms in terms of wooden structure-function is wholly satisfactory, but while in all probability the classical architects did have a general conception that these details had had a functional existence in wood or wood and brick architecture, they themselves were not so much depicting the forms of that architecture in stone as employing them to clarify the structural logic of the functional system of the new material.

The more fundamental question, then, is whether the shapes of stone column, architrave, frieze, and cornice are formed according to the structure-function they fulfil. In this sense it is one of the qualities of Greek architecture that the structure-function is immediately apparent in the form: the base of the building, with its stepped, pavement-like foundation providing a platform and floor for the structure; the normal design of masonry in the wall with the bottom course higher and often slightly thicker, revealing the special function as support for the wall above; the columns shaped in terms of shaft and bearing-members (and, in the Ionic order, a base supporting the shaft); the entablature designed in forms which lie transversely across the columns supporting the cornice, projecting to carry rainwater and drop clear of the supports; the roof structure, sloping in the simplest, most concise manner with sima, antefix, and ridge palmettes, a direct development of the system of tiling. Even ornamental moldings are arranged to mark transitions—major joints in the structure—and hence are direct outgrowths of structural logic.

In short, as the forms of volumes are drawn from the use-function, the structural forms are drawn from the structure-function, while the plastic forms of ornamental detail are modeled to some extent on the external world of nature. Thus in every respect the conceptual forms are iconic and naturalistic.

SENSORY ELEMENTS

MOTION

In considering the stimuli to the kinaesthetic sense, it is hardly necessary to dwell on sculpture. Apart from the movement of the figures understood as human beings (as conceptual form) running, twisting, stretching, and sitting, the graven lines or carved ridges and hollows that delineate anatomy or drapery constitute lines of the flow of energy and movement. The repeated occurrence of various accents, whether the elements of conceptual form like the feet of a troop of horses or the serried legs and bodies of marching or fighting men, or of formal lines and shapes, establish rhythmic movements. But there is nothing exclusive or novel about the Greek devices for stimulating the sense of motion through sculpture.

With regard to painting, much of what may be said about drawing on vases would doubtless be true of the fresco and panel paintings, and this would be little different from what may be said about sculpture. There is the movement of the conceptual form itself, of the figures *qua* figures; there is the movement of accent and rhythm and flow of line among and through the figures and elements of formal pattern. There is, also, the greater emphasis on drawing—line drawing—and emphatic contour, which carries a larger proportion of movement than in other styles. But there is nothing significantly different in kind.

Perhaps it should be emphasized that even figures conceived as being at rest may contain some implications of movement. At the one extreme, standing figures, particularly draped female figures like the Nikandra statue of the earliest period, are utterly immobile, though in this immobility is a negation of movement, an emphatic affirmation of fixation; and the Moschophoros from the Athenian Acropolis, though the figure stands apparently still and quiet, suggests rest by failing to suggest motion. Among the earliest of these Archaic figures (Plate 71) there is an exaggerated emphasis on those parts of the anatomy which are most significant in movement—the knees, elbows, wrists, and waist. While the figure may be generally conceived as entirely or nearly at rest, these parts of the human form serve as a reminder, a suggestion, and a stimulus to the kinaesthetic sense. In other examples, the exaggerated, unreal, formal, angular running position of Archaic gorgons, or the stiff-legged stride of the cattle in the cattle theft metope of the Sikyonian treasury at Delphi, by their very stiff artificiality suggest the quick staccato movements of some gay dance.

From the latter part of the sixth century on, in addition to the varied obvious and subtle movements of standing or moving figures, there is an increasing variety in the movement and potential movement of seated or reclining figures. The various degrees of relaxation, the casual turn or alert poise of the figures on the Parthenon (Plates 73–74) include a wide variety of the possibilities, but the s-curves of the Praxitelean style, the internal tensions in contorted or even quiet bodies of Scopaic or Lysippan figures, stimulate awareness of the kinaesthetic sensation of muscles in various states of tension. We are aware of them internally, in the moments of readying the body for an action, as distinct from the actual execution of the movement. The possible complexities of the repertoire of movement thus augmented appear in the Pergamene group from the Acropolis in Athens, with its rendering of men or women in a broad scale of movement, from violent action through collapse and decline to utter lifelessness and death, or, more subtly, the implication of the torsion of the Tyche of Antioch, balanced so lightly on the river Orontes. Hellenistic nymphs seated while satyrs dance; Marsyas hanging; Ariadne sleeping; boxers resting, and waiting; all produce a great variety of movements in conceptual form beyond the ordinary and obvious kinds of movement in which figures engaged in traditional kinds of activity would naturally be seen. The development of attitudes of internal movement provided opportunities for devising complex patterns of movement beyond the thought of earlier artists.

Movement in architecture, considered first in its external relationship, aside from the movement of approach inherent in the conceptual form, would be partly a matter of visual progression along the avenue of approach or from building to building, partly a visual reaction to the building itself. Thus the procession of points marked by the edge of the outlying elements—the terrace in front of a stoa, for example—and the accelerated accents of the steps, the recession between the columns, and the repulsion of the wall behind returning the movement to the external area would be a strong stimulus. Similarly, the broad expanse of the building "looking across" the area in front of it would constitute a movement from the building outward. More vivid, though, would be the movements of the façade itself. The long, low, thin horizontals of the steps, rising from the earth; the higher but still broad and horizontal rectangle of the colonnade, its shape and rhythm carrying out the contrasting horizontal movement of the steps, strongly marked with the bold verticals of column and intercolumnar spaces, light and dark; the fluting of the columns subdividing the horizontal rhythms and accentuating the verticality of the columns; the horizontal lines of the entablature, broken in the upper reaches into shorter verticals by triglyphs successively halving the spaces, or doubling the number of the elements below, vertical to carry on the movement of the columns, low to be reconciled to the culmination above, more numerous to compensate for their slighter bulk, and by their greater number accelerating the rhythm of accent, finally merging with the sky either in a triangular pediment over a temple façade, with the sloping lines of the gable breaking the horizontal toward the arch of heaven, or in the long roof line of the stoa or temple flank, where the tiling system finally reduces the movement of line and accent to a shimmering generality that is dissipated, as it were, through the ridge pole palmettes, as lightning rods dissipate static electricity.

In terms of the external volumes, the horizontal and vertical lines of the façade serve to define the external space by establishing height and breadth to the volume, one side of which is formed by the façade; this definition is naturally reinforced when created by a stoa of L or U shape. Apart from the solids of the particular buildings, the spaces around them and among them are part of the composition of shapes, solid and empty, with the concomitant flow of movements.

Internally, a simple lateral movement would be most prominent in a stoa, and in a non-peripteral temple there would be little more than the limited progression from door to interior. But in a peripteral temple there would be the movements of the volume along each peripteron colonnade, and around the cella within the colonnade, that might be composed in more or less elaborate forms; and the movement of successive enclosures in the presence of the mass of the cella within the volume of the outer colonnade, and the movement of variously, if slightly, ordered progress from the exterior through the colonnade and pronaos to the interior, through increasingly confined spaces. All this, of course, without taking into account the movements of the vertical forms in their real though restrained complexities among the shafts of columns and volume of the peripteron corridor, and into the volumes behind the architrave and frieze, into the hollows of the coffered ceiling.

Since the conceptual form in Greek architecture is derived from the basic concept of a container or shelter, the element of movement of the conceptual form of the interior space is not extensive. And yet even in the temple, or at least in those of any complexity, there are some stimuli. There is the sense that the cella of the temple is withdrawn and enclosed by the peripteron—a box put inside another box; there is progression from the exterior, up the steps, through the columns, and across the peristyle colonnade (or around it), up and through the pronaos, up and through the cella—perhaps even to an inner adyton. The horizontal and vertical lines of the steps rising on all sides are not only a visual stimulus but suggest the movement that their intended use implies; and the columns, constituting a screen but a universally penetrable one, similarly suggest by the realization of their normal use the movement in and out. In the stoa, the realization of the function of the structure in enclosing an area strengthens the sense of movement in and out of the colonnade at right angles to the façade; awareness of the colonnade as a promenade supplements the lateral movements in the lateral lines of the structure.

Finally, among the significant movements in Greek architecture are those of the exterior spaces generated by lines of progress for processions through propylons, along roads between sculptural groups or small buildings, to the altars. Such movements in Greek architecture are not as rigorously channeled as in other architectures, or as might be expected from the simple, regular design of the temples and stoas themselves; the ceremonial roads are not sharply defined or laid out by calculation; they follow lines of spontaneous movement and respond readily to accidental diversion.

In literature, one fundamental movement is the rhythm of the words as sound, together with the actual rate at which they are spoken. In poetry, of course, there is the basis of the metric system. Greek poetry developed great variety of formal metric patterns, all based on the quantity of each syllable rather than the stress or tonic accent, though these accents were important in syncopating the metric rhythms so that monotony and singsong were avoided. Metric feet, each consisting of one or more long syllables, and/or one or more short syllables, were combined variously into lines of usually no more than six feet; there were not only the iambics, trochees, dactyls, and anapests familiar in English, but feet of five times (e.g., two longs and a short; a long, a short, a long; etc.) six times, and even seven times. The total made available an unusually large potential for various rhythms and indeed various paces. A spondee, of two longs, though it takes actually no more time to speak than a dactyl of a long and two shorts, moves at a more leisurely pace because the same time span is covered in two rather than three units. It is as easy to produce something light and tripping in iambics as it is to produce something ponderous and solemn in feet of six times or something intricate and sparkling in feet of five or seven times. The variety of Greek rhythms, in fact, is unparalleled.

In prose writing, of course, movement and rhythm of word quantity and stress are less evident; but here, as indeed also in poetry, in addition to the sound rhythm there is a rhythm based on meanings. Even in Homeric verse the basic phonetic rhythm is elaborated by the more or less rhythmic repetition of stock lines, half-lines, phrases, and epithets of gods and heroes, and to encounter these is to recall the others and feel one's place in the rhythmic succession of accents of concepts. When a god or leader issues instructions to a subordinate, and the subordinate delivers the instructions to the intended recipient, he repeats the entire conversation with the commander; or when a ship lands the procedure of furling sail is often reported in the same or similar terms, and when the ship puts to sea again the sail is meticulously unfurled with equally complete and repetitive explanation. These recurrent words, phrases, whole passages, though they may be monotonous in a sense, and though they may derive from the peculiarities of oral composition and transmission, nevertheless contribute effectively to the cumulative effect of ceaseless, wave-like rhythm, with an almost unlimited series of overtones and undertones, harmony and counterpoint, of various but mutually integrated rhythms.

So in succeeding poetry and in prose rhythms, movements slow and fast, monotonous, accelerated, crescendo, are developed by the increasingly elaborate patterns of meaning. To a considerable extent, this is the basis of various formulations in the intricacies of sophistic, Aristotelian, and post-Aristotelian rhetoric. The more elaborate complexities of these rhythms (commonplace though most of them have become) were not evolved until the period beginning with the later fifth-century sophists. Herodotus sought calculated patterns of meanings. His particular quality in this sphere is the eager spontaneity with which his tale moves rapidly through its many episodes; the compelling advance of his narrative is hardly sensed until the reader is deep in the vast flood of human event which he recounts. Thucydides is more conscious of the rhetorical patterns of smaller scale. His basic rhythms are in the sequences of the years, varied by the shift from one theater of war to another, and the alternation of action and reflection represented by the dispersal through the narrative of expository and argumentative speeches, the latter paired in pros and cons to throw the force of movement first in one direction and then the other. The over-all organization of his *Peloponnesian War* is a vivid illustration of the possible change of tempo of movement and its effect; the introductory paragraphs of Book I are calm and static, theoretical and abstract; then comes the broad, distant view of all history; then the tense, concentrated events leading to the causes of the war; then the rapid summary of the rise of Athens; then the moment of discussion when all hangs in the balance and men try to get a grip on themselves; then the catastrophe, followed by a comprehensive, detailed, and measured account of the war itself. Within this, too, there are changes of pace, of which the most notable is the Melian dialogue. This seems to occur outside time and space, like a dream, with motion suspended; in terms of word sound, it is presented in a dry, abstract, schematic succession of observation and response, wholly unlike the fluid, continuous style found elsewhere in this volume. Immediately thereafter begin the long, methodical, careful preparations for the Sicilian expedition, the excited rush of departure, the delays, the gathering concentration of energies in the siege, and the wild agony of the cataclysm. It may be that this is what did happen, that it is part of the conceptual form, but Thucydides need not have presented it so. He must have felt the pulse and change of pace and tension and power of movement; at least, it is embodied in the rhythms and pacing of his composition.

From the latter part of the fifth century the conventional devices of rhetoric were analyzed, described, and used quite generally, and many of these are instruments of movement. Choice of words of long or short syllables; assonance; parallelisms of various kinds; antithesis; repetitions and repetition by indirection (anaphora and antistrophe)—all are means of establishing accents of word or meaning by which rhythms are set in train. When the rhythms are compared to normal usage, they are seen to constitute fast or slow movements of greater or lesser intensity. The periodic style is a complex manner of building such rhythms into elaborate structures, multiplying them to compound, accelerate, and direct their force. Often this involves the element of suspense; the direction of the gathering forces is not revealed until after a moment of poise at the climax.

The special form of Greek drama requires particular notice, since the form involves not only words but direct appeal to the eye in the movements of actors and chorus. Perhaps one should not speak of the movements of the chorus as paralleling the movements of the words or of their speech and movement as a synthesis. One should attempt to conceive of the words and physical movement as an integral entity manifested in different ways, as the music and action and words of Wagnerian opera are an entity. Of course the elements can be taken separately, and one can read a choral ode as one reads the libretto of an opera or perform the choral movements as one plays an operatic melody on the piano; but they were conceived as an entity, as a single rendering of one concept in a composite language. We have no way of visualizing today the exact physical movement of the members of the chorus and the extent to which movements of the hands and body developed the movements of the feet, but there can be no question that the visual impact of the performers stimulated the kinaesthetic sense. So, too, the movements of the actors depicting the various parts of the play.

Viewing now the movement of the conceptual form itself, there is the movement in the *Iliad* that we experience in visualizing the armies pouring into the plain, the surge of battle back and forth, the bright swiftness of the course of some hero through the fray, the suspended animation of camp and field at night, the sudden immobility of death. Indeed, the movement described in the *Iliad* is continuous, ever-different, and always vital, so that to analyze it would be to repeat the poem. In addition to the inclusion of the full panorama of human movement, we might mention here examples of at least a few other kinds of movement; the ethereal effortlessness with which a god moves from mountain peak to plain or sea and the dream-terror of the awful surge of Skamander's flood across the plain in pursuit of Achilles. Of such unreal movements which yet fall within human experience the *Odyssey* adds its own examples—the pitch and crash of stormy waves, the tense race from Cyclops or Laestrygonian, the summer afternoon calm of the land of the Lotus Eaters and Calypso's isle, and the lapse of reality as the ship is buffeted through the storm from known lands to unknown, from Scheria to Ithaca.

In the poetry of succeeding generations, the movement of conceptual forms reveals yet different aspects: the wanderings of Leto, Apollo, and Demeter in the Homeric hymns, the chariot of Aphrodite in its cloud of whirring wings in Sappho's lyric, the grim maneuvers of citizen soldiers in the odes of Alcaeus, Tyrtaeus, and others, the intricate figures of Alkman's dancers, his still mountains. In the drama there looms a curious inconsistency already noted: an art based on action and yet devoid of action. Little of the series of events constituting the plot occurs on the stage; the movements on the stage are for the most part those of the chorus in its character as choral accompaniment, not in its character as participant in the action. Not that this deprives the audience of the impact of the movement; indeed, the habit of reporting action by word of mouth instead of displaying it in progress widely expands the possibility. Thus the leaping signal fires from Troy to Mycenae suggest the quality of the sweeping majesty of divine progress that could never be shown on a stage; Aeschylus' reports of the sack of Troy and the battle of Salamis, Sophocles' story of the chariot race in which Orestes was reported killed, Euripides' description of the sacrifice conducted by Aegisthus and of his subsequent murder, are simply among the more outstanding "messenger's speeches" in which vivid movement is contributed effectively by purely narrative means. At the opposite extreme is the immobile, chained figure of Prometheus whose visible inertness stands in immediate contrast to the imagined wide wandering of Io or the stirrings of cosmic forces.

In Greek comedy, as might be anticipated from the greater importance of plot in the conceptual form, the movement is more naturally immediately present in the spectacle: all the actors perform in full sight of the audience. Thus much of the stimulus to kinaesthetic sense in the comedy derives directly from the visual experience of the performance, even when it coincides with the formulation of the conceptual form as such. But in such scenes as of the procession of the mystae in *The Frogs,* the spectator's conception of the real movement of the Eleusinian mystae, either on the road to Eleusis or on the road to the hereafter, must have affected his reaction to what he saw; what he knew of local processions in celebration of Dionysos added scope to the mock festival in *The Acharnians;* his knowledge of the business of groping down a dark alley in Athens would have enlarged his picture of the jurors assembling in *The Wasps.*

In the work of Greek historians, the movement of the events which are the rational content is usually exploited to assure an aesthetic effect. The pains taken to make explicit not only major but minor movements of troops (the Persians filing through the path above Thermopylae as well as the tactical maneuvers at Plataea, the wild course of the ships at Salamis or the disciplined circling at Naupaktos or the calculated thrust and withdrawal at Aegospotami, the rush of the Plataeans over the Spartan wall, and the subsequent pause while the pursuing Spartans hurry down the wrong road in the dark, the racing ships of the Athenians as they set out to Sicily, the painful struggle of the defeated Athenians along the road after Syracuse) produce tangible sensory effects; they are not simply informative.

Even Plato took time to depict his disputants walking along the road to Athens from Piraeus, strolling in the colonnade of a gymnasium, coming in from the street to a party, and after a night of varied discussion, a dawn of subdued, desultory activity amid general quiet. Moreover, the central concept of the philosophic argument is projected in some sort of motion: in the *Republic* there is the varied activity of the state, illumined by the more dramatic movement of certain inserts such as the experience of Er; in *Crito* the Laws themselves move about the scene; the erratic movement of a spirited team of horses enlivens the *Phaedrus* as it illumines the concept of the soul.

In the Hellenistic period, movement of the conceptual form continues to contribute to aesthetic effect in increasingly elaborate and developed ways. In the *Argonautica,* there is the picture of Medea roaming the palace at night struggling with her emotion. In the Idyls, there is the conventional pattern of people moving quietly and gently through country scenes or of the nymph playing on the beach with her excited dog racing alongside; but there are also the tense, mysterious manipulations of the enchantress, and in such details as Theocritus' carved cup a glimpse of the fisherman straining to gather his net or the foxes creeping stealthily upon the boy preoccupied with his cicadas, the quick drop of fruit from the trees, the cool rush of water from the spring, and the flutter of leaves in the light breeze.

LIGHT AND COLOR

Stimulus of the sense of light is provided in a considerable variety of ways, though with conspicuous limitations. In sculpture, the range of light and dark may range between the bright gleam of smooth-polished material and, at the other extreme, the blank shadow of the space between two figures or the hollows of the drapery or bodily form. Within these extremes are the slighter but more freely manipulated shadows within the folds of drapery of various depth or amid the locks of hair—sharp, thin, and fine if desired, or full and deep, of varying intensity as the depth and boldness of cutting varies. These lights often constitute the visible form of lines of movement, especially the contours of shadows that fall across and around a form, but they also function as light for strong contrast or subtle modulation. Such particularly is the effect of a shadow cast by a large form (a breast, head, or arm) whose successive surfaces receding from the light take on gradually darker and darker tones. Almost all the varied possibilities of luminosity—different degrees and qualities of light and shade, created by carving, pose, composition—are dramatically exploited in the frieze of the great altar at Pergamon (Plate 75). The material itself has a definite role in the luminous effect of sculpture: in the varieties possible among gleaming bronze, with bright, sharp reflections, and the deep, soft, internal luminosity of highly crystalline marbles which glisten even in shadow.

It is this variation of light which constitutes the color in sculpture; in tones of white, black, and gray, these colors are inherent in carving or modeling itself. But Greek sculpture, of course, also used chromatic colors. Not only was bronze in various alloys exploited, but gold and ivory and woods were incorporated. In stone sculpture, buff-gray limestone and white marble were almost universally employed, perhaps because of their properties in carving. But stone sculpture was also painted so that the forms varied chromatically with a distinctness and boldness that we cannot realize today, now that the color is largely gone. In the lack of well-preserved examples of such work, it is fruitless to discuss it, except to observe that it must have increased the brilliance of these figures.

Once again, it is pointless to discuss monumental painting, for examples are rare; we know in general that it was colorful, though it lacked the luminosity of oil. Nor, so far as is known, were light and shadow developed. It is, of course, possible to study the light and color of Greek vases as examples of graphic art. In the geometric period, and the late sixth and fifth centuries, the colors were those of the ceramic fabric itself and the black mat or glaze paint with which the ornament was laid on; in the seventh and sixth centuries, a limited polychromy of mat colors was employed. The black glaze and firm terra cotta of the late sixth and fifth centuries had luminosity, with clear gleams of light. In the drawing, however, there was little light or shadow; some textures were developed by manipulation of lines—soft, billowy fabrics at some times, stiff, hard, pleated, corduroy effects at others.

Light is especially significant in architectural design—brightly illuminated columns set against the shadowed space behind and the graduated shadows cast by the flutes on the cylindrical form of the shaft, so that parts of the surface are in almost full light, parts merge with broader and deeper shadows to the full shadow of the intercolumniation. The details of the entablature are duplicated by the shadows they cast, and the shadow of the cornice falling over the columns or frieze adds new lines to the façade as well as new plane surfaces and different intensities of dark. Moreover, the whole composition is constantly changing as the sun moves on.

Color, again, may be understood in some of the luminous effects, as in sculpture; pigment was freely applied to the buildings to pick out various details. The intent seems to have been twofold—to enliven the surface with bold, brilliant color and to accentuate the structure-function of certain elements.

In the drama, the physical presence of the actors and members of the chorus provides sensory stimuli. The costuming of Aeschylus's *Persians,* of the returning army in the *Agamemnon*—and the red carpet; the costuming in the other plays of the *Oresteia* must have been spectacular indeed. The richness of the costuming in the plays of Aeschylus and Sophocles and their contemporaries may be inferred from the disapproval of the "realistic" costuming favored by Euripides. In general, the importance attached to spectacular effects, that is, color, texture, and kinaesthetic stimuli, may be realized unequivocally from the importance of the liturgy of the choregos and from Aristotle's recognition of the role of spectacle. Little of this can be recaptured now, but there is at least one fact about the spectacle of ancient drama which we know clearly and to which the modern mind finds it difficult to adjust: since all the plays were performed in full daylight, in outdoor theaters, there could have been no "lighting effects." Rarely, as seems possible with the *Agamemnon,* the play itself began at dawn, the hour of the opening of the action, so that the sun dissipated the surviving shadow of morning as the watchman ceases his night's vigil, though the timing would have had to be faultless to produce this effect. In any case, the spectacular gloom which commonly characterize the modern presentations of a play like *The Trojan Women* would have been impossible in antiquity.

Apart from the spectacle of the drama, the color, light, and texture—in the drama itself as well as in other literature—came in part from the words themselves. In comparison to the range of possibilities, there are few color words in Greek literature as a whole. Those which do occur are usually the simple primary colors, and often these are of somewhat dubious color value, as the "xanthos" (does it mean yellow or blond?) Menelaos; and is "glaukopis Athena" gray, dark, or owl-eyed? Phrases like the "white-armed Helen" almost lose color meaning. It would be easy to overemphasize this circumstance, but it is a curious fact: so much color, so much of it from conceptual form, so little from color words.

Another kind of color, from strange and elaborate words and phrases, a color not chromatic and appealing to the visual sense but striking and vibrant for its novelty, was familiar to the Greeks. Aeschylus was noted for his use of unfamiliar and exotic words, and in plays like the *Persians* or *Prometheus Bound* he makes much of foreign names of persons and places. As we have seen, these may be colorful from the point of view of conceptual form, as the names Samoa or Tahiti are colorful to the modern reader for what he knows or thinks he knows of these places; it is also colorful in being strange and foreign, like Xanadu in *Kubla Khan,* with an unusual combination of sounds. So Xerxes, Artembares, Mardonius, Susa, and Bactria must have had a multiple effect on the Athenian listener.

In general, however, one has the impression that Greek literary men did not frequently resort to this kind of color. The verbal oddities of Aristophanes were conceived at least as much for their kinetic qualities as for their color; perhaps also for their texture, which is, as we have observed, sometimes simply another aspect of movement. The rich vocabulary of Homer and of Greek writers in general seems directed toward precision rather than oddity, and to variety, the avoidance of monotony. In this last regard it may be understood as a kinetic device, to make repetition more vividly apparent when it does occur, to avoid unvarying succession when it is undesired. Still, this too may be conceived as a kind of color, a prismatic dispersal of the elements of vocabulary, creating by its variety of tones and shades of meaning something comparable to the subtle modulations of color and light in painting.

Still another kind of color is given by similes and metaphors and other figures of speech. Here Greek literature is rich indeed. The relatively elaborate similes of Homer need no further discussion; succeeding writers employed figures of increasing variety; the poets of the Hellenistic period went to unusual lengths in casting intricate and elaborate figures of speech. Indeed, the speciality of the period, the epigram both funereal and otherwise, often is simply a slyly contrived metaphor.

But the chief source of light and color in literature is the conceptual form. This does not provide as great a play of light as might have been achieved, but the effects are significant. It is the light of full day which prevails, and is naturally, normally, to be assumed, without statement or comment. By way of contrast, in the works of Homer, the conference at night, the Trojan camp at night, the night raid between the lines, the night-shrouded visit of Priam to Achilles, are momentous events; the gloom and obscurity of the situation are keenly felt and ominous. The "light of day," which is the equivalent of life, and the "dark shadow" that covers the eye with death are telling contrasts, but broad and forthright, with little modulation or contrivance. So, too, the stark contrast between sight and blindness in *Oedipus* is overpowering, but not elaborated, and is perceived as light by indirection. The more delicate and subtle variations of light are usually secondary, undertones, so to speak, in the composition. Thus the stars whose light fades before the approaching moon, and the other moon effects in Sappho and other lyricists, seem subdued; Homer's gleam of armor, his "rosy-fingered dawn," the workshop of Hephaistos; the lights and colors and sounds of terrestrial explosions in the Hesiodic battles of the divine powers; the wasting night giving way to dawn in Apollonius' *Argonautica,* and a host of other similar allusions to luminous phenomena throughout Greek literature are vivid and effective, though usually obscured by the more dominant concerns of the work. Even the gloomy rites by which Odysseus invokes the shades of Hades, and the shadow-mists in which he sees them, significant though they may be in the development of the theme of the *Odyssey* in contrast to the clear light of the world and of Odysseus' true sphere, is granted only a restricted role in the poem.

Though classical literature never produced anything so fundamentally, pervasively, and meaningfully luminous as, for a supreme example, Dante's *Divine Comedy,* the development of Aeschylus' *Oresteia* reveals some of the potentiality of treatment and use of light in conceptual form which was easily available to the Greek writer had he been interested. The *Agamemnon* opens just before dawn; full light arrives quickly, but throughout the play episodes of dark are introduced in one way or another—the reference to the night through which the fires brought the news, the references to the night of the sack of Troy. All this is heightened, to anticipate, by the color, the strong, bright red of the slaughter at Troy and of the blood of Agamemnon and Cassandra themselves, quite apart from the carpet and the costumes. The *Choephoroi,* on the other hand, is drenched in gloom; the action is largely what amounts to a memorial service for the dead, an invocation of the departed, and the remainder is a morbid plot between two unstable persons to effect the murder of their mother. The emotional atmosphere is dark and depressed. The *Eumenides* opens on a similar note, with Orestes and the monstrous Furies asleep before the altar of Apollo in emotional as well as physical exhaustion; then follows the frustrating, unsatisfactory wrangle over the rights of the case, which is suddenly forgotten in the bright, almost blinding vision of untarnished, gleaming peace which Athena and the Furies describe as the destiny of Athens under the protection of the transformed, now benign, Eumenides.

In sculpture and painting, the conceptual form in its own capacity contributes little of light or shadow. Save for the gloom of grief that may be felt in funereal representations of various kinds and the shadow of death that is suggested in wounded or dying figures, there is little effective suggestion of light and dark. Indeed, in certain circumstances where the implication of light and dark is intended in the broadest possible terms, as where Night and Day are represented by the chariots of Helios and Selene in the corners of the Parthenon pediment, the allusion is substantially lost and plays no real part in the composition as far as luminosity is concerned. With regard to architecture, since in a considerable proportion of the instances the major use of the building was external (in the full light of day, which could not be manipulated), there is no implication of light or shadow in the use-function of the temple. In its capacity as a vessel for storage, the opposite would hold true; the interior would be unchangingly dark and unrelieved by light. In the buildings or parts of buildings whose primary use-function was shelter from the weather, as the stoa and peripteral colonnades of large temples, the use-concept would no doubt vary according to conditions —sometimes the thought of shadow would seem paramount, sometimes that of bright sun, protected from the wind.

The presence of color and texture in the conceptual form is less marked in architecture, painting, and sculpture than in literature. In architecture, to be sure, we have little idea of the kind of color that would be evident in a religious ceremony: we can visualize the scene, in a general way, as one of gaiety and richness, with colorful costumes, elaborate ceremonial equipment, and gilded and festooned sacrificial animals. The scene was doubtless a colorful one, but it is hard to be definite. In painting and sculpture, the pigment would stand for the color of the conceptual form itself, though no doubt often purposely altered.

Literature, however, abounds in colorful conceptual form. Most conspicuous is the frequent mention of various kinds of flowers, more often than not unaccompanied by any adjective indicating the true colors. We know, or generally assume, that Greek roses are red—and so on, through a long list of flowers whose color we know or think we know; and thence through a longer list which we can hardly identify but to which we attribute a quality of color, though we may be unwilling to specify just what color. All this is so habitual that we think we are reading a color word—the "rosy-fingered dawn," for example, though rose is a flower, not a color. Much later, Theocritus describes his Bombyka as "honey-colored" rather than "tan"; his allusion to the violet raises a color response, though he describes the flower as black or dark; his inscribed "hyacinth" is colorful enough without a color word. In short, a vast amount of color is introduced into literature by the simple mention of flowers, though their colors we do not know.

In the same way, the mention of fruit and countless objects of the world of nature, wine, fire, blood, bronze, operates to contribute color through conceptual form alone; one thinks of the "wine-dark sea" (though this probably should be "wine-*like*" sea, which, incidentally, stimulates the sense of smell and temperature) and the elaborate palette of Achilles' armor in various metals. Another rich source of color is geography, where any allusion to a place known to the listener or reader will evoke the complex color panorama of the place in question. Thus the catalogue of ships must have contained vivid color for every listener, especially for those who had traveled; even to the untraveled, "grassy Haliartos" and "lovely Mantineia" must have evoked images of landscape, however inaccurate. So, too, accounts of or references to places even farther away in the real or imaginary world, and to strange folk and customs, would contribute their unspoken color.

TEXTURE

Texture is most evident in sculpture, and Greek sculpture exploits it through a wide range. The extremes—high, glossy polish and rough tooling showing the physical texture of the stone, or heavily roughened surfaces—were usually avoided, in marble, at least. It is not clear what effect the waxed tint applied to flesh parts of marble statues would have had on the texture. It is known that bronze statues were kept polished, and the textural effects of the gold and ivory in the rich cult statues would have been vivid, but in general Greek sculptors tried to establish in stone equivalents of the texture of the conceptual form, the flesh, and varying textures of flesh, and various kinds of cloth. Where there is no attempt at some degree of equivalence of this kind, the plain surface is smooth but not polished.

Another kind of texture is achieved through the forms of the conceptual forms—rippling ribs or taut flanks; the smooth hang of a garment or the bunched and gathered folds over a girdle or the clinging and wrinkled material over the body. In such treatment there is perceptible the texture of the conceptual forms themselves as well as the modulated surface of stone and the relative smooth or vibrant light.

In architecture, the texture of the material is prominent, whether the soft crystalline smoothness of marble or the hard, flat coat of flinty white plaster over porous stone. Indeed, in certain kinds of architectural form, like fortifications and retaining walls, a full range of texture was developed, from almost polished surface to roughened protrusions of bull-nosed rusticated work. The more dramatic examples of these studied effects are Hellenistic. The texture of a colonnaded façade with the alternation of massive column and open space; the column itself, of receding surfaces rippling with the flutes and shadows of varied width and depth; the varied surfaces of flat architrave, projecting richly modeled metopes and pediments, the cornices, roof and all, are extraordinarily variegated. In fact, the contrast of light and shadow between the exterior and interior of a colonnade emerges as an almost physically tangible sensation of texture—the hard, bright light, the soft, cool shadow.

Perhaps there is no need to discuss the textures of painting; much of its character may be inferred from sculpture, and we have some idea of the variety of texture that would distinguish encaustic painting on wood or stone. We know much more clearly the various textures produced on terra-cotta vases, ranging from the soft velvet of orientalized pottery to the deep, glassy sheen of the best black glaze of the sixth and fifth centuries, with the firm, hard, ceramic smoothness of the red ground.

A great deal of texture in literature is derived from the conceptual form. Any allusion to nature brings with it a sensation of textures, and we have seen that Greek literature contains many allusions to flowers and trees of all kinds as well as to man-made objects of particular textural quality like armor, cloth fabrics, and objects of ivory and wood and metal. Furthermore, though it would be hard to demonstrate this, there are fewer direct statements of texture than of light: the soft necks and flesh of Homer's heroes, their hard bronze, are frequently mentioned, but the delicacy of many lyric poems may not necessarily be textural.

It is fairly easy to see a pervasive concern for aural texture in the use of words and rhythms. This is evident in the appreciation of the sounds of the words themselves, revealed partly by the extraordinarily rich vocabulary and by the obvious preference for certain kinds of words—the mouth-filling sonorities of Aeschylus and the tripping words of Euripides, satirized by Aristophanes in *The Frogs*. Even more apparent is the textural quality of the varied metric patterns—the trills of many Aristophanic choruses, the intricate rhythms of lyric poetry, the resonance and liquid melody of some poetry. Such qualities can hardly be demonstrated in translation, and even in Greek the reality is difficult for the modern to approach, but one is constantly aware of it. In another way, different textures may be felt in the crisp, solid objectivity of many writers, of which Thucydides is the extreme, and the mellower warmth of Herodotus, Plato, and the idyllic poets.

SOUND

The importance of sound in Greek art, too, is almost impossible to analyze, but that it was a significant factor is beyond doubt. It hardly emerges in sculpture, and but slightly in painting, though the boisterous songs of the figures appearing on vases is often striking. In literature, sound emerges largely through the conceptual form, the clear or reedy (however we understand it) voice of Nestor and other Homeric orators, the clang of Apollo's bow, the much-resounding sea, the hymn of the host departing for Syracuse, the volcanic thunders of Hesiod's battles of the gods, the song contests of the shepherds, surrounded by the plashing of springs and the sound of wind in the branches of trees. Perhaps the clearest documentation of the importance of sound to the Greek himself is the attention paid to sound in the drama. The drama was operatic, with musical accompaniment (as, indeed, was lyric poetry), and great value was placed on the quality of enunciation. An actor was estimated more on the quality of his speech than on other aspects of his performance. This is reflected, furthermore, in the importance given to oratory and the attention paid to all details of oral delivery. Even prose literature, in certain periods at least, was composed to be read aloud. Herodotus "published" his work and gained his reputation by public recitals at the great festivals. Unfortunately, most of this is beyond recapture; we can only recognize its existence.

MANNER

In summary, then, Greek art is marked by a naturalism restricted to human character and experience even more than human action; there is a wide range in the stimuli to the kinaesthetic sense and a somewhat more restricted range of those of color and texture; there is a preference for full, even light rather than shadow and modulation; an extraordinary proportion of the sensory stimuli are provided through the conceptual form rather than directly. Still more definitive individualities of style emerge from a consideration of the manner in which the elements are used. Most are familiar enough in one way or another; it may be rewarding, however, to review them.

ONTOLOGY

There is no disputing the idealism of Greek art. Indeed, considering the indeterminate nature of the meaning of the word "idealism" in our context, it would be more convenient simply to define it as "the ontological character displayed by Greek art." Whatever it is called, its character is clear enough and certainly significant in the history of art and the analysis of aesthetic phenomena.

The idealism of Greek art is not, of course, a matter of creating an impossible, exalted image superior to any reality. It is rather the identification of the type—the form possessed in common by all individuals apart from their imperfections and eccentricities. Insofar as the conception is divested of these imperfections, it is in fact superior to any existing example, but the "ideal" is not something which has never existed and can never be achieved; it is that which actually does exist, though in damaged state. It is "a subtle heightening of the typical in reality . . . a profound realism . . . so close to the object that its results are barely distinguishable from the object." [1]

Moreover, the idealism of Greek art does not remain constant throughout its history. It ranges from a strong abstraction at the beginning to a tendency toward particularism in the Hellenistic period. But from the sixth century the range is, on the whole, not great.

Idealism is most quickly recognized in the conceptual form, especially the rendering of man. In sculpture, from the mid-fifth century to the mid-fourth century, the depiction of the male figure is in terms of a simplified anatomy in which all the visible structural physical forms are rendered as in theory they ought to be as determined from the examination of healthy, well-trained, unblemished individuals. Not all details are rendered—not all veins and arteries. The pubic hair may be indicated, but the hair under the arms is not. On the other hand, many details that would escape examination are included because they are involved in the functional structure represented by some more conspicuous element that has to be rendered. There are seldom particularizing features, even though the figure may stand as a portrait. Broad distinctions may be made, sometimes underlined by special attributes; drapery or armor combine with beard to indicate the senior statesman and citizen, though bearded figures of as late as the mid-fifth century may still be athletes. But the faces are not particularized, even when they are not all the same and may be said to have some individuality. What they

[1] Voegelin, *Order and History,* II (Baton Rouge, 1956), p. 368.

reveal is the underlying structure, the basic forms of various faces, and never the particular details (the scar on the lip, the pinched nose, the cast in the eye), the clues that give expression, by which we distinguish our acquaintances and which we weave into our conception of their personalities.

Action, too, is depicted in generalized terms, indicating the kind of thing that happened but not precisely what did happen. We have already noted the scarcity of depictions of historic events as such; the theme of the Greeks battling the barbarians, or Persians, is common enough in sculpture but never particularized to the extent that one can identify a historic moment. It is known that there once existed paintings of particular battles, and that some, like the painting of the battle of Marathon in the Painted Stoa in Athens, seem to have included tactical information. One wonders, however, whether it was possible to distinguish the full onslaught of Boeotians and Persians from the depiction of a similar clash in another battle, or whether the Athenian pursuit of the Persians through a swamp would have differed from some other pursuit through a swamp. No doubt there were some respects in which these paintings, and much sculpture, were exact and specific, so that Pausanias was able to identify each of the scores of figures in Polygnotos' great painting of Homeric scenes in the Lesche of the Cnidians at Delphi, but this was certainly by rational means—even to the extent of labeling the figures in the painting. The several details of the scene were presented as kinds of action—man falling, horse rolling, and so forth. An illustration of the point in question is the group on the pediment at Olympia depicting the Lapith woman struggling with the centaur (Plate 72): neither the centaur nor the woman exhibits the slightest awareness of pain, fright, or tension. In the struggle of Greeks and Amazons on the frieze at Bassae, the expressions on the faces and the action of the body are crude stereotypes.

All this is true also in literature. The figures in tragedy are simply types of humanity in various types of situations. As in sculpture, we see character accurately and completely insofar as it pertains to the situation at hand. The events are depicted to show the situation in its basic form but do not include unnecessary detail or show the situation in some purely local example. Thus the plots and figures come from mythology, not history; they concern (like most of mythology, to be sure) circumstances of larger than ordinary scale—kings and murders rather than clerks and blows—involving the same basic emotions that pervade all action at all levels. It is revealing, however, to compare three treatments of the Electra theme, to observe how each dramatist embraced a wider and more detailed sphere than his predecessor.

In spite of Thucydides' slur on the motives of Herodotus, it is probable that both historians had in mind to preserve for posterity typical historic events. Herodotus' avowed purpose is to record the deeds of exceptional men that they might not fade from memory, and he does this conscientiously and in a methodical way. Moreover, his faithful industry in assembling data on the customs of the Egyptians and other strange peoples has certainly resulted in the accumulation of an astonishing array of particulars. On the other hand, it may well be that he was in fact a proto-Aristotle and his book a collection of data to help to understand the kind of people involved in his story. In any case, Thucydides is explicit in indicating his intention of showing the kind of thing that is likely to happen under certain conditions; it is true that he lays himself open to a charge of particularism in selecting the Peloponnesian as the greatest of wars, and his treatment of it is certainly detailed and exhaustive. However, even some of his most fascinating episodes—the siege of Plataea and the escape of the besieged—captivating though they are as accounts of ingenuity and daring, are, first of all, *examples* of the kind of thing that was happening. It is evident that, like Hippocrates in his analysis of disease, Thucydides was analyzing human events (faction and its course; democracy and its tendencies; aspects of leadership), not simply recording a revolution that happened to occur in Corcyra, the adventures of Kleon, the interesting personalities of Pericles and Alcibiades.

In architecture, the conceptual form is conspicuously idealistic in the absence of change. The development of the Ionic and Doric orders, temple forms, even stoas, was achieved by the mid-fifth century; from then on, save for the introduction of the Corinthian capital, the external form of these structures remained substantially the same. Stoas varied freely, as we have seen, for their particular use-function, but from the point of view of exterior design neither temple nor stoa altered considerably save in proportions. The typical, ideal, form of the structures was accepted and preserved unchanged.

It is much more difficult to describe the idealism of the aesthetic sensory elements. It might have been more clearly revealed in an element which is now nearly lost to us—color. The painting on buildings, statues, and even mural or easel paintings were in broad, more or less elementary, pigments, employed as color effects but not highly individualized. The restricted range and limited variety of light and color in literature might also be an expression of this idealizing tendency. So, too, the tendency of the movements to be formulated in definite, geometric shapes; a specified number of specified metric patterns, no matter how numerous, may express the same tendency.

All this, however, has to do with the central period of Greek art centering around the end of the fourth century. Earlier and later there were notable deviations from the norm. In geometric vases, for example, the human and animal figures which begin to appear in conceptual form in the later phases are highly abstracted, quite as much as Egyptian or more primitive figures might be. A good part of this impression, however, is due to the linear rendering, since it is necessary to simplify the figure in reducing it to line. That identical repetition is used in the presentation of figures shows that particularization was far from the artist's mind; each figure is composed of the same anatomic elements in the same proportion, indicating general agreement as to what were the essential parts of the figure. Finally, the deployment of the figures in the same kind of regular rectilinear rhythms as the geometric ornament itself reveals that the figures are treated as decorative motifs. A further suggestion of this is the way in which familiar birds, often holding worms or snakes, are used as pure decoration; quickly they become stylized as zigzag lines, no longer recognizable as birds.

In the seventh and sixth centuries, there was a rapid development toward a fuller depiction of the imagery and idealism that reached an apogee in the fifth century; but there continued to be a strong tendency to abstract and emphasize those elements with decorative possibilities. The statues of ca. 600 (Plate 71) present hair, ears, elbows, knees, hands, wrists, and (in a broader way) faces that are not so much anatomical forms as ornaments; the underlying geometric shapes are isolated and rendered for their own sake. It is possible to recognize an ear when one sees it on the side of a head, and to perceive that the sculptured ear displays the basic pattern of the anatomical ear; but if the same ear was broken from its statue, it might not be so quickly recognized as a part of a human body. There was a considerable period when the process of abstraction went beyond the familiar idealism of the classical period, tending especially to abstract the elements of the subject constituting its geometric pattern rather than its conceptual form.

How may these conclusions be applied to the literary arts? Are the figures in the *Iliad* and *Odyssey* abstracted to the degree that the figures in geometric vases are, and can it be said that the figures of epic and Archaic lyric are depicted in terms of the aesthetic elements abstracted? More is to be said for the notion than might seem at first. Of course, all this is relative and comparative; it is simply a question of whether Achilles is depicted in a more elemental form than Oedipus. The matter is further complicated by the effect of the difference in configuration—the problem of the *Iliad* is presented in chain, events seriatim, movement constantly forward, whereas the problem of Oedipus is presented in masses, with examination from several sides and exploration of ins and outs, cause and effect. Still, it is probably true that the problem of the *Iliad* is simpler and more elementary. The wrath of Achilles for the insults and dishonor heaped upon him is a more straightforward and simple reaction than the emotional disturbances of Oedipus, Clytemnestra, and Orestes.

It is a commonplace that Homer's minor characters are usually known by one or two characteristics—blond Menelaos, the wide-ruling Agamemnon, the white-armed Helen. Many kinds of incident, as we have already observed, are quickly reduced to a few significant details, like the landing of a ship, the fall and death of a hero, and are repeated whenever the occasion arises: they constitute the concise statement of an important event reduced to some basic essential. Again, it is not important that these mannerisms are useful to a poet composing orally as he recites, or that they may have developed as a consequence of this very need. It is important that they were accepted as adequate to the high purposes of the work; they fit the wants and expectations of poet and auditors and express the conceptions they understand.

Conversely, in the Hellenistic period there are tendencies toward particularization. Indeed, a school of portraiture developed in which highly individualized portraits of the most detailed character were produced, in addition to more conventional portraits of orators, statesmen, and the like. But the development of portraiture, significant as it is as a symptom, is a highly specialized diversion. In typical sculpture of the period there is the production of studies of many specialized types: men and women of different ages, from very young to very old, from different walks of life—peasant, athlete, warrior; in different poses—standing, leaning, kneeling, sitting, crouching, reclining, lying. All this seems a long way from the few basic types of the fifth century, and yet to make a statue of a middle-aged boxer seated in a twisted position is not necessarily to depict or be concerned with any particular individual. The hair in the armpits of a giant on the Pergamene frieze, the hair of Marsyas as he hangs waiting to be skinned, are not particularizing elements in the formulation; they are elements of conceptual form intended to stimulate an organic emotion. In spite of the obvious fact that many more ideal forms or types are recognized in the Hellenistic period than in the fifth century, they remain essentially types and never become particular. It is in fact a reflection in sculpture of Aristotle's influence to classify and subclassify, and his conception that behind each irreducible type was its molding form.

In literature there is increasing concern for relatively trivial things, for genre and varieties of scene and locale. The extreme manifestation is in the epigrams reflecting almost every conceivable kind of emotion under every condition. The composer of the elegiacs on the *Ruins of*

Corinth does not speak with the personal intimacy of Childe Harold viewing the sites of ancient fame, and yet it is inescapable that the growth of the lyric is an expression of greater individualism.

EPISTEMOLOGY

Another well-recognized quality of Greek art is its objectivity. It is not the conception or opinion in the mind of the artist or the audience that is paramount; it is what the artist has perceived in the subject he has chosen, which he tries to incorporate in material form and from which the audience is expected to form its own impression. In conceptual form, the starting point of creation is to ascertain the features of the thing to be depicted and reproduce them as nearly as possible in the same form. It is not a matter of establishing an arbitrary pattern to which the real thing is keyed (as in Egyptian work), or the particular feeling which the artist himself may happen to have about it. Behind this lies a conviction from which not even Plato escaped: physical substance is real, flesh and blood and vessels of bronze and wooden ships in which to sail exist, and "material things" have value as well as, or perhaps in harmony with, the less concrete reality of the ideal form. In the more purely sensory elements of the work of art, this objectivity is revealed in the palpable form of the various stimuli. Although a movement may be suggested or implied by a gesture or glance or pose, if a line is to be drawn it is drawn or carved in the object. The basic rhythm of the language, based on quantity rather than stress accent, preserves a physical continuity of sound from stress to stress rather than relying solely on the beat to make the continuity.

The objectivity of Greek art is thus a more material objectivity than the logical objectivity of Egyptian art. Whereas the Egyptian artisan admitted the objective reality of various features of a human body, he combined them according to logical principles, not as they are in the human body. The Greek sculptor was keenly aware of the anatomical form of the body and strove to reproduce it in the statue according to the same principles that exist in the organization of the material body and in its entirety, as indicated by the practice of finishing even the hidden parts of a statue. Moreover, he attempted to reproduce it so that it presented itself to the observer as the body presents itself, so that the observer may draw his conclusions about the sculptured body in the same way that he draws his conclusions about the human body. This is not altered by principles of idealism and abstraction: the simplified, typical forms of anatomy in the Greek statue are distilled from the physical form of the living body, according to the special problems of each figure; the more abstract forms of the Egyptian statue, once derived, are imposed arbitrarily on all statues—indeed, the relatively few standardized types are reproduced as symbols of bodies rather than as depictions of bodies. On the other hand, the Greek statue is not distorted or modified to make specific some opinion of the artist about it; it is not attenuated beyond the range of actual proportions of normal figures to seem more tense or dynamic; one figure in a group is not made unreasonably larger than another to emphasize his relative importance; expressions of grief or pain are not exaggerated beyond ordinary experience for effect—indeed, they are more likely to be more subdued than normal.

To most of these and similar observations about the visual arts of the middle period exceptions (real or apparent) may be found in earlier times. Geometric figures are attenuated and constructed on lines paralleling the Egyptian logical objectivity. Archaic figures (Plate 71) exhibit anatomical details strikingly different from those apparent in nature—the elaborately patterned ears, for example. But this is not a distortion to reveal a special opinion about the figure; it is a simplification, with some modification, to reveal a basic fact in the material form of the figure. Later on, in the Hellenistic period, there are statues from the Pergamene school with more muscles than are to be found in the human body, presumably to make the statue look especially powerful; and there are many extreme poses, like the bursting chest and hollow abdomen of the figure on the Pergamene frieze (Plate 75), the tautly stretched Marsyas, or the sensually developed Aphrodite (Plate 76). All this doubtless reveals a particular opinion or attitude of the sculptor, but rarely is there an example of serious distortion of form beyond its normal range.

This tendency is more apparent in literature than in the visual arts. Homer conveys a world of feeling about the experiences of war by describing a woman saying goodbye to her husband, men dying, struggling, victorious. Even in his similes, where his thought might be expressed by allusion or implication, he selects concrete terms of trees crashing, flies swarming. Sappho writes of love in clinical terms. Her allusions to flowers, the moon, and night are inevitably haunting, but they are presented with almost complete objectivity: "The moon has set, and the Pleiades; it is midnight—the hour has passed—I lie alone." In the drama, the most powerful force controlling the emotion of some of the more violent scenes—Medea with her children, Oedipus in his blindness—is that the action, speech, the general rhythm and pace moves relentlessly on, with no attempt to accommodate to the particular situation despite its exceptional character, so that the spectator, like the writer, remains apart and watches the event *sub specie aeternitatis*.

In the works of Herodotus and Thucydides there is an avowed intent to present a personal understanding of events and occasional comment on developments. But these judgments are presented through the speeches of the participants and embody opinions held by the partici-pants. Otherwise, both men faithfully recorded facts as they could ascertain them, fully assuming that the facts would speak for themselves. If Herodotus' statistics on the size of the Persian army are excessive, it is hardly to be supposed that he falsified them, though of course he may have yielded in accepting the highest of several estimates.

Finally, one should note the objective quality of the technical use of material in Greek art. As fully and carefully as the Greek sculptor may have worked out the anatomy of figure, he did not strive to make the surface of the statue resemble skin; instead, he developed some inherent quality of the stone or bronze itself. Bronze was polished for its gleam, stone was rubbed for its velvety texture and particular degree of translucence. Seldom was the stone polished. The surface and texture most desirable in the material was the surface and texture chosen, provided that this did not conflict with the surface and texture of the body depicted. Words too were things of beauty and loved for their own sake; we have alluded to the particular joy taken by Aeschylus and

Aristophanes in discovering and devising new words; and the variety and richness of Greek vocabulary, and the vocabulary of almost any writer, is a testament to their recognition of the value of their basic material.

SIGNIFICATION

In addition to the factors of idealism and objectivity, we must speak of the manner of signification—whether Greek art is literal or symbolic. This, of course, is a matter on which it is impossible to form definite conclusions, since the meaning of "symbol" is so elusive and the degree of conscious symbolism in a work of art depends on the intent of the artist. But the balance of probability seems to be that, in Greek art, whatever is being rendered is rendered for what it is, not for what it might stand for. It is sometimes said that such a subject as the battle of the Lapiths and centaurs is symbolic of the struggle of the forces of barbarism and civilization, but this is hardly demonstrable. Indeed, when a real struggle between barbarism and civilization, between the Greeks and Persians (as the Greeks would have defined it) was depicted, there is no very obvious distinction between the two sides apart from their costumes, a part of the conceptual form. Dio Chrysostom says of Pheidias' statue of Zeus at Olympia that "our Zeus is peaceful and mild in every way, as if it were the guardian of Hellas when she is of one mind and not distraught with faction." He does not say that the statue "represents" Hellas in this happy state, or that it "symbolizes" the happy state itself; he says that it depicts the agent who preserves the happy state—that is, Zeus. By the middle of the fifth century, many Greeks no longer recognized the physical existence of divinities such as Zeus and Apollo and Aphrodite, but they did recognize the existence of the powers and values traditionally attributed to Zeus and Apollo and Aphrodite. It may be said that as the *names* of these divinities were basic symbols, as all words are symbols, so the *forms* of the gods were basic symbols in which the existent powers were visually conceived.

In the corners of the Parthenon gables are the horses of the Sun and Moon and the personified rivers of Attica. Are these symbols of time and place, is a human figure the symbol of a river? Personification is a rather literal form of symbolism; whatever is understood to be endowed with will may be endowed with other human attributes, and the Greeks sensed the wilfulness of most things in nature. We may admit an element of simple symbolism in the figures as indications of time and place. As such, however, they throw into bold contrast the lack of symbolism in the major subject. Emblematic symbols of a simple kind were widely used in Greek sculpture in the numerous attributes by which one recognizes this divinity or that—the thunderbolt, spear, and trident—but these are hardly more than labels. They have an important role, for one has a different impression of a statue if it is known to be of Poseidon rather than of an unknown athlete. But the attribute itself is ancillary; the same difference in impression might be created by a label on the base of the statue or a phrase in a guidebook. Knowing that it is Poseidon invokes past experience and creates a rational position that establishes a particular control of reception of the sense stimuli that come directly from the statue. But in the absence of the label, the Greek Poseidon can be seen only as a human figure. It is not the statue which is symbolic, in the sense of the distinction made above; it is some small part of the statue which indicates something about the statue. Symbolism, in short, to the extent that it exists in Greek art, is a minor element.

The problem becomes more difficult in literature, where the nature of words as a kind of symbol is inherent and inescapable in the very substance of the work, and where in some degree any serious work can be related to an idea or situation larger than itself. It is impossible for critics to agree on the matter of symbolism in Greek literature. There are considerations, however, which suggest that Greek literature is literal and not consciously symbolic even to the degree that the plastic arts seem to have been.

For example, today almost everyone recognizes in the story of Oedipus a symbol of a complex of psychological phenomena, but Sophocles could have had no real inkling of this; the myth could not have been, to Sophocles, a conscious symbol of a psychological pattern.

Even apart from the Freudian implications of the Oedipus story, there is to us an evident symbolism in the manifestations of physical and mental or spiritual blindness, so that we would readily admit one as a symbol of the other. But the blindness was not Sophocles' invention—it was in the myth—and it is not necessary to suppose that Sophocles was consciously employing symbolism. Of course, even if he did not intend physical blindness to stand as a symbol of spiritual blindness, he may have recognized the usefulness of its literal irony as a shock to the emotions. Analogy rather than symbolism may have been the intention. "As Oedipus is physically blind, so mankind is spiritually blind." It is one thing to say that "Odysseus is a symbol of the human spirit," another to say that "as Odysseus experienced, so all men experience." The figures in Plato's writings, simple and elaborate, are conscious analogies—the cave, the charioteer, the state itself are analogies by which justice and the soul are discussed.

If symbolism is to be found in Greek literature, it rests in Aeschylus' *Prometheus.* Its elusiveness, to be sure, and the consequent impression of symbolism, may be due in part to the fact that only one play of the trilogy is preserved. We are presented with the demigod Prometheus nailed to a rock and tortured by Zeus the ultimate god—Prometheus the creator of man and all that is human stiffly resisting the crushing authority of the Omnipotent Divine. That Prometheus is more than human and yet seems to represent humanity gives a strong sense of his being a symbol of humanity or human values or some human value. It is true that this kind of interpretation allows inconsistencies: Prometheus is man; he suffers to redeem man; he has courage in enduring his ordeal by the knowledge that there will come one who will redeem him, Prometheus, by some act, perhaps of sacrifice and suffering. So who is redeemer, who the redeemed? Who is man and who is the god? Or, conceivably, as the symbolist has a fairly free field, may all be one? On the other hand, it is altogether possible that there is no such symbolism, man does not enter the picture at all: it is as it seems, a conflict among superhumans—divinities or semidivinities, an account of the conflict between certain powers and values, one lot named Zeus and the other named Prometheus, visualized in anthropomorphic rather than geometric terms, but no more symbolic than this universal process and conceived concretely and literally.

DEFINITION

Of the qualities pertaining to sensation, the quality of definition is the clarity which is invariably recognized as one of the outstanding characteristics of Greek art. This is not the precision of Egyptian art; the clarity of the Greek style is the lack of ambiguity, the lack of vagueness or equivocation; it is the thorough and painstaking care that all elements and their relationship shall be quickly and accurately comprehended. But Greek artists did not go beyond this to the sharp, emphatic precision characteristic of Egyptian work, nor did Egyptian artists care so much whether the elements and relationships of his work were clear to the beholder so long as the execution was finely and mechanically precise.

In the rendering of the drapery of a figure, the Egyptian sculptor may cut certain outlines more distinctly and with sharper and bolder precision to bring out the pattern itself. The Greek statue may have more complete differentiation of modulation in the contours, and more forms, to bring out all relationships among all elements. The Egyptian sculptor, to sharpen the outline of a pattern, may eliminate a fold or an edge of the costume so that the draping of the material is difficult if not impossible to comprehend; the Greek sculptor normally takes care to indicate directly or indirectly both the costume and its draping. The Egyptian sculptor, rendering drapery over a body, may on occasion simply etch the patterns of the drapery on the contour of the body, as though the drapery were adhering to the flesh, or he may omit to render some edge of the drapery for one reason or another, so that where the garment ends and the skin begins is not apparent. The Greek sculptor, if he wishes to develop a composition of drapery over flesh, leaves no doubt about the difference: the drapery, though it might lie close to the figure, is made clearly apparent by obvious gathers and folds of the material (which, incidentally, are plotted to indicate, as though by line drawing and by shadow, the contour of the flesh beneath), and the exact extent of the material is nowhere in doubt. There are, to be sure, some notable exceptions to this, conspicuously the mid-Archaic Moscho-phoros in the Acropolis in Athens, whose drapery is indicated (plasti-cally) only by the edge of the garment falling from the neck down each side of the torso. The lack of differentiation is so great that it is necessary to follow the outer contour all around to know which surface is inside the contour and which outside; which surface is cloth, which flesh. To be sure, in its original state the drapery would have been painted to distinguish it from the flesh, as would be an Egyptian figure. The Moschophoros stands out rather conspicuously among Greek sculptures for this very peculiarity and should not be thought to represent Greek art as a whole. So also in the conceptual form of painting, architecture, and literature there is a bright clarity which leaves without ambiguity the identity of all the forms and their relationships, in general and in detail.

There often seems to be an ultimate obscurity in Greek art, in spite of the general clarity that pervades the immediate perception of it. In spite of the clear delineation of the human forms in a statue, it is often an insoluble problem whether the statue depicts a man or a god—or what god. Frequently there are appurtenances with the figure to show whether a male figure depicts Poseidon or Zeus or an athlete or a warrior or a statesman. But without such attributes there would be no way of distinguishing; the statue would simply depict a man. In literature, in spite of the fine delineation and development in the *Oresteia* and *Oedipus the King,* there remains sufficient doubt as to the meanings of these plays to have supported generations of classical scholars in their debates. One is inclined to wonder why, if the Greeks were such masters of clarity, they could not have made their plays transparently and unequivocably clear. Here again one must recall that, insofar as the conceptual form is concerned, it is the experience of the persons of the drama which is delineated, and this is never in doubt. What the "meaning" of the play is, rationally approached, or in terms beyond the sphere of the persons of the drama themselves—whether, indeed, there is such a meaning—is another matter, to which we may allude again. If a sculptured figure becomes ambiguous with the loss of some attribute, we must conclude that whether it depicted a god or man was unimportant in the eyes of the sculptor: what it did depict—or where his efforts in depiction were concentrated—was the human figure in its most excellent form.

In any case, the clarity of elements other than conceptual form is abundantly evident in Greek art of all kinds. Even in the technical aspect this clarity is conspicuous. In the visual arts, the cutting and drawing of line and plane is clean and brilliant and true; so also in verbal expression. There is an economy, a habit of expressing as directly and simply as possible. Where one line is sufficient, one only is used; where one word fills the requirement, it is seldom that we find two. It is true that many of the repetitive words in the works of Homer—the stylized epithets and repetitions of stock lines, or longer passages—do not always seem necessary to the sense of the poem, but they are important to the rhythms, as we have seen, as well as being a functional element in the oral tradition of the work. In later literature, word duplications are relatively rare, the rhythms being achieved in other ways. It is also true that an inflected language, by showing its relationships through word inflections instead of auxiliaries, prepositions, and the like, allows for the composition of sentences using fewer words (though not necessarily fewer syllables) than English; conversely it is true that a Greek sentence is likely to have a swarm of conjunctive and adverbial particles which express shades of relationship so subtle that they cannot be conveyed by English words alone, though they may be conveyed by intonation and expression in speech. Thus such words may seem unnecessary, but their availability provides Greek literature with a potentiality for delicacy of expression which was used to the full.

The kinaesthetic stimuli in poetry are clear enough; the metric and other rhythm are well marked in spite of their intricacy. That modern scholars cannot always agree on scansion reflects a defect of our knowledge, for it is evident that, whatever the exact manner of rendering the forms, they were rigorous and clear to the ancients themselves, even in mathematical proportion. With all the variety, there was no blank or free verse. As we have seen, there is commonly a number of movements or rhythms of various kinds operating in a work of any magnitude, but never to the extent of being baffling or bewildering; one may be carried away on a tide, but not in a tide-race. Whether it is the word rhythm or movement of meaning or the choral dance in Alkman's *Partheneion* or Aeschylus' *Persians,* intricate though the patterns may be, their pattern is clear and unconfused; the waxing, waning, freshening, always developing movement of the *Republic;* the various patterns in Hellenistic idyls, all move with the same simple, direct clarity.

In sculpture, painting, and architecture, the neat, clear-cut, distinct line with its implication of clean, unequivocal movement is an obvious characteristic, as is the trim, starched, swallow-tail costumes of "Archaic" maidens, with their sharp, angular, zigzag movements running diagonally across the figures, over the lucid, rippling movement of the lines of the undergarment (with concomitant, clearly contrasted texture). The full, abundant movements of the rich drapery of the women of the Parthenon pediments swell out from behind and beneath their bodies, rising over their thighs, receding between their legs, rising again to disappear behind, to be clearly resumed by those of a neighboring figure. In the Pergamene altar, in the plunge and surge of figures and swirling drape and light, there is an essential clarity of rendering. It is hardly necessary to pursue this point through other premutations; the clarity of Greek art is among its best recognized characteristics.

CONFIGURATION

Throughout its history Greek art exploited a wide range of dimensions of configuration. A broader study of the art of the world would quickly reveal that this change in preference for different kinds of configuration was not peculiar to Greek art, and it has even been suspected that such a change, in just the sequence we find revealed in Greek art, is natural in the development of style. Nevertheless, Greek art is almost unique in that its history encompasses almost the entire range of possibilities.

Greek art first emerged with a preference for configuration in one dimension—in line; then interest turned to configuration in two dimensions—in expanse; then three dimensions—in mass; and finally, in four dimensions—in what may be called space-time. The picture is complicated by several facts: the interest in mass, once experienced, was never entirely dislodged, so that the style of space-time differs in certain ways from other styles of space-time, as we shall see in discussing Roman art; second, in some arts which were late-born, so to speak, like drama, there seems to have been a hurried rehearsal of the whole experience of configuration, up to the point reached by the other arts.

In the earliest aesthetic objects of classical Greece, the geometric vases and figurines, the rendering is almost exclusively one-dimensional, i.e., linear (Plates 63–70). All the ornament on the vases is executed in line. In the fully developed geometric style, it is one effect of line to divide the surface into smaller surfaces, geometric shapes like triangles, circles, and the like, and these are filled with lines, so that the triangle or circle is distinguished from the pure form that it would be were it a solid color. Although the ornament is arranged in bands which are ribbon-like and hence have breadth and two-dimensional surface, they are filled with lines which dominate the impression, and they are themselves one-directional movements around the vase. In later vases, where the entire surface is covered with band after band, an over-all tapestry-like pattern is produced, but clearly to be distinguished from an over-all tapestry which would have been some kind of radial or axial symmetry or a completely generalized organization instead of the inescapably horizontal linear movements. Finally, in the relatively late phase when human and animal figures become common in decoration, these too are linear, reduced to wirelike constructions, exactly as are the figurines of the time. Groups of figures are arranged in series, never in depth. Only rarely, as in the attempt to depict a chariot or a bier with the corpse lying on it, does the problem of three dimensions arise, and then it is solved by a purely arbitrary, abstract logic of providing in the foreground views of what otherwise could be concealed.

There is little architecture known from the period that may be counted as art; most known buildings are of purely practical construction. Late terra-cotta models of buildings, however, show painted decoration in the same style, and it is even more significant that some of the earliest monumental buildings known, like the earliest temple at Samos, are designed with very long, very narrow spaces. Even as late as the Archaic period, some buildings were designed with a single row of columns down the middle of the cella, an arrangement which could not fail to emphasize the longitudinal character of the space. This kind of space, surviving into the Archaic period, may be understood in some degree as a conservative survival of the earlier feeling.

The literature of the time is the Homeric epic. This, too, is one-dimensional in many ways. The rhythms, the hexameters and the meaning rhythms, are all direct, forward-surging; there is a kind of monotony about them—not boredom but a continuing, growing relentlessness that becomes hypnotic and absorbs the listener in its ceaseless, endless pulse. As for the conceptual form, the *Iliad* develops according to a single thread; there is Achilles made wrathful—unreasonably, inhumanly so—by his quarrel with Agamemnon, and then come the events, presented in chronological sequence, leading to the reconciliation of the quarrel and the internal reconcilation and readjustment of Achilles. Much happens, many people are involved, and much that happens, like the relations between Hector and his wife and family, seem to have little to do with the relations of Achilles with himself; but in the *Iliad* the affairs of no Greek or Trojan are followed independently of the main theme; everything that happens to them does so because of their relation to Achilles, and is discussed when it is relevant to that connection and not in the order appropriate to the man they concern directly. Although the plot moves with changes of pace calculated to provide suspense and release, and ultimately a climax of tension with subsequent relaxation, it is essentially one line of movement.

In the *Odyssey,* to be sure, there is a different arrangement. The story begins simultaneously in three places, heaven, Ithaca, and Ogygia, with the gods, Telemachus, and Odysseus each pursuing an independent line of action. True enough, it is all related to Odysseus' final installation at home, but the several threads are followed independently. The gods have their plan, which they discuss and formulate, remaining aloof for the most part but moving in to intervene when necessary. Telemachus sets off from Ithaca to find his father—quite in the wrong

direction, as it turns out—and travels about almost forgetfully, it sometimes seems, until ultimately he returns to Ithaca to meet his father. At
the same time Odysseus himself is released from Ogygia and brought
through various adventures until he, too, arrives at Ithaca. There the
three threads are woven into one; the three agents move in concert to
the achievement of the common goal. Although there are several independent themes, each moves in the same direction. The contrast is
evident when one examines a modern version of the story, Eyving
Johnson's *Return to Ithaca,* in which the several strands are presented
in briefer episodes in such a way as to make clear that here are several
series of events occuring in different parts of the world simultaneously;
one has the impression of being on a mountain watching, in a single
vision, three groups of people converge unseen by each other in the
plain far below. The *Odyssey* itself is more like watching three events
taking place on three different slopes of the mountain; one cannot
watch all three at once.

The plot movement of the *Odyssey* is further complicated by Odysseus' recital of his early adventures at the banquet of Alcinous; this
brings the beginning of his adventures before us near the end of his
travels, a device that might have added depth. Homer presents the
stories simply as part of the evening's entertainment, like the ballad of
Ares and Aphrodite. Although it provides much for our understanding
of Odysseus and his fate, it is not presented as though opening a door
into the past or into the depths of his personality; it is a straightforward
chronology of his adventures.

The basic conceptual form of the *Iliad* is not involuted. Achilles is
hardly complex by modern standards. His single conflict, between pride
and humanity, he faces with single mind, and this Homer develops
with subtlety and penetration. It is a simple problem, destructive
though it may be; it is solved not by involutions but by a series of
cathartic experiences. As for Odysseus, complex though he may be in
our own eyes, viewing him from what we think we know of psychology,
to Homer he was far from complex. To Homer, Odysseus was a man
whose struggle was to live a full life; we follow his quest and sense the
quality of his driving power as a single compulsion. We know that
Odysseus has lived a year or so with Circe and seven with Calypso, but

the temporal expanse is not differentiated. If there is anything more profound than the evident exhilaration of a life of sun and storm and adventure and treasure, Homer does not say so. Whatever complexities we sense in Odysseus, Homer may have felt, but he did not develop them by introspection, analysis, and reflection. Instead, he created a much-suffering, godlike Odysseus, pursuing steadfastly by craft and might a fixed idea, not simply return to his wife and family, but the living of his life.

Thus in plot and movement Homeric poetry is basically linear, and in many other respects this characteristic emerges: grammatically and rhetorically in the paratactic construction, the linking of series of similes, the recital of a battle in terms of a series of individual conflicts fought by a series of heroes; the list of contingents on each side from the catalogue; the quick chronological narration that constitutes much of the freshness of Homer's work.

In the following period poetry had a distinctly different configuration. Hesiod's poems, though he wrote in the same meters as Homer, are much shorter, and the subject matter is more clearly defined. One poem deals with how to make a living, another with the gods, another with famous women, and so on. Each has a limited subject with beginning and end and sides, which is surveyed and brought to a completion. The *Iliad* is not a comprehensive account of the story of the Trojan War; but *Works and Days* is a treatise on a definite topic.

The lyricists chose even shorter topics to treat with special care. One of the new meters, the elegiac couplet, is a device to break the continuous flow of dactylic hexameters by short alternate lines with a halt in the rhythm that has the effect of making the movement progress by broad steps rather than even continuity. The same breaking up of the smooth continuum was accomplished by other lyricists in other ways. Among the iambists, Semonides, in spite of the unbroken meter of unvaried iambics, divides his poem on women into quasi-stanzas by taking up various type of women, each discussed for approximately the same length, so that the sense rhythm breaks the poem into more or less regular stanzas, each representing a separate topic. Alkman, the later Alcaeus, and Sappho write quasi-stanzas, breaking their poems into sections, an effect accentuated by the choral dance patterns accompanying the poems.

Vase ornamentation becomes two-dimensional. The zones of decoration become fewer and wider, and large panels become common. Linear patterns disappear, to be replaced by rosettes and broad, flat, colorful floral designs of other origin; animal motifs become common, the animals full-bodied and flat, with no depth or modeling. Among the special varieties may be found wares with special predilection for lines, but these are arranged in scale patterns or the like. Panels or zones are fully and evenly covered with ornament, so that the total effect is that of an oriental rug or tapestry (Plate 64).

In sculpture, the figurines are broad and flat. Female figures are more characteristic than male. The costume is ornamented with broad, flat rosettes like the pottery; hair is arranged so that it falls on each side of the face in a broad triangle, the face itself a reversed triangle. There is no side view; the figures resemble planks. Architectural forms, of which there are all too few, are similarly broad and flat.

By the early sixth century, full three-dimensional mass was favored. Statuary is designed with both front view and side view, so that the depth and solidity of the figure is fully recognized. Each view is still wholly flat, so that the figure seems to be composed of flat silhouettes on each side. Detailed forms also are predominantly interesting for their surface, their texture and outline, though they often are carved to suggest the fulness behind them. By the mid-sixth century the concern for showing the relation of the frontal and lateral silhouettes developed, and from then on through the fifth and into the fourth century this was a dominant theme in the development of sculptural art—to make clear the solid forms of which the body is composed, both anatomical (i.e., muscles and bones) and geometrical (i.e., prisms and cylinders), and how they are related to each other. The early phases, indeed, present some interesting variations out of which a common preference grew. "Eastern" figures, of which the Hera of Samos is an example, are conceived in the fewest possible generalized solids, curvilinear where possible, the surfaces being treated as continuous sheets of textures of various kinds encompassing the figure, with a predominant fluid vertical movement of contour and internal movement. "Western" figures, of which the Kore No. 593 from the Athenian Acropolis is an example, are constructed of more rectilinear solids, with heavy recti- linear patterns on the surfaces and a stronger separation of the massive forms. Between are the Attic figures, like the Berlin Kore, with a kind of mean between the curvilinear fluid unity of eastern work and the chunky western style, and with the further peculiarity that the lines, where possible, have plastic mass—they are not merely etched in the surface or formed by intersecting planes.

But from the mid-sixth century there is, practically speaking, only one style—the Attic. In the female figures we have full, rich surfaces with intricate patterns of lines and planes developed out of the costume, hair, face, and so forth, with an increasing tendency to build up the lines as plastic solid forms in themselves and even, toward the end of the century, for solid forms of drapery, arms, and legs, to project over and into space to create an organization of masses that extends beyond the confines of the body in its most compact form. By the time of the Persian Wars the development of the anatomical masses has become so extensive that it distracts attention somewhat from the geometrical masses, though as late as Aegina torsos are formal patterns more than bone and muscle. Through the fifth century the anatomical forms are more and more completely differentiated, and depicted in their massive extension into the interior of the figure, or around the sides, but the geometric masses have re-emerged, now fused with the anatomical. The bone and muscle of the Parthenon "Theseus," for example, reveal clearly the distinctness of the muscular and other bodily forms, in which there is a strongly geometric character in the emphatic solidity and fulness of the masses of material. Drapery, too, has developed into full solid forms alternating with strong hollows, and is employed in great profusion to model in linear terms the depth and contours of the shapes of the figures. Thus the whole development from early sixth to late fifth may be described as a movement to fuse all elements of sculptural design into a concerted, unified, rendering of masses.

A similar accounting might be given of drawing on vases and painting, though this is perhaps unnecessary (Plates 65–66, 69). In architecture the plastic forms of the building in the sixth century are broad, flat, sweeping plane or curved surfaces; the proportion of a temple façade are broad and low, with a large part taken by the entablature and pediment—the physical plane surfaces. By the time of the Parthenon the columns have become more prominent and the entablature smaller in proportion. The columns are taller and not so thick, though the word thick is misleading because the "thick" Archaic columns with their broad fluting become gently curving surfaces, while the more compact later columns, with more and deeper fluting, are more tangibly molded into cylindrical solids. The broad, relatively shallow moldings of Archaic times have given way to narrower, more boldly projecting members, which with the aid of their shadows emerge as distinct, plastic elements instead of mere bands. The interior volume of Archaic buildings must have been low and hence with a predominant emphasis of horizontal extent. In the fifth century the ceiling was higher, the cella shorter; the space was more compact, a "solid" or "massive" volume, so to speak.

Literature in the sixth century is represented chiefly by lyricists who continue the tradition of the orientalizing period, but the century was also the birth-epoch of tragedy. Tragedy developed from the dithyramb, which was a kind of choral poem recounting a story to which a chorus of dancers performed. The literary features are reflected in the fragments of Bacchylides of the fifth century. Stories of moderate length and complexity are recounted partly in straight narration, partly in some kind of antiphony between a leader and the choros, giving a dimension to the rendering which is absent in straight narration. Even in odes like those of Pindar, in which, though they also were choral, there is no dramatic antiphony of quite the same kind, there is a series of tripartite patterns of ode, antistrophe, and epode which gives again a new dimension to the movements. Moreover, the stories told by Pindar in these odes usually are introduced in some relation (not always apparent today) to the theme of praise to some victor. Here again is an interplay between two elements that gives dimension.

The drama, however, provides the most vivid illustration of the new configuration. The works of Aeschylus, especially the earlier ones, are, compared to those of Euripides, one-dimensional. The *Suppliants* is largely choral ode with a simple plot developed in simple conversation; so too the *Persians, Seven,* and *Prometheus Bound.* The characters are not very complex, the problems simple if difficult, the action brief and uncomplicated. In the *Oresteia* there is much greater complexity, exaggerated to us, perhaps, by the fact of our having all three plays of the trilogy. And yet the action moves quickly from phase to phase; there is a high percentage of choral dancing; the characters are not complex. Even Orestes suffers the major change of his personality between the plays. Nevertheless, the fact of the presentation of one crime in one play, another in another, and the debate on the problem created in a third has the effect of the Archaic statue in presenting one silhouette, then another, then a third. There are three sides, but they are exhibited separately. In general, the broad, rugged forms of the *Oresteia* associate it with Archaic style in sculpture.

Recapitulation of the earlier phases of Greek art in the works of Aeschylus reminds us of the theory that each art must go through these states to reach its maturity; drama beginning late had nevertheless to traverse the same road as the other arts, though more rapidly since it could see its goal.

In any event, in the plays of Sophocles we find a style comparable to the Parthenon. The choral odes have sunk into a position where to some extent they simply block off the sections of the action, though they do more than this by providing contrast (i.e., dimension) and form of their own in their antiphonal construction. Apart from this, the action is more fully developed in time and space; there is more concern for accounting for the various events and traits of the characters. The Electra of Sophocles is "studied." She is revealed as a person of character in a difficult situation; in reacting to various strains she reveals various facets of her character. Aeschylus' Electra was an embodied passion, an agent of heaven to bring about a desired end, for whom we felt, no doubt, but of whom we had little knowledge.

Euripides, going still further and indeed beyond his century, depicts not only the Electra of the event, but reveals the changes that she went through and contrives explanations for them. He is concerned not only with the full figure of the heroine but with her relation to her environment, both physical and human. He depicts her as a person who is part of a temporal and spatial organization of things, people, and events. This is evidenced by his concern for "realism" and "local color," the action in the sense of movement on the stage, and perhaps especially by the messenger describing the death of Aegisthus. He begins, for example "After we had set out from this house we struck onto the broad highroad and came to the place where was the far-famed King of Mycenae. Now he was walking in a garden well watered, culling a wreath of tender myrtle sprays for his head, and when he saw us he called out 'All hail.' " In short, suffused with atmosphere and temporal and spatial movement.

But such treatments are in advance of the fifth century generally, and many of Euripides' plays, like *Medea,* are more sensibly simply three-dimensional like those of Sophocles and the pediment of the Parthenon.

Finally, an interesting contrast can be made between the writings of Herodotus and Thucydides. Herodotus approaches his subject in a leisurely way, to encompass all and spread before us whatever he has learned. He does not forget the thread of his narrative, to be sure, and the bulk of the work, however else conceived, swells that stream to overwhelming strength. But the idea of dwelling leisurely on Egypt for a book, on Scythia for another, of taking up in turn the great civilizations of the world and viewing their history and character in their totality, is something that might be felt as an "expansive" treatment of the theme. In contrast, Thucydides formulates his account, as we have seen, almost as a plastic composition: the broad foundation of early history; the full treatment of the few years' events precipitating the war; the quick survey of the fifty years of Athenian growth; the solid, complete, and compact statement of the beginning—and so on. These formulations give a size and shape to the various events in relation to one another; some sections seem solid and massive, others light and thin, mere transition. It is clear that Thucydides felt that his subject matter had a beginning, a middle, and an end (or would have an end), and was otherwise composed of parts, with full dimension of length, breadth, and depth.

The road into the following centuries, and the dimension of relationships of space and time, foreshadowed by Euripides, is revealed most clearly by the philosophers. The philosophers of the sixth and early fifth centuries had been largely concerned with the substance of being. Socrates, however, put his emphasis on human relations and probably was led to a conception of a system of form as ultimate reality, creating the problem of the relation of material phenomena to this non-material form. These problems Plato continued to explore, formulating them in greater and greater detail, but always beginning and ending with the same problem. The subjects he considered—love, justice, epistemology—all are problems in relationships. Aristotle solved, in a way, the problem of the relation of the form to the material phenomena by the conception that it was the formative principle of material things, but he was fundamentally and always concerned with relationships: the establishment of definitions of different forms—political, biological, social, physical, artistic—by analysis of existing phenomena and their relationships. He was predominantly concerned with the problem of becoming—and principles of procedure—the relationships of things, genetically speaking, in time. There was no real successor to such thinkers who could comprehend all being, but their followers, by pursuing the closer analysis of various categories, made more vivid the significance of differences, as Theophrastos explored the varieties of human personality.

Insofar as they are aesthetically conceived, the writings of these men parallel their thought. The conversational presentation of his views of immortality by Socrates through his last hours in prison, the setting for the *Republic*—beginning on the road from Piraeus and continuing in a dining room—and the whole conception of the problem of justice in terms of the intricate patterns of a society are illustrations. Aristotle, as we have said, refrained from aesthetic devices in his writing, but Theophrastos introduced a large measure of animation and interplay of human occurrences in his Characters.

The most notable illustration of the tendency comes in the account of Medea's encounter with Jason and her falling in love in Apollonius' *Argonautica*. In this poem, consciously imitative of Homeric epic,

Apollonius did what Homer never did: he reveals not only the actions and words but the feelings of Medea in all their complexity, from the first mention of her when she is completely unconcerned and indeed oblivious of Jason, through the first awakening of love, the torture of her mind as she is torn between the new emotion and her filial feelings, through the long night, her final yielding, and her subsequent single-hearted devotion to Jason's interest. In contrast, the episode of Nausicaa, though we are inclined to understand in it a good deal of our own conception of a young girl's reaction to the situation, Homer actually disposes of by a concise direction from Athena, a vivid but matter-of-fact account of the trip to the beach, the discovery of Odysseus, and his introduction into the palace. Calypso's feelings are closer to Medea's but expressed in a few brief sentences; Andromache's emotions for her husband are plumbed even more keenly, but certainly lack the deep probing in all directions, the sympathy which broods over Medea's tumultuous, gnawing indecision.

All this, it is clear, is an extension of interest into another dimension. The problem now is of relationship, temporal or spatial, or both. That is, attention is no longer simply on the individual, but on his relations to other things, and on the processes of the changes he undergoes. Among the things to which the individual is related are non-material things like ideal forms or a soul or emotions. It is not the same as in Sophocles' *Electra* where Electra is delineated largely by being put into contrast with other characters of different quality; this is merely a device to illuminate the nature of Electra in and of itself. What is new is the recognition that the relation of an individual to his soul, to the world around about, to other people, is in itself part of the individual.

The same concern appears in sculpture, too, with the work of Praxiteles. In his figures the tendency is perhaps only incipient—the vague suggestion in the cast of the glance that the figure is thinking of something—which implies in the first place the real existence and importance of a non-material element of the individual which *does* think, and in the second place the existence of something remote and not actually depicted in the sculptural group about which the individual is thinking. The style imputed to Skopas, of figures charged with emotional frenzy, the agonies and fury of the Pergamene frieze (Plate 75), the morbid sensationalism of the Pergamene battle group at Athens and the group of the flaying of Marsyas; the erotic interest of the adaptations of Praxiteles' Aphrodite (Plate 76), where the goddess is shyly or blatantly self-conscious of her nudity, or of the satyrs and nymphs familiar in Hellenistic sculpture; the sultry brooding of the Medusa or the implications of the sleeping Ariadne—all these emotionally charged conceptions are exploiting a fourth dimension, the psychological relation of the figure itself to something else in his own mind. Moreover, it is perhaps to the point to suggest that this dramatic, sensational, psychological, conceptual form works to include the spectator in the composition. The spectator no longer stands apart and regards the statues as things in themselves; he is drawn into their experience, and participates directly in it. Thus the relationship—spatial and temporal—of the piece of sculpture and the spectator becomes an element in the aesthetic formulation.

Apart from the conceptual form, the sensory elements of design in fourth-century and later sculpture exhibit the same tendencies. In the works of Praxiteles, the s-curve has added an element of lightness, potential spring, as it were, to the figure; the lines are more subtle, less commanding, more mobile. By the mid-fourth century this characteristic is generally evident. Especially revealing are the friezes from Halicarnassos with the strained, angular figures, set wide apart with heads well below the top of the frieze: they are in space, have room to move, and the movements of the composition are taut and tense; they do indeed charge the space in which they exist. Finally, the array of fourth-century grave stelae, though not dated and therefore not really reliable, seem to reveal a growing tendency from the conception in which the figures are carved in half-relief projecting from the surface of the stone, with any border of the stone light and well behind the figures, to the kind where the figures are in full relief, in half relief, or in very light relief, arranged within the deep projecting sides of the monument as though in a box, and even with doors in the background opening upon still more distant vistas. In the Pergamene frieze (Plate 75) are greatly heightened effects of swirling, dashing lines contrasted with more stiffly angular and relaxed movements; violent contrasts of light and shade and various textures, all combining to create a kind of Wagnerian storm. Other Hellenistic compositions are much calmer, but always subtly novel, and always contrived to emphasize the fact or potentiality of movement. Figures are bent and twisted, though not always obviously so; from any point of view there are movements leading around the figure in either direction, compelling a continuous inspection of every minute aspect, maintaining a constant stir of movement in space.

It is particularly suggestive that painting figures on vases almost dies with the fifth century, and gives way to plastic ornamentation with a full spatial component (Plate 67); and interest in extended spatial form begins in monumental painting, too, in the fourth century (Plates 68–69).

Even in architecture, spatial effects become more conspicuous (Plate 79). In general, columns become more slender and hence less massive, more mobile in their upward thrust; the space between columns, and between colonnade and cella, becomes wider so that there is more air, more movement, more space in the composition. Occasional structures, like the temples at Sardis and Didyma, present relatively complex spatial systems (though these may have existed in earlier versions of the temples as well). The temple at Teos had the unusual feature of being raised on a high platform ascended by many steps on all sides, constituting a spatial novelty. It was not until the fourth century, and then increasingly in the third, that multiple-story, complex-plan stoas were built. But perhaps the most significant fact architecturally is the emergence in the third and later centuries of the agora surrounded on three sides by a continuing colonnade, with a long stoa across the fourth. This is a spatial conception with a predetermined spatial unity; it makes of the agora, so to speak, not a square but a compound. The conscious effort to compose the volume is a novelty, for previous spatial compositions no doubt had been more or less instinctive.

The foregoing has been almost a systematic sketch of the history of the Greek arts, and as such it may have some use, but its purpose was to call attention to one fact only: that through its history Greek art varied in its preferences for the several kinds of configuration. Beginning with a preference for linear, one-dimensional configuration in the geometric period, it came to prefer two-dimensional configuration of expanse in the seventh century; then moved to a preference for three-dimensional massive configuration during the Archaic period, when survivals of the two-dimensional preference were long evidenced, through the fifth century, when a full consolidation of all devices in massive formulations was achieved. In the fourth century and following we find a lively interest with experiments of all kinds in configuration in four dimensions—space-time. From this it is clear that configuration itself cannot be a criterion of the Hellenic in art, although fundamentally it is likely that the Greeks preferred the mass.

DYNAMICS

In its dynamics, Greek art is characterized by a quality of poise: an equilibrium of forces which is not an inert balance in which the forces have lost their energy, but a resolution in which the forces remain alive and yet mutually absorbed. The energies are pervasive, free and continuously active, but kept within broad, simple patterns. Movements are in terms of straight lines and simple curves; complex curves are formed of sections of straight lines and simple curves. Movements are channeled and controlled, not volatile and elusive; they are alive but not restless. Their interplay ends in a harmony of all elements, not in inspiration of unsettlement. This again is a quality which is commonly recognized from classical times to the present. It was expressed in antiquity—not, to be sure, in a direct evaluation of art, but as an ideal of being, in such aphorisms as "Nothing in excess" and the concept of the mean. It is variously described in modern criticism of antiquity under some such term as "balance" or "restraint" or "moderation" or "sanity." Thus it hardly demands further discussion, save to point to certain qualifications and to the particular formulation in the special terms of the present discourse.

One of the qualifications is the warning to distinguish between this poise and the static balance of some axially symmetrical designs as, for example, in Egyptian art. The façade of an Egyptian temple, with its twin pylons flanking the entrance, is mathematically symmetrical but with an entirely different effect from the mathematically symmetrical façade of a Greek temple. In the Egyptian building the balancing elements are substantially inert forms, firmly resting on earth and devoid of any but the minimum movement of the outline, and the gravitational downward forces which are in themselves fixed and determined and in relation to each other precisely equal. The scales are balanced and inert. The ornament on the face of the pylons provides some movement, but this also is a relatively static one. The Greek temple, on the other hand, is alive with internal movement: the horizontals and verticals emerge from the ground and rise through the columns to the entablature and roof in continually separating forms to merge with the sky, horizontal and vertical constantly interplaying. At the same time, there are the movements in depth, establishing the masses of the forms and the structure within, and the movement and color of the light and shadow and pigment. In addition, there is the effect of the "refinements," present to some degree in most Greek buildings: the varied spacing of columns (and, in a Doric building, triglyphs and related features); the entasis and inclination of the columns; and in some buildings the curvatures of steps and stylobate and occasionally of the entablature. All this creates a composition of continuous activity; the façade may be rigidly symmetrical on the axis, but the corresponding halves are vital, as one might say of a man who is sitting quietly except for his breathing, the pulsing of his blood, and the slight, involuntary movements of eye and muscle.

It is significant that these forces are restrained and slight, often barely perceptible or even consciously imperceptible except to the most careful observation; they animate the design without establishing an independent, almost disembodied motion as, for example, does the Gothic building. Moreover, again unlike the Gothic building, the movements are all contained within the composition—even the steps which might extend to the horizon save for the pervasive ingathering of the receding vertical faces that begin the upward movement of the sides. In the Gothic building, the larger movements sweep upward with such concentration as to establish a single ascending force which hardly terminates with the spires; the interior space rises to such a height as to have left the ground behind.

The same effects are evident in sculpture and drawings on vases. There is, to be sure, often an axial symmetry but never absolute balance. There is, as in architecture, always a play of movement, light, color, and texture which prevents this, and furthermore, unlike architecture, there is seldom an exact axial symmetry. Normally, even in compositions which might tend to such symmetry, as in the pediment of a building or in a vase composition like Exekias' Ajaz and Odysseus (Plate 65), there is a careful difference in the design of the two halves in which, however, the totality of forces is brought to equilibrium. In a single figure, if one leg establishes a stronger movement by being straight and supporting the weight of the figure, this is compensated by some special force in the opposite arm. Such balanced design is, of course, a commonplace in many styles; it is less common, but of course not restricted to Greek art, that all of the forces are ultimately returned to the center of the composition. These principles are to some extent renounced, or apparently renounced, in some Hellenistic work, as we have seen, when the composition is extended by the conceptual form or the aesthetic movement to include the spectator or some relation to external environment, or when figures are designed to be off-balance, as in the Pergamene dedication on the Athenian Acropolis. Some of these compositions, however, must be understood as experimental. The extremes are rare and by no means characteristic of Greek style. Even in Hellenistic art, the principle of confining the whole complex of forces within the frame, so to speak, of the design, and in equilibrium about some approximately central point within the design, was preserved.

The quality of poise, then, as apparent in the visual arts, is a matter of pervasive, vital energy in terms of movement and intensity and variety of light and color and texture, self-contained and in equilibrium. In the literary arts, it is evident, first of all, in the conceptual form. In general it is the absence of extremes. The characters in Greek literature are rarely eccentric or perverted or malformed by nature or society. Obvious exceptions immediately leap to the mind—Cassandra, Thersites, Sophocles' Ajax or Philoktetes, the Orestes of Euripides' *Orestes,* and even these are displayed with notable restraint. They are not "advanced" or "difficult" cases of their kind, and their excessive symptoms flash out only briefly. As for the characters in drama in general, they are never colorless and neutral—hardly words to describe Clytemnestra or Orestes or Oedipus or Medea—but the dynamic factors in their personality and experience, when violent, end in catastrophe. Moreover they are always shown in relation to normality—either the pseudonormality of the sisters of Electra and Antigone, or the normality advocated or implied by the playwright—and always there is an ultimate resolution in which the distorting factor is in some sense subdued, though not necessarily killed. The violence is compensated by the broad simplicity of their character and problem, the simple pattern to which the treatment is reduced. Even the *Bacchae,* often interpreted as an exposition of the irresistibility of the "Dionysian" element, is really an affirmation of the rightness of such a spirit in life if accepted and integrated to the whole. By itself, it will destroy.

Similarly, with regard to action and situation, though the drama admitted violence of the most extreme kind, its effect was carefully restrained by removing it from direct vision; and though the repressed as well as conscious psychological tensions of the Oedipus theme are employed by Sophocles, or at least not rejected, they are not allowed to absorb the play as they well might have, and are compensated by the theme of mystery and ultimately brought to a state of quiescence, however pained and fitful. Herodotus and Thucydides—and Greek historians in general—are at pains to present both sides of a problem, either formally in argumentative speeches, or more generally in setting forth the activities of opposing parties with equal care. Although some historians may have had a conscious or unconscious bias, they present their matter in terms of conflicting forces in which ultimately, presumably, they intended to discover a suitable resolution.

In short, the conceptual form of literature is generally depicted in "moderation." There is an attempt to bring out various aspects of a figure or a problem, an avoidance of uncompensated extremes and of uncontrolled violence. Sometimes the compensation. the control, over a potential sensory extreme, as the almost overwhelming pathos of Andromache's parting from Hector or the inhuman frenzy of Achilles as he goes into the battle with the river, are subdued in part by the unchanging rhythm of the poetry and the calm elevation of the diction. Indeed, it is this firm anchor of formal movement which balances the passion of Sappho's lyrics or the agony of the Athenian defeat at Syracuse or the sentimentality of Medea as she falls in love in the *Argonautica.*

The sensory elements, without losing their vitality, find some kind of compensation and harmonious resolution within the work. There are always broad, over-all patterns that are clear and simple; they provide large, major rhythms confining the other elements in a measured pattern. Thus in the drama there is seldom, outside of Aeschylus, a real change of scene, though allusions in the speeches may provide a great variety of scene. The action is broken into a few major sections by the choral odes, so that however intense the emotion or rapid the action or agitated the sensory elements, the ode always comes in formal stride to intervene and provide a relieving contrast of imagery and sensory stimuli, including the major change from dramatic action to choral action. The odes themselves, like much other poetry, are divided into measured, and carefully balanced, ode and antistrophe, and these elements are repeated so that no ode or antistrophe or epode gathers undue momentum.

In prose, every completed work obeys the Aristotelian principle of having a beginning, a middle, and an end, though these may not always be as carefully designed in terms of movement as Thucydides' *History.* Herodotus, for example, has a much slighter introduction than Thucydides, and the broad, often languid movements of his work in its larger patterns sometimes seem to lack equal compensation for all parts—the *Egyptika* and the *Scythika* balance each other but seem too distinct from the rest of the work to have effective compensation taken together. But it is difficult to see how the ending, or any other projected ending, could close the climax of the Persian Wars. It might also seem that both the *Iliad* and *Odyssey,* with their rhythmic movements that seem to be only an arbitrary section of infinity, have no adequate ending, but in each there has come an end to the struggles and frustrations of the heroes, the tension and relaxation of emotion and intensity of color and movement in a lull or subsidence of feeling. There is a sense that all is not finished, that there is more to come, whether in the life of Odysseus or the siege of Troy and the career of Achilles, but this is for the moment compensated by the realization that Odysseus has won through to home, that Achilles' wrath is appeased and he has found—not his old self, but a better self. Thus again the balance is achieved—not static, but living and poised.

SYSTEM

In composition or arrangement we continue to encounter familiar qualities. One aspect of the composition is its system. This is, it will be recalled, a matter of whether the elements of a composition are distributed in an even, regular manner or whether the elements occur in random, miscellaneous quantities and order. In this scale Greek art is obviously conspicuous for its regularity. Indeed this regularity, taken with the concentrated centrality of focus, is a large part of the "order" and "balance" of the art. The composition of sculpture and painting will normally have the focus in the center, with an approximately equal number of figures on each side and with the forces of movement, color, and so on systematically distributed. In literature, characteristically, the patterns of movement, from meter to composition, the marshaling of the elements of conceptual form, are systematically ordered according to some regular pattern of relationships.

In architecture, the regular arrangement of columns and other elements of a façade hardly requires comment. Volumes are arranged on consistent principles. In contrast, the composition of exterior spaces was usually wholly irregular and irrational. Temples and other buildings in almost any complex were erected almost at random, without any attempt to rationalize the relations among them. There are evidences that the Greeks were aware of the problem of planning exterior space, and sometimes planned groups as a single design, sometimes to give some organization to the space in front of the principal building, sometimes to create a space for its own sake, like an agora. But these compositions, at least until the Hellenistic period, are by no means always regular; indeed, as often as not they are characterized by a prominent inequality of some kind. This complete willingness to accept the random arrangement inherited from the accidents of tradition in the location of buildings, and the evidently conscious preference for some irregularity in some freely created designs, may mean that the architects were allowing the subordinate structures to ease the transition from the architectural chaos of the city as a whole to the unimpeachable regularity of the chief buildings. In any event, it is in architecture too that the supreme examples of regularity in the visual arts are to be seen—in the moldings at transitional points along the walls of a structure, around doors, and occasionally elsewhere. The long bands of various types of ornamental motif, carved with an astounding and fascinating precision and delicacy, were also designed with meticulous accuracy so that the elements of the motif in a series, always precisely the same in size, have been calculated so that they come out even at all corners. When several bands with different kinds and sizes of motifs were involved, to be arranged in parallel on adjoining walls of different length, this must have called for considerable ingenuity in calculation.

FOCUS

Greek art is notable, too, for its concentration of focus; there is almost always a well-established dominant to which all else is subordinate and related in a definable scale. In the characteristic forms of the fifth century, the central axis of the temple is strongly marked by the peak of the gable and the symmetrically sloping sides, the wider central inter-columniation and the door behind it. The façade of a stoa seldom has a central dominant of this character, though occasionally there are project-ing wings at the ends which become twin foci, flanking elements at the expanse of the façade in general; where such wings are lacking, a short return of the end walls along the front distinguishes the colonnade as one element between flanking members, the real dominant being the forward movement of the structure as a whole. In sculpture, the treatment of single figures find obvious focus in the scheme of the conceptual form itself, as, normally, the head of a man, although almost any single figure will be depicted in some form of action. The concentration of the elements of the conceptual form and the sense stimuli on the figure in action establishes the major focus. In group composition, however, there is greater possibility of variety without the loss of insistence upon a dominant focus. In a pedimental composition, obviously, the axis of the gable makes the major dominant, and to this all other elements contribute their force. In a frieze, on the other hand, there is no externally imposed dominant, except perhaps on the short ends of a building and especially over the door, where the axial dominant is almost invariably accepted. Generally there is a fairly continuous longitudinal movement toward the front, which thus becomes a focus. In panels like metopes some fairly simple event is usually depicted in distilled concentration, and the sensory elements of the work are normally focused on the center of interest. In drawing and painting on vases, there is normally a focus on some one part of the vase—the shoulder of an amphora, the bottom of a kylix—where the most important and conspicuous design is placed, the other ornamentation being subordinate and contributory to the primary ornament and the forms of the vase itself. The point of focus, moreover, usually occupies some central point of a bilaterally symmetrical scheme. Within the focal panel, again, the design of figures is concentrated on some single point as in sculpture.

In literature, the concentrated focus of the style is most obvious in the selection of a particular theme, the elimination of everything unessential to the theme, and the careful hierarchy of all elements to focus on the central point of the theme. This is especially evident in tragedy, which often seems stark and bare according to modern standards because it is stripped of all atmosphere and the numerous characters that seem to us so necessary in creating an illusion of real life. Rather, the Greek play is reduced to the bare minimum of characters, and the effect is heightened by arranging that there shall never be more than two or three on the stage at once. This effect is, of course, immediately mitigated by the presence of the chorus, which, however, is different in kind and distinctly supports the actors. It has almost the character of an abstraction and does not serve the same function as a swarm of people. In these and other respects tragedy is conspicuously intensified in purpose and economical of means. All this, of course, also contributes to the clarity, poise, and objectivity of the play. In the lyric, the same intense concentration on a single feeling or thought; in the writings of Thucydides the rigorous discipline of attending to the theme; and in all of these a similar focus of the sensory elements on the common end is the quality which seems to characterize this aspect of Greek art.

There are, of course, authors whose work does not seem at first to have this unrelenting discipline of concentration. Homer's poetry encompasses scores of characters and events whose relation to Achilles or Odysseus often seems remote; Herodotus accepts anything that comes to his attention. But the searching inquiry of Herodotus had a single purpose—to ascertain the nature of the peoples with whom he was concerned and formulate from the particulars the pattern in which might be perceived the essence of the great conflict. Achilles' and Odysseus' struggles with themselves were purged in their experience of the external world, and it was to the point to depict life at large. Although one may admit that the concentration of Homer and Herodotus does not involve so drastic a paring away of event as the concentration of the dramatists, their objectives are, in a sense, larger. It is also true that everything in their work does relate in fact to the ultimate end; there are no discursions that are mere afterthoughts or by-the-ways.

COHESION

Lastly, with regard to the qualities of arrangement or composition, is the strong sense of cohesion in terms of architectonic structure. Not only is the composition centrally concentrated and regularly ordered, but the arrangement is such as to emphasize the component elements and bring out strongly their particular character and function and their relation to each other in building up an architectural whole. It is thoroughly different from the monolithic unity of Egyptian art, the fluid, dynamic unity of Gothic art, or the vegetable, organic unity of Minoan art. It is a unity of structural relationship—of mutual support and bond, of separate parts added to each other and composed with each other, not simply in series but in structural logic.

As the figure comes from architecture, so it is clearest in architecture. The major divisions in the design of the façade always come at points of structural differentiation—between foundation and steps to the general floor of the building, between floor and supporting elements, between supporting elements and ceiling elements, between ceiling elements and roof. Within these broader divisions, parts are boldly distinguished, so that organization of the design in terms of building blocks, as it were, is emphatically brought out. In the interior forms, the relation of the cella of a temple to the peripteron space to the pronaos to the interior space is rendered in terms of fully distinguished separate spaces, fitted one to the other.

Perhaps a more striking demonstration—though the concept of "architectonic structure" will never be striking to the Westerner, who accepts this kind of cohesion as "normal"—is in the design of the vases. The emphases placed on the distinction of parts with different structural roles—the foot, the stem (if any), the body and shoulder, the neck, the lip—are in Greek pottery far more compelling than in many other ceramic styles, particularly, for example, Minoan. Moreover, not only are the parts emphasized, but also their distinction, their separability.

In sculpture and figure drawing, the matter may be illuminated by contrasts within Greek sculpture. In the Archaic "eastern" school, the human body is rendered with some depiction of anatomical form, to be sure, but the forms are smoothed down and merge to flow into a sweeping continuum of surface and movement. In the "Western" style, the various sections of the body are indicated with strong horizontal lines, so that the statue gives the impression of having been built up out of blocks. Even detailed elements, like the hair, or lips, or drapery, are full and chunky and separable. In the developed Greek style of the later sixth and fifth centuries, these tendencies have fused. It is difficult, in a way, to distinguish the "structure" of the statue created by the sculpture from the "structure" of the anatomy dictated by the conceptual form. Statues of youths are generally less strongly articulated than statues of more mature men, a difference obviously deriving from the conceptual form. However, the statues of mature men reveal a structure of parts which is only rarely clearly apparent in the physical man. The abdominal section is rendered by Polycleitos, for example, as essentially a truncated cone fitted firmly into the cavity between the masses of the upper thighs; the masses of muscle are everywhere finished off in contour and outline a little more distinctly than would be perceptible in nature, so that their independence as forms among forms is unequivocal.

The same quality is inherent in the manner of composing the sensory stimuli. The lines and rhythms that arouse the sense of movement are patterned in the same clearly defined component parts. This is apparent in the construction of complex curves by successions of straight lines angling from each other, suggesting the structure of the curve; but more obviously it is indicated by the concentration of movements and textures in fairly distinct channels and areas and by the close harmony of formal sensory stimuli and conceptual form, each bringing out the structure of the other, as when lines of drapery are arranged over the contours of the body so that the drapery helps draw the contour of the body and the body helps give shape to the lines of drapery.

In literature, the architectonic quality is familiar enough, though perhaps not generally recognizable under this name. In Homer—even in Homer, one might say, since the linear style of his epic might easily have been composed in a thoroughly fluid continuum—the component parts are not only present but fully marked in the development of the narrative. In the *Iliad,* there is the invocation, the opening incident, the preliminary adjustments—the general groundwork; then another beginning, with the catalogue and its invocation, the breakaway into the full action of the narrative; and so on through the poem. The whole falls into clearly apparent sections which constitute the broader elements in the pattern of conceptual form and sensory stimuli; and, of course, within each section are smaller units, equally perceptible.

It is true that the history of the poem and its composition have had a certain effect in this regard. Originally there were a great many relatively short sagas in circulation, and Homer took from these whatever he found useful in expounding the wrath of Achilles. It is altogether possible that the catalogue was incorporated *en bloc* from an independent poem; so also the "aristeia of Agamemnon" and some of the other "aristeiai." The unity of style, to be sure, makes it appear that if these episodes were simply adopted by Homer from a previous existence, he must have rephrased them thoroughly in his own way of speaking. Nevertheless, the separability of such sections was surely not unwelcome to Homer.

Aristotle's insistence on the "beginning, middle, and end" is based on a preference for evident structure, which he obviously found to be characteristic of the best literature—and not only the beginning, middle, and end, but the evident internal structure of the subdivisions that in themselves have beginnings, middles, and ends. Once again, perhaps the most complete and clearest example in literature is the structure of Thucydides' *History*. It begins with a preliminary foundation of the broad review of world history; then a brief but solid body of events constituting the eve of war; then the "fifty years"—a quick survey of the growth of Athens, which might just as well have come at the beginning except for the special architectonic character it has here in providing a block of material, as it were, of less bulk or at least different texture to make the transition between the events leading up to the eve of war and the events of the eve and dawn which follow, in full detail and extent. Then comes a relatively even succession of events, place by place, year by year—the events of different places discussed seriatim— the transition from year to year marked by some special notice. And so the structure rises—not grows or develops, but is built—through the Peace of Nikias with its conclusion of the first phase of the war, to the Melian incident where the dialogue, unique in form and staggering in content, brief as it is and subdued and restrained, marks by its special form the transition to the culminating episode. This is, of course, the Sicilian expedition, which has its own beginning and middle and end, and rests on the previous structure as an entablature and cornice rest on a wall. To an extent our analogy is vitiated, for not only does the history go on from there, but there is no way of telling how much farther it would have gone on. Moreover, if Thucydides in fact did begin writing at the beginning of the war he could have had no notion of when to start building his entablature, as it were. But this reservation is beside the point, for it is not the purpose to show that Thucydides' *History* is designed with the lines of a Greek temple, but that it is designed according to a principle of emphasizing structural segments and their interrelation, and this Thucydides does in a most striking way.

ROMAN ART

In the attempt to identify the peculiarities of the "Roman" style, we encounter a situation which, while not new to us, has not been unduly difficult in our survey so far. This is the question of what, historically and geographically, is meant by "Roman"—a question, in this instance, of peculiar subtlety. The most natural meaning, and that most consistent with the concept of "peoples" with which we began, would have it refer to an Italic folk resident on the lower Tiber and their achievements in their chief city, Rome, and other places where they settled and made their homes, preserving their ethnic identity. Another meaning of "Roman," however, would refer to the world empire which these people created, comprehending almost the entire civilized Western world during the first few centuries after Christ—but here there are really two meanings involved: one chronological, denoting simply an era in the history of the various regions, as we might speak of the Roman period in Greece or Egypt; one cultural, if we wish to refer to the phenomena which constitute the unity of culture throughout the empire beneath or above the local diversities.

In this account we shall take the position that "Roman" does indeed refer essentially to the Italian inhabitants of the city of Rome and their achievement, including among the latter the Empire, considered not only as a political but a cultural force. That is, the unity of the Empire, consisting of elements deriving partly from the Romans themselves, partly in various degrees from various peoples within the Empire, and partly from the creative forces of the Empire itself—this is also "Roman."

We shall not take into account, for the most part, the temporal phases of the local styles—Greek and Egyptian and Gallic and even Italic—of the imperial period, though these, too, often participate in the imperial movements; we shall concern ourselves primarily with the style that is characteristic of the Roman people, ethnically speaking, and of the ecumenical element in the culture of the empire they created.

The Romans emerged in Italy as a people among the Indo-European tribes, closely related to the Greeks, during the early years of the first millennium before Christ. For long they were scarcely to be discerned among the other peoples of the land, especially overshadowed by the Etruscans who dominated central Italy around the middle of the millennium, or the Greek colonies in Sicily and southern Italy which were founded during the eighth, seventh, and sixth centuries. But the Romans were in fact there, and recognized this early phase of their history in semilegendary, semimythological tales that saw the germination of the Roman stock from the alliance of fugitives from Troy under Aeneas with the native Latins, the founding of the city itself by Romulus and Remus in 753, and the subsequent reign of kings until about 510.

About 510 begins the growth of the free and independent Republic. The first century and a half were busy with experiments in the social and political institutions that distinguished the people both in kind and quality. Around the middle of the fourth century, the city began to associate to itself, by a great variety of bonds, in all of which Rome remained dominant, the other states and territories in Italy; around the middle of the third century, she began to acquire territories beyond the seas. By 146, Rome found herself substantially in control of the Mediterranean world. The next century was one of internal conflict—social and economic unrest. Around the middle of the first century B.C., Julius Caesar, after establishing himself through the conquest of Gaul, incidentally adding a vast European territory to the expanding state, substantially took personal control of the machinery of state and became a dictator.

Caesar's adopted son, assuming the name Augustus, took over absolute authority, giving himself the title only of Princeps—First Citizen. His administration, from 27 B.C. to A.D. 14, was devoted to creating a system of administration which, in the first place, would remain ultimately at the control of a single man—the Princeps; second, be adequate to cope with the vast and intricate problems of the worldwide interests and responsibilities of the Roman state; and third, preserve as much good as might be out of the political experience of the Romans during the preceding half-millennium. The result was the Roman Empire.

A kind of Golden Age was marked by the reign of Hadrian in 117–138, but affairs were more difficult during the third century, culminating in another epochal revolution, according to which Diocletian established two co-emperors and two regular assistants. With all this went a complete abandonment of any recollection of republican days, and an exaltation of the concept of autocratic emperor in its purest form. Constantine contributed to the division begun by Diocletian by abandoning Rome for his new capital, Constantinople, in the east. His most crucial act was the recognition of the long-growing, long-suffering, but no longer to be ignored new religion, Christianity. With this event and the merging of the Oriental religion with the Roman state, a new world begins, and Rome and the classical world are, not dead, certainly, but no longer separate, unique entities.

During this long process there occurred a drastic evolution in the term "Roman," and the character of those who were understood as Romans. In the earliest phase, the inhabitants of the city of Rome maintained a dire devotion to their racial integrity and their tradition, though they were inevitably overshadowed culturally by the Etruscans. With the beginning of their expansion in Italy, they confronted the problem which remained alive from then on: how to weld the varied folk that came to be attached to the growing state into one people—to what degree, and how, to make them "Roman." In general, the policy of the state continued to be to reserve a special distinction for those who were Roman by birth and tradition from the days of the past, but nevertheless to develop an effective fusion of the entire population. In this some things were imposed on the newcomers and some things were absorbed by the "original" Romans. This policy continued, with the gradual effacement of one distinction after another, until by the second century after Christ there was no real distinction, political or otherwise (apart, perhaps, from a pride of birth among those who could still demonstrate the integrity of their descent from the mythic past), and if a Spaniard or Illyrian became emperor there was substantially no mark of his particular provincial origin; his real tradition is the developed tradition of the world state that Rome had become.

In the meantime, these Romans, already ethnically and linguistically close to the Greeks, from their first contact with the Greeks of Magna Graecia had adopted intact many Greek cultural forms, with little or no effort to modify them; among these was the developed Hellenic style of art. There persisted a relatively thin stream of art in a direct line from the unadulterated tradition, but there was a larger stream that was Greek—or Hellenistic—in almost every sense: it was made by Greeks, or Hellenized Orientals, much of it in Greece or the Hellenized east, but some of it in Rome itself. This Graeco-Roman, Hellenistic art was bought in increasing quantities by Romans, who accepted it as produced and had no wish to impose their own taste upon it. There was also produced a certain amount of Hellenistic art, slightly modified to appeal to the latent native Roman taste, and a few men strove to effect a fusion of style.

This is evident in literature as well as the visual arts. There were the Greeks who came, sometimes as slaves, to Rome to teach, and some of them had talent and opportunity to write. They might write a simple translation of Greek things, as Livius Andronicus wrote a Latin *Odyssey*. Like Terence (who was not a Greek), they might adapt Greek works with some very slight variation to accommodate the special preconceptions of the Roman audience. Other men might write the strictly traditional *saturae,* grimly resisting influence; or, like Plautus and Ennius, they might strive to effect a genuine synthesis. Essentially this condition persisted throughout the Empire, though as we come to think of Rome as consisting integrally of the lands and peoples from Gibraltar to Palmyra and England to the Sahara, it becomes more complex, for there are a multitude of local traditions, few of them very strong, to be sure, operating in the same way. Everywhere and at all times, one finds work in the purest Greek style possible at the time accepted uncompromisingly because of its prestige; everywhere there are occasional products of purely local tradition; everywhere there are attempts to fuse the local and the Greek. There is also, however, the strain descending from the original native Roman tradition, modified more or less by Greek and local influence, but never losing the inspiration from the Roman past. This is the "Roman art" of our study, impervious to time and place, but permeating the Mediterranean world throughout the time of the Empire and not wholly gone today.

CONCEPTUAL ELEMENTS

The conceptual form of Roman art is, like Greek, iconic and overwhelmingly devoted to mankind. Animals of various kinds are not infrequently treated, and with sympathy and interest, but almost entirely in a secondary order of interest. There is perhaps, as we shall see, a greater interest in "nature" in the sense of landscape and floral forms than in Greek art, but essentially the unflagging concern is for humanity. There is, however, a slight difference in the aspect of humanity which is of interest: in Greek art it is the experience of man which is paramount; in Roman art there is a definite, prevailing attention to his activity.

For one thing, the most primitive and original, purely Latin contribution to literature, the satire, is a commentary on some aspect of human conduct. Personal activities are described at length and in detail, and this makes the satire of the late Republic and early Empire a mine of information about daily life, along with the closely related epigrams of the kind for which Martial is famous. Things that people do, and the way they do them, are the subject matter of all this extensive and peculiarly Latin body of literature. Closely related in the earliest major Latin literature is the comedy, and comedy was the form of literary drama that chiefly pleased the Romans. Of course Plautus and Terence, for the most part, were simply adapting the Greek "new comedy" of Menander and his followers to Roman idiom, and the differences are too subtle to be useful in our immediate inquiry: certainly there is no substantial difference in conceptual form. Therefore, to say that what are practically Greek plays represent something unique in Latin feeling may seem illogical, but out of the range of Greek literature it was the comedy—and this kind of comedy, in which action is especially important and intricate, and the savor lies in the touches of ordinary daily activity—that was seized upon most keenly by the Roman public. Furthermore, the earliest Roman tragedy, never so popular as comedy, in contrast to Greek, took its plot largely from near-at-hand history, evidently relishing "real" action.

Later, when tragedies more closely following the Greek were written by foremost artists like Seneca in the first century after Christ, the plays ordinarily were not performed but recited; this might imply that something other than the action of drama was more appealing. But Senecan tragedy, though not written to be enacted on a stage, depends more than Greek tragedy on the melodrama of plot, setting, and action, even if this must be imagined rather than seen; literary drama after Plautus and Terence had little vogue in any form, but gave way rather to the mime, farce, and extravaganza whose roots lie in Roman culture before the Greek influence.

Another indication lies in the development of the novel, or something closely akin to it, during the period of the Empire. It is true that the advanced form which we see in the *Metamorphoses* of Apuleius had its origins in Hellenistic, non-Roman novellas, and in a sense even in the epic poems of Homer and others; but, once again, that it was the Romans who selected what had been a minor form of Greek literature and created out of it a major form is a revelation of their attitude. Again, the fact that not only the Latin Apuleius but the Asiatic-Greek Lucian and other Greek and Oriental, non-Latin authors wrote extensively in the novel form, and in shorter forms in which action was predominant, may seem to contradict the suggestion that this interest proves something about Romans. But what we are discussing, it must be recalled, is not a local or ethnic matter exclusively; it is a new spirit, emanating from the particular people of a particular town in Italy and penetrating the world which they had formed.

It would be impossible to discuss in detail the whole of Latin literature, pointing to examples or indications of a greater interest in action than is evident in Greek literature. Such a discussion could never be a demonstration, for it would inescapably be a matter of relative quantity, a thing impossible to measure. One might, for example, feel that the story of the *Aeneid* is of a quasi-historical event—the foundation of the Roman people—and not simply a human experience. Another might feel, also of the *Aeneid,* that the compression of much of the content of the *Iliad,* the *Odyssey,* and the *Argonautica* into one work is indicative of an impatient appetite for action. The meticulous concern of Caesar for the events of the campaign might be shown to be greater in amount or degree than Xenophon's in his *Anabasis,* who sketches his battles in more vivid style, but with less system and detail, and surely has nothing to compare with Caesar's specifications for his Rhine bridge. One might think also of the growth of biography, Greek and Roman. Striking, too, is Ovid's reduction of mythology to a library of short stories, or his exposition of ways of making love. Equally striking is the development of the historical epic, beginning with the lost *Punica* of Naevius and the *Annals* of Ennius, through Lucan's *Pharsalia,* Silius Italicus' *Punica,* and other less distinguished work. These encompass vast and complex action in which one minute detail of a naval stratagem or military maneuver is as fully exploited as the sweep of historical forces. The complication of Greek themes, like the *Argonautica* by Valerius Flaccus or the theme of the *Thebaid* by Statius, reflects similar taste.

In sculpture, this interest in action is most obvious in the great historical reliefs, notably the columns of Trajan (Plate 93) and Marcus Aurelius, in each of which a long and complicated campaign of action is illustrated in great detail, depicting all manner of events and situations, in order to present a whole history in visual form. The degree to which this and other historical reliefs fall short of being purely illustration of particular events will be considered later but, whatever the limitations, the gulf which separates the interest in action for its own sake in these columns and anything in Greek art is vast. The comparison is actually much closer with Egyptian and Assyrian work.

Not all sculptured compositions are so extreme in this regard, of course. If one compares the Arch of Titus (Plate 92), for example, with the frieze of the Parthenon, which is the "most narrative" of any of the major Greek reliefs, it is difficult to specify the exact difference in conceptual form. Each represents a procession, and in fact the four hundred-odd feet of the Parthenon frieze undoubtedly depict the Panathenaic procession more completely than the panels of the Arch of Titus, each about fifteen feet long, could possibly depict the whole extent of the triumphal procession of the emperor. And yet one panel, of the Spoils of Jerusalem, seems more concerned with what is going on than the whole of the Parthenon frieze. In the latter we have represented a moment of the event in suspension, as it were. The priestesses preparing the garments to be offered, the gods looking on, are depicted in terms to satisfy our curiosity as to what is happening but hardly to raise the question of how or where. The Athenian magistrates stand about—looking on, no doubt; everyone else is simply walking or riding along, carrying things quietly and inconspicuously, or keeping the sacrificial animals in order (not that they are making any trouble). The only people in the procession who are doing anything that attracts attention are the marshal urging people into position and the man lacing his boot. In the panel of the Arch of Titus, people are carrying exotic spoils, or band instruments, lagging or pushing forward, relaxed or strained; swinging out of one street and disappearing through an arch at the other side. The procession of the main frieze of the Ara Pacis (Plate 91) is only slightly distinguishable from the Greek in this respect, but in the panels flanking the door at each end the interest in varied action for its own sake is prominent. Particularly in Aeneas' sacrifice of the sow (Plate 90), each individual takes an active part, not only participating in the central act but also preoccupied with some concern of his own, and all thoroughly interested in the central action. In general, the long series of sacrificial reliefs depict, even in the simplest examples showing only the animals and priests, an action which is interesting and important in and of itself, and in which the proper forms of the action are the real importance. And the reliefs faithfully record this.

Not only historical and sacrificial reliefs, but compositions depicting scenes from ordinary life (the relief of the Haterii, for example) and literature or mythology are common. There is still a question as to the relation of these reliefs to the Hellenistic "Alexandrian relief," but whether or not the latter is an original product of Hellenistic culture before the admixture of Roman influence, the fact remains that this kind of conceptual form belongs to the period of the Empire and represents the pervasive, common taste of that era.

In painting, too, this interest in event emerges as a striking new characteristic. Leaving aside the Roman versions of Greek or Hellenistic work—a large part of the body of Roman painting—one thinks of the Aldobrandini Wedding and the paintings from the Villa of the Mysteries at Pompeii as embodying a variety of actions which draws the attention; in the Odyssey landscapes and related paintings (Plate 84), the narration of the story in detail is conspicuous; in paintings like the scene from the Isis cult at Herculaneum, or of the amphitheater panorama at Pompeii and the late Roman hunting scenes, action from life is obviously of leading concern. Especially striking are the frescoes depicting fullers, dyers, and others at work, and above all the putti in the house of the Vetii at Pompeii, where the variety of activities, combined no doubt with the fanciful incongruity of having the activities performed by cupids, inevitably captures the interest at first sight.

The most originally creative artistic activity of the Romans was in the field of architecture. In conceptual form, Roman architecture is essentially naturalistic, as is the Greek; and the Romans had no difficulty in adopting freely Greek details and structural forms like columns and friezes. The Roman temple, however, was originally something quite unlike a Greek temple, in ways which persisted through all the later Hellenizing influence. The Roman temple characteristically rests not directly on the ground but on a prominently raised podium (Plates 95, 100), thus distinguishing it boldly from the environment and, furthermore, making it natural if not necessary to approach the building from the front only, rather than from any side, as in the Greek temple. A natural corollary of this is that normally the Roman temple is not peripteral, like the larger Greek temples, but had columns only in front, across the porch. In later, Hellenized versions, half-columns or pilasters were commonly engaged to the side walls, producing the superficial lines of the design of a Greek building and contributing other effects that may be discussed later, but as conceptual form they are redundant and meaningless from the points of view of both structure-function and use-function; essentially there was but one entrance, one approach— from the front. This distinction in itself implies a stricter concern for the specific use-function of the structure—it is a place of divinity, to be used only for worship and not also for relief from the weather; it should be remote from the human plane, and should be approached with special dignity.

The Romans came to develop a number of other kinds of architectural forms even more distinct from Greek practice. Prominent among these was the basilica (Plates 99, 100), characteristically a large rectangular structure completely enclosed, often with one or more apse-like extensions at one end or on the side. Especially if the apse should be at one end, the building would be divided lengthwise into a nave and two aisles, usually by columns though later sometimes by piers supporting groined vaulting. If the apse(s) were along the sides, the columns might enclose a rectangle within the over-all rectangle of the building. The structure was roofed, but often designed with a clerestory. These buildings, which were characteristic of Roman and Romanized towns throughout the Empire from republican to late Imperial times, usually provided space for administrative and, normally, judicial functions. The courts, apparently, would sit in the apses, and free space throughout the building was provided for conferences and business of all kinds among administrative officials, lawyers, and the people in general.

Another characteristic Roman development was the bathing establishment (Plate 102). Essentially, this consisted of three rooms adapted to the various stages of the bath—hot, warm, cold. But by late republican times the baths had become the center of a wide variety of social and cultural activities; in the large public baths the arrangements were magnified and elaborated on a vast scale. There might be two sets of the basic units of three bathing rooms; there would be dressing rooms and lounging rooms and lecture rooms and antechambers and interchambers; the building might be designed as a part of a complex including complete outdoor athletic facilities, parks, lecture halls, galleries, and so forth. Normally, as the complexity of the arrangements increased, so also the scale increased, until the great central halls of the baths of Caracalla or Diocletian may be counted among the largest spaces ever brought under a single span.

In addition to the basilica and bath, other less complex structures with a strong element of originality characterized a Roman town: the amphitheater, an open oval "bowl" of seats around an arena, for gladiatorial combats and similar spectacles; the odeum, or relatively small enclosed theater for concerts and more intimate dramatic performances; the macellum, or typical Roman market building, consisting of a space surrounded by a colonnade along the outside of which ran rows of shop rooms; and other peristyle buildings for various purposes. That these peristyle structures are distinctly Roman rather than Greek, especially since the columns were ordinarily of Greek type and the arrangement would seem to be substantially that of a more or less complex stoa, may not be immediately obvious. The macellum, however, was a single building, not a square surrounded by buildings, but an inward-centered structure with the middle open to the sky. In this it was similar to the Greek palaestra and some gymnasia built on the pattern of a palaestra, but the Greeks themselves did not commonly make buildings on this plan until relatively late.

In domestic architecture, the Romans had some distinctive contributions. One of these was a native kind of house. The most characteristic feature of this was an atrium (Plate 97), a rectangular room with a hole in the roof to admit light and to emit smoke. Behind the atrium was a smaller, more or less square room called the tablinum, a shrine to the ancestors, living and dead, the special retreat of the master of the house and the repository of the most important property. On either side of the atrium and tablinum were living rooms, facing on the atrium; behind might be a garden or, in the well known Pomeiian form which shows much late Hellenistic influence and creative development, a peristyle room, surrounded in its turn by other quarters.

The mansions of the cities might not follow this form, because of the pressure of population or possibly because of some other tradition not clearly known. Palatial dwellings, erected without regard to cost, would be likely to have at least one great hall called an atrium, whether or not it had a hole in the roof, and a series of halls, galleries, and chambers of various shapes and kinds arranged around it (Plates 98, 101). In late republican and early Imperial times, an original form of architecture appeared in the Roman cities, born no doubt in answer to congestion. This was the apartment house in three to six stories. Usually the ground floor on the street was devoted to shops; there was a small courtyard in the center from which the various floors were reached by stairs. The individual rooms were small and characterless, purely "rational" in our sense, but the façade was relieved by balconies; and the court, with balconies and stairs, had a simple and attractive design directly related to its use-function.

Finally, as among the memorable symbols of Roman culture, should be mentioned the aqueducts and bridges, and the triumphal arches, erected for the ceremonies of recognition of conquerors who had won public admiration or fear.

In so brief a survey of the conceptual form of Roman architecture in terms of use-function one impression stands out—how vividly they reflect the variety and activity of Roman life. They are more or less highly differentiated, specialized structures for the varied activities of life, taking form from the nature of the activity. It is not that the Romans engaged in more activities than the Greek; the Greeks also had bathing establishments and courts and concerts and aqueducts. But the Romans undertook through and by their architecture to distinguish and magnify, as it were, these activities. The most striking example of this, perhaps, is the aqueduct, which was often given a quite unnecessary architectural monumentality.

Another aspect of the conceptual form of Roman architecture is in the structure-function. The Romans had two structural devices that were original with them: concrete and a certain kind of brick. The latter was technically superior to Mesopotamian brick, harder and more resistant to weather. With these separately or in combination, the brick used as facing for concrete masses, the Romans had an almost completely flexible material, and one of strength and stability to span tremendous spaces. Of these potentialities they took full advantage, discovering and developing all the principles of construction and vaulting needed for the material. It should be observed that these materials, though plastic and receptive to a high degree of molding and modeling, became monolithic masses when dry. There is little play of localized and channeled stress and strain in a concrete vault, as there would be in one of masonry or wood; generally it rests like a stone on its supports. These principles, then, are made fully explicit in the design: piers and buttresses, arches, vaults, groins and domes are all conspicuously evident. Of course Hellenic forms of columns and entablatures were often used, in structurally unnecessary ways, for pure decoration and in contribution to the general conception of magnificence. These aesthetic functions we shall consider later, but the borrowed and extraneous Hellenic forms were usually designed to correspond to the structure itself and often were given work of their own.

In general, then, we may say that in architecture as well as in the other arts the Roman style was characterized in the conceptual form by a frequent emphasis on activity as well as human experience and character. In this it shares a preference in common with the Egyptians, although the rational interest in Egyptian art is perhaps more profound and more thoroughgoing.

In another respect the conceptual form of Roman art differs from the Greek. There is a greater interest on the part of the Romans in nature, in the sense of physical enviroment, and in vegetable life. Above all, Virgil's *Georgics* is an indication of this; primarily it is devoted to a depiction of the values of country life and the beauties of nature. There seems to be nothing at all like this in Greek literature; Hesiod's *Works and Days* is a farmer's manual, in a sense, not a description of a rural environment.

But after this the distinction is not quite so clear. Virgil's *Eclogues,* for example, seems to give a more prominent role to the floral and other natural imagery of the setting than do the writings of Theocritus, where the descriptions of settings are more clearly a background and not the central theme, though this may seem a tenuous distinction. Virgil seems to dwell longer and more sensitively upon his descriptions of natural phenomena in the *Aeneid* than do Homer or Apollonios—the storm in which Aeneas' fleet is wrecked, the hunt and the storm preceding the mating of Aeneas and Dido in the cave. Horace's *Ode* I, 9 (and III, 13) has a poignant description of a seasonal landscape, but it might be hard to distinguish this from something in Alcaeus or Anacreon from the point of view of conceptual form, especially because of the obvious direct influence. Lucretius describes the world of nature with more sensuous completeness than might seem necessary to his theme, but we have no way of comparing his approach with that of his Hellenic predecessors.

It is impossible to demonstrate any distinction objectively, but few who are familiar with Latin literature will deny the general recurrence of an appeal to country and nature, often only in reaction against the tension of the city, as part of the stimulus of a poem. Horace's *Satire* II, 6, on the country life, Tibullus' romantic vision of rural prosperity in his first ode, and to a less romantic extent in II, i, are explicit statements of this feeling. But there are multitudes of allusions that reflect it indirectly through most of the body of Latin literature. The epic of the early Empire, the "vignette" poetry like Statius' *Silvae,* and the later romantic literature, both Greek and Latin, especially Longus' *Lesbian Pastorals,* devote increasing space to the development of landscape. The theme is more prevalent in Latin literature as a whole than it is in Greek literature as a whole.

In painting, the interest is reflected in the numerous works embodying some degree of landscape setting, though usually it is the human interest which is primary. In the Odyssey landscapes and some other mythological scenes, human beings are small and insignificant; nor is the landscape itself detailed. There are, however, a number of paintings at Pompeii in which landscape is the primary interest, especially the villa at Prima Porta (Plate 85) with its garden compact with vegetation. As well as such genuine landscape paintings, we find a significant amount of painted decorative motif in floral forms—garlands and flowers, vines, and the like. Indeed, this floral and rustic imagery was one of the significant legacies of Roman to early Christian art through such monuments as the mosaic ceiling of the ambulatory mausoleum of Sta. Costanza (Plate 103).

In addition, one may recall "Alexandrian" reliefs and their successors, though in these the interest seems to be rather in the content than in rural nature, and the paintings and mosaics, which seem to be primarily studies of animals and birds. Finally, mention should be made of the important but still smaller class of still-life, in which floral motifs like bowls of flowers are depicted alone or combined with glass vessels, animals, and other things in the familiar manner of a modern still-life. But this class hardly represents a major tendency.

Even in architecture, the interest in floral forms is apparent in the form of sculptured ornament. One of the remarkable achievements of Roman design and craftsmanship was floral ornament, combining great verisimilitude and exquisite delicacy of form and pattern, used as the ornament of panels, pilasters, and the like. Such work is already beautifully developed on the Ara Pacis (Plate 89) and in examples preserved from the Flavian period, like the "Rose Pillar" in the Lateran. Some of the finest of this work was in molded plaster, which has now disappeared, but the practice of floral ornament as an independent primary motif was widespread, if only in the simple form of a wreath. From the point of view of use-function, conceptual form came to include landscaping as an integral part of design—the garden peristyles of houses, the palaces of Nero in Rome and Hadrian at Tivoli (Plate 98), the Praenestan sanctuary, the villas described in Statius' *Silvae,* and the park spaces of public buildings like the Baths of Caracalla and the Library of Hadrian—in all of these, landscape, natural or formal, is a conscious element in architectural composition.

Sensory Elements

The conceptual form of Roman art, then, is distinguished from the Greek by marked emphases on action and nature. Among the sensory elements themselves, however, few sharp distinctions can be made between Roman and Greek art.

MOTION

In movement, for example, all the Roman arts exhibit the same kinds and varieties, produced by the same means, as in Greek work. Architects frankly adopted Greek design and, in republican days, even plundered

Greek buildings for columns and other structural elements, thus incorporating physically into their own buildings much of the rhythmic and linear patterns of Greek work. In Imperial times, even the most original Roman designs in terms of space and concrete construction were accented by columns and entablature of Greek type, thus again incorporating some of the movements of Greek work. In sculpture, also, the kinds of movements embodied in the work are essentially the same as in Greek work. In painting, if we compare the surviving examples—which is hardly sound since most Greek "painting" is known to us in the form of drawings on vases, and most Roman in the form of fresco—the Greeks seem to use drawn line as outline or drawing more extensively; in Roman work the "lines" are more often the intersection of planes or surfaces.

Motion in Roman literature is evident in about the same ways and degrees as in Greek. So far as basic stress and flow patterns of metric rhythms are concerned, there is little difference, since most Latin verse meters are adopted from the quantitative systems of the Greeks and forced upon the somewhat resistant Latin. The movements of rhetorical figures are elaborated beyond the norm of Greek and, particularly in later Latin, become extremely complex and subtle. It is hard to demonstrate the degree of difference, if any, between Greek and Latin literature in word-imagery of motion; to do so would require as a beginning exhaustive statistics of the occurrence of words of motion, which might very well be indecisive anyhow, at least if we are trying to comprehend the more sensitive perceptions of Latin and Greek audiences. The conceptual elements, however, do seem to be perceptibly more volatile. This is a corollary of the greater interest in activity, although the Egyptian interest in activity, by contrast, is expressed with far less mobility. The fluidity of Caesar's casual traversing and re-traversing of the continent of Europe may have constituted one of the agreeably piquant qualities of his commentaries. In the *Aeneid,* not only is travel more prominent than in Homer, but an episode like that of Nisus and Euryalus, perhaps properly compared to the Rhesus episode in the *Iliad,* is a more strikingly disembodied dream-movement in a vague and shifting scene. The movement of the epithalamia of

Catullus is more prominent than in Greek predecessors. But these are all much affected by Greek tradition; more purely Roman would be the wide-roaming action of Lucan's *Pharsalia* and Silius' *Punica* as well as the intricate movement of individual actions like the sea-fight at Marseilles or on the Dalmatian coast or the battle of Pharsalus and Pompey's flight, and the freer, more elaborate, and more numerous movements of the action in Flaccus' *Argonautica* and Statius' *Thebaid* beside comparable Greek works.

It is worth observing that the genre of satire involves a lighter touch—the quick dart of wit and the rapid, sparkling shift of imagery against a tense undercurrent of seriousness, and the sharp turn of thought as the climax is reached. It is also pertinent that the Empire saw the rise of epideiktic oratory—speeches delivered chiefly for their own effect, like chamber music, as it were, or for the formal adulation of an official. Such rhetoric, in a way, is "pure" literary art, without any significant rational aspect, designed to no other end than aesthetic effect. In the genre of oratory, the dominant aesthetic element is kinaesthetic—the pattern of the time and rhythm of the frequency and intensity and volume of sound and image. This element is indeed characteristic of all oratory, including that of Demosthenes and Cicero, but in Dio Chrysostom and his imitators, Greek and Roman, to Ausonius and Boethius it is fostered and developed and affected for its own sake.

LIGHT AND COLOR

Again there is some difficulty in establishing any significant difference between Greek and Roman work in the matter of light and color. There is too little Greek painting preserved to justify extensive inference from what remains, though what is preserved consists of work done in flat rather than elementary colors, and this stands in some contrast to the more modulated tones and values of Roman work, though even this is rarely as fully modulated as most post-mediaeval European work. To be sure, this suspected differentiation agrees with the similarly insufficiently observed facts from architecture: fine Greek work, though built of white marble or smoothly plastered limestone, was boldly colored in full, flat colors; Roman work, though it too may have been painted, took much of its color from the variegated stone facing of colored marbles, porphyries, and granites.

Closely related is the matter of light, where it is much easier to see differences between Greek and Roman work. In architecture, for example, Greek work takes advantage of light, as we have seen, in several ways: line, plane, and movement on a façade, in the form of shadows of different kinds; tone and depth of light and half-light as between the exterior of a building, the space behind the columns in a peripteron hall or within a stoa, and the interior—but goes little beyond this. Roman work, particularly in the more complex spatial forms like the baths, or palaces and villas, produced more elaborate and dramatic effects in the vistas through a series of halls and chambers, each differently illuminated, so that there was an extensive pattern of different quantities and qualities of illumination contrasting and supplementing each other (Plates 97–99). In painting, outlines of figures are often shadows, modeling is in highlight and shadow; the illumination of backgrounds is studied and varied, in contrast to the empty neutrality of Greek backgrounds. It is uncertain to what extent work produced in Roman times, even when it is known to have been copied in some sense from Greek work, may have reproduced the chromatic and luminous character of the Greek original and to what extent it may have modified these aspects of the original in the reproduction. It does seem clear from Etruscan painting (Plate 83) and such works as the stelai of Mnason and Rhyncon, the Girls Playing with Knuckle Bones at Herculaneum (Plate 68), the Alexander mosaic, and others, that there was a Greek style largely devoid of chiaroscuro and other luminous effects, depending largely on line drawing and flat colors, at least into the third century; but there may well have been a strong movement toward more luminous effects after that time within the Hellenic sphere. Nevertheless, these qualities, whether original with the Romans or not, were certainly favored by them and were characteristic of Roman painting wherever it appears. In sculpture, particularly in later times, sharp contrasts of highlight and deep shadow are conspicuous—the quality of "colorism."

In literature, color comes chiefly from conceptual form. Few colors are specified in description, though one readily perceives the color of blood, flesh, and bronze, as in Greek work. Moreover, the more extensive attention in Roman work to strange lands and peoples, to the variety of everyday life and to nature, introduces a broader, more varied palette, more frequently in evidence. Nonetheless, it can hardly be said that color is among the more conspicuous elements of conceptual form in Roman literature. Perhaps the only direct color that stands out as more vivid in Latin than Greek is green; otherwise we have the familiar gold, silver, white, and red. Insofar as variety of vocabulary, phrase, and figure are color, these are much elaborated, and increasingly, through the Empire in both Latin and Greek.

Far more significant than color in Roman work, and more attentively modulated in Roman than in Greek, is light. In the *Aeneid,* the fires of burning Troy in the murky night are a vivid and relatively simple example. Much more revealing are the passages at the end of Book VI and the beginning of Book VII: after the shadows and gloom, the weird and fitful lights and colors of the Underworld, Aeneas sets sail on the gleaming sea under the tremulous moon; then the sea reddens under the rays from the rosy chariot of the shining dawn and becomes smooth as marble; then the ship sails to Tiber's yellow sands round which birds with varied songs and colors fly; then, sails up, back into the shade again. All this is thoroughly impressive. The misty gloom that foreshadows Lucan's version of the battle of Pharsalus, in contrast to occasional gleams of light during the conflict, and the murky shade and fitful lights of Statius' siege of Thebes, and the stormy obscurity of many passages of Seneca are other examples.

Apart from the contribution of conceptual form, light and dark are hard to identify in literature; once again we are not in a position to take statistics of word meanings. More apparent is a kind of gradation of what might be felt as luminosity in the varying degrees of simplicity or turgidity of expression; the, perhaps subjective, effect of the periods of a

Cicero, rolling and swelling like a cumulus cloud, or the thin, clear shafts of expression of a Martial; the open clarity of Caesar or the relatively opaque turgidity of Lucan.

Finally, the varieties of texture are significant in Roman art. This is most conspicuous, of course, in sculpture, where apart from the textures of the conceptual form a wide range of physical textures were exploited, ranging from high gloss to tangibly roughened surfaces. The range was increased by the use of different materials, as in Egyptian work: the gloss of a Greek marble differs conspicuously from that of an Italian marble, and the Romans used not only both of these but a wide variety of granites, porphyries, and the like. So also in ceramics, a variety of materials and treatments of the material, glass as well as terra cotta, were exploited to the same taste. In architecture, too, different kinds and treatments of stone were employed in conscious variety, so that a wall might be built of heavy, bull-nosed masonry in its lower portion, a smoother texture for the main section, and a different texture at the top. The use of concrete and brick provided still other textures. Non-structural, decorative elements contributed further sources of variety: the choice between carved stone or plaster or painted surface, the use of pilasters or columns in the round along a wall. In literature, the effect of texture is evident in words themselves, particularly in the onomatopoeia and alliteration which is more common in Roman than Greek, though not pervasive, and in rhetorical varieties, as we have mentioned in relation to light—the range from sharp, clear statement to relatively involved turgidity.

MANNER

Whatever the specific differences, if any, between Hellenic and Roman work in the kinds of imagery and sensory elements employed, the more important difference we would expect to find in the manner in which they are used. Here again, however, there is, on the whole, an essential similarity, which is not due solely to external Greek influence but which exists in some degree in the earlier, relatively pure, uninfluenced, original, native Roman style. But in spite of this similarity, which makes it proper to speak of a "classic" style as opposed to other styles, and including both Greek and Roman, there are certain emphases in Roman art which ordinarily distinguish it from Greek work. Nor do these differences consist exclusively in technical manners of working the material, although such differences are frequently the most conspicuous and objective ways of distinguishing a Roman monument from a Greek monument; they extend to most of the aspects of manner that we are accustomed to consider.

ONTOLOGY

Among the qualities of manner which relate to perception rather than sensation, we encounter immediately one distinction of Roman art: although it is based on the same kind of idealism we have observed in Hellenic art, it has a definite element of particularism.

There is a danger of overemphasizing this particularism in an effort to distinguish it, essentially and over all. Roman art is conceived in types, like Greek art. But within these types there is discernible a leaning toward particulars that goes beyond Hellenic manner. It is clearly evident in the earliest phases of the art, extending back to the dawn of civilization in Italy and the Italic plastic funeral urns (Plate 87), which often bear heads with what seems to be marked individuality. By the fourth and third centuries, both Etruscans, as vividly exemplified by the "obesus Etruscus," and Romans, as exemplified—perhaps later—by the so-called Brutus, were creating portrait statuary of a most accomplished kind. The particular origin of portrait sculpture, presumably from the death masks made of the departed to provide likenesses for the household rites of ancestor worship, no doubt gave a special stimulus to this branch of art; and it is true that portraiture remained, throughout the Republic (Plate 88) and Empire, one of the most distinguished achievements of Roman art.

The Greeks also developed portraiture in the Hellenistic period. Prior to that time, statues had been made purporting to depict individuals, like Pericles, Harmodios, Aristogeiton, or Olympic victors. But until the end of the fourth century, these statues were rendered in the most general terms, with the elimination of most marks of individuality, preserving only the basic humanity and the quality for which the individual was distinguished—physical prowess, intelligence, and the like. Even the portraits of the late fourth century, like Lysippos' Agias and the studies of Alexander, reproduce only the broader forms. Afterward, to be sure, portraiture of what appears to be highly detailed individualism appeared throughout the Hellenistic world. Thus it may be questioned whether there is, in fact, anything uniquely Roman in their production of portraiture.

Two considerations may be advanced. It seems significant that portraiture was apparently the first and most deeply rooted sculptural development in Rome, whereas it was the last to appear in the Hellenic world, and that at a time when the social condition had developed to something thoroughly cosmopolitan, in which the Greek tradition was only a part, if the dominating part. Second, the cosmopolitan world in which Hellenistic portraiture developed was one which Rome had already begun to infiltrate; among the centers of Hellenistic portraiture were Delos, at that time a center of Roman trade, and North Africa.

But whatever the position of portraiture in the Hellenistic world, its position in Rome and the Roman world is unambiguous. It establishes in the most objective terms a predilection of the Romans that can be discerned in one form or another on almost every side.

At the same time, it is worth noting that, as in Egyptian portraiture, the Roman interest in the individual normally stopped at the neck. There are no "spare heads" as have been found in Egyptian tombs, but there are innumerable portrait heads and busts for which no body was ever made, and it was the practice to carve bodies of standard type to which the portrait of some or any individual might be affixed. It is clear that the particularism of the Romans was limited and circumscribed by the same kind of idealism we have found in Greece.

Of course portraits form a special case, and may even, in the most extreme attempts to reproduce the features of an individual, be thought of as dominated by the rational content, and hence not really art. The tendency to particularism, however, reappears in the narrative reliefs—those that depict sacrificial ceremonies, scenes from daily life, historical events. Here it usually seems as though a specific event is being depicted, or at least an activity with some specific connotation. Thus the Ara Pacis presumably depicts the ceremony of the sacrifices in thanksgiving for the peace won by Augustus; the Arch of Titus depicts the triumphal procession after the conquest of Jerusalem; the columns of Trajan and Marcus Aurelius depict the story of their wars in the Balkans. Moreover, the events are depicted in such detail that they seem to be quite literal illustrations of what occurred; one can describe the activities in the friezes and have the sense of describing the events themselves. And yet they cannot be actual illustrations in the sense of reproducing the very occurrence they purport to record: the frieze of the Ara Pacis was installed before the ceremony of dedication took place; the artist could not have predicted what the little boy would be doing at any particular moment, and even if he had predicted it accurately his rendering would be of his prediction, not of the event. The detailed chronicle in the columns of Trajan and Marcus Aurelius are rendered in an epic manner: one group of soldiers is floundering in a river while another is fighting on shore and a third gallops toward a town which a group of soldiers is attacking under the defense of the inhabitants. And it may very well be that this is just what happened, but it is not to be supposed that each of the groups depicts exactly or even approximately the appearance, position, and action of the several individuals who were there; the groups are, as it were, vignettes: (1) soldiers floundering in the water; (2) soldiers fighting on land; (3) soldiers defending the city, etc.

Though it is beyond question that these reliefs were intended to be thought of as depicting particular events, and in fact give the impression of depicting particular events, in execution they depict someone's free formulation of an event—a kind of idealism.

The central part of the Great Trajanic Relief showing the emperor in the midst of his officers in battle is an example of a slightly different approach. No doubt a particular event is being depicted, but the affair is formally staged with the officers in full dress instead of battle dress and the emperor displayed to good advantage. The relief also illustrates another kind of particularization: in one corner, the emperor is welcomed back to Rome, received by the Dea Roma, and crowned by Victory.[2] Obviously neither "Roma" nor Victory appeared in any ceremony at Rome, yet this is a specific event depicted as though in literal illustration.

In general, then, we find this pervasive interest in the particular not strong enough to overcome the tendency to idealize the form of not only person but of event, but strong enough to manifest itself in some degree almost everywhere.

In considering painting we encounter the familiar dilemma that it is impossible to distinguish with complete confidence the degree of influence of Greek and Hellenistic work on Roman art. Particularly from the point of conceptual form, the preserved paintings, though they include an appreciable number of scenes from daily life, are predominantly mythological in subject, and hence lack the obvious touch of the particular historical event.

The elements which do give a particularizing character to the conceptual form of Roman paintings are the elaboration of the setting, so that time and place—not necessarily sharply specified, but the fact of time and place as part of the action—are fully implied by the setting and furnishings of the scene. This is, of course, more distinct in some paintings than in others (the "putti dorati" scenes are rendered upon a completely abstract, black ground), but it is generally true in some degree. We should not confuse this with the aesthetic quality of space-time configuration, for it could be given by a relatively few points to establish the spatial forms; conversely, the setting could be particularized in any kind of configuration. Thus indication of the time and place of the event, as differentiated from the indication of spatial and temporal relationships among objects, is in fact a departure from pure idealism. In Roman painting, as in sculpture, the departure is not great. We cannot say that the event took place in Knossos or on Mt. Ida, but we can see that it took place in a city or on a mountain or along the sea, and usually we see a little more than this about the nature of the setting.

The most marked particularism in Roman painting is in the sensory

[2] G. Hamberg, *Studies in Roman Imperial Art,* pp. 8, 56–63.

stimuli themselves. There is a wide variety in the kinds of movement—by continuous flow or widely separated accents; firm lines, blurred lines, rough lines. Light is sometimes used to model in evenly modulated shadows, sometimes in bold, flaring highlights against solid somber black. There is, in general, a pursuit of novelty. Painting seems to present the reverse of the characteristics of sculpture: in the latter, the particularism is more evident in the imagery than in the sensory elements; in painting, it is more evident in the sensory elements than in the imagery.

In architecture, the particularism is evinced in the variety of group plans created. There was of course a strong uniformity among the various types of buildings, and even in the plans of towns and elements of towns like the forum, colonnaded streets, and the like. But if particular conditions suggested, it was possible to design a complex forum like Trajan's in Rome, and oval one like that at Jerash, or one co-ordinated of structurally diverse elements like that at Corinth. This is not simply a matter of ignoring preconditions, as the Greeks did on the Athenian Acropolis, except for basic structural and functional needs; this was adapting and harmonizing a standard design to specific functional and structural conditions, so that a new formula was produced for a specific situation.

The tendency may also be seen, less in temples than in other buildings, in the devices to introduce variety within the types. The bath, the basilica, the odeum, are usually recognizable quickly enough by their general features, but each one has its own individual adaptations of spatial organization, ornament, and functional devices that are more consciously conspicuous than the relatively subtle variation in proportions and detail that distinguish Greek buildings.

Finally, although it has only a secondary place in the aesthetic aspect of the work of art, it was the common Roman practice to display prominently on a building the name of the individual who built it or the name of the god or person to whom it was dedicated, a statement of the function of the building, and other such information. This not only reflects the interest of the Roman in particulars, but aesthetically the information plays a role in starting a train of associations that may interplay with other emotional responses in the mind of the observer as he examines the work.

The inclination toward particularism is most vivid in the satiric tradition in literature, where individuals are singled out and attacked for specific idiosyncracies that constitute the conceptual form of the work. Moreover, the success of the satire depends on the novelty and special aptness of expression. But, at the same time, the basis of the satire in constituting an attack on a kind of manner that is at odds with an approved manner, the conscientious development of a *form* of satire and the preservation of the traditional meters, indeed the meters which are oldest and most solemn, reveals the overriding idealism.

In other literature, the conception of Aeneas as an historical figure founding a particular nation, and the application of this concept to the particular figure of Augustus, is an aspect of the work which differs from the unidentifiable and hence universal world of Homer. But again the concept of Aeneas and his achievement is couched in terms of the experiences and exploits of the Homeric world—i.e., as types. In Roman lyric and elegiac poetry, the choice of themes involving particular emotions and experiences with particular people is more evident than in Greek. Catullus' Lesbia was a particular individual, though whether Sappho was writing for herself or others may be in doubt. Of course the universality of the feeling in Catullus' experience is an evidence of the idealism, as is, again, the recognition of the validity of the themes of tradition, the acceptance of the standard metric and other patterns.

Finally, one may recognize an example of particularism in the development of biographical literature, with its concern for individuals (though usually studied so as to clarify the *kind* of persons they were, rather than to establish their impregnable individuality). And beyond biography may be seen the autobiographical element in Apuleius' *Metamorphoses,* which beneath its elaborate narrative seems to reveal the special conversion of Apuleius himself. Yet, again, this is not offered, presumably, as an interesting and unique curiosity, but as the kind of thing that people can and should experience. The witch and the robber are types having little individuality; but we have vivid glimpses of streets and houses and stables and theaters, and some of these scenes seem to be drawn from life. Finally, it is worth recalling Roman fondness for historical epics about real individuals.

EPISTEMOLOGY ✓

In considering the epistemological factor in Roman art, we encounter frequently the terms "impressionism" and "illusionism." In general they have been variously employed with reference to Roman art, synonymously or otherwise, with relation to various kinds of rendering of space and narrative and to certain kinds of work in which the conceptual form is indistinctly or incompletely depicted.

But by now "impressionism" has been so variously used in discussions of art that it has lost any value in analysis unless it is carefully defined in each context. "Illusionism" is a singularly unfortunate term because almost any naturalistic work is to some degree concerned with creating an illusion of reality of some sort. The term "illusionism" might be arbitrarily restricted in some way, as for instance to refer to depictions of men or other things so as to create effectively a conviction of the actual presence of an actual man, as in the many stories of great artists who painted a bunch of grapes or the like so skilfully that some animal came to steal them. This might be a workable usage; although even so, what might constitute an effective deception to people of one group might not seem so to another. Hence we may reject either of these words in any particular technical sense.

In our own terms, on a scale between objectivity and subjectivity, on the objective side the artist puts into the work everything that he wishes to have registered on the observer's consciousness, so that the pattern of the observer's impressions exists also in the medium. At the subjective extreme, the pattern is formed in the observer's mind by arbitrary stimuli calculated to evoke indirectly in the observer a sense of having perceived something. Thus in the rendering of a sculptured head the objective artist indicates the hair by carving strands; the sculptor with a subjective approach would carve a rough surface. In either case the observer would have the "impression" or "illusion" of having seen hair—not real hair but sculptured hair, of course—but in the former case a close examination confirms the impression, and in the second case a close examination reveals the deception. In any painting depicting a three-dimensional configuration, the observer who examines the work closely will naturally fail to find an opening or regression behind the picture plane, but in the objective work he will find the lines and surfaces which form the configuration; in the subjective work he will fail to find even these.

In this light, Roman art is thoroughly objective and indistinguishable from Greek. In sculpture, the forms of the imagery are reproduced in the stone, or if not—as in the rocks and trees of some landscape reliefs—they are conventionalized and rendered so distinctly that it is the conventionalized form which is apprehended and there is no allusive suggestion to perceive them more "naturally." The action is depicted "as it happened," with little suggestion or innuendo. The lines of the drapery exist in stone; occasionally a wad of cloth may be rendered with a disorganized crumpled surface, but this is an objective reproduction of the mass of cloth, not a suggestion of roughness. In narrative and in four-dimensional reliefs, not only do some figures *seem* farther away and more vaguely outlined, they *are* farther away and more vaguely outlined. The same is true of painting, with exceptions which we shall consider later. In the more common kind of work, the factual content of the conceptual form is depicted with impersonal accuracy; what seem to be lines and solid forms are fully modeled by light and tonality and color along every contour. In architecture, shapes and relations of shapes are depicted by walls and supports and moldings with physical substance; only rarely are shapes and scale manipulated by perspective designs or other suggestive devices. Occasionally, as in the Lechaion road at Corinth, one finds converging colonnades, with the effect, whether intended or not, of an attempt to control the illusion of perspective, but this is rare, and the intention remains in doubt.

In connection with architecture, two special problems arise. One is the situation created when paintings depicting vistas of various kinds are used on the walls of a room, like the Odyssey landscapes, which are depicted as stretching beyond a colonnaded gallery along the room; or the more conventionalized architectural vistas. Are these not "illusionistic" and hence subjective? Illusionistic they may be, in the sense of "opening out" the wall; and yet this illusion is created by objective means. There are real lines delineating the perspective, and the details of the architecture of which the observer is aware are fully draw on the wall.

Another problem lies in the use of colored marble revetment over stone or brick or concrete walls; the use of half-columns and entablatures or detached columns, as on the façade of the Library of Hadrian, as ornament on concrete buildings, the false façades like those behind fountains, the Septizonium of Septimius Severus, or screen façades before unsightly or unintegrated spaces. Are these not all deceptions in some sense or other? Do they not create an impression of something that does not exist? To some degree this may be so, but not entirely. The problem of revetment brings up a question as to whether the function of the concrete might not include the display of colored marble slabs. It is not so much a question of concealing the concrete as it is of providing the marble. The false façades do not so much constitute a pretense of a building behind as that of an element in the enclosure of the space in front, and these are rendered in full, substantial actuality designed in terms of their real function, whether that function be structural or ornamental.

In literature, objectivity is apparent, first of all, in that thoughts are almost invariably expressed externally to the author, who appears but rarely and even then, like Caesar, as "he"—and fully and directly, not by suggestion, general allusion, and implication. Of course there is some use of suggestion, particularly in the satire and lyric, and in oratory, but generally speaking ideas are openly and intelligibly developed. This is not to deny the possibility of some symbolism, as we shall see later, nor the fact that many ideas are expressed in terms of specific allusion to mythological or historical figures or situations that seem vague and obscure to us. To the properly prepared reader, however, these would not be vague and misty, but forthright and factual. For the rest, the imagery in the poets is in terms of external phenomena rather than internal reaction, though there is a more subjective quality to Latin elegiac than in most Greek poetry outside the Hellenistic epigrams. The movement, color, and light that is effective in the writing can be specifically identified there; it is not given as the author's reaction, and is not created as "mood" by the reader himself from unrelated stimuli in the work.

In short, for the most part Roman art shares the objectivity of Hellenic art. There are, however, two exceptions worth noting. One is in certain classes of painting, which do have much of the quality of nineteenth-century "impressionistic" painting, in that the pigment is laid on not in continuously modulated line and surface but in splotches that in some subclasses of these paintings might be numerous and small and in others might be few and large. In the former, like a Pompeian fresco with roosters or a still life with fruit, the effect at a distance is of full modeling, but each is rendered in terms of spots of light and shadow that fuse optically at a certain distance. This technique quite possibly is intended to adopt the effects of mosaic, in which, of course, tesserae of different colors were used. There can be no continuous drawing or modulation of color or shade; it must be done in successive, varied tesserae, and the merging must be optical. Successful results were achieved by mosaicists in what is astonishingly like the nineteenth-century impressionist, particularly the pointillist, technique, using stone tesserae instead of dabs of paint. Some of the painting, then, does resemble tesserae in its effect and may have been copied from mosaic. What may be an extension of the principle may be seen in the Odyssey landscapes (Plate 84) and some of the Alexandrian landscapes, to a much greater extent in the Isis fresco from Herculaneum and the Trojan Horse fresco, and to some degree in many others (Plate 86). In modeling a figure, this involves the use of broad splashes of light to highlight rather rough, heavy outlines and a general tendency to distort the figure in some expressive manner. This is verging on a definitely subjective, expressionistic style, and it is especially significant in relation to the genesis of post-classical, early Christian art.

The other exception has to do with the development of colorism, which began in the latter part of the second century after Christ and perhaps was related to the movement in painting just mentioned. Colorism in sculpture and architecture is the creation of visual stimuli of vivid, vibrant light, in part subjective, with the sharp contrast of bright light and deep shadow. Hair is no longer hair but a pitted surface; folds of drapery are no longer folds but furrows. Thus subjectivity enters the style, although it does not become a controlling force in pagan art.

SIGNIFICATION

In signification, Roman art exhibits a tendency which is markedly different from Hellenic, though it is not a universal characteristic. Whereas Greek art is essentially literal, as we have seen, Roman art is frequently characterized by conscious intellectual symbolism of various kinds. Both contain unconscious emotional symbols, as must almost any art, but neither would seem to use emotional symbols in a conscious way.

This characteristic of Roman art, to be sure, may not be "native" in the sense of having developed independently among the Italian people; it may have been developing in the Hellenistic world and come to maturity coincidentally with the emergence of Rome as the world power. Thus the first prominent example in sculpture would be the Altar of Domitius Ahenobarbus of about 32 B.C. The frieze on the front of the altar depicts a sacrifice in honor, presumably, of a naval victory; the sides and back depict Poseidon and Amphitrite in a swarm of sea nymphs. The mythological scene does not depict the gods and nymphs doing anything in particular; they are simply there and call to the spectator's mind the sea and its majesty by a process which, while it is largely intellectual, is so easy and spontaneous as to circumvent any actual reasoning process. Thus they establish an association for the ensemble in the same way as a trident in the hands of a male figure would establish an association identifying the figure with Poseidon: they constitute, in short, an emblematic symbol of a largely intellectual character, and they were surely used in this way with conscious purpose.

Another kind of symbolism common in Roman sculpture is the formally emblematic symbol, the personification of Fides or Providentia of Salus or Victoria or Roma. It may appear in an allegoric depiction of some event, with real human figures or with other personifications (Hamberg's allegoric paraphrase),[3] or it may stand alone for a whole event (Hamberg's hypostatized norm). We see such figures as Roma and Victory frequently, as in the Trajanic Frieze from the Arch of Constantine, the River Danube in the Column of Trajan, and so forth.

On the Ara Pacis (Plate 89), the relief of Terra Mater is more than emblematic symbolism, although included are countless emblematic symbols, like the bits of vegetation and the animals which symbolize the fruits of agriculture. As the goddess presides over the scene and welcomes the little children on her lap, she becomes an allegorical symbol of the beneficence of nature. In this she has a prototype in the Arcadia of the Telephos fresco from Herculaneum, or, rather, from the probable Hellenistic source of this fresco. Then, too, the relief depicting the sacrifice by Aeneas is almost surely a conscious analogical symbol, in the sense that it is intended to allude not only to the sacrifice conducted by Aeneas but also to a modern analogue, the sacrifice conducted by Augustus.

Finally, there is the kind of symbolism evident on the sarcophagi, particularly of the second and third centuries, in which mythological scenes are depicted with obvious secondary meanings. The story of Dionysos becomes an analogical symbol of resurrection, with unconscious emotional symbolic strains in the sleep of Ariadne, and with an increasing development of minor emblematic symbols in the vine and ivy and other appurtenances of the cult. In similar fashion, if to less degree, the myths of Orpheus, Adonis, Meleager, and others came to be used in this way.

In the field of painting, there is, perhaps because of the accidents of preservation, rather less symbolism. Most of the preserved paintings are apparently literal depictions of mythological or realistic scenes, though it is always possible that the artist or some individuals understood their secondary meanings. A few works, like the Telephos and Arcadia from Herculaneum, which may be an adaptation of a Hellenistic original, are allegorical. Other compositions, like the Aldobrandini Wedding or the

[3] G. Hamberg, *Studies in Roman Imperial Art*, pp. 41–45.

frescoes in the Villa of the Mysteries at Pompeii, may embody some symbolic meaning, though it is uncertain just what it is.

In architecture, the most conspicuously symbolic structures are the triumphal arches. They symbolize the city gate of the early town, the submission of the vanquished to the conqueror and of the conqueror to his government; and perhaps unconsciously, the might and glory of Rome. They differ from Greek victory monuments like tropaia or choregic monuments, which in a basic sense were symbols of victory but were intended as specific memorials and devices to display achievements.

The extent to which other architectural monuments were conceived symbolically may be debated, but does not appear to have been great. In a way, perhaps, the construction of towns and cities of Roman design in all parts of the Empire was in itself, in the totality of each town rather than in particular buildings, the conscious and effective symbol of Roman rule.

In all this, of course, we have been dealing with the symbolism of the conceptual form of the visual arts. The extent to which purely sensory stimuli may have been symbolic in the visual arts is dubious, but would appear to have been slight.

In Roman literature, there is rather more conscious emblematic symbolism than in Greek. Superficially the distinction may not be obvious, but when Sappho spoke of Aphrodite she almost surely meant something that was to her a real power of nature and life, as when we speak of God. When Catullus spoke of Venus he was alluding directly to the emotion "love" by reference to an unreal being who was, he understood fully, a poetic equivalent of the emotion. Sappho speaks directly to the evening star, accepting it for the moment at least as something with which one might have converse; to Catullus it is simply a symbol of evening. Thus Latin lyric and other literature are filled with allusions to the sea and the celestial bodies and phenomena of life and nature in terms of mythological figures which were clearly understood to be imaginative substitutes, created for that purpose. In beginning the tenth eclogue, Virgil calls on Arethusa, taking the fountain for the island, as though it were a person. Elsewhere he seeks to create a force with a personal entity when he describes at length and in detail the spread of rumor and gossip in terms of a distinctly conscious allegorical symbol, "Fama." In satire, there is a great deal of analogical symbolism, obviously self-conscious in the very nature of satire, in the use of selected features to denote the whole of a character or situation.

There are a few works in which the conscious symbolism is much more complex and profound. Such would be the *Aeneid,* which is, literally taken, the narration of an historical or legendary event, and the depiction of the character and experiences of individuals involved. Quite evidently, however, the individuals are analogical symbols of Roman character and Roman history—of the dangers and blandishments to which Rome has been subjected in its contact with Carthage and Italy and the rest of the world, and of the properties necessary for triumph. More specifically, it is an analogical symbol of the triumph of Augustus, the full realization of Roman destiny. "An inevitable civil war—all the participants were Italians, all ancestors of the Romans— had happily come to its period. All had fought well, and, according to their best lights, justly. All bitterness and all passion was now laid at rest, and all could now join hands as comrades and together walk to meet the shining future." [4]

Within this structure there is much symbolism of more restricted scope but often deeper intensity. It is hardly to be supposed that Virgil was aware of the symbolism of the golden bough in the same degree as was Frazer, but it must have meant something to him, and the experience of Aeneas with the Sibyl and in the Underworld involves an emotional symbolism of death and resurrection which was probably unconscious but must have been more alive to Virgil than it was to Homer, if only because he had read and reflected on Homer. Much of the mythological and historical allusion in this and other passsages may be considered symbolic in a way, though on the whole one is likely to be impressed with the apparently literal objectivity of an account which could very well have become nothing but symbolism.

Perhaps the extreme in symbolism in Roman literature is Apuleius' *Metamorphoses.* In this, the general story of a man turned into an ass

[4] M. Hadas, *History of Latin Literature* (New York, 1952), p. 159.

and his final recovery of human form, followed by his conversion to the worship of Isis, is obviously a conscious, analogical symbol of human salvation from depravity. Without the conversion to the cult of Isis, to be sure, the story could easily be taken simply as literal, somewhat fantastic, and picaresque, but there can hardly be any question of its allegorical intent. This interpretation is strengthened, of course, by the insertion of the story of Cupid and Psyche, which is a more specifically allegorical symbol in that most of the main characters have the names of that which they are to symbolize: soul, love, pleasure, etc. The story of Cupid and Psyche, then, tells of how the Soul is saved from degradation and death by Love (Psyche actually descends to Hades, it will be recalled), with the definite interpretation of the time and artist that the result is Pleasure. This story then simply parallels and reinforces the main theme that Love saves the Soul and stands in contrast, since salvation promises not pleasure but a kind of peace. It is not without significance that the initiation into the cult of Isis follows a somewhat similar pattern.

That the Cupid and Psyche story is a version of the Indo-European Märchen of Beauty and the Beast, and that this folktale had its original inspiration in some year-daemon myth, perhaps with an admixture of the myth of a corn queen, cannot have been known to Apuleius, but having heard the story he undoubtedly felt the unconscious emotional symbolism and recognized its value for his theme.

In literature, it seems easier to recognize the symbolism of sensory elements, especially light and color, than it is in the visual arts. The transition in the *Aeneid,* from the end of Book VI to the first of Book VII, is not only a striking example of light and color in conceptual form, but it is clear that the particular differences in this particular place are to be understood symbolically as expressing analogically as well as emotionally the character of the setting, the experience, and the meaning of the experience.

On the whole, then, we are constantly aware in Roman art of simple symbolism of several kinds, and occasionally of much more complex and profound symbolism. And yet, as is true of any contrast between Greek and Latin, the deviation of Latin from Greek in the matter of symbolism is not extreme. The basic signification in Roman art is generally literal, and the degree of symbolism when it occurs is seldom enough to make it completely foreign to Greek style.

DEFINITION

The difference between Greek and Roman art is least, perhaps, in the quality of definition. Here the same kind of clarity which is characteristic of Hellenic art characterizes also the Roman. The difference is again a quantitative one; in this case it does not extend to so many details. In rendering the drapery in a statue or painting, the Roman artist was not always meticulous in revealing explicitly the exact arrangement of all parts of each garment, the articulation of the body beneath, the full development of every fold. He might be satisfied with indicating clearly enough the major outlines, and indicating the connections by relatively sketchy, mechanical devices. A striking indication of the fundamental attitude, though not typical of really fine work, is the custom of turning out large quantities of headless figures in routine, almost mass production, to be completed by affixing portrait heads made on order. That a statue could be articulated in this way reveals a lack of concern for the closer refinements of articulation. In painting, the more extensive use of light and shadow often resulted in the broadening and obscuring of contours and internal lines, though in a general way the relations would be perfectly clear. In architecture, the sharp accuracy of cutting at corners and joints that is characteristic of Greek work is missing; the larger forms are clear and bold, but the details are often vague and unfinished. In literature, it would be scarcely possible to establish a difference of this sort and degree, even if it exists.

CONFIGURATION

It is in the quality of dimension that one of the most conspicuous distinctions of Roman art emerges. We have followed the development of Greek art through several stages: the linear dimension of the primitive geometric period; the expansive dimension of late geometric and orientalizing; the massive dimension, beginning in the Archaic period and continuing; the space-time dimension, beginning in the fourth century and continuing and developing through Hellenistic. It should be recalled that interest in a new dimension does not necessarily mean the abandonment of interest in the old dimension, and in Greek art it does not. In orientalizing art, line and linear pattern are still alive; in the Archaic period mass is co-ordinated with surface so that there are still full surfaces interesting in themselves and a basis for the play of line; in the fifth century, the massive form is developed more subtly by line and surface; in the fourth century and later, none of this is abandoned but a new interest is added. In Roman art, however, in the time of the Empire at least, not only did the relationships of space-time become strong but qualities of mass are subordinated and sometimes lost.

Predilection for space-time relationships appears in Etruscan tombs of the sixth century, even though the paintings in these tombs are largely adapted from Greek art of the same period. The bird-hunting scene in the Tomb of the Fishers in Tarquinia (Plate 83), for example, represents a boat holding four men floating along a sea filled with fish while a man standing on a rock tries to bring down some of the swarms of birds in the air with his sling. The scene is rendered wholly in two dimensions, and in many ways it is reminiscent of Egyptian hunting scenes, from which indeed there may have been some influence. But the important thing is that already there is an interest in depicting a variety of actions in a complex spatial relationship. The pose of the Apollo from Veii has more of a swing forward than a contemporary Greek statue would have been likely to have. The man and his wife on a pottery sarcophagos from Cervetri, in the Villa Giulia, are arranged in a looser composition, with open gestures, the relationship between them not only physical but giving a sense of intimacy and affection and a definite tie to the spectator by the gaze directed, as it were, toward the camera and the admiring family. The Arringatore, with poised left arm and outslung right arm, eager, earnest head, feet ready to step forward, the deep, loose folds of the garment, is fully conceived in its relationships in space as well as in mass. An interesting relief from Aquila is thought to be a survival in late republican or early Imperial times of an earlier Etruscan tradition of rendering complex spatial relationships.[5] The manner is that of the Egyptians or geometric Greeks, with different zones for different depths, but it reflects the basic interest.

On the frieze of the altar of the Ara Pacis are depicted figures in a sacrificial ceremony, each figure of substantially compact form, and although there is perhaps more space around most of the figures and over their heads than would be true of a fifth-century Greek relief, there is nothing strikingly different in the quality of dimension between the Roman frieze and a Greek one. On one of the panels flanking the doors of the enclosure is a depiction of Terra Mater (Plate 89) surrounded by birds, beasts, and flowers, as well as by children and personifying figures, compatible with later Greek work. Although the setting on a hillside is depicted, the figures dominate the whole, almost filling the panel, with rocks and vegetation showing between and with a minimum of empty space. The two flanking figures are strikingly enveloped in the hollow of billowing drapery, though the children playing on the lap of Tellus are little different in kind and degree of spatial, temporal, or emotional relationship than much that is found in Greece after Praxiteles.

On the outer sides of the enclosing wall is depicted the sacrificial procession (Plate 91). Superficially, it is strongly reminiscent of the Parthenon, with its figures completely filling the space from top to bottom, no empty space anywhere on the frieze, and with the same quiet, measured rhythms. But a second glance reveals that, even within these difficult limits, the figures are arranged in space. They stand behind each other, the head of one man visible over the shoulder of another, with a whole forest of feet appearing below the line of the edges of the togas. This disposition of figures in successive logical planes is evident in the Parthenon, but in the Ara Pacis the figures indicated as farther away are in different depths of relief, varying according to the presumed distance. Some figures look in, some out, some backward, some forward, creating not only movements of conceptual form in and

[5] I. S. Ryberg, *Rites of the State Religion in Roman Art*, American Academy in Rome, *Memoirs*, XXII (1955), Plate IX, Fig. 196.

out but also recession and reprojection of physical line and plane in and out of depth. All this is far more significant, in a way, than the Tellus relief, since it reveals not simply a readiness to accept a spatial organization in its own terms but also a determination to enforce a spatial organization both novel and difficult.

Then, finally, in a panel to which we have already alluded, depicting Aeneas' offer of the sow to the Penates (Plate 90), there is a thorough rendering of spatial relations—Aeneas and his companions around the altar in the foreground, with a tree behind it and a temple on the hill in the distance. Whatever its imperfections and technical theoretical basis, it depicts a scene in depth, a complex spatial arrangement on a large scale. There is still a strong concern for the massive form: the chief figures dominate the scene and are fully and carefully rendered; it is not yet time for the dwindling of the massive form in favor of the spatial.

We should not neglect the floral ornament on the lower zones of the enclosure of the Ara Pacis, for the tendrils and flower and leaves are rendered to seem separable, like open ironwork rather than relief on stone. The contrast of mass and space is emphasized. A considerable number of narrative and landscape reliefs exhibit almost uniformly some concern for the depiction of a scene as taking place in space. In the Arch of Titus, the figures come out of a street, bend around and go through an arch, with full space above, figures in depth, and diverse movements running back and forth (Plate 92). In the Arch of Trajan we see figures standing in front of each other and in front of an architectural background. In the Aurelian panels, we see a scene before the Temple of Jupiter Optimus Maximus, other scenes in front of other buildings or in and around arches, groups of men gathered around platforms, all with perspective or overlapping or changes in scale, or all three, resulting in an emphasis upon the spatial pattern.

But in the Aurelian panels, and in the columns of Trajan and Marcus Aurelius, we begin to see the disintegration of mass. This may come about, in part, because in the depiction of the large scene and spatial and temporal relationships, individual figures must be either crowded together or diminished in size; on the other hand, it is probable that as the problem of spatial and temporal relationship became more important to the artist—seemed to him a more significant element of reality—the massive, substantial form of the figures became less important. It was no longer a matter of thinking that importance lay in the relationships among the elements; importance lay in the relationship itself, abstractly conceived. This positive rejection of the value of mass and substance may be indicated particularly by the beginning, even in the Aurelian reliefs, of coloristic carving, the contrast of deep-shadowed cuttings with even, brightly lighted, projecting surfaces. It is the light and shadow which are important, and the drawing that the lines so formed produce; there is nothing in the depths of the shadows—no cloth, no flesh, no finished stone. Drapery, hair, features lose their substantial existence and become simply patterns of light and shadow, line drawings in part, but with dramatically agitated passages, faces and bodies drained of substance to be converted to energy. This description, of course, is too extreme to characterize the Trajanic or Aurelain monuments, though it is not too far from the Severan arches at Rome and Leptis Magna (Plate 94) and represents a tendency that begins to swell through the third century A.D. and into the fourth and later centuries, and extends to the composition as a whole in monuments like the Balbus and the Ludovisi sarcophagi.

The optical depiction of space itself is augmented by the time-space factor in the events depicted. While spatial relationship in themselves are time relationships, the occurrence of events also involves time and space, though often in different ways peculiar to the nature of the events themselves. In Roman art, we find a variety of methods employed in dealing with the time and space of events. There is the method of the Aurelian panels, where there is a close approximation of real perspective, and one sees, for the most part, what he might have seen from a real or imaginary standpoint at some fixed time. Then there is the method exemplified by the columns of Trajan and Marcus Aurelius, where several events taking place simultaneously but at different locations are represented side by side by some distortion of perspective, or quite arbitrarily, as when the soldiers outside a fortified town are depicted from a more or less natural point of view while those opposing them are depicted inside the walls as though seen from above. Here the space relationships of the conceptual form are replaced by the purely physical space relationships of the composition and carving. Another method is to represent several incidents from a series of events in one composition as though in a single panorama. In the Great Trajanic Frieze, one sees Trajan fighting with the enemy in the center while at one side he is being welcomed into Rome, though the figures are disposed as though they were all one crowd. Here the time relationships in the imagery are replaced by purely physical space relationships of the composition and carving. In the columns of Trajan and Marcus Aurelius, of course, both are combined. As the frieze unrolls, we are confronted with scene after scene with no separation, as though it were a single panorama beheld from a single standpoint, but obviously the successive scenes depict events of which some are distinct in place and others successive in time.

There are, then, several ways of dealing with the time and space of events. The Egyptians had a purely arbitrary, rational, logical system. The Greeks confined themselves to the idea of a single point of view, though this is commonly not always a unique point of view but a theoretical or ideal one. The Panathenaic procession, for example, is depicted on the Parthenon with the head of the procession arriving at the Acropolis and the tail just getting started at the city gate. Since the frieze itself cannot be seen without walking from one end to the other, there are complications and contradictions in the verisimilitude of what one sees and the order it is seen, but physically it is conceived in the abstract way we have indicated, as are all narrative scenes in Greek art. The Romans never settled on a single way of rendering the relationships they were so avidly interested in, but almost always they put some kind of spatial relationship into their sculpture.

From Pompeii to Antioch come paintings and mosaics in which there are only a few figures which occupy most of the space and are arranged in a kind of perspective as though seen from a single point of view; these no doubt are Greek or copies of Greek work. Such are the Herakles and Telephos from Herculaneum and the Perseus and Andromeda from Pompeii. Also with a single point of view are many paintings, like that of Achilles concealed at Skyros, in which in addition to the figures, which are large in scale, there is a good deal of architectural or other background. Finally, though no later in beginning than the time of Christ, are paintings from a single point of view in a kind of perspective which depict figures in architectural or landscape settings in approximately natural scale. In some the figures are as large as might be possible and with houses and trees in the same view in something like natural scale, like the Concert of Pan from Pompeii; in others the figures are tiny and almost lost in the landscape, which assumes the proportions of something vast and limitless, reaching out to the horizon. Such would be the Odyssey landscapes, depicted as though the observer were inside a portico looking out across the landscape.

In the Odyssey landscapes, of course, there is a fusion of the time relationship with that of space; Odysseus is depicted several times participating in several events, but in a continuous panorama. This is characteristic of many of the paintings in which the figures are small in scale.

Perhaps the most extreme indication of Roman interest in spatial organization is in painted decoration of the interior walls of houses, at least at certain periods. Columns and other architectural devices are depicted in a kind of perspective to give the appearance of being a real façade with colonnades in front and windows through the wall behind, through which one can see vistas or pictures. Sometimes, in other periods, the architectural motifs depicted on the walls are obviously not intended to seem real; they are too slender or fanciful to be understood as architectural members. But in their allusion, and the spatial illusion of their lines, they, too, open the wall so that one looks into depth or feels that there is an open space between the ceiling and the painted part of the wall of the room. The space is made to seem more complex and airy.

In architecture, the concern for space is conspicuous and appears early. It will be recalled that we are dealing here with volume, to begin with, and trying to distinguish between linear, expansive, massive, or "spatial" space, which creates a verbal difficulty. We need to hold fast to the notion of volume as a "substance" and space as a quality of the substance. In contrast to the earliest Greek buildings of monumental character, which we have seen to be long, narrow, and thin, the early Roman temples are broad—for example, at Cosa (Plate 95)—and almost square in plan. The total volume is organized against a back wall along one side of the square; from the wall project three parallel halls in the center, flanked by colonnaded halls on the side which merge into the open volume of the front half of the building under a roof supported on three rows of columns. These are divided to leave a wider volume down the middle to the central cella, narrow corridors leading to each flanking cella, and middle-sized corridors to the side colonnades. They are divided crosswise, moreover, so that there is a wider transverse passage between the second and third ranks of columns than between the first and second or the third and the cella doors. This is quite a complex organization of volumes within the limits of the square plan and columnar system. Its primitive character is betrayed by the narrow cellas and the division of the volumes in terms of corridors rather than rooms, but the organization of volumes is perhaps the most complex of any building that we have met within so severely restricted an over-all plan.

Our next clear view of Roman architecture finds it in a period when studied adaptation of Greek principles and motifs curbs the full exploitation of arrangements of volumes. But even in the manner of adapting the Greek forms the tendency emerges. Though the temple may be Greek in appearance, its position on the podium raises it above the surrounding area, and to ascend the podium involves conspicuous change, ascent within a volume, in addition to the actual entry of the temple by one or two steps. There are not likely to be columns along the sides, but there is likely to be a deeper pronaos, perhaps with two rows of columns. Often, instead of a peripteron corridor, which would be inconvenient if not useless, the peripteron columns are engaged to the wall. Thus the aesthetic effect of the column in developing massive and spatial relationships is preserved, but the actual volume, being useless, is eliminated. Almost invariably, the Roman temple is located in an area architecturally formed, usually by inward-facing colonnades, rationally related to the temple itself in terms of the same principles that govern the design of the temple itself. The basic principles are symmetry and axial movement, but these may vary from a simple, rectangular, colonnaded court to a series of grand and varied elements like the steps, octagonal court, gates, and main court of the sanctuary at Baalbek or the series of elaborate terraces and steps that we see at Praeneste (Plate 96). The environment of Greek temples was never organized so thoroughly.

The settings for temples and shrines are paralleled and exceeded by the great planned fora like the Forum of Trajan in Rome (Plate 100), with its fusion of temple, column, library, basilica, and forum proper into one symmetrical scheme, with integrated movements and counter-movements given by the various axes of the particular elements, their façades, and the colonnades. Characteristically, a number of buildings were planned as a unit, but sometimes the individuality of the several buildings would be recognized, and integrated in another way. Such, for example, was the situation in the forum or market at Corinth. Here the total area was subdivided longitudinally into two sections, the lower separated from the upper by a row of shops of which the fronts faced on the lower agora and the roof served as a promenade approached from the upper agora. The upper agora was a governmental area, with administrative offices housed in quarters devised within the space of a vast Greek stoa that ran the whole length of the agora. Near the middle of the central row of shops was a rostrum from which administrative officials from the upper agora would be able to address the ordinary populace in the commerical agora below. At one end of the central shops was a monument; at the other a shrine. The lower agora was bounded on the east by a basilica, on the west by a row of temples, on the north by colonnades and shops, broken near the middle by the entrance to another basilica and a triumphal gateway to the main road north-ward. The whole plan, carefully separating various functions according to combined considerations of convenience and design, with variations from mathematical symmetry in the planned architecture to provide compensations for the lack of symmetry imposed by natural features and inherited monuments, is exceedingly intricate and thoroughly co-ordinated, even though it was not planned as a unit but developed in terms of individual buildings added over a period of years.

Equally characteristic of the Roman interest in organizing volumes "spatially" is the design of the great baths (Plate 102). It is not simply a matter of combining a hemispherical and a cylindrical volume, as in the Pantheon, which one might conceive as a "massive" volume, or of devising hemispherical or oval or even quatrefoil rooms or the like; it is a matter of combining volumes of these kinds in different compositions, and with different kinds of vistas from one to the other, to produce the effect of a series of volumes varied in shape and other characters, but composed in spatial relation to each other. Similar designs characterized some of the great palaces, like Hadrian's villa at Tivoli or Diocletian's palace at Spalato, and to a more restricted degree some of the basilicas, especially the Basilica Nuova of Maxentius (Plate 99).

Preoccupation with spatial organization is revealed in many smaller ways: the use of attached or semidetached columns in a façade or as ornament on concrete piers; the deeply cut ornament that makes the ornament seem detached or detachable; the smooth column shafts that eliminate the emphasis on mass that fluting contributes and allow a continuous flow of movement of free space.

In literature, interest in space is conspicuous in both the conceptual form and in the sensory elements. In neither respect is it different in kind from what may be found in Greek literature, but it is far more prevalent in occurrence and spacious in extent. One expression is seen in the broader conceptual form—for example, the wide wanderings of Aeneas, which are actually no more extensive in distance than those of Odysseus, perhaps, but more carefully depicted and connected, so that there is a more plausible suggestion of true geography. Aeneas may be storm-tossed for three days, but he is not spirited by magic ships from the unknown to the known. So, too, Valerius' Jason follows a more closely charted path than Apollonius. The geographical range of Lucan's *Civil War* and Silius' *Punic Wars* might be attributed to the subject, but conversely may have helped to determine the choice of subject. In most of the Greek romances of the period, the far-flung travels are obviously invented; the landscape settings of some scenes, notably Longus', are also compositions of spatial relationships. Another reflection of this interest is seen in the cosmological subjects of Lucretius and Pliny. Viewed more closely, there is often more abundant detail in the description of an event, like the sack of Troy, so that the scene is more crowded and hence the sense of the volume is more vivid, with many things happening, many figures moving about, side by side and around and among each other. Specific descriptions exhibit a greater consciousness of extent of space: a remarkable example is this passage from Valerius' *Argonautica* (I, 495):

claraque vela oculis percussaque sole secuntur scuta virum, donec iam celsior arbore pontus immensusque ratem spectantibus abstulit aer

("immeasurable space takes the vessel out of their sight," as Mozley translates the last line), but a comparison of a Virgilian storm in Aeneid I and a Homeric storm also reveals a more direct consciousness of the vastness of heaven and sea. Lastly, a poem is addressed directly to the reader, so that a relativity between the poem and the reader is created, giving the poem, as it were, a definite spatial position. This does not make the poem subjective in the sense to which we have tried to adhere. The poem is still an objective statement of circumstances which created the poet's feeling, and from this the reader may become aware of that feeling. But the direct address to the reader (not only in lyric, but frequently in other kinds of writing as well) explicitly establishes the reader as an external element in the process. When the situation is described by the poet in the first person, a third locus comes in, so that the consciousness of transmission is accentuated and with it a sense of spatial disposition.

Closely related to the conceptual form in its restricted aspect is much of the imagery, so that when, as is common in lyric, the imagery is geographical, with allusions to Gades and the Ganges and innumerable, far-flung places, there is a clear awareness of wide range and broad horizon.

Seen in terms of the sensory elements, Roman four-dimensional configuration is evident chiefly in the tendency toward more complex organization than in Greek literature. The organization of the *Aeneid*— the last six books repeat the form of the first in the same order, implying a parallel but not identical development later in time—and Horace's composition not simply of poems but of books of poems with intricate relations among the poems within the books, are examples that have been already analyzed by scholars; and, generally speaking, the elaborate attention of Roman writers to periodic structure not only of ideas but of kinds of sentences and parts of sentences, the development of introductory, closing, climactic, and various kinds of subsidiary and auxiliary elements, is well known and immediately apparent.

In all this, it is perhaps again desirable to emphasize, there is no difference in kind between Roman and Greek work. But, generally speaking, as we have seen, spatial organization is rare and sporadic in earlier Greek work and never fully developed; in Roman work it is evident from the beginning in some degree and often elaborately developed in the later phases.

DYNAMICS

There is no very perceptible difference between Hellenic and Roman art in the matter of definition, but a fairly substantial difference in the matter of configuration. As for the dynamics of Roman art, there is a slight difference. It consists in a lack of the subtle variations on the theme of balance which gives Greek art the quality of breathing, sensitive life. Roman art has a more studied balance than Greek art, a firmer stance, though not the static immobility of Egyptian art.

In architecture, an important factor is a more complete axial symmetry in group plans; where the Greek compensated for the complete symmetry of the design of a building not so much by plan as by avoiding symmetry in the surroundings, the Roman imposed complete symmetry on both. Thus the forces are all entrained, in exact equilibrium, with no release. The result is greater discipline, great concentration of force, but no elasticity. Nor is the situation relieved by the refinements of Greek architecture—the deviations from straight lines, not merely casual and haphazard, but calculated and controlled, which yet relieve the relentless precision of an absolutely straight line. There is a substitute for this kind of relief in the colored stone facings, the architectural ornament in the form of attached columns, entablatures, coffers, and the like in the brick and concrete structure of a bath, but these are normally horizontals and verticals in fairly large rectangular patterns which maintain the essential stability of the whole.

So, too, in sculpture and painting, there is an equilibrium and composure of forces which results in a steady balance, usually without the subtler variations and delicacy of workmanship that contribute to the poise of Greek work. Compositions usually have a simple geometric form—pyramidal, rectangular, occasionally circular—centrally and squarely established in the field. In imagery or disposition of aesthetic forces, the patterns are firm and self-contained; the conception is restrained, calm, neutral.

In literature, there is a closer approach to Hellenic poise, particularly in the relatively spontaneous work of the satirists and writers of epigrams. Above all, Horace, in his aptness for phrasing and rephrasing, injected old thoughts with new life by purely linguistic and semantic means. Moreover, the lyricists and elegists maintained a sensitivity toward their imagery and a delicacy in use of words that animated the formal patterns of their works, handicapped as they were by their self-assumed respect for Hellenic originals in form and content. Virgil, in his consciously solemn purpose in the *Aeneid,* has everything planned so exactly and so finely polished, and on a plane so exalted and dignified, that there is none of the restless surge of Homer; instead, there are the sober measures of a solemn march.

It is true that the eccentricities reflected in satire are stimulating rather than harmonious, but the *mens sana in corpore sano* in conceptual form is always present as the measure of the eccentricity and the ideal. The horrors and stupefactions of Lucan, Valerius, Silius, and Statius are simply blocks in a ponderous edifice, and though Seneca used such matter for its own sake, he stands as an exception. Cicero is powerful in his periods and his imagery, but he swept men to reason, not to madness. In general, there is a completion, a rounding of sensory and conceptual elements, in Latin literature which creates a stability, a finality; it does not begin an action that is not completed.

SYSTEM, FOCUS, AND COHESION

The qualities of arrangement—of system, focus, and cohesion—are so similar in Greek and Roman art as to be meaningless in any distinction of styles; there is the same range of deviation, around the same norms of regular system, concentrated focus, and architectonic structure, in Roman as in Greek. Indeed, these qualities are prominent among those by which the "classic" style is commonly recognized.

The measured rhythms, the careful symmetry, the systematic order are all general and familiar. In the visual arts, they are first seen in the invariable symmetry of design, then in the prevailing repetition of similar elements, the neat geometry of pattern. In literature, the basis of regularity is the formal, balanced language and metrical and rhetorical patterns. But it is evident also in the careful correspondence of works grouped together—the *Odes* of Horace, the *Biographies* of Plutarch. The collection and ordering of materials on similar themes, like Virgil's *Georgics* and *Eclogues*, Ovid's *Metamorphoses*, Statius' *Silvae*, and even the encyclopedic studies of Pliny and others, represent an interest in establishing a regular, systematic order.

Throughout, the design is in terms of a dominant with graduated subordinates; rare is the author, sculptor, painter, or architect who lacks a central theme of conceptual form or sensory stimuli and fails to maintain its unique prominence or allows inadequately related subordinate material to distract from the climax and to reduce the composition to a generalized continuum. It is true that the organization of the material in a composition like the sculptured friezes of the columns of Trajan and Marcus Aurelius cannot very well have sensory dominants, since one sees so little at a time, but there are graduated dominants in terms of conceptual form. The floral ornament on the Ara Pacis and similar monuments, where the tendrils are displayed quite evenly over the whole surface, is in itself a clear example of a non-focused, generalized, free-field pattern, though among the units there is gradation of focus. The floral panels must be conceived not as whole works of art in and of themselves, but as elements in the total composition of the whole wall of the altar, so that they stand in a subordinate relation to the figured friezes, as a molding does in a wall design.

Finally, the articulation of a composition is always in terms of clearly and emphatically distinguished parts, the identity and nature of the juncture of each unit boldly delineated. This tendency may explain the anomaly of columnar and trabeated forms used as apparently superficial ornament in concrete buildings like the baths. The monolithic character of Roman brick-concrete meant that there was an inseparable structural oneness among supports, vaulted ceilings, and walls. But the Romans felt so strongly the need to distinguish aesthetically the forms of volume, mass, and structure that it was necessary to shape the surfaces of the homogeneous concrete monolith in some way, and the obvious way was in terms of the Greek orders. Similarly, works of literature are formed of closely subdivided sections and subsections of imagery and sensory patterns fully distinguished by various devices.

Summary

In general, Greek and Roman art stand so close together that only their extremes are clearly distinguishable; it is natural to think of them as constituting a single, "classic" style. In searching for the distinction, we must isolate and magnify and, hence, distort. But the distinctions are, nevertheless, important historically.

Broadly speaking, the classic style is characterized by a preference for iconic conceptual form drawn particularly from humanity; the Greek concentrates on the man and his experience; the Roman views with equal fascination his activities and his natural environment. The sensory elements are chiefly movement and texture; color is limited and specialized—so also light. The Romans had more varied interest than the Greeks in color and light. In the qualities of the manner of aesthetic representation which pertain to perception, the classic style is basically idealistic, though the Romans had a native tendency toward particularism. The classic style is thoroughly objective; it is characteristically literal, though the Romans developed an increasing fondness for various kinds of conscious symbolism. The definition is conspicuous for its clarity; the configuration runs the full range from one through two and three to four and five dimensions; it would seem that characteristically the Greek preferred mass, the Roman space-time. Common to the classic style as a whole is a balance, regularity, concentration of focus, and architectonic cohesion; the difference between Greek and Roman is in the emphases which produced in Greek art a calm poise of free and vital movement and in Roman art a firm discipline of vigorous power.

In terms of a view of the world, the classic vision, in the widest sense, beheld the true world as literally and objectively existent, in clear, regular, sharply focused, logically structured, balanced order. Both the "ideal" forms and the material substances of the cosmos are real. The history of Greek and Roman art within this "classic" framework exhibits a wider range of fundamental varieties of world outlook than any of the other arts we have examined, if perhaps not so great a variety of relatively superficial stylistic differences as we noticed in Hither Asia. Thus we find that the reality of substance was denied in primitive and Archaic times; in Hellenistic and Roman phases, the validity of non-substantial relationships among substantial things was affirmed in many ways—and in the end the Romans themselves, or many of them, again came to deny substance and affirm the non-material. We find, too, that reality to the Greeks, though in ordered balance, pulsed with vitality, whereas to the Romans it stood in rigid discipline. Again, among the Romans there was a marked tendency to recognize the reality of the particular and the possibility of subjective, intellectually unknowable aspects of reality, whereas the "classic" view in general, and that of the Greeks especially, inclined toward the truth of the objective reality of formal types. To classicism in general, mankind is the most important reality: to most Greeks it was his own nature that was paramount; to many Romans, his activity in and his relation to the world about him, and that world itself, were no less important.

CHAPTER V

The Art of the Early Christian World

OUR CONCEPT of the ancient Mediterranean properly concludes with a view of the early Christian world. Although it is true that these centuries—the fourth through the sixth of our era—in many vital respects look forward to the Middle Ages and modern times, it is also true that in equally logical ways they belong rather to antiquity than to what came later. It was in this period, under Justinian, that for the last time the Mediterranean basin formed something like a unit of culture which was the focus of all other known cultures; afterward, the growth of cultural centers in northern Europe and elsewhere left the Mediterranean either a peripheral area or a "land between." It was during this era, too, that the diverse cultural tendencies of the earlier Mediterranean world, largely native to that region, finally merged in a relatively self-assimilated and equally balanced unity, a new thing formed from the native elements and but little adulterated by foreign influences.

This development began with the first interrelation of Aegean, Egyptian, and Hither Asiatic cultures of the second millennium before Christ, but its most conspicuous and distinctive element is Christianity. The first two centuries of the new religion were dominated by two problems. One was to conquer or disarm the active resistance, or will to survive, of the pagan environment, political as well as religious and moral; the second was to create the most effective possible way of life from the social and spiritual materials available.

By the beginning of the fourth century, Christianity was a power to be reckoned with among the forces affecting humanity, and when Constantine gave it quasi-official recognition the movement was ready to assume a dominant role in the control of affairs. Perhaps naturally, the new position opened the field for internal dissension, and for some time troubles within the movement attracted at least as much attention as dangers from without. But, apart from the brief reaction of Julian in 361–63, these external dangers were not, as before, from the Imperial administration; they were from outside the Empire and threatened the body politic as a whole as much as the new church. The dynastic confusion which obscures the latter half of the fourth century, complicated by invasion and threatened invasion of Goth, Hun, and Vandal through the first half of the fifth, could still put a man like Augustine on the defensive—to show that it was not *his* religion which was responsible for the cataclysm. But in spite of this and for all the desperate handling that even a princess like Galla Placidia could receive in the struggle to adapt policy to conditions, her court and the life of large parts of the Empire could prosper in certain ways and pursue a by no means hopeless existence.

The last legitimate successor of Augustus in the west gave way in 493 to a frankly usurping Goth, Theodoric, though he and his successors were so well assimilated to the Mediterranean culture of their time that they lived and reigned and held their court within the evolving Roman tradition. But the Empire was largely reduced in area by the incursion of invaders from almost every side, and internally it was completely riven into eastern and western sections—no longer by administrative plan, as under Constantine, but by dynastic and even ethnic rivalry.

It was the tremendous achievement of Justinian (527–565), however dearly bought, to restore, if briefly, an ecumenical empire within the Roman tradition throughout the Mediterranean basin and to bring to the highest expression the cultural movements of the time. His reign saw the dramatic reconquest of the Empire, the development of an administrative system and an imperial idea embodied in a code of law, a hierarchy of office, and a symbol of monarchy; an extensive program of public works of social and religious as well as of artistic worth in the highest degree.

The implications of all this for the arts are numerous and complex. At a superficial level, the suppressed but aggressive movement of the first centuries, relatively poor and at the mercy of an unfriendly law, could not produce monumental public expressions of itself, even had it desired, without risking their loss. Literary expression was more feasible and extensively developed, but in strictly limited ways—apologetics, directed toward the pagan world, and homiletics or inspirational writing directed toward the Christians themselves, intended to clarify problems of the faith, encourage the much-beset believer, and help him develop his way of life.

During the fourth through the sixth centuries, public expression of all kinds was not only possible but driven by urgency, in order to cement the triumph of the new ideas over the centuries-old pagan tradition. For pagan tradition was not, even yet, easily obliterated. Not only were devoted pagans still active through most of these years, but many newly professed Christians were so in name and social form alone, lacking the real spirit, and many who were truly Christian in spirit preserved perceptible traces of the pagan mold.

Thus, beginning with the first century of our era, we begin to find sporadic expressions of the Christian movement, though sometimes dressed in Roman forms for a Roman public; and we may detect modifications in the classical forms reflecting the changing values of the pagans themselves as they prepared to accept the new order. And, later, after Constantine, we see the rapidly broadening flood of the new culture, with persistent but diminishing tints of the waning classical spirit. This new early Christian culture, then, is less distinct in boundaries and definitions than other cultures, but amid the currents of the age its stream formed and grew to absorb them all.

CONCEPTUAL ELEMENTS

Through all the variety and vicissitudes of this art, in its nascent as well as its florescent period, the conceptual form is natural. Predominately human, it includes "nature" in the sense of landscape, vegetation, and animal life. Superficially, its range is that of Roman art, but there are some important differences. There is, for example, little interest in activity per se; scenes of action may be depicted or described, but there is little indication of what happened or how; simply the fact of the action or scene is depicted, to identify a situation which is significant only at another level of its meaning, and without significance at the level of natural being.

The conceptual form in early Christian art is in a sense spiritual: it is the spiritual man, not the physical; the spiritual event, not the phenomenal; the spirit—whatever it may be—of the floral or animal form, not its leaves and stem or flesh and blood. This physical form is adequately suggested by a conventional indication of the natural form of which the spirit is presented; form dwindles into insignificance as the floral motifs disintegrate in formal patterns, and the content of a poem is forgotten in the intricacies of pattern of word and syllable. The very existence of the naturally based conceptual form is almost forgotten, and an illusion of aniconic form seems about to emerge.

In the literary and visual arts, the conceptual form comes, of course, largely from the Bible and perhaps a few other religious writings and concepts. Stories from the Old and New Testament and the lives of martyrs and saints are the normal visual formulation of most aesthetic production. Moreover, as we shall see in greater detail later on, a certain amount of symbolic material appears early—the basket of the loaves and fishes, the feeding of the multitude. In related fashion, elements in the conceptual form of pagan art—Apollo, the god Helios, Orpheus, Dionysos and his appurtenances—are endowed with a symbolism appropriate to the formulation of Christian aesthetic concepts. (Pagan conceptual forms still persist in their own right and character in pagan literature, like Quintus Smyrnaeus' *Fall of Troy,* or in "literary" literature without Christian ideological content but composed by Christians, like Nonnus' *Dionysiaca.*) Finally, an increasingly important role is taken by frank abstractions or personifications of Virtue and Sin and Faith and Philosophy, particularly in the writings of Prudentius and Boethius.

In much of the literature of the first two centuries, the conceptual form is not heavily emphasized. The participants in a discussion are seldom prominent, as they are in Minucius' *Octavia,* but are more or less in the background, as when in the more common epistle or apologia the author, in the first person, addresses some vague and quiescent opponent. At another extreme, the New Testament Revelations and the *Shepherd of Hermas* are elaborate visions teeming with manifold creatures and action in extravagant settings—but these figures are far more forceful and intense than "real"; the basic form is less apparent and comes from the eschatological world. The tower in the *Shepherd* for example, is a tower only by deference; its architecture and engineering may be admitted, but this is far less determining than the structure of the church it represents. The last vision of mountains hardly composes a landscape, though the several elements are recognizable as mountains, however successful may be the allegory. Eusebius' "Oration on the New Church at Tyre," insofar as it does describe the real church, is remarkably clear, but it is not so much the physical church as it is the spiritual Church of the Body of Christ that is the conceptual form of the oration. Similarly, Augustine's "cities" are, first, not stone and mortar but constitutions and, second, no effort is made to form the material to correspond to the physical pattern of a city or constitution; instead, Augustine shows the moral growth of the pagan and Judaeo-Christian communities. Even in the *Confessions,* biographical material is highly selective, focused on the inner life of the subject. In his *Psychomachia,* Prudentius follows with extraordinary consistency the external forms of Homeric epic, but his contestants have no physical substance, are mere names, albeit with virtues and vices. So striking is the contrast that the work seems a mock-epic rather than a serious composition. So also in the writings of Boethius, the participants in the dialogue are Boethius himself, in somewhat abstract form, and various abstractions in only slightly concealed anthropomorphic form; the shape of the content is that of the problems involved and the myth that is in process of creation.

Special problems are involved in some of the most crucial works because of their peculiar role in the development of the Christian faith. Thus the Gospels and the Book of Acts in the New Testament, like the

Martyrdom of Polycarp and some other works of the pre-Constantine period, are cast in a conceptual form that is usually taken as being the external lives, actions, and experiences of the individuals depicted in terms of their own logic alone. Of the Gospels, however, it is increasingly realized that it is the spiritual Jesus, not the "physical," which is the subject of the account.

In later years, only the pagan Julian and the semi-pagan Ausonius wrote, or often wrote, with focus on physical matter; Ausonius' descriptions of the Moselle and other scenes of his native land are concerned primarily with physical configurations, although it is true that his catalogues of family and professors are more names than persons. Namatianus' account of his voyage home, so far as it is preserved, is full and detailed and concentrated, so that it is in fact the trip which occupies the scene and the interest. But one needs caution: even an *ekphrasis*—a description of some work of art—is molded on the observer's reaction rather than, or at least as well as, on the object depicted.

In the pictorial arts little remains from the period before Constantine. But in the catacombs at Rome there is some material rather widely varied in its range, from traditional Roman-Hellenistic ornamental work through several of the special Roman-Imperial developments to some specific Christian expressions. Of all these we need mention only the last—simply to note that the material comes largely from the Bible, and is chiefly confined to individuals and incidents with particular theological significance. The theological conception freely shapes the pattern of figure and incident, as distinct from a historical or scientific conception. So, too, in the chapel at Doura. In the post-Constantinian world, formal manuscripts like the Joshua Roll and the Paris Codex (or their originals) are cast in conceptual forms recalling the classical, where the human figure, and even its drapery, appear in substantial form; the battles and other activities are full of detail and the intricacies of actual transactions; even mountains and trees and flowers have some physical qualities recognized and preserved by the artist. Of course these interests have become isolated and unrelated; they are mechanically, almost absent-mindedly, worked out by increasingly conventionalized

321

devices; the real interest is in the spiritual events depicted by the picture. This attitude is much more apparent in such MSS as the Vienna Genesis and the Rossano Gospels (Plate 109), where the human figures and their actions are indicated by a number of conventions variously intermingled as most convenient in paralleling the written matter. The figures are not flesh but names or integers—not in action, but in a paradigm of an action. In sixth-century MSS, like the eastern Rabula or Etschmiadzin Gospels, the conceptual form, though still natural, is predominately ornamental, with a minimum of allusion to the real substance of the source of the form.

From the world of mosaic, the same general impression is confirmed. In the decoration of Sta. Costanza, the rustic vignettes have some interest of their own, as human activities, as well as other possible meanings, but of course there is some question whether at their inception they were anything but pagan (Plate 103). The depictions of Bethlehem and Jerusalem in Sta. Pudenziana (Plate 104) convey, at least to modern scholars, an intense fascination with the topography represented. Although their real form in the minds of the original audience was surely more spiritual than architectural, the degree of architectural verisimilitude that does exist implies some interest in the mundane substance of the scene. The nave mosaics of Sta. Maria Maggiore contain a good deal of narrative content which probably was of interest for its own sake, but the relatively remote position of the panels, high up on the wall, made it impossible to follow the action closely. At Ravenna, in the Mausoleum of Galla Placidia (Plate 105), it is again not so much the physical being or event that is depicted but the spiritual.

In Sant' Apollinare Nuovo, the concept "procession" is vivid in the lines of martyrs along the nave, though it is not a procession in the natural world as are the processions of the Ara Pacis or even the Parthenon; indeed, one would not think of the martyrs as in procession were it not for the gates of Ravenna from which they proceed.

The mosaics of San Vitale are more of the world of nature (Plates 107–108). In the scenes in the apse, where Justinian and Theodora with their companions participate in a ceremony in the very building, there is a special reality to the presence of the figures as in an actual ceremony. And yet what they are doing, and the form and features of the individuals, is not fully formulated; that they are present and participants is sufficiently shown. In the choir scenes from the Old Testament, significant events are depicted in fairly full settings, though once again we gather no information about Melchizidek's meal or the sacrifice of Isaac. We are reminded that these events occurred, and continue to occur, in the world of the spirit.

The extreme example of this general tendency is to be seen in the apse mosaic of Sant' Apollinare in Classe, where the cross is displayed as the central, unique, spectacle of the apse (Plate 106). It is the Cross, depicted according to the forms of the Cross at Calvary, and is thus naturalistic. But the transformation of that Cross into one of wholly different material reminds us that in a profounder reality it is not the Cross of Calvary that is depicted but the Cross of Christianity, a concept whose real being is more of the world of spirit than of the world of substance.

Sculpture dwindles to a minor role in the art of the period, which is a phenomenon of some interest and a result of tendencies in the aesthetic character of the time. Here, the decline in interest in the substantial physical form of things in nature renders the essentially tactile substance of sculpture relatively useless, and, in fact, to a large extent sculpture becomes a matter of drawing or engraving rather than of carving or molding. In one of the still creative and productive areas of sculpture, the carving of architectural moldings, capitals, imposts, screens, and the like, although there is an extraordinary fertility in the invention of new and different floral forms arranged according to increasingly varied and intricate patterns, there is a consistent tendency to depict the material in schematic rather than natural form, in pattern rather than natural arrangement. So, too, in the ornament of sarcophagi (Plates 110–111). The few preserved sculptures of figure scenes, like Orpheus (Plate 112) or the Good Shepherd or the Nativity (Plate 113) in the Byzantine Museum in Athens, have a strong appeal in terms of action; this modern reaction, however, must be treated with reserve, for it may reflect only the archaeological novelty of these rare pieces, which in actual fact are fairly barren of curiosity as to the figures or events in themselves.

In the sphere of architecture, the characteristic monuments were churches or places of worship. Our knowledge of the pre-Constantinian church is limited—indeed, apart from the catacombs, which are not, strictly, places of worship, almost the only monument of which we have any full knowledge is the chapel at Doura. Here in all probability the spatial arrangements were determined in part by the particular history of the building and in part by the immediate use-function. That the building was probably a house originally, and later adapted to the needs of a church group, may explain some of the house-like features that survive, whereas the enlargement of the large assembly room and the special arrangements of the chapel or the baptistery were contrived to fit the ecclesiastic needs of the group. It is probable that the close seclusion of the structure is a survival of the house concept, but whether this was required also by the ecclesiastic concept because of current political conditions, or because of the idea of community or family unity that existed among the members of the group, would be hard to debate objectively at this distance.

On the other hand, once in the post-Constantinian period, a distinct form—or two forms—of structure rapidly crystallized, the basilican (Plates 115–116) and the central types (Plates 103, 114). Of an example of the former at Tyre we have a verbal description of Constantinian date by Eusebius in his *Ecclesiastical History* (X, iv, 37–46), which gives some idea of the contemporary understanding of the forms of the structure. It was surrounded by walls of defensive character; it had monumental, open gates, affording a view inside the enclosure, leading to a colonnaded courtyard in which were basins for washing—an "adornment and an appropriate place of waiting for those still in need of first instruction." From this "open space" (aithrion, atrium) more magnificent gates led to the "royal house," which, unfortunately, Eusebius considers too well known to require description, and which we may visualize as a nave and (perhaps) aisles. Within were thrones and benches, a "holy sacrificial place of holy things, in the middle," surrounded by lattice work so as to be unapproachable and yet visible. Presumably these seating arrangements were around the foot of the large apse, a characteristic of the earliest churches, and the altar was in the fenced "templon" extending from the apse part way into the nave. Eusebius does not speak, clearly at least, of the pulpit, and he includes some rooms around the church which are not known from preserved remains of churches. Apparently Eusebius does not refer to anything resembling transepts, nor are transepts found in all early Christian churches. In general, however, his remarks are clearly understandable reactions to well-established characteristic forms of the basilican church of the fourth through the sixth centuries.

The central type of building is characterized by some kind of dome as the dominant feature, set over a cylindrical, square, or polygonal structure, with or without aisles or other internal subdivisions, variously adapted to support the dome by columns or diagonal arches or partial vaults over the corners. A structure so conceived was most likely to be used as a baptistery, with the font in the center; but, especially if adapted by the insertion of a small apse at some point, with entrance opposite, it might also be used as a church.

The adaptations of the central type of building (Plates 117–118) suggest the nature of the problem of use-function. To serve as a "church," a building must have an axis according to which the participants in the liturgy can be arranged in line, the clergy at one end and the laity at the other, with the altar between. Normally, the clergy and the altar were established in an apse, or an extension of the apse floor space into the interior of the building, by fencing of some kind; the laity faced this, with their entrance door behind them. To make a structure having a true central focus suitable for the liturgy in its spatial organization, an apse must be provided to create a horizontal spatial axis, even if this remains more or less arbitrary and secondary to the central focus of the essential architectural volumes. On the other hand, for a baptism, when people gathered around a point of central interest without the separation and opposition of laity and clergy created by the physical and spiritual presence of the altar between (the person baptized was a fellow human, brought, literally, into the midst of the group), the central type of arrangement was perfectly suitable.

A remarkable example of architecture was the Constantinian Church of the Holy Sepulchre.[1] It was a complex consisting of a basilica, behind which was an open colonnaded court ending with a great hemicycle at the rear; immediately behind the apse of the basilica was the "bema" or episcopal throne on the Calvary; and in the hemicycle was a small monument over the tomb. This is a combination of the new creation, the basilica, and traditional Roman monumental design arranged to accommodate the ritual features and the unique tradition of the site.

The plan and general composition of volumes in both church and baptistery were direct and functional outgrowths of the liturgy, the nature of the buildings. And, yet, once again, one is brought to realize that the liturgy, though often indeed a thing of material substance in its pomp and richness, was essentially an activity in the world of the spirit. The central feature was a meal, but not (in the eucharistic meal) one in which there was actual dining or any but token participation in food and drink; the baptism was in water, of course, but equally in a water of the spirit, and the real event which occurred was not the drenching of a body but the cleansing of a spirit.

The structural forms also take their shape from their function and hence are naturalistic, though these functions are less substantial and material than in earlier architectures. This is evident in colonnades of more slender columns with wider spacings, frequently carrying arches rather than architraves, and often supporting plain, flat walls which may in turn carry other colonnades or clerestory windows. In a building like Hagia Sophia in Constantinople, the intricate complex of domes, half-domes, arches, and vaults, carried on tremendous piers, is a dynamic thing of forces, not a shape of inert concrete. Indeed, the ribs supporting the structure of the dome are fully visible, but it is the windows ringing the base of the dome, or rather the light, that seem to support the dome, not the ribs. The screen walls across the arched spaces along the side of the nave are obviously screening, not bearing weight.

[1] K. J. Conant, "Original Buildings of the Holy Sepulchre in Jerusalem," *Speculum*, XXXI (1956), pp. 1–48, esp. Plates III, VIII–X.

Generally speaking, then, the structural functions of the building are more concerned with energy than with mass, the non-material element of structure, not the substantial.

SENSORY ELEMENTS

MOTION

In what may seem, at first, illogical contrast to the deprecation of the physical and substantial side of the conceptual form, early Christian art exhibits a strong emphasis on the sensory elements of the work of art. The emphasis appears in the variety and the intensity of the various stimuli. To consider first the element of motion, we may begin a review of its role in literature with the New Testament itself. Here, in the Synoptic Gospels, the movement comes chiefly from the conceptual form—the events of the life of Christ, recounted in simple, straightforward narrative. The same quality appears in the *Martyrdom of Polycarp* and indeed much of the literature, to some degree: a plain, even advancement of the theme according to its own terms. Even in the Gospels, however, are reflections of some of the specifically sensory kinds of movement, conspicuously in the listing of the ancestry of Jesus at the beginnings of Matthew and Luke and the Beatitudes of the Sermon on the Mount, and more pervasively and effectively in the paratactic constructions, with phrases like "and answering he spake unto them," that in some way recall Homer. There is a more forceful movement in the cadences of Paul's discourse, especially in his chapter on love, and although a similar cadence appears in Agathon's discourse on love in Plato's Symposium, and it is not impossible that Paul was in a sense following Plato here, there is no denying that the manner of repeated parallelisms building on one another is less characteristic of Greece than of the Orient (whence indeed Plato himself may have been influenced).

In any case, in the Revelations of John, as in the *Shepherd of Hermas,* the kinetic stimulus of the rhythmic successions of cities, horsemen, angels, trumpets, plagues, and so forth, and the successions of visions, mandates, and parables, casts the works as wholes into processional movements of varying tempo, while interwoven minor rhythmic parallels of expression introduce a continuously moving, always various series of subordinate movements.

In the full stream of post-Constantinian literature, certain kinds of kinaesthetic stimuli are common. Familiar in classical tradition are the movements of conceptual form, as in the broad passage of Ausonius' *Moselle* or Namatianus' *Return;* the violent Homeric turbulence of Prudentius' *Psychomachia* or the wider, freer transports of Nonnus' *Dionysiaca.* Less obvious, though the same in essence, is the movement of the argument, or the development of the thought which constitutes the conceptual form of Augustine's *City* or Boethius' *Consolation.* Of a different order, but recognizable from both classical and non-classical work of certain periods, are the serial rhythms of simple repetitions, most obviously the groupings of rhetorical questions and assertions and other phrasings; the marshaling of biblical passages in witness of a point, the catalogues of learned men and relatives presented by Ausonius, the pulsating alternation of narrative and reflective passages in Augustine's *Confessions,* the alternation of prose and poetry in Boethius' *Consolation.* Still another more particularly characteristic and certainly a prominent and striking area of kinaesthetic stimulus is in the elaborate verse forms which are so extravagantly exploited that the rational content of the poem is neglected almost entirely and the conceptual form dwindles to a distinctly secondary role. Not only are there new and involved metrical patterns of quantities, but also an accentual rhythm; rhythms are built on the repetitions or contrasts of words differentiated according to their number of syllables, their spelling (whether they contain a given vowel or not), or their strict meaning; large compositions involving numbers of poems as well as passages in prose are contrived so that almost every component will be of a unique rhythmic pattern—that is to say, with a unique kinaesthetic stimulus.

Other kinds of kinaesthetic stimulus are employed, of course; words, and images, of motion, for example. These are particularly striking in such a work as an ekphrasis of a building, where the subject matter is objectively static, but where the author, as does Paulus Silentiarius, lavishly employs words of motion and a conceptual form based on the account of a grand ritual in the church.

Kinaesthetic stimuli in mosaic and painting have basic as well as superficial analogies to those in literature. In the catacomb paintings, line is prominent, not only as such—in purely linear floral motifs and borders—but also in the attenuated figures, mannered gestures, and often serried ranks of components in the realm of conceptual form, and in the strong distinction and emphasis of linear components in the depiction of the figures, lines of drapery, and the like.

In post-Constantinian mosaic, the linear outlines of the various elements of the pattern are usually bold, and the tesserae within a form are aligned in concentric circles or other patterns. This is technically characteristic, to be sure, of mosaic in general, but by no means subdued in early Christian work, and in general the lines of "drawing" are conspicuously and generally sharp, clear, and numerous. Indeed, in the choir mosaics of San Vitale not only do outlines and lines of drapery pattern—to say nothing of eyebrows and such minor details—come out brilliantly, but modeling and shading in three-dimensional objects like trees and rocks are done in terms of slashing bands of distinct color. Elsewhere, the conventionalized ground line suggesting the brow of a rocky cliff establishes a strong, regular, and staccato rhythmic movement.

The long lines of martyrs on Sant' Apollinare Nuovo are notable examples of the kind of processional rhythm exemplified with equal boldness in the catalogues of Ausonius. The rhythm, of course, is far from naïve and simple, with the delicate variations of the kinds of crowns, the ornament of various details of the garment, and even the shape and attitude of head and face, together with the background of trees and occasional flowers.

Other kinaesthetic stimuli emerge from the total conception of the long narrow band sweeping the length of the nave (in other churches, a band of panels, perhaps, rather than of martyrs); and within the band not only the lines of martyrs and trees, but the band of green at the bottom, gold at the top; the line between the colors and the line of writing above; the bands of border patterns, these too in long sustained lines of sharply defined rhythm.

The kinaesthetic stimuli of manuscript illumination comes chiefly in the strong line in the depiction of drapery, in the compact rhythms of closely arrayed people in crowds or groups, with overlapping heads or haloes, and the repetition of drapery or figure forms of closely similar, parallel shape and pose. There is also a greater intensity in the colors and textures of manuscript work than in most mosaic, thus introducing another basis for rhythmic organizations than that of continuous line or the accents of conceptual form. It should be borne in mind, of course, that manuscript illuminations are arranged in conjunction with written sheets, whether rolls or codices, whether interspersed vignettes or framed illustrations. These possible combinations introduce another system of movements, whether the several scenes constitute, as it were, a series of "moving pictures" or a running commentary, or whether they constitute a series of set pieces for individual inspection.

Similar qualities are well evident in another kind of ornament—that carved in stone. Most dramatic are the moldings of the Syrian churches that envelop a building in tenacious, snaky movement not only around the structure at some logical point but following up and around obstructions like doors or windows in a continuum disturbing to modern taste. In general, such moldings draw immediate attention, though they are seldom obtrusive; and commonly they consist of endlessly flowing lines, joining their constituent elements, based on floral forms, by more or less arbitrary attachment. Thus there is the continuity of the molding, that of the line of attachment, that of the series of motifs, and the internal movement of the lines of each motif. On broader surfaces, like capitals, designs in foliage often are developed to swarming nets of leaves and tendrils, though among patterns of this kind the more starkly simple designs of crosses, monograms, circles, and the like provide bold contrast and punctuation.

The basic kinaesthetic effects of architecture derive in part from the forms of the walls and supports and in part from the forms of the volumes themselves. In the basilican churches, especially effective are the colonnades and moldings, the expanses of wall surface and window leading lengthwise along the nave, and the rounded lines and surfaces of the apse absorbing or returning the longitudinal movements. There are relatively few verticals; in colonnades, the verticals are rhythmic accents in horizontal movement. The transverse horizontal lines of the ceiling beams also constitute a strong succession of rhythmic accents along the length of the building. On the exterior, the lines are normally straight and clean and more or less rectangular, with large, clear, smooth parallelograms of wall surface. In buildings of the central type, the patterns of wall and support are inevitably more complex and predominantly curvilinear or even circular. Fundamentally, there is the horizontal circle of the base of the dome and the vertical arcs of the supporting arches; within these may be any of a great variety of more or less complex arrangements of columns or wall surfaces on straight or curved-line plans, usually with curved lines of arches connecting groups of the columns in ranges. To some extent, in some buildings, this complex of circular arcs, of varying degrees of completion in horizontal and vertical planes, is countered by horizontal, rectilinear moldings or even rectangular patterns of decoration in marble or mosaic.

From the point of view of the movement of volume, a basilican church presents some notable features (Plates 115–116). In the first place, it must be emphasized that the atrium is—if not equally important as the interior of the "royal house"—an integral, functional, and aesthetic part of the whole. Thus the outer gate, as mentioned specifically by Eusebius and as is evident in contemplating restorations of such churches as that at Jerash, Phthiotic Thebes, and elsewhere, opens a vista of the interior from the street, with passages and stairways aligning and inviting movement. Within the atrium, the broad, low space defined by the colonnades, like classical architecture in the splintering of the horizontal continuum by the verticals of the columns, comes in strong contrast to the narrow, low, transverse, rectangular volume of the narthex—and then suddenly the direct, horizontal, longitudinal volume of the nave, broad, high, and open, closed by the cylindrical and spherical segments of the apse. In large churches, these movements would be supplemented, but always in parallel, by aisles in one or even two stories.

The central church is far more complex, because of the mutual adjustment of curvilinear and rectilinear volumes (Plates 114, 117). Excepting in the simplest forms, like St. Stefano Rotondo, which is purely a composition of cylinders, there is almost always the problem of adjusting the central dome to a square or polygonal outer wall by cutting across the corners with niches, colonnaded or otherwise, squinches and pendentives, and even timbers, with or without aisles. By the fifth century, exhaustive consideration was devoted to solving the additional problem of combining with this arrangement some cross-like arrangement, so that some longitudinal axis, and some perceptible but not conflicting sense of cruciform symbolism, might be woven into the composition. In this search, the most successful solution was achieved in Sta. Sophia in Constantinople (Plates 118–119), though the problem remained for succeeding centuries of Byzantine architects to exploit under somewhat different conditions. But in general any solution involves the inscription on a single square plan of at least three systems of combined forms; one from the cross, one from the circle, one from the square, all completely consistent, mutually adjusted, co-extensive. In this composition, the disposition of these volumes on the horizontal plane provides a certain stimulus to the kinaesthetic sense, as one moves or looks from one part of the building to another—from the corner space to the nave or crossing, for example. But the most effective movement is vertical, not only upward through each segment of the subsidiary volumes, but cumulatively to the highest and largest, the central cylinder and the hemisphere of its dome. In a building of the type of Hagia Sophia, the semi-cylinders and quarter-domes of the ends of the nave contribute an upward supporting flow as well as an opening horizontal movement.

In general, in all of these architectural movements, we may often observe some of the characteristics already mentioned. Chief among them are the recurrence of passages of limited extent in rhythmic cadence, like groups of three or four columns in niches or in the screen walls on the sides of the nave of Hagia Sophia; repeated groups of more intricate accentual rhythms of volumes in the peripheral areas of the central church, in contrast to the open, unrestrained sweep of movement in the central volume; and the long, even rhythms of the colonnade in a basilica or the rhythms of the windows at the base of the dome of a central building.

It is interesting to observe the Constantinian Church of the Holy Sepulchre as a structure emerging from pagan classicism. New forms are developing in the basilica; the old are evident in the broad open court to the rear, with the low enclosing colonnade, the great sweep of the hemicycle, and the strong, massive accents of tomb monument and bema in relation to each other and the space.

LIGHT AND COLOR

Both light and color are vividly conspicuous in early Christian art. This is especially true of mosaic and book illumination, and perhaps architecture; in literature their role is less apparent. In mosaic, however, the effects are obvious in several ways. There is the contrast of the light from the relatively flat, opaque tesserae of marble or terra cotta, one of the most notable examples being the pavements from the great palace in Constantinople, and the deep inner luminosity of tesserae made of glass with gilt or other colored backs, or of other translucent stuffs, of which a dramatic example among many is the niche vaults of St. George in Thessaloniki. Then there is the total luminosity of a space enclosed by mosaic-ornamented walls, with the whole atmosphere alive with the gleam and pulsation of light. This shimmering effect is a result, in part, of the way in which the tesserae are built up by hand on a plastered wall so that the wall surface is not precisely plane and flat, but undulates slightly—enough to suggest the ripple of the pile of a carpet. This, and the way in which the mosaic may be modeled plastically around corners or on the curving surfaces of dome or pendentive, means that the reflections from the tesserae are not precisely regimented but converge and diverge in unpredictable ways. Light is varied, too, by the various colors used, of varying intensity.

Color is vivid and abundant—partly, again, from the conceptual form, in the design of garments, trees, flowers, and the like; partly in the physical color of the tesserae. Conspicuous is the gold of the ultimate background of most scenes and the purple or blue of the sky or background of other scenes; the brilliant green of vegetation, and many jewels and garments, the bright maroon of roofs, borders, and other passages, constitute only the beginning of a long and intricate list. Nor is it sheer volume of color, but, even more, intensity: the strong concentration of contrasting colors in jewels and ornament, flowers, and the like. Furthermore, it should not be forgotten, in this novel flood of physical color, that there can be a color effect in the vivid contrast of white and black in the drawing of drapery, for example, or of features or landscape.

In manuscript illumination, the Rossano Codex, for example, has gold in lavish quantity and a rich expanse of purple which constitutes the all-pervading background. There is also some richness of variety of color, though one misses a brilliant green, and few colors have the intensity of the mosaic (though if the coloring of the Paris Psalter reflects an early Christian original, there must have been powerful and intense colors in some manuscripts). An effective factor in creating an atmosphere of intensity is in the contrast of white, or blue-white, and dark in gleams and shafts. A peculiar intensity, resulting in part from "dirty" colors applied occasionally in smears through which the ground may show, is evident in some work; the Rabula Gospels is an example. In contrast is the relatively flat, pale colors of the Joshua Roll, on its plain ground, which in this as in other respects reflects a pagan tradition.

In architecture, the luminosity of mosaic is important, to the extent that the mosaic covers much of the wall surface and animates the atmosphere of the interior volumes. In many churches, however, the walls were covered in considerable part by panels of varicolored marble, and the effects of this, while colorful, would be of a different order of luminosity—firm, mat, hard. When highly polished, even these marbles, and the porphyritic stone of which columns were often made, produced deep, soft, gleaming gloss, with flecks of brightness streaming off at one point or another. In other phases of the ornament—moldings, balustrades, capitals—where designs were cut in bright, coloristic techniques of bright highlight and deep shadow, another kind of effect would be produced. All contribute, in varying proportions, to the total effect.

The broader effect was dependent upon the arrangement of windows. In a basilican church, there might be windows in rows along the walls of the aisles, in the clerestory above the nave, and occasionally in the apse or the front end wall. The degree of illumination resulting depended, in large degree, on the number of windows; one has the impression, for example, that Syrian churches and even Italian churches had less fenestration than some Greek churches. The amount of light ranged between extremes, from churches which were dark to churches which were almost totally illuminated, like Hagios Demetrios in Saloniki, where light flows in from almost every side and pours downward in a golden flood.

The illumination of a building of the central type is a different matter. Theoretically, if the dome is supported on four arches as in Hagia Sophia in Constantinople, the sides can be entirely open, with unlimited light. In fact, however, domes were supported on cylindrical drums, which were not ordinarily pierced with a number of windows, or on piers or pendentives over a volume reduced from a larger square or polygon, so that the outer walls lay beyond the system of supports for the dome. This was necessarily so in any adaptation of the cross plan, of which Hagia Sophia is one. Illumination from the side walls was indirect at best, and it seems never to have been lavish. The main illumination usually came from windows in the base of the dome. The effect of this is most striking; it creates a band or ring of bright light at the base of the dome, in the wall surface, and a glow of luminous atmosphere through the upper part of the volume, with diminishing intensity and precision in the lower reaches. Ordinarily, there would be subsidiary sources of light, as the few, almost random, windows in the apse dome and niche domes beside the apse of Hagia Sophia, and at the top of the screen walls between the piers on the side of the nave. There might also be windows in the outer walls lower down, allowing shafts of light to reach the interior of the building. The general effect, then, would not be the somber gloom of a dark basilica but a general atmosphere of relative obscurity, broken by gleams and strata and merging forms of different fulnesses of light. A special quality of illumination should be recorded: the soft, live, mobile light of candles at night, from candelabra or from the devotional tapers of the worshippers, as described in the *Ekphrasis of Hagia Sophia* of Paulus Silentiarius. The fitful glow, warm, scented, like a cloud of light within the pervading gloom, striking fleeting reflections from metal, marble, and mosaic, creates a presence, an animation almost unique.

Before turning to the particular problems of literature, we may note briefly the luminous effects in sculpture: the colorism of the flat, two-plane relief with bright forward planes and deep-shadowed recesses; the variation in intensity, an ornamental motif of close-set, fine lines in contrast to one of broad, full volumes of light or dark.

Against this background it is at first difficult to account for the apparent lack of color and light in literature. There are, to be sure, some vividly colorful passages in descriptions of the Eternal City of the New Jerusalem, such as that in the Revelations of the New Testament or in Prudentius' *Psychomachia,* and there is much color and even light in the *ekphraseis*. But many opportunities for this sort of thing are ignored, as in the *Shepherd of Hermas,* and here, as frequently, opportunities to exploit the colors of natural imagery are barely recognized, as, for example, in the elaborate vision of a mountainous landscape in the latter part of the *Shepherd*.

Of course this first impression of contrast is soon seen to be excessive, due to the extraordinary color and luminosity of mosaic and related work. Even so, early Christian literature is richer in color than the other literatures we have examined. Once again we must yield the point of the light and color of sounds and local or temporary connotations. Apart from this, there is throughout a perceptible contribution of color values from the conceptual form, allusions to things in nature and civilized society that have their own physical colors—clothing, buildings, and the like. This is more effective, because more sympathetically and affectionately treated, in works of semi-pagans like Ausonius in his *Moselle* and in his and Sidonius' descriptions of villas and court scenes than in the works of more devoted Christians to whom the phenomena of the world were less real and hence less vivid. The suggestions of color in the landscapes of Namatianus are slight and fleeting but peculiarly telling, perhaps because of his nostalgia, or mixed nostalgia, for two ways of life, neither of which he can wholly possess.

In the work of more overtly Christian writers, although the colors of this world are less consciously introduced and original color compositions like those of Revelations are less common than might be expected, there is development of the contrast of white and black, or light and dark. This is frequently present in the many near-trite allusions to the forces of light and to divine and human inhabitants of heaven garbed in white and is sometimes heavily emphasized in conceptions like the allegorical hosts of Prudentius and Boethius, with the good distinguished by their white robes. There is frequent allusion, too, to the light of day and the dark of night, but far less is made of this than might be expected in consideration of what seems an obvious analogy to the illumination of conversion and achievement of knowledge of God. Indeed, Boethius was perhaps the first to introduce on a significant scale the sun and the stars, the light of day and the darkness of night, as sensuous images.

There is another element in much of early Christian literature which has a luminous effect of a sort, though in a sense it is at least as much kinaesthetic. This is the expansive, the explosive, release that comes in the climax of an argument. After the case is presented in more or less intellectual terms, according to some set scheme, with exhaustive, devoted fervor and concentration, there comes the real solution—the glory, the triumph, the complete resignation to the ineffable beyond. This is so much in contrast with what went before, in its confidence careless of any criticism, its belief needless of demonstration, its free, its boundless, rarefied, amorphous spirituality in contrast to the strictly applied, labored attempt to cope with worldly matter and fact, that it has, in a sense, the release of a bright light after a dark room. It is the sort of thing that is found, by exception, in Aeschylus' *Eumenides* and rarely elsewhere in previous literature, but is characteristic of Christian expression of the triumph of salvation.

Finally, and most peculiar to the particular tradition and culture of the age, and in fact the most abundant body of color in early Christian literature, are the allusions to the Bible. Much apologetic and homiletic writing is heavily loaded with quotation after quotation in endless sequence; it should be realized that to the Christian himself these were not simply the accumulation of the weight of authority, although they were doubtless that, but in the Christian world these verses from the Old and New Testament were the Gades and Nile of the Roman, the Lydia and Babylon of the Greek. They represented the topography of the real world in which he lived, with the local and physical color the details of such topography has, albeit the color is an inner, emotional one to a larger extent than it is optical. Nevertheless, the "color" of the literature, in the sense of its variety, novelty, brilliance, and aptness, or somberness and solemnity, to a large extent came from the intrinsic and allusive images of these citations of Holy Writ.

TEXTURE

Texture, too, has a prominent place in early Christian art. Again, it is conspicuous in mosaic and painting, in ways that have been alluded to, at least indirectly. There is, first of all, the texture of the conceptual form, but less tangibly and specifically, since the casual and incomplete manner of rendering such forms gives little consideration to shape and texture. But the texture of the material elements is vivid and various. The large-grain surface of a mosaic, with its tesserae of different substances each with its own specific texture; the rippling, almost yielding, pile-like surface of the whole expanse; the plastic modulation around corners; the various light-frequencies to which we have referred—all are textural effects intrinsic to the material aspect of the art. In mosaic as well as in book illumination, and particularly in the minor arts of jewelry-making and metal-working, the sheen of gold leaf and other metallic substances, the enamel-like gloss of some pigments or enamel itself, and other varieties of texture are presented in a wide assortment. In sculpture, the range from close, fine engraving in accents of varying frequency to broad, large forms is the chief mode of variety. In architecture, the variety of building materials—marbles, porphyries, metal; the use of mosaic, painting, glass; the handling of light, shade; the size, shape, and arrangement of space—all contribute sensations of texture. Literature, again, is less direct; the textural effects derived from conceptual form are at a minimum, as we have seen, and the chief effects (apart from sounds, which must elude us) are in the kinds and degrees of acceleration and rhythmic progression.

MANNER

In summary, then, early Christian art reveals a conceptual form drawn broadly from nature, but not the physically substantial aspects of phenomenal nature; and an emphatic richness and intensity of sensory stimuli of all kinds.

ONTOLOGY

Under the heading of ontology we undertake to characterize the mode in which things are understood to exist. Early Christian art presents us with an ambivalence in this regard that is more than a little confusing. From certain points of view, the artists of the period seem to understand reality as existing in the particular, whereas from another point of view they seem to understand reality as existing in an essence. This ambiguity is a fused duality in which both the essence and the particularity of things as they exist reside in distinguishing features of an order different from that by which things in the physically substantial world of nature are distinguished by others. Particulars exist, but in essential forms.

The quality of particularism appears in a variety of ways, though not with perfect consistency. In literature, it is one aspect of the common form of discourse in which the author in his own person addresses some other person. The interchange is among individuals, not on a general basis. It also appears in the tendency which produced Ausonius' catalogues of teachers and members of his family; in the collections of prayers for the several hours of the day written by Prudentius and others; in the accumulation of multitudes of examples and precedents as the basic form of argument, whether the visions, mandates, and parables of Hermas or the endless citations of biblical and pagan history which constitute the artillery of the apologists and homilists. It is not simply that large numbers of facts are adduced but all these persons and events are recognized as individually existent and significant.

The same or a similar attitude is reflected in the pictorial galleries of saints, whose individualities were significant and carefully preserved, if in arbitrary ways. The martyrs are quickly identified by the instruments of their martyrdom (though there is little curiosity as to the application of these instruments in literary sources where the details are accumulated to impress by the length of the list rather than the intensity of any one experience). They may even be identified by the neat inscription of their names: the friezes of martyrs in Sant' Apollinare Nuovo is as complete and as highly particularized a parade of individuals as Ausonius' professors, though the individuality in both series stops at the name. Innumerable details of the stories of the Old and New Testament were reduced to highly specific formulae of portrayal; though a particular formulation might vary little among innumerable manuscripts, the tendency toward particularization expresses itself in the identification of the scenes to be depicted.

In another area, the tendency toward particularization expresses itself in the fashion of striving for novelty in poetic form: Prudentius, Boethius, and others contrive endlessly to invent new patterns of word and stress, with a different rhythmic pattern for each prayer of the day, and by separating the several prose sections of a work. Somewhat related to this may be the fondness of Augustine for distinct sections of prosaic and poetic prose.

In architecture, although the variety of general types, and the major forms of buildings within each type, may be small, there is infinite variety of detail in the ornamentation on capitals, imposts, and moldings. The borders of mosaic panels, if not the program of scenes depicted, is varied with equal assiduity. The plan and organization of

340

volumes, at least in the central type of building, and particularly those on the cross plan, were constantly under experiment not only in terms of proportion but of interadjustment of volumes and illumination.

There are some other features involving particularization that naturally occur to one, like the portraits of Justinian and his court in S. Vitale, but it might be difficult to distinguish these particular monuments in kind from Imperial portraits in other media from other ages; it is only in the perspective of the more pervasive, if erratic, particularism of early Christian art that they take on importance.

In contrast to the impressions that such observations as these might produce is that, after all, there is very little personal individuality involved in all this particularism—no realism in the portrayal of these numerous historic figures and events that we can identify by name and experience. Any one of the male figures looks like any other, apart from such tokens or emblematic symbols, or positions, that may have been formulated to identify him. In other words, it might seem that only "a man" is depicted, not Melchizidek or Abraham (Plate 108) or some other historic individual. Iconographically, scenes are repeated with little variation. Usually the similarities result from what is almost literally a mechanical repetition of the same scene—a direct copy extending to mannerism of rendering—so that it is not a matter of re-creating the scene according to identical principles but simply of reproducing it. This is especially evident in manuscripts, and indeed even more so when the style of an earlier period may be followed in a later manuscript, though the palaeographic characteristics, perhaps, may change. In such mechanical repetition of iconographic patterns, the particularism or individuality of the incident depicted may seem a sham, for there is apparently no vital concern for the incident as a historical happening, but only, somehow, for a quintessence of some kind, a subvisual or experiential element in the event.

It is obvious that the "a man" which is the visible reality in the conceptual form of Melchizidek or Abraham as depicted, or the quintessential element in the event of the embarkation of Noah, is somewhat different from the ideal reality which Hellenic art would have understood in such situations. There would have been more of earthly human experience perceptible in the Greek depiction of Old or New Testament history. The "essence" in early Christian art is the "ideal" type form of classic art drained of the physical qualities existent in this world. (The ambiguity may seem to parallel that of Egyptian art, where type and particular were so strongly exemplified. But in Egyptian art the particular and the type are kept distinct; the head is in particular, the body a type.)

The resolution of the ambiguity in Christian art is of a special order. The fact of particular individualization is recognized and even insisted upon, but the essential similarity, the underlying oneness, is also affirmed. Neither the terms of the individuality nor the terms of the similarity or oneness are defined. Abraham and Melchizidek are distinct individuals, and each is "a man"; the incidents of history and human life are unique, but it is not the differences that are of chief interest to the artist. Every particular is eternal, and it is the eternal that is important. The novelty in the position is the uncompromising dualism, in the sense that reality (one in itself) has obverse and reverse facets, its particular aspect and its essential aspect, both of truly equal and genuine significance not only theoretically but actually.

EPISTEMOLOGY

Knowing, however, is fairly well at one extreme of the scale we have adopted, and is emphatically subjective. This is clear as another aspect of certain characteristics we have already noted—that so much of the literature is couched in the first person, whether in debate or persuasion or in recital of experience. The most monumental example is Augustine's *Confessions*. Its subjectivity appears most conspicuously in its nature as an autobiography, a mode of composition the more striking coming out of the immediate background of the classical world than it would seem from the world of the Old Testament or even, recalling Sinuhe, Egypt. Even more significantly, it is not an objective study of a self, nor even an objective depiction of the experience of a person. Rather, it is a series of impressions and moods, some created by events in a life, some by the revelations of God through history and the Old

Testament. It is, again, not so much a description of these moods and impressions or yet a recreation of them; it is a record of events in terms of the moods, the impressions, the reactions they caused, an account of a man's recollections of experience and of his imperfect and incomplete understanding of them.

The subjective character of the *Confessions* appears also in the rhetoric—the invocation and expostulation, in which not only is a subjective state revealed but emotion is created in the hearer, not so much by concepts of a kind to call forth emotions of pity or terror or reverence as by indirect and incomplete allusions which nudge and suggest rather than lead and direct, inspiring an emotional state within the hearer by causing his own feelings to work upon him.

Though Augustine is the grand example of this characteristic of early Christian art, it is embodied equally in other writings of the time. Although the Gospels seem to be objective narrative, they are closer to statements of an idea of Jesus than to historical data. They contain little information about Jesus, theologically or historically; most of our impression is built up in our own minds from the circumstances surrounding the various incidents, and from the circumstances of the parables, from our impressions of the moral and religious injunctions, and from what people are reported as having said or felt about Jesus. In the Epistles, the reader's reaction is as much from the fervor as from the argument; the vision of the Apocalypse is of a great brilliance in which the particular shafts of light and their structure are soon lost. Hermas' experience through his several visions is depicted as one of changing impressions, though they are usually objectively described. In the post-Constantinian era, Prudentius' personifications are figures existing only as embodiments of his own values; Boethius' discussions with Philosophy are in a sense an autobiographical account of his own spiritual life presented in the form of an argument in which the effects of and the effect on his emotions are prominent elements in the general tone and spirit of the work. So, too, in writers essentially non-Christian: Ausonius' pictures of his world and accounts of events are chiefly in terms of how they affected him and his feelings; Namatianus' *Return* is narrative and descriptive, but in terms of his reactions to place and event. Even in so traditional and pagan a work as Nonnus' *Dionysiaca,* the proportion of attention to the thoughts of the participant is high in comparison to that in earlier pagan epic, and there is often an emphasis on the development of some sensation or sensuous experience as if an end in itself, rather than as an element in the whole, and by suggestion and indirection rather than explicit statement. In illustration, one might compare, as extremes, Homer's episode of Hephaistos in bed with Aphrodite and Nonnus' account of the seduction of Semele by Zeus (Bk. vii).

In mosaic art, the subjective quality is especially telling, though perhaps exaggerated unduly by the technique. In a design of small blocks of stone or glass, there are limitations to the possibility of "drawing" or delineating a form fully and objectively. It is necessary to work in a quasi-pointillistic manner, relying upon the distance of the observer from the mosaic plane and upon his imagination to supplement imperfect shapes. The "peacocks" on the garment of a court lady like the one attending Theodora in San Vitale on close examination prove to be almost shapeless blobs of color; to execute the outlines of a peacock more closely would be impossible upon the scale involved. Thus the observer's imagination is a fully recognized element in the scheme. Nevertheless, that this situation should be accepted freely, that the major pictorial art should be in a technique in which such a situation is unavoidable, is in itself an indication of at least acquiescence in and fondness for this kind of effect and its implications. On a larger scale, the chalice in the hands of Theodora may be recognized, after only a moment's adjustment, as a chalice; it has a certain shape and is gold and is decorated with green jewels. Compared to the basket which the youth is offering the donkey on a floor mosaic from Constantinople, the evidence by which we recognize the chalice is seen to be drawn largely from our general idea of what is going on, whereas the basket is represented objectively in its own terms. Many people will never recognize what Justinian is holding, though given the suggestion that it is a bowl they see it perfectly clearly. Still more thoroughly and characteristically subjective is the sense one has of seeing this Imperial group in an architectural setting, though the columns on right and left are fantasies of pattern and not recognizable columns in any respect excepting the capitals. Even these are mere wiggling swirls of gold, but when located where Corinthian capitals often are located they call to mind the light and shadow effects of Corinthian capitals. The neutral sort of rectangular pattern at the base *becomes* a base since it is at the bottom of a column. Across the top is a molding which suggests architecture, though it is neither an architrave nor a lintel, and some curtainlike shapes add to the suggestion that there is a roof or ceiling of some sort above. The totality of these impressions, having no internal coherence of their own, stimulates the mind to supply a structure of an essentially different order, a more logical one, in which thenceforth the mind understands the scene as taking place. In the same way the jewelry on Theodora's head and shoulders we recognize for what it is supposed to be and endow with all our own preconceptions of what jewelry might be, all at the stimulus of a wholly arbitrary pattern of colored chunks of stone and glass.

In short, much of what we think we see—costume, patterns of line and color, soft, undulating textures—are not depicted in the mosaic but developed in our minds.

In a somewhat different way, manuscript illumination has the same subjective character. A crowd consists of three or four figures with a sea of heads; eyes and mouths are not drawn to any shape but are amorphous blobs of pigment. In the Rossano Codex, the thirty pieces of *silver* which Judas casts before the Sanhedrin become ten or a dozen flashes of *gold* tumbling to the ground.

In both mosaic and manuscript some general characteristics recur. Those parts of a body which are covered by drapery are in no way apparent. The drapery covers them completely, and the patterns of folds of the drapery are not designed to make apparent the pose of the body beneath. The result is that a leg issuing below a garment may have a position inconsistent with the pose of the shoulders at the top. Moreover, the body, or that part of it represented by drapery, is likely to be out of proportion—too long and thin or short and stubby. The artist assumes that only that which the observer can experience can be known or communicated. In rendering the setting (if, indeed, it is not omitted entirely), the landscape—stones, hills, trees—may be rendered as a jumble of lines and colors, more or less schematic or free, to which we again quickly assign suitable roles in the representation according to their intended function. So, too, with colors; the lines representing shadows under Theodora's eyes and chin are of gold tesserae, but we see them as darkness; the colors and movements in the rocks and peaks behind Moses as he receives the Tables of the Law are hardly those of nature but those imagination conjures in visualizing a state of turbulent drama.

Of course just such manipulation of form and color and movement and the rest constitute a large part of perception in general and the perception of art in particular; these devices and adaptations we call subjective might rather be called aesthetic. All art requires simplification of form and visual interpretation. The point is that in the objective style the artist tries to construct in the work of art forms that correspond as far as possible to those of the thing to be apprehended; in the subjective style the artist puts into the work forms that correspond to the observer's reaction. In other words, things are depicted in terms of the reaction anticipated, not in their own terms.

In architecture, the quality of subjectivity is most prominent in the central churches, where the structure is so complex that it can hardly be perceived in any large part from any point of view and is not easy to comprehend under any circumstances. One has at best a series of impressions of changing vistas and varied volumes, each important to the observer from his particular position, though structural forms and forces are elusive and only vaguely indicated. The smooth, often polished columns are apprehended not as shafts of stone but as flashes of color and texture, perhaps light. Capitals may be carved in metal-sharp patterns suggesting basketry or rough forms suggesting floreation; occasionally, in the wind-blown acanthus motif, an impression of eerie non-substantiality is created not only by the carving and pattern of leaves but by the suggestion of strong currents of air in the room. More generally speaking, the church, basilican or central, produces various impressions from place to place and time to time and observer to observer; and there is relatively little effort to establish some fixed, definite, unchanging, independently existing form or reality.

The subjective attitude of the Christian toward architecture is evident in a special way in the *ekphraseis,* as we have observed. Paulus Silentiarius' description of Hagia Sophia is objective in the sense of providing definite information about the actual structure and form of the building, but apart from the use of such imagery as imparts to structural forms movement and action which the observer feels—as to say that a molding "runs around" the wall, or "the helm [of the dome] strides above the house"—he is constantly speaking of what one can see, how astonished one is, what one would think. There is no systematic analysis of his subjective reaction, and the reported reactions or impressions of the observer are not what everyone would be inclined to regard as the most important. The point is what the observer felt, rather than the building itself.

SIGNIFICATION

There is little equivocation, however, about the rich and elaborate variety of symbolic signification in early Christian art. We have a full array of symbols both emotional and intellectual, and among intellectual symbols there are those which are emblematical, allegorical, analogical. Indeed, there is almost nothing that is to be taken literally. The Constantinian Church of the Holy Sepulchre makes a particularly interesting point in this connection. Here the holy places are present actually, not in symbol only, and yet the *raison d'être* of the church is to make possible the symbolic re-enactment of the holy mystery.

We begin with emblematic symbolism as it appears in the New Testament. This is a consideration complicated by credal differences as to the degree of literalness or symbolism involved in the record. Thus to some the bread and wine of the Last Supper, insofar as Jesus may have said "This is my body, this my blood," is emblematic symbolism; to others it is emphatically literal. The dove which appeared at the baptism of Jesus seems to have been variously understood even among synoptic evangelists. In the Pauline Epistles, there is an obvious kind of emblematic symbolism in the equivalence of "the Law" for Judaism— not that this is original with the Christians—and to the Cross for Christianity. Whether the Judgment Seat and the Day of Judgment, among other eschatological terms, should be considered emblematic symbolism or "imagery"—the difference, to be sure, is slight—is perhaps again a matter of judgment. So, too, in the Gospel of John, when the Baptist greets Jesus as "the Lamb of God," we may think this colloquial or literary "imagery" or more formal symbolism depending upon the date we assign its composition. In the Revelations of John, there can be little doubt that the Lamb is indeed an emblematic symbol, as in fact almost all of the elements in John's vision are symbols of something in one or another of his worlds.

In the visual arts, emblematic symbols are more frequent and clearcut than in literature. Thus the Cross itself, from an early period in the catacombs throughout subsequent Christian history, its various monograms (†⳨⳩), and the closely related Constantinian monogram IHC. More complex is the fish, with its ΙΧΘΥΣ — Ι ησους Χ ριστος Θ εου Υ ιος Σ ωτηρ —anagram, its allegorical and analogical relations to the Eucharist and the Passion, and its emotional symbolism. The symbol appears early, in some context or other, in the catacombs, although its connotations may be more recent. So, too, the vine appears early as a symbol, perhaps first as a purely decorative device but soon realized as an emblem of the wine of the Eucharist. The lamb also makes its appearance fairly early, under circumstances that leave its precise nature as an emblem in doubt; is it first the "Lamb of God," or the charge of the Good Shepherd, or simply the emblem by which we identify the Good Shepherd, or some conflation of these? Probably by the time of the tomb of Galla Placidia, and certainly by the time of Sant' Apollinare in Classe, "sheep" as distinct from "lamb" has become, so to speak, an *ad hoc* emblem of a person.

By the fifth century, too, the endless array of symbols by which one identifies the martyrs—not only the crown of Sant' Apollinare Nuovo but the instruments of martyrdom displayed in the tomb of Galla Placidia, the symbols of the evangelists, the haloes of various shapes, and the keys of Peter—have become even more narrowly standardized.

In architecture, monograms soon became common motifs in decoration, and other motifs acquired symbolic character. Grapevines and ivy and tendrils were common in moldings. Though they were not common ornaments in classical times, even then they had been endowed with some allusions to immortality and were doubtless adapted by the Christians for this reason. So, too, the acanthus, which had been an ornament of Corinthian capitals, was widely used in Christian churches, in part because of its perennial habit, in part because its thorns or spines gave it the force of an allusion to the Passion of Christ. Finally, continued efforts to develop a church plan that would be cruciform obviously are based on a symbolic conception.

As for allegorical symbolism, we should bring first into view the fact that all the emblematic symbols may take on allegorical roles the moment that that which they symbolize is in turn understood as allegorical. That is, a fish, which may be the emblematic symbol of Christ, assumes a role in the allegory of salvation, if the Passion of Christ is taken as allegory; perhaps less controversially, a symbol of some martyr assumes a role in an allegory (or analogy) of salvation as soon as the martyr symbolized is understood as an allegory of salvation or an analogy of the Passion of Christ.

Proceeding beyond such material, we may quickly identify new allegorical material, though once again the New Testament provides certain obstacles because of the doctrinal significance of the material. Whether the parables by which Jesus taught are allegorical or analogical may be important to doctrine, in some instances, at least. Is the story of the sowing among the rocks an allegory of election to salvation or an analogy for sensible action? The point is that some kind of symbolism is characteristic of the communication of Jesus. Much more difficult is the question of the life and actions of Jesus himself. Was the miracle at Cana a "fact" or an allegory or analogy composed by the evangelist? If it was a fact, did Jesus perform the miracle as an allegory or an analogy? And so with other episodes, including the accounts of the Nativity and the Passion.

In the Epistles, allegory is rare, but the Revelation of John is a tremendously complex allegory composed, as we have seen, of emblematic symbols in considerable part. It is enough to call attention to the vitality that many sections of the allegory have had—the Four Horsemen, the veils and trumpets, the Adoration of the Lamb, the New

Jerusalem. Of similar nature, but much less effective in part as well as less unified, is the *Shepherd of Hermas*. Lactantius' *Phoenix,* if it is his, also represents the allegorizing tendency of Christian art. Although the phoenix had had symbolic character among the pagan Romans and Greeks, the first attempt to construct anything extensive on the theme occurs when Christian style begins to emerge. It would be difficult to find a more literal allegory than Prudentius' *Psychomachia,* and his *Hamartigenia* has much allegorical material in it. So, too, Boethius' *Consolation* is obviously allegorical. Less easy to read as allegorical symbolism is Augustine's *Confessions,* though it would seem likely that his own life and its salvation are to be understood as a kind of "pilgrim's progress."

In the visual arts, the figures of Church and Synagogue in Sta. Pudenziana are allegorical, as are the personifications of place and elements in the Paris Psalter. The symbols in the latter are taken directly from classical originals, but they are used as mere labels, not as classical personifications. But in the Rabula Gospels, the scene of the Ascension, for example, with its angels escorting the figure of Christ into heaven, trappings from the vision of Ezekiel, and Night and Day breathing on the scene from the corners, is something of an allegorical elaboration of the written account. More complex is the story in the Good Shepherd mosaic on the tomb of Galla Placidia, where much can be read of the story of Christ and his message through the symbols, few and simple though they be. Still more elaborate are the political hagiology of Sant' Apollinare Nuovo and the highly compressed and exalted statement of the high nature of Apollinaris set forth in his church in Classe. So, too, the political statement as read by von Simson [2] in San Vitale suggests the complexity of allegory that might be achieved in a mosaic program as a whole.

In architecture, one recalls Eusebius' allegorization of the church at Tyre and its social and later its religious associations, though whether Eusebius' interpretation is his own rhetoric or represents the interpretation of the Church generally may be in doubt. Apart from this, it is probably sound to see some allegory of heaven, and hence salvation, in the dome of the central church and its special illumination.

[2] Otto von Simson, *Sacred Fortress* (Chicago, 1948).

Analogical symbolism is perhaps the most abundant, since it is by analogy that most of the argumentation of the Christian writers is conducted (Plate 110). The method of establishing a point by adducing every conceivable analogy from history and precepts of the Old and New Testament is basic for the early Christian apologist or homilist. So, too, in the visual arts, the development of a complete collection of illustrations of scenes from the Old and New Testament is based on the concept of analogy. Jonah and Noah are analogies of the death and resurrection of Christ; Melchizidek of the Last Supper; Abraham and Isaac of the sacrifice of Jesus by God the Father. So, too, incidents from the Gospels, in the earlier life of Jesus, become analogies for the crucial events of the Passion: the wine of Cana and the feeding of the multitude become analogies of the elements of the Last Supper, the raising of Lazarus, the Resurrection, and so on. In a different vein, the sufferings of the later martyrs become analogues of the Passion of Christ—and, perhaps rarely, some pre-Christian motifs, like Dionysus, Apollo the Shepherd, and their attributes become involved in some of the same analogies (Plates 103, 111–112). Beyond that, analogical imagery is added *a novo*. The peacock, for example, known for its longevity, takes a place in Christian ornament; the splendor of the emperor and his court becomes a worldly analogy of the Kingdom to come, and so figures in the pictorial material.

Perhaps the supreme analogy in literature is Augustine's *City of God,* though it is difficult to press the conception very far. The City of God is the Right Life which has emerged from the Judaeo-Christian part of human history; the Wrong Way is that of the pagan world. The Right Way of life, presented in its pure form that we may have an ideal toward which to move, is seen as an analogue of the Right Steps that have been taken in the past. Perhaps it is impossible to describe the City of God as a clear analogical symbol, or organized as such, but the spirit of symbolism seems to pervade the work.

In all this we have been speaking of the symbolism of the conceptual form; there is equally strong symbolism of the sensuous elements. The gold background in many a mosaic, both in its aesthetic and in its material and rational aspects, symbolizes the timelessness, the splendor, the value of the conception in general. A blue background may be equally timeless, but less rich; a red ground, as on the Imperial codices, adds a sense of absolute power. The color of a crown or a chalice or a cross is a symbol contributing in any of several ways to an understanding of value or quality; so the splendor of a jeweled cross, as von Simson points out in describing the apse of Sant' Apollinare in Classe, leads one to think of the glory rather than the bitterness of the Passion.

We come, finally, to the emotional symbolism, that which is perceived directly and subconsciously and not by intellectual association. Here, too, there is a wealth of material. Perhaps we should omit such particular details as Paul's discovery of an Oedipean match at Corinth (I Cor. 5:1), the Oedipean dilemma of Abraham, and a host of what may be termed Freudian elements in the martyrologies. We may omit, too, the story of Jesus—wholly to the point but too controversial. But already in the Revelations of John there is much of the repertoire that will be used by succeeding generations. Prominent is the blood of the Lamb, since blood, quite independently of any particular construction we may put on it ritually, is a deeply disturbing substance; so, too, the fire and pestilence, massing of numbers, the blaze of light, the springtime which is perpetual in the New Jerusalem. These are psychologically effective without reflection, from our inborn reflexes of our earliest history. The symbolism of the fish, the flood, and Jonah we have mentioned in other connections; the emotional symbolism of fish and flood lies far beyond Christianity, in the sense of the sea and water as the womb of life, and of fish as a primal, boundless fertility in that element. We have spoken, too, in another connection, of the dome in the central church; no doubt the early Christian felt also, though perhaps no more explicitly than we, the maternal warmth and safety of its rounded form hovering protectively above and the quickening promise and life of the blaze of light penetrating the gloom within.

DEFINITION

Although it is difficult to hit upon a designation for the quality of definition that will be brief, neat, and incontestable, there is little difficulty in seeing that the quality of these elements of early Christian art differs markedly from that of the other arts we have surveyed. There is none of the clarity, the sharpness, the precision that we have encountered earlier. In contrast, the dull, blunt, broken, and uneven edges of many carved patterns are likely to seem negative, to be the result of lack of care or even of technical incapacity. And yet this view can hardly stand in the face of some of the exquisite carving of many Theodosian capitals, or the basket capitals of the Justinian period, or even of the perfectly controlled, crisp contours of less ambitious work observed in more provincial places. Or compare the quick, broad delineation of the Rossano Codex and the even more sketchy work of the Rabula Gospels with the close, careful drawing (in some parts) of the Paris Psalter and the Joshua Roll, inherited directly from the classical tradition. A negative quality must be admitted, it is true, in that the less precise execution was widely accepted, but the negation is not in inability but lack of insistence. Even in ivory carvings of the highest quality, many details are broad and unfinished; the finest jewel work on boxes and reliquaries features shapeless stones of uncertain outline and obscure pattern. The very nature of mosaic, as we have seen, precludes precision and clarity in line. In the conceptual form, again as we have seen, there is simply no effort to make clear the articulation of a body or a tree or a crowd except for some specific reason. One should not look for clarity in the catacombs, and it is certainly not to be found: lines are often smeary, conceptual forms incomplete, colors indistinct. Nevertheless, in the catacombs and in mosaics high on church walls any refined precision of definition, in detail at least, would hardly be useful; only broad forms can be distinguished, and these have a distinctness, even to the point where individual figures are framed apart, as are the martyrs in the processional friezes of Sant' Apollinare Nuovo and the apostles as usually arrayed in a dome devoted to the Baptism. In architecture, too, the large forms are distinct enough, but the lines and edges are often casually rounded, moldings may be bulky, heavy patterns or finer patterns which in normal light and at a distance are suffused into a blurred band rather than an engraved design.

In literature, again, there are broad distinctions of certain elements, like the alternation of prose and poetry in Boethius, autobiography and psalmody in Augustine, and the visions and mandates and parables in the *Shepherd of Hermas*. And, too, there may be a sharp brilliance in some particular bit of conceptual form or sensory experience, as in many verses of the Revelations of John. But, to take a well-known example, though there is a vivid brilliance in many of the images in Paul's account of love—the sounding brass and tinkling cymbal—and the whole has a crystalline, vibrant glow about it, in actual fact neither the meaning nor the structure is clear; one has a strong impression without definable shape. So too in the ordinary language of the New Testament and other homiletics, the thought and feeling is likely to override grammar, thereby sacrificing precise formulations. Even in Augustine, whose thought is sufficiently subtle and accurate to serve as an adequate translation of Platonic concepts and a base for much Christian philosophy, the precision of these subtleties is well-cloaked in a verbal framework whose organization and distinctions are loose, broad, and often obscure. Even in the classical writers of the fifth and sixth centuries, verbal virtuosity and other considerations stand above clarity of expression and organization.

To characterize the early Christian kind of definition as inept carelessness would be manifestly wrong, as it is in many cases a free choice and is almost always positively effective. But "care-less-ness," in the sense of a lack of concern for the refinements of clarity, might be accurate; and "bluntness" might describe the optical form as well as the forthright, uncompromising, moral conviction that black is black, right is right, and a difference marked by no more than an iota is nonetheless damnably wrong.

CONFIGURATION

The characteristic configuration of early Christian art is two dimensional, one of expanse or surface. Most prominent is the manner of rendering the conceptual form, which is in almost all examples flat, without depth or body, whether in mosaic or manuscript illumination. Even crowds or scenes are depicted without any kind of forceful perspective. A crowd may be represented by lining up several rows of faces above each other upon a single row of shoulders; a landscape will be either a horizontal line or a series of superimposed flat outlines of rocks or other natural forms, literally on top of each other in the vertical plane of the picture, and without any serious indication of depth. Occasionally there will be some degree of intimation of volume by some kind of quasi-perspective, as in the placing of the grill in the Martyrdom of St. Lawrence in the tomb of Galla Placidia, or in the spectacle of Jerusalem and Bethlehem in Sta. Pudenziana, or (very slightly) in the wall encircling Ravenna in the mosaic of Sant' Apollinare Nuovo. But normally a scene is rendered as though on a backdrop, with no depth of its own. And not only the groups but the individual figures lack depth. A figure is normally only a silhouette with an internal pattern; rarely is there any indication of the solid bulk of the object depicted. Occasionally, as in the male martyrs of Sant' Apollinare Nuovo, the hem of the drapery may seem in places to hang free, or in others to lie over the arm; parts of the bodies of the female martyrs seem to have some solidity. But these passages are unrelated and accidental; they seem to be mere disjointed, chance survivals of an earlier manner which is being copied piecemeal rather than in entirety or with any interest.

This quality of early Christian art in general is, as it were, brought into relief when contrasted with certain relatively unusual phenomena in the period—for example, the manner of the Paris Psalter or the Joshua Roll, in which an almost startlingly full-bodied rotundity emerges, not in the scene as a whole but in details. In the Paris Psalter, the figures of Night and the Red Sea and the Depths, in the scene of the crossing of the Red Sea, are Hellenistically three dimensional; even Moses and the central group of Israelites are no less so. Another illuminating contrast is furnished by the floor mosaics in the palace at Constantinople, where among other "classical" qualities the figures are definitely modeled in three dimensions, with easy profile and three-quarter views, effective shading and linear modeling, and a strong suggestion of space by simple superposition of limbs and other objects. But the most startling contrast is the turgidly massive forms of some Coptic sculpture, almost blasphemously fleshy and earthy amid the dematerialized abstraction which is the norm of early Christianity.

In architecture, the quality of expanse is evident in several ways. One is in the decoration, on both large and small scale. In the carved ornament, for example, as on capitals and moldings, the tendency is to cover flat surfaces with shallow carving at uniform depth. Sometimes this is worked out in relatively brilliant contrasts of smooth light and deep shadow—"colorism"; sometimes it is more evenly graded in swarms of linear movements—but always in the same plane, never in depth. Larger carved surfaces, like balustrades or screens, are equally flat, with intricate linear patterns moving in two dimensions. Large wall surfaces are sheathed with mosaic which in several ways draw attention to the face of the wall rather than to its bulk. The knowledge one has of the mosaic technique—the application of the visible tesserae to relatively unsubstantial plaster; the intangible, shifting, sparkling luminosity of the visual surface; the undulating, fabriclike surface of the tangible substance; the limp, unskeletal plasticity with which the mosaic is molded around a corner; the two-dimensional character of the conceptual form depicted. Wall surfaces sheathed with ornamental marble slabs also denigrate the substance behind, without the correcting influence of pilasters and architectural formulae such as endowed a Roman bath with its substance. On the exterior there is a continuous expanse of wall in which the openings, the windows and doors, are practically flush with the masonry and hence part of the same film; there are few if any recesses or extrusions, certainly nothing like the systematic modulation of a colonnaded façade to develop a consciousness of depth. It is true that the major forms of the structure—the nave, aisles, and apse, and the dome above the cylinder or polygon or cube of the central building—are visible from the outside, but in the basilican structure these are closely harmonized and preserve the maximum continuous expanses. The central structures lack the intricacy of later Byzantine compositions and indeed are frequently criticized for their "plainness"—the lack of geometrical form that they exhibit from the outside.

Once again, the Constantinian Church of the Holy Sepulchre is an illuminating structure in revealing the new style emerging from the old. The basilica, set in the over-all enclosure, reveals the relatively undifferentiated continuum of space and movement on the interior, the relatively moderate distinction of mass on the exterior. The conception, though, of the basilica and other structures within the enclosure, is spatial. Though the enclosure, broad and low, is a matter of horizontal expanse rather than volume, its function as containing the focal elements is evident. In the later version, when the great rotunda had been erected over the tomb, even this spatial quality was lost; the quality of the buildings as existing within an enclosure was gone, and there remained only the two great structures, which could be apprehended only from within.

Within the building, one is more clearly aware of the division of nave from aisles and the separate shape of the apse in a basilican church, but the relatively slender columns, widely spaced, make a minimum of separation, so that there is an open unity in the basic expanse of the floor. Nevertheless, the screen of the columns and the walls are apparent as a screen, an expanse. The definition of the nave as a formed volume is relaxed by the easy flow of space from nave to aisle and (when the ceiling is not closed), through the open joists at the ceiling plane, to the "attic" above. In the central building, the effort to achieve a genuine fusion of the several cubical forms gives an unusual importance to the floor as the one tangibly common element among all the volumes. Although the entire floor is not visible from any one point, the presence of the floor receding in every direction to a visible or invisible common boundary of the whole complex contributes to the sense of expanse. So, too, the volumes beyond volumes, where the particular shape of each volume is not always clear, gives a special importance to the rhythm of recession itself—the general movement away from the observer. The forms of the structural members—the broad faces of piers, the polished faces of columns, elements like the palpable screening walls along the nave of Hagia Sophia, the lack of emphasis on fundamental structural masses as differentiated from subsidiary forms—all tend to draw attention to the surfaces, the planes, the skin of substance, not its solid substance and bodily form. Finally, although the cylindrical and spherical forms in various segments would inevitably create shapes of solid geometry, the effect is minimized in a variety of ways. One way is the relative lack of strong definition at corners, so that the semicylinder of an apse merges without seam or obstruction, in a kind of sweeping flow, with the cube of the central building or the rectangular prism of the basilica. The domes and half-domes and quarter-domes, the segmental squinches and the like, inevitably in their complexity, and especially with the lack of strong delineation, tend to fuse with each other instead of establishing separate forms. Domes are not always complete hemispheres, or when they are, they merge almost unmarked with cylinders. Sometimes, as in the case of Hagia Sophia, the windows around the base of the domes introduce a transitional phase of structure and light so that the tangible surface of the dome itself seems much flatter than a full hemisphere, and hence a less determinate solid shape. All such factors tend to draw attention from the very definite geometrical composition of the volumes and, without eliminating awareness of these volumes, draw a large measure of attention to the undulating surfaces as such.

In literature, "expanse" is an aspect of the lack of objective substantiality, the lack of "depth," which is commonly felt in depiction of character or personality. This appears in such obviously unexplored and unfelt personalities as Ausonius' family and professors, and even in Augustine himself, where his fairly ambitious autobiography is so definitely selective to depict a particular facet of his experience and takes no account of so much that would "round out" the personality. Our impression of Boethius, not to deny the profundity of his thought in some respects, is definitely one-sided. Prudentius' *Psychomachia* is, for all its Homeric spirit, and for all its intended profundity of meaning, a shallow picture. The character, and only the necessary facet of the character of each figure, is provided simply by the name; the vivid painting with which it may be further embellished is simply color to the same silhouette. We have, in a way, a repetition of the orientalizing period of Greece, where small subjects are treated largely to exploit one aspect in full—one emotion, one idea, one conceit, one hour of the day—but not to explore the relationships, the internal substance, or all the facets. The *City of God* is more like Herodotus than like Thucydides: it roams exhaustively over its two planes, but though its intent is to throw the two into relief, this is accomplished more by the reader, as if comparing two works, than by the author, as if fashioning one structure against another. And if one speaks of historians, one is reminded of Procopius, who evidently conceived of two levels of reality in history, not interactive, so that one had its existence independent of the other. So, too, he felt a unity in a compendium of the buildings erected by Justinian, which, like Ausonius' catalogues, reminds us more of Hesiod and the catalogues of orientalizing Greece than of the genuinely encyclopedic Roman, Pliny.

In a negative way, the lack of three-dimensional form in literature is exemplified by the rather generalized movement of such a work as Paulus Silentiarius' *Ekphrasis of Hagia Sophia*. Moving through several introductory phases, invocation or dedication first to Justinian, then to the patriarch, then another invocation, it proceeds to the festival, then the architecture, the ornament, and the light of the building. Although there is a "conclusion" in the final peroration to emperor and patriarch, the development is sequential and discursive.

It is fairly obvious that this affection for the surface film, the expanse, is more akin to the oriental than to the classical world. In early Christian art, to be sure, it is a more light and yielding surface—the surface of the mosaic fabric as contrasted with the polished granite; but in going no deeper it should not be characterized by our deprecatory word "superficial"; rather, it should be understood as an affirmation of a value other than physical substance.

DYNAMICS

From previous observations it will be obvious that the dynamics of early Christian art are in truth "dynamic"—that is, there is a tense, volatile, mobile energy in it that is distinct from anything we have encountered previously unless, in some respects, the early Aegean world. This energy is a component of two elements: a high degree of movement or released force of various kinds, concentrated (and thus brought under pressure) in two or at most a few lines of interaction to achieve a restless equilibrium. In other words, it is similar to the poise of Hellenic art, but the forces are more active and the equilibrium therefore less easy to maintain and more intense.

Prominent in the visual arts are the endless linear patterns of architectural moldings and other carved designs, long continuous movements formed where none previously existed, as when circular or floral motifs are divided at focal points and joined at tangents to resolve what had been a row of similar motifs to a fluid, current, and shifting line and light and shadow. In mosaic, too, there is the ceaseless, restless movement of light and color, and of the very fabric of the stuff, as well as the endless lines of borders. In the conceptual form of mosaic or manuscript illumination, it is the continuous, often electrically angular and flaring movement of line of drapery, shape of figure, pose, and grouping (and, incidentally, the increased mobility of de-substantialized form), and the restless accumulation of erratic line of contour of rock and vegetation in a landscape. In architecture, it is the flow of movement in the nave of the basilica, the less solid, more mobile proportions of the nave columns, the lines of archivolts which "spring," as we say, from column to column by light rounded lines (contrast the sedate dignity of the more classic Sta. Maria Maggiore). In the central church, the ultimate objective—seldom achieved, as at Hagia Sophia—of clearing support from beneath the ceiling and roof structure, results in complex circles and countercircles animating the upper air without wholly engaging in the supporting lines from below. The lofty elevation of even the average dome compels the observer to strain to behold it, an intensification of the sense of upward movement. In literature, the intensity is in the fervor of the evangelistic conviction and the outpouring of image and rhetoric to carry the points; in the exhaustive accumulation of analogy in the development of argument; the uncritical accumulation of mythology by a Nonnus; in the sustained rhythm of rhetorical form and imagery, even in such works as Boethius' *Consolation*. From another point of view, it is in the strained effort to achieve novelty by far-fetched devices of rhythm and poetic form, the strain for novelty in other ways.

On the other hand, the counterbalance, the restraint, is again easily apparent. In the visual arts, it is the almost unvarying bilateral symmetry, so that forces are disposed equally on both sides of a center. This is especially conspicuous in apse mosaics; and in panel mosaics the bilateral equivalence is not always obviously precise, but there is almost always some central or near-central dominant, with approximately equal forces flanking it. In some compositions this fact is not apparent within the bounds of a single scene, as in the nave mosaics of Sant' Apollinare Nuovo, but in this case, as in others, the real center of symmetry is between the two compositions; the two friezes are themselves the balancing elements. Similarly, the Justinian and Theodora panels balance each other, though neither is precisely balanced, in any obvious way, within itself. In manuscript illumination, further complexities are introduced as we encounter the peculiarities of arrangement of the pictures: whether as separate scenes (with or without frames), or as casually interspersed vignettes, or as a continuously unrolling, interconnected panorama of events through time, like the reliefs of the Column of Trajan. In the more formal set pieces, the bilateral symmetry is usually apparent, though not always a simple equation of equal weights. In the Judgment of Pilate in the Rossano Codex, the greater tension and vividness is on the side with Christ; but on the left is the more solid weight, and the secondary tension is substantial. In other kinds of scenes, anything like bilateral symmetry is neither possible nor attempted, though there is almost always a successful contraposition of forces, either conceptual or sensory or both. In architecture, the bilateral plan of the basilican form is simple, as is the corresponding symmetry of the façade. In the central type, there is a radial symmetry, except where a strong axial plan has been established, as at Hagia Sophia in Constantinople, with a distinct conflict between the central and the longitudinal axes. In the central building, however, the greatest tension is between the horizontal and vertical; in this the vertical is invariably stronger, but the relaxation it brings releases the observer to the horizontal movement and re-engages him in the conflict.

In earlier Christian literature, the tension is basically that of the evangelizer or apologist against the non-believer; later, it is the perennial and pervasive conflict of the city of God and the city of man, the struggle of good and evil, time and eternity. This is the non-substance and substance, rational conflict, in which every effort of the Christian is required to overbalance the opposition. In form it is evidenced in such phenomena as we have previously noted: the open division of a composition into conspicuously different forms, prose and poetry; the opposition of the historical and emotive expression in Augustine's *Confession;* the tight pattern of numerical quantities in the Revelations of John; the preservation, in general, of classical forms of prose and poetry to contain new emotional and spiritual content. There are, moreover, no "eccentrics" in character—in Christian terms, at least; unless one feels the fortitude and goodness of some martyrs are excessive, and the ferocity of their persecutors—but here, again, the opposition is diametric. Rather, norms of behavior are quickly established, and discourse and conceptualization are henceforth in these terms, without preoccupation with the abnormality. The ending is a direct outgrowth of the forces involved—not a surprise or inexplicable in terms of preceding events. In short, all forces in literature are channeled ultimately into the same main stream, whether after long, parallel, and separate courses, like the two cities of Augustine, or after a constant series of parallel assaults on some single objective.

SYSTEM

About the system of early Christian art there is perhaps little that need be said. The essential regularity and order of it, as opposed to any tendency to erratic, haphazard disposition of elements, is hardly to be questioned. It is obvious, of course, in such compositions as the martyrs in Sant' Apollinare Nuovo, in the array of dignitaries in the courts of Justinian and Theodora in San Vitale, even in the systematic disposition, all things taken into account, of the figures in the scenes from the Old Testament in the same building. The generally regular order of arrangement of elements in practically all composition in the visual arts are so matter of fact and intimately accepted as to be hardly noteworthy; the regular arrangement of the elements of the church, of either type, is self-evident.

In literature, there is quickly perceptible plan and regularity in the ordering of the elements of conceptual form, the figures in a plot and the facts or data in an argument, as well as of the sensory progression of elements, as distinct from any haphazard, erratic, or spontaneous arbitrariness of choice and selection.

FOCUS

So also in the matter of focus, there is little that can be added at this point that has not already been broached in some other connection. There is, as a general characteristic, some dominant, and usually this dominant is central rather than peripheral. In architecture, it is the longitudinal axis of nave or façade of a basilica, or the longitudinal or central axis of a central structure; it is the point of division of bilateral symmetry in such pictorial compositions as possess this feature. The dominant focus in the manuscript illustrations of the consecutive form is often in a point of the drama in the action or event but may also be in a relatively casual feature such as a door or baldachin on which color or movement is concentrated. In literature, the dominant may be the "point" or objective of an argument or demonstration, or perhaps the very virtuosity of some novel form. It is certainly characteristic of early Christian literature that although it may often be diffuse and long in development, it is seldom ultimately discursive and rambling. The chief quality of Christian literature, as we have seen, is its intensity, its powerful, unrelenting movement toward some rational and sensory climax. Even though the end may not be visible, as halfway through Augustine's *City* or Boethius' *Consolation,* there is a current moving in a direction from which one cannot deviate easily.

COHESION

In the quality of cohesion, however, we may perhaps perceive something significantly distinctive in early Christian art. Although in the design there may readily be perceived the parts, the structural integration of these parts is seldom distinguished, as we have frequently observed, as it is in classical art, for example. Nor is there the monolithic, or rather monoidal, unity of Egyptian art. The cohesion among the parts of a basilica—the apse and nave and aisles—or among the parts of a central church—the divisions and subdivisions of the square, the hemispherical, and quarter-spherical forms of the dome structure, with their curved profiles and surfaces—is not formulated architecturally in terms of mass on mass, bearing surface on supporting surface, nor in terms of thrust against thrust, of energized skeletal structure. Rather, it is a matter of fusion of parts, as glass is fused or as metal is welded. The roof ceiling structure of Hagia Sophia, as we have already suggested, is a single web, incredibly complex, spanning like a sheet of honeycomb a vast nave and supported, apparently, not on piers but on shells of wall structure that have strength from their fusion with other walls, not from their brute, solid bulk. The entire fabric is a film, a sheet, a complex of films or sheets, joined by fusion and pressure at the corner until they form a single film capable of supporting itself. The apse and its half-dome are, in a sense, extrusions of the flat end wall of a nave, not appended structures of masonry abutting onto the end, but shells, half-tubes, welded to the opening at the end of the nave.

In pictorial compositions, too, the parts cohere not in terms of block resting on block, or section impinging on section, but in terms of one element attached to the other, not always with the intimacy that fusion implies but with the lack of an articulated juncture. In manuscript illumination, it is possible for scene after scene to unroll in a mixture of chronological and topographical succession, and with less specific divisions than in the Column of Trajan—indeed, so careless of divisions that even in the catacomb wall painting, to say nothing of manuscript illumination, one part of a given scene may play a role in an adjoining scene. The effect is perhaps less obvious in mosaic, except in the fairly obvious lack of any other kind of organization. In the Justinian scene at San Vitale, where a structured hierarchy might be expected, the figures flow from one to another in continuous movement, one overlapping the other but without strongly silhouetting the emperor or establishing a structured pattern of relationships. The group has a unity which would be hard to break or dissolve, in spite of the obvious differences between such groups as the soldiers on the right, Maximian and Justinian, and the other dignitaries.

In literature, the absence of architectonic structure is one of the conspicuous differences between early Christian and classic work, except in the most "classicising" products. The difficulty of detecting the joins, so to speak, in the development of Augustine's career in the *Confessions*—not that there is not a development—is characteristic. The beginning, middle, and end, and various subparts are not easy to disjoin. Even the *City of God,* which in its conception has the beginnings of a sturdy architectonic structure, loses this definitive form as it gathers force and the impetus of its swelling movement carries one toward the end. The parts are there and can be discerned but are hard to separate. The cohesion is one of fusion: the transitions are long and gradual and interwoven. It is true that units of a certain kind—narrative and invocation in the *Confessions,* prose and poetry in Boethius' *Consolation*—are sharply distinct, but these are not structural units having tectonic integration; they are successive accents in continuous rhythm.

This quality of fusion as the manner of cohesion is evidenced, too, in purely sensory realms. It is especially vivid in the effect of mosaic in a building in which the lights and colors fuse and blend not only with distance but with the minute inclinations of the tesserae and the changing angle of light. It is effective also in establishing the total unity of the central type of structure, where the final fusion is between the horizontal and the vertical expanse, a merger which takes place at no point but is continuous throughout and is effected uniquely from every diverse point of view.

SUMMARY

It remains, then, to summarize the aesthetic character of early Christian art in our accustomed categories. Its conceptual form is iconic—naturalism concentrated on humanity and on the spiritual life of humanity. It employs all the sensory stimuli—movement, color, light, texture—in great variety. In its ontology it presents a dualism of particularism and abstraction; it is highly subjective and relies heavily on symbolism in many forms. It has a bluntness of definition, a preference for configuration in two dimensions, and is characteristically tense and highly charged in its dynamics. It is regular, concentrated in arrangement, cohering by a fusion of parts.

The true and real world envisioned by "the early Christian" is thus a subjective one, existing in his own experience. If there is an ultimate reality with a wholly objective existence, it is "that which is beyond our power to imagine," and is known only by faith. For all practical purposes, reality is the working within us of the Unknowable and can be realized only in the experience itself or in symbolic allusion. Or, perhaps, in a truer focus, it should be considered that there is no reality, even including ourselves, excepting subjectively to that Unimaginable, and our knowledge and awareness of anything is part of a series of reactions between us who are imagined and the Unimaginable by whom we are imagined, in His own mind. In any case, these realities are broadly, not sharply, defined in relationships that are regular and structured though inseparably and indissolubly fused into a single entity which is not frozen and static but charged with energy and power. Reality, moreover, is non-material, non-substantial, existing, so to speak, in the form of individual particles of various kinds of basic essences. Thus to the early Christian we are not so much "man" as "men": we are all—all of us—of one essence, but all of us are also, individually, our own particular quanta of that essence. And in the list of realities the chief is the spiritual life of men, which is the activity of God Himself.

To say all this is to leave in abeyance the peculiar historical position of early Christian art. Previously we have been dealing with the arts of independent peoples; with early Christian art we are dealing with a "people" composed of members of all the other peoples we have considered, distributed through all the lands we have considered and heirs to their traditions. Is the style of early Christian art, then, a selection and fusion of survivals from this inheritance? Or is it a new generation spontaneously developed to meet new needs? From another point of view, as we observe the Christian style emerging from the pagan world, are we to think of some of the phenomena of Roman art—for example, symbolism—as transmitted to Roman art from the Christian or its sources, or vice versa, or resulting from impulses in the cultural situation stirring both pagan and Christian?

The Art of the Early Christian World

The broader historical situation is clear enough. Christian culture ultimately did permeate the entire geographical expanse of our interest, absorbing all earlier traditions. In it we see readily values and attitudes known in each of these traditions, though related in new proportions. The various regions of the Mediterranean world, whatever diversities still remain, participate on terms (in part at least) compatible to each. As long as we approach the problem from the point of view of the Mediterranean and its earlier history, the early Christian vision of the world is clearly its own, fashioned from what it chose to accept from the Mediterranean world before it and what it had need to create anew.

So much is clear. The investigation of the details of such problems is beyond our scope, important though they may be, for our purpose has been primarily analytical and descriptive. Of course, the full accomplishment of the announced purpose—"to discover the basic and meaningful characteristics of the several styles of art of the ancient Mediterranean world"—would indeed require a full comprehension of the entire historical situation, not only with reference to art itself but to politics, economics, society, philosophy, religion, and so on—even to matters of fashion, manners, and language. Our own investigation can hope only to have added the basic elements of two contributions. We glimpse, first, through the styles of the ancient Mediterranean world, something of the vision of the world seen by Western man in various episodes of his youth, as we also discern, in some such terms and with whatever difficulties, the ethos of each culture through its art. And, second, we see the causative forces in the formation of style: changes in style represent changes in the conception of the nature of the order of truth and reality among those who espouse the style. This is the explanation of why style changes, if it changes, and why it does not, if it does not—a question that cannot be answered simply in terms of technique and forces and practices of art itself, but must be understood in relation to visions of the world in the profoundest sense.

Bibliography

I. Some works, listed in chronological order, containing material and views relevant to problems in the interpretation of art:

ARISTOTLE	*Poetics*		
———	*Physics*		
HILDEBRAND, ADOLF	*Das Problem der Form in der bildenden Kunst*	Strassburg	1893
WÖLFFLIN, HEINRICH	*Kunstgeschichtliche Grundbegriffe (Principles of Art History)*	New York	1915, 1932, 1950
PINDER, WILHELM	*Das Problem der Generation in der Kunstgeschichte Europas*	Berlin	1926
DVORAK, MAX	*Kunstgeschichte als Geistesgeschichte*	Munich	1928
STACE, W. T.	*Meaning of Beauty*	London	1929
COLLINGWOOD, ROBIN	*Principles of Art*	Oxford	1938
FRANKL, PAUL	*Das System der Kunstwissenschaft*	Leipzig	1938
FOCILLON, HENRI	*Life of Forms in Art*	New Haven	1942
LANGER, SUZANNE	*Philosophy in a New Key*	Cambridge	1942
MARITAIN, JACQUES	*Art and Poetry*	New York	1943
CASSIRER, ERNST	*Essay on Man*	New Haven	1944
FREY, DAGOBERT	*Kunstwissenschaftliche Grundfragen*	Vienna	1946
———	*Grundlegung zu einer vergleichenden Kunstwissenschaft*	Innsbruck	1949

368

Bibliography

PEPPER, STEPHEN	*Principles of Art Appreciation*	New York	1949
SCHAPIRO, MEYER	"Style" (pp. 287–312, in *Anthropology Today*, ed. A. L. Kroeber)	Chicago	1953
ARNHEIM, RUDOLF	*Art and Visual Perception*	Berkeley	1954
NESBIT, FRANK	*Language, Meaning and Reality*	New York	1955
PANOFSKY, ERWIN	*Meaning in the Visual Arts*	New York	1955
PEPPER, STEPHEN	*The Work of Art*	Bloomington	1955
READ, HERBERT	*Icon and Idea*	Cambridge	1955
SYPHER, WYLIE	*Four Stages of Renaissance Style*	New York	1955
COBB, JOHN	"Toward Clarity in Aesthetics" (*Philosophy and Phenomenological Research*, 18, 169–89)		1957
GILSON, ETIENNE	*Painting and Reality* (Bollingen Series, XXXV, 4)	New York	1957
LANGER, SUZANNE	*Problems of Art*	New York	1957
HAUSER, ARNOLD	*Philosophy of Art History*	New York	1959
GOMBRICH, ERNST	*Art and Illusion* (Bollingen Series, XXXV, 5)	New York	1960

II. Some works concerning particular styles, listed according to subject matter,
   A—developing matters of principle, and
   B—largely for convenience in illustrating monuments.

Egypt

(A) FRANKFORT, HENRI (ed.)	*Intellectual Adventure of Ancient Man*	Chicago	1946
SCHÄFER, HEINRICH	*Von Aegyptischer Kunst besonders der Zeichenkunst*	Leipzig	1922
WORRINGER, WILHELM	*Aegyptische Kunst*	Munich	1927
SMITH, E. B.	*Egyptian Architecture as Cultural Expression*	New York	1938

(B) MEKHITARIAN, ARPEG	*Egyptian Painting*	Geneva	1954
PRITCHARD, J. B.	*Ancient Near Eastern Texts Relating to the Old Testament*	Princeton	1955
RANKE, H.	*Art of Ancient Egypt*	Vienna	1936
SCHÄFER, H., and ANDRAE, W.	*Kunst des Alten Orients* (Propyläen Kunstgeschichte, II)	Berlin	1925
SMITH, W. S.	*Art and Architecture of Ancient Egypt*	London	1958

Hither Asia

(A) FRANKFORT-GROENEWEGEN, H. A.	*Arrest and Movement*	Chicago	1951
(B) AKURGAL, EKREM, and HIRMER	*Art of the Hittites*	New York	1962
——	*Kunst Anatoliens*	Berlin	1961
FRANKFORT, HENRI	*Art and Architecture of the Ancient Orient*	London	1954
PARROTT, ANDRÉ	*Sumer*	London	1960
——	*Nineveh and Babylon*	London	1961
(See also *Egypt:* FRANKFORT, PRITCHARD)			

The Early Aegean

(A) GRAHAM, J. WALTER	*The Palaces of Crete*	Princeton	1962
(B) MARINATOS, SPYRIDON, and HIRMER	*Crete and Mycenae*	New York	1960
MATZ, FRIEDRICH	*Kreta, Mykene, Troja*	Zurich	1956
(See also *Greece:* LAWRENCE, RODENWALDT)			

Greece

(A) CARPENTER, RHYS	*Esthetic Basis of Greek Art*	New York	1921
——	*Greek Sculpture*	Chicago	1960
——	*Greek Art*	Philadelphia	1962
KITTO, H. D. F.	*Form and Meaning in Drama*	London	1956
MATZ, FRIEDRICH	*Geschichte der Griechischen Kunst* (esp. vol. I, Introduction and further bibliography on pp. 9–11)	Frankfort a. M.	1950

Bibliography

MYRES, J. L.	*Herodotus Father of History*	Oxford	1953
SCRANTON, ROBERT L.	*Greek Architecture*	New York	1962
WORRINGER, WILHELM	*Griechentum und Gotik*	Munich	1928
(B) ARIAS, P. E., and HIRMER	*Thousand Years of Greek Vase Painting*	London	1962
LAWRENCE, A. W.	*Greek Architecture*	London	1957
LULLIES, R., and HIRMER	*Greek Sculpture*	London	1957
PFUHL, ERNST	*Malerei und Zeichnung der Griechen*	Munich	1923
ROBERTSON, MARTIN	*Greek Painting*	Geneva	1959
RODENWALDT, GERHARD	*Kunst der Antike, Hellas und Rom* (Propyläen Kunstgeschichte, III)	Berlin	1927, 1944

Roman

(A) BRENDEL, OTTO	"Prolegomena to a Book on Roman Art" (*Memoirs of the American Academy*, Rome, XXI)	Rome	1953
HAMBERG, GUSTAF	*Studies in Roman Imperial Art*	Uppsala	1945
RIEGL, ALOIS	*Spätrömische Kunstindustrie*	Vienna	1901
WICKHOF, FRANZ	*Wiener Genesis* (Translated in part as *Roman Art*)	Vienna	1895
STRONG, EUGENIE		London	1900
(B) BROWN, FRANK	*Roman Architecture*	New York	1962
DUCATI, PERICLE	*Die Etruskische-Italo-Hellenistische und Römische Malerei*	Vienna	1941
MAIURI, AMADEO	*Roman Painting*	Geneva	1953
PALLOTINO, MASSIMO	*Etruscan Painting*	Geneva	1952
STRONG, EUGENIE	*Art in Ancient Rome*	New York	1928

(See also *Greece:* RODENWALDT)

Early Christian

(*A*) MICHELIS, P. A.	*Aesthetic Approach to Byzantine Painting*	London	1955
(*B*) DALTON, O. M.	*East Christian Art*	Oxford	1925
GRABAR, ANDRÉ	*Byzantine Painting*	Geneva	1953
RICE, TALBOT	*Beginnings of Christian Art*	London	1957
SIMSON, OTTO VON	*Sacred Fortress*	Chicago	1948
VOLBACH, W. F., and HIRMER	*Early Christian Art*	London	1961

Index

INDEX

INDEX

INDEX

Fall of Troy (Quintus Smyrnaeus), 319

Fantasy: in Egyptian art, 50, 60, 104; in art of Hither Asia, 100–102, 104, 114, 147

Fishers, Tomb of the (Tarquinia), 301

Form, 41

Form, conceptual: aniconic, 12, 13, 14, 15, 100, 153–54, 158, 188; Egyptian, 15, 66, 77, 79, 92; Greek, 15, 158; iconic, 12, 13, 14, 15, 66, 112, 188, 201, 202; Minoan, 15, 153–54

Forum: of Corinth, 289; of Jerash, 289; of Trajan (Rome), 289, 308

Frazer, Sir James G., 298

Frogs, The (Aristophanes), 222

Galla Placidia, 317; mausoleum of, 322, 348, 350, 355

Georgics (Virgil), 277, 313

Gebel el Arak, 96

Gilgamesh, Epic of, 103–4, 106, 116–17, 122, 141, 143–44

Girls Playing with Knuckle Bones (Herculaneum), 282

Gizeh, 55, 57, 81, 87, 92

God and His Unknown Name of Power, The, 51

Good Shepherd, 323

Gospels (N.T.), 320, 321, 327, 343, 348, 351

Grave stelae, 251

Great Trajanic Relief, 287, 288, 305; *see also under* Trajan

Greece, art of, 166, 185–265, 266–315 *passim*; Archaic period, 186, 231, 239, 240, 246, 253; architecture, 13, 159–60, 188, 196–208 *passim*, 215, 219, 226, 239–46 *passim*, 252–62 *passim*, 275, 276, 281, 282; Attic period, 245; Classic period, 186; color in, 214–19, 223; geometric period, 188, 215, 227, 231, 240, 241, 253; Golden Age, 186; Helladic period, 152, 153, 158–60, 183; Hellenic period, 188; Hellenistic period, 187, 188, 191, 195, 202, 217, 221, 224, 231, 251, 252, 255, 268, 285, 286; human activity in, 188, 190, 191, 192, 195, 196; idealism in, 223–27; influence on Etruscan art, 301; light in, 214–19, 223; line in, 239; literature, 4, 37, 188–195 *passim*, 208–43 *passim*, 246, 247, 248, 250, 255–65 *passim*, 283, 309; minor arts, 188; movement in, 204–14, 253, 263; Mycenean period (Late Helladic III), 153, 160–84 *passim*, 201; nature in, 188, 189, 190; naturalism in, 223; neolithic period, 152, 153; painting, 4, 188, 204, 215, 219, 221, 239,

257, 262, 281, 282; philosophy, 249; portraiture, 285, 286; sculpture, 188, 190, 191, 201, 202, 204, 205, 206, 214, 215, 219–39 *passim*, 244–63 *passim*, 285; summary of style, 252–53, 300–301, 314–15; symbolism in, 233–35; texture in, 216, 219, 220–22, 223; vase painting, 158, 183, 188, 190, 191, 192, 221, 222, 240, 244, 252, 255, 265; 7th century B.C., 215, 227, 228; 6th century B.C., 215, 222, 224, 227, 244, 245, 246; 5th century B.C., 215, 222, 228, 233, 244, 245, 246, 259, 262; 4th century B.C., 224, 244, 251, 252, 253; 3d century B.C., 252

Gudea of Lagash, 99, 121, 133, 135, 141, 142, 145

Gymnasium, 198, 199, 275

Hadrian, 267; library of, 279, 293; palace of (Tivoli), 279

Hagia Sophia, 327–28, 332–33, 335, 347, 357, 358, 360, 361, 364

Hagia Triada sarcophagos, 171, 174

Hagios Demetrios (Saloniki), 335

Halicarnassos, 251

Hamartigenia (Prudentius), 350

Hammurabi, 99, 149; Code of, 136; Stele of, 103, 115, 121, 130, 134

Harvester vase (Crete), 154, 168, 175

Haterii, relief of, 272

Hatshepsut: Mortuary Temple of (Deir el Bahri), 56, 57, 65, 66, 83; reliefs of expedition to Punt, 69

Hebrews, art of, 116, 125, 127

Hellenic Europe, 187

Hellenism, 187

Hera (Samos), 244

Herculaneum, 273, 282, 294, 296, 305

Hermas, 340, 343

Herodotus, 194, 209, 222, 223, 226, 232, 248, 256, 257, 261

Hesiod, 218, 223, 243, 277

Hesire, Stele of, 78

Hierakonpolis, 47, 77

Hither Asia, art of, 98–150, 162, 176, 185, 186, 187, 190; abstraction in, 120; animals in, 101–2; architecture, 106–20 *passim*, 123, 127, 129, 132, 133, 137–39, 143, 145–47; Assyrian period, 99 (*see also* Assyrians, art of); color in, 118, 119, 133, 147; colorism in, 118, 119; divinity in, 100; Early Dynastic period, 99, 107, 133, 148; fantasy in, 100–102, 104, 114, 147; human activity in,

INDEX

378

INDEX

INDEX

INDEX